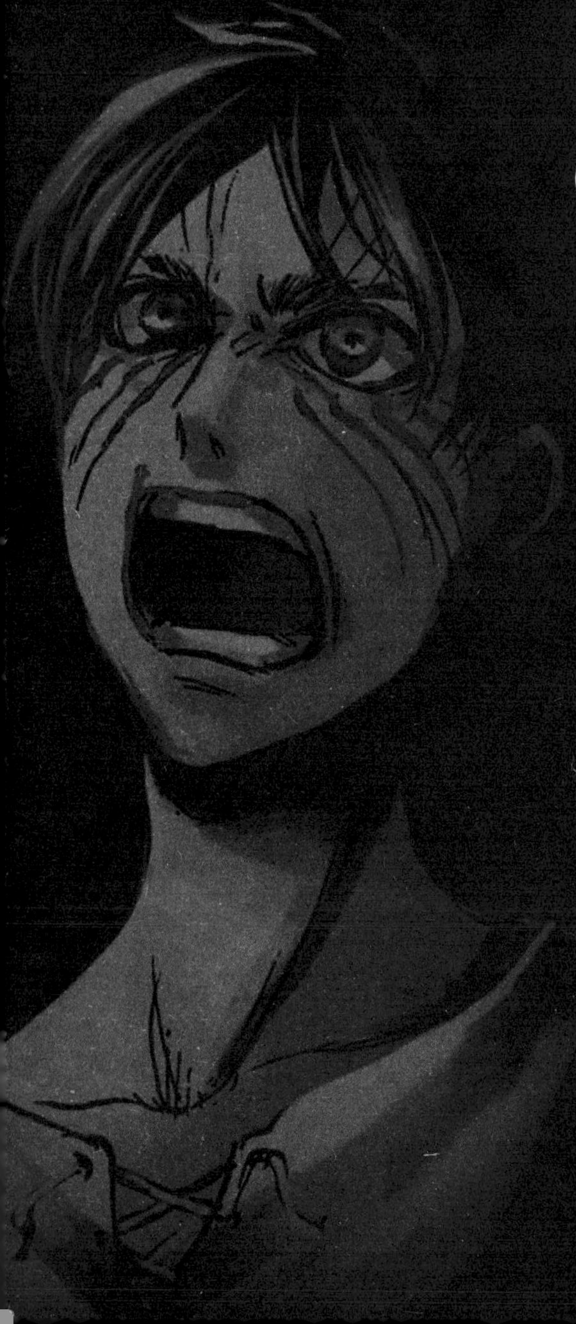

ATTACK ON TITAN
12

HAJIME ISAYAMA

ATTACK on TITAN

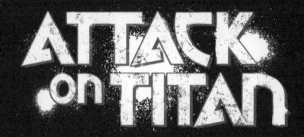

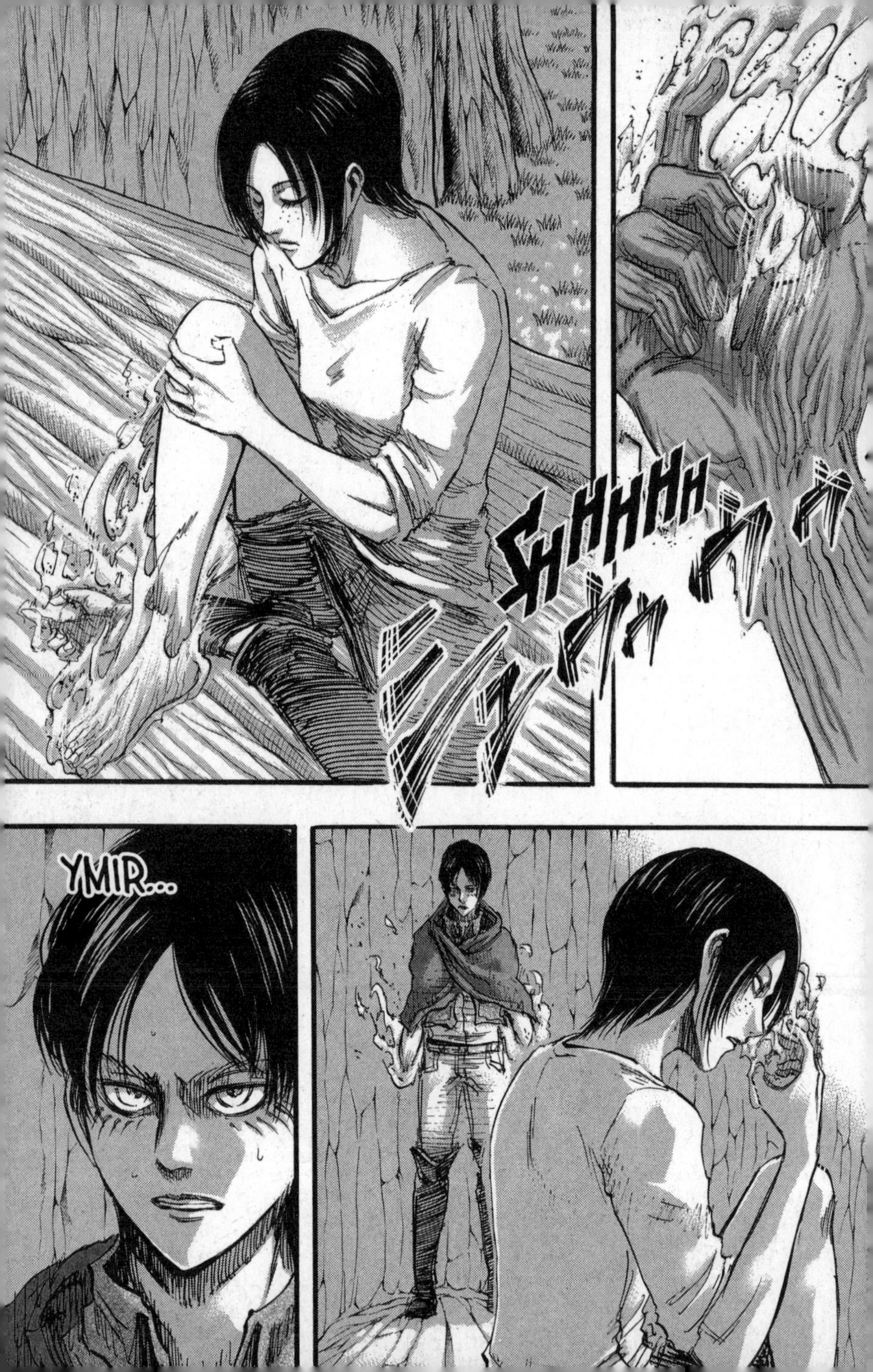
SHHHHH
YMIR...

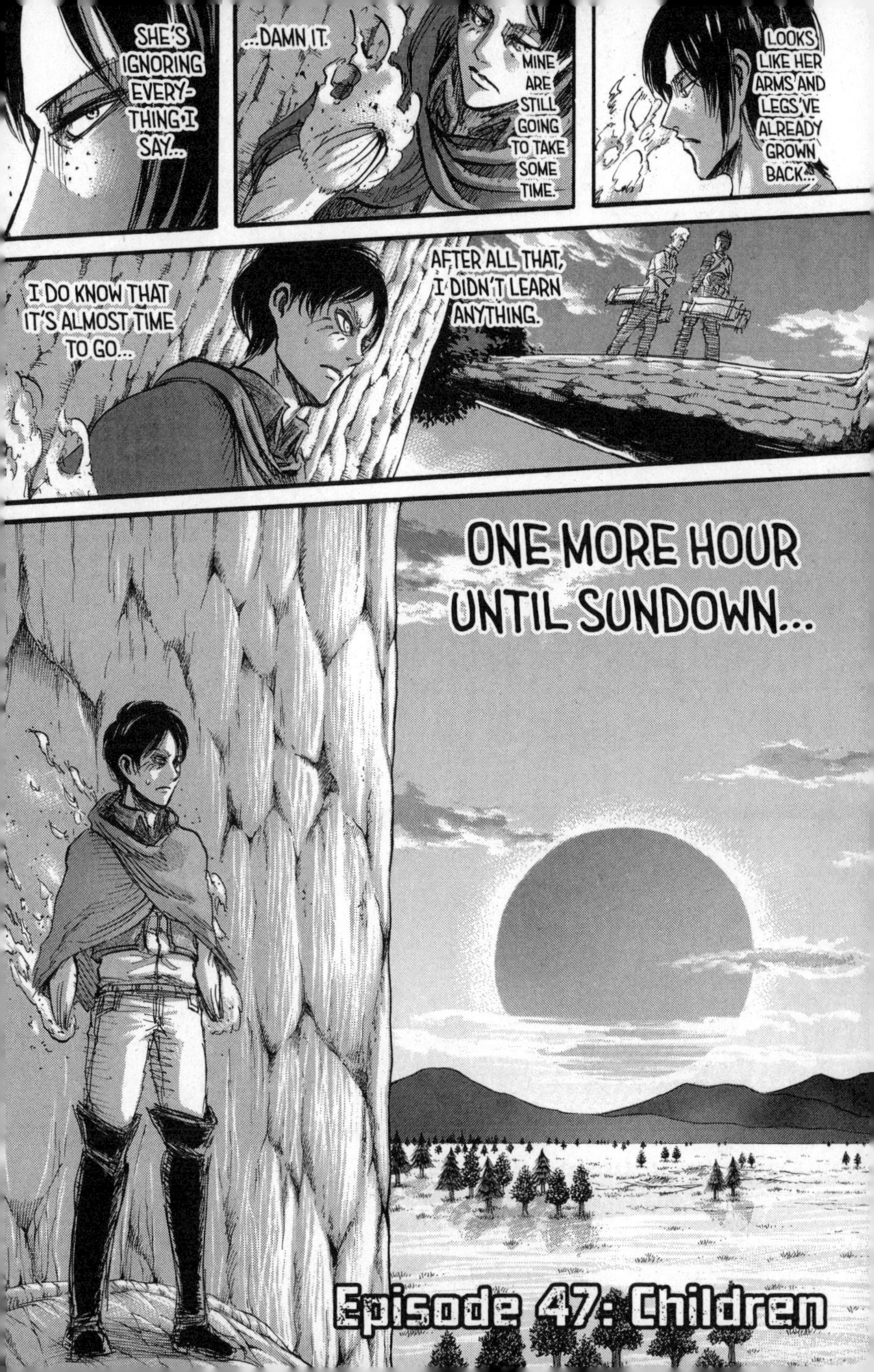

LOOKS LIKE HER ARMS AND LEGS'VE ALREADY GROWN BACK...
...DAMN IT.
MINE ARE STILL GOING TO TAKE SOME TIME.
SHE'S IGNORING EVERYTHING I SAY...
AFTER ALL THAT, I DIDN'T LEARN ANYTHING.
I DO KNOW THAT IT'S ALMOST TIME TO GO...
ONE MORE HOUR UNTIL SUNDOWN...
Episode 47: Children

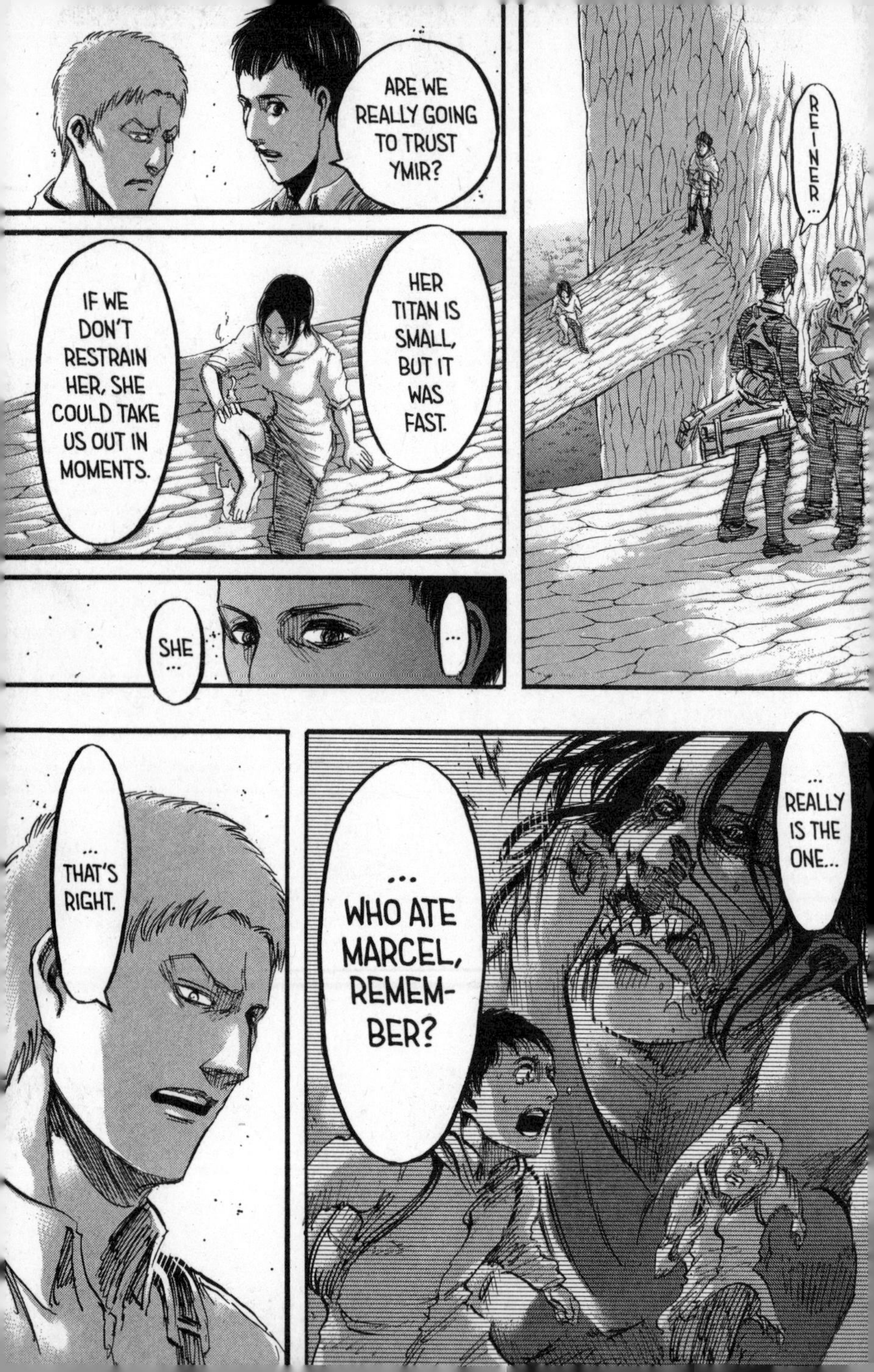
REINER...
ARE WE REALLY GOING TO TRUST YMIR?
HER TITAN IS SMALL, BUT IT WAS FAST.
IF WE DON'T RESTRAIN HER, SHE COULD TAKE US OUT IN MOMENTS.
...
SHE...
...REALLY IS THE ONE...
...WHO ATE MARCEL, REMEMBER?
...THAT'S RIGHT.

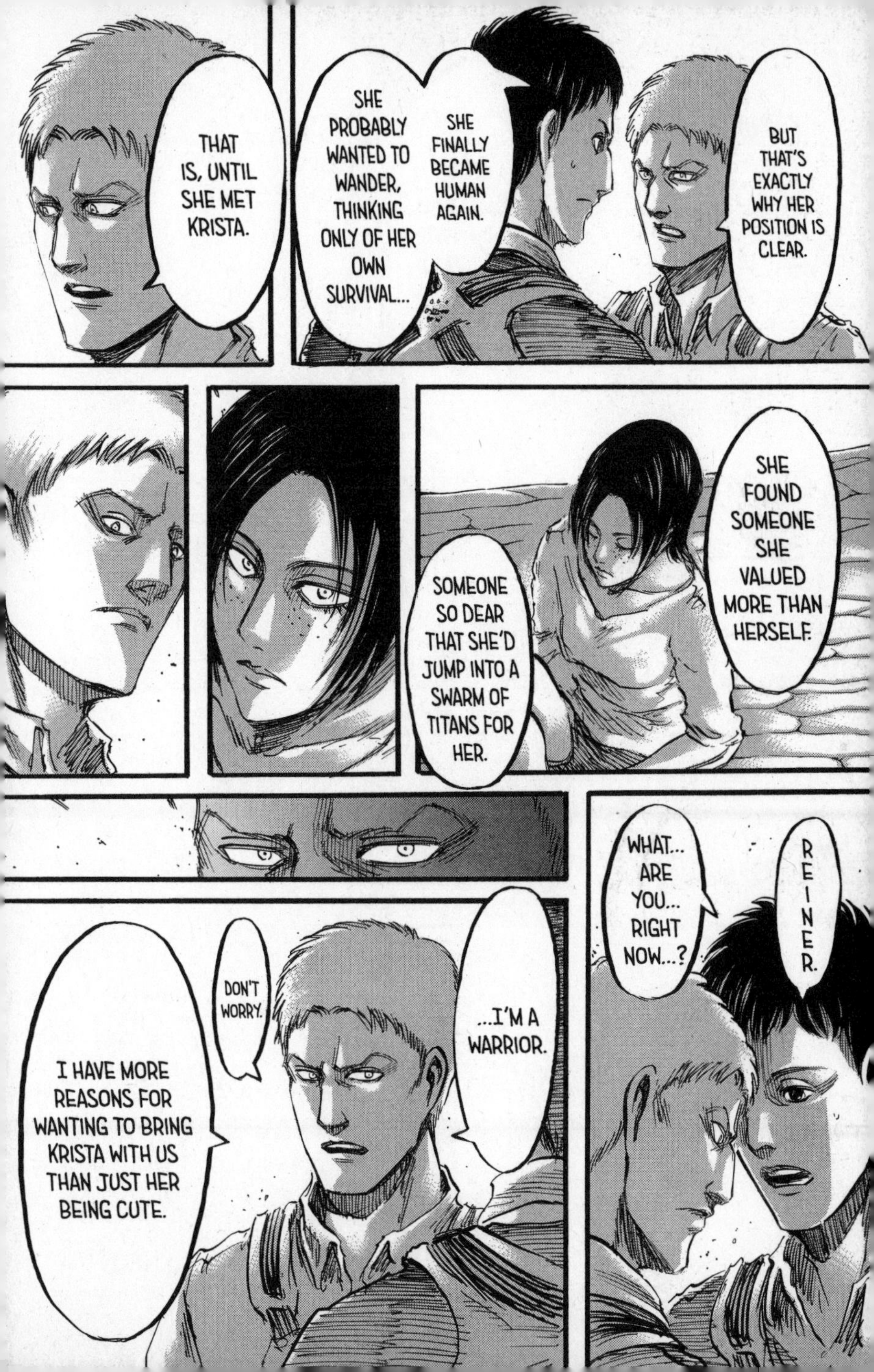
BUT THAT'S EXACTLY WHY HER POSITION IS CLEAR.
SHE FINALLY BECAME HUMAN AGAIN.
SHE PROBABLY WANTED TO WANDER, THINKING ONLY OF HER OWN SURVIVAL...
THAT IS, UNTIL SHE MET KRISTA.
SHE FOUND SOMEONE SHE VALUED MORE THAN HERSELF.
SOMEONE SO DEAR THAT SHE'D JUMP INTO A SWARM OF TITANS FOR HER.
REINER.
WHAT... ARE YOU... RIGHT NOW...?
...I'M A WARRIOR.
DON'T WORRY.
I HAVE MORE REASONS FOR WANTING TO BRING KRISTA WITH US THAN JUST HER BEING CUTE.

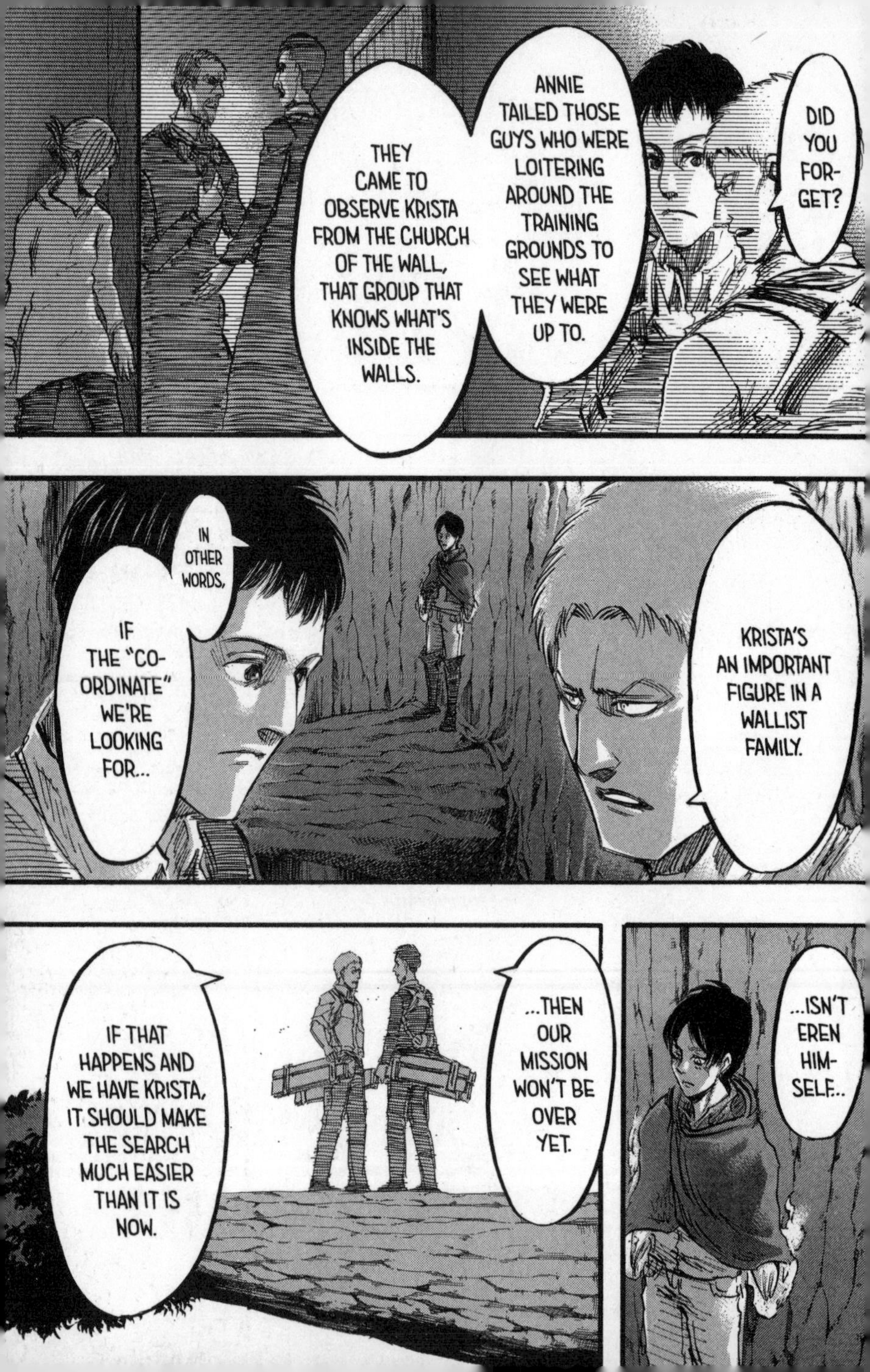
DID YOU FORGET?
ANNIE TAILED THOSE GUYS WHO WERE LOITERING AROUND THE TRAINING GROUNDS TO SEE WHAT THEY WERE UP TO.
THEY CAME TO OBSERVE KRISTA FROM THE CHURCH OF THE WALL, THAT GROUP THAT KNOWS WHAT'S INSIDE THE WALLS.
KRISTA'S AN IMPORTANT FIGURE IN A WALLIST FAMILY.
IN OTHER WORDS,
IF THE "CO-ORDINATE" WE'RE LOOKING FOR...
...ISN'T EREN HIMSELF...
...THEN OUR MISSION WON'T BE OVER YET.
IF THAT HAPPENS AND WE HAVE KRISTA, IT SHOULD MAKE THE SEARCH MUCH EASIER THAN IT IS NOW.

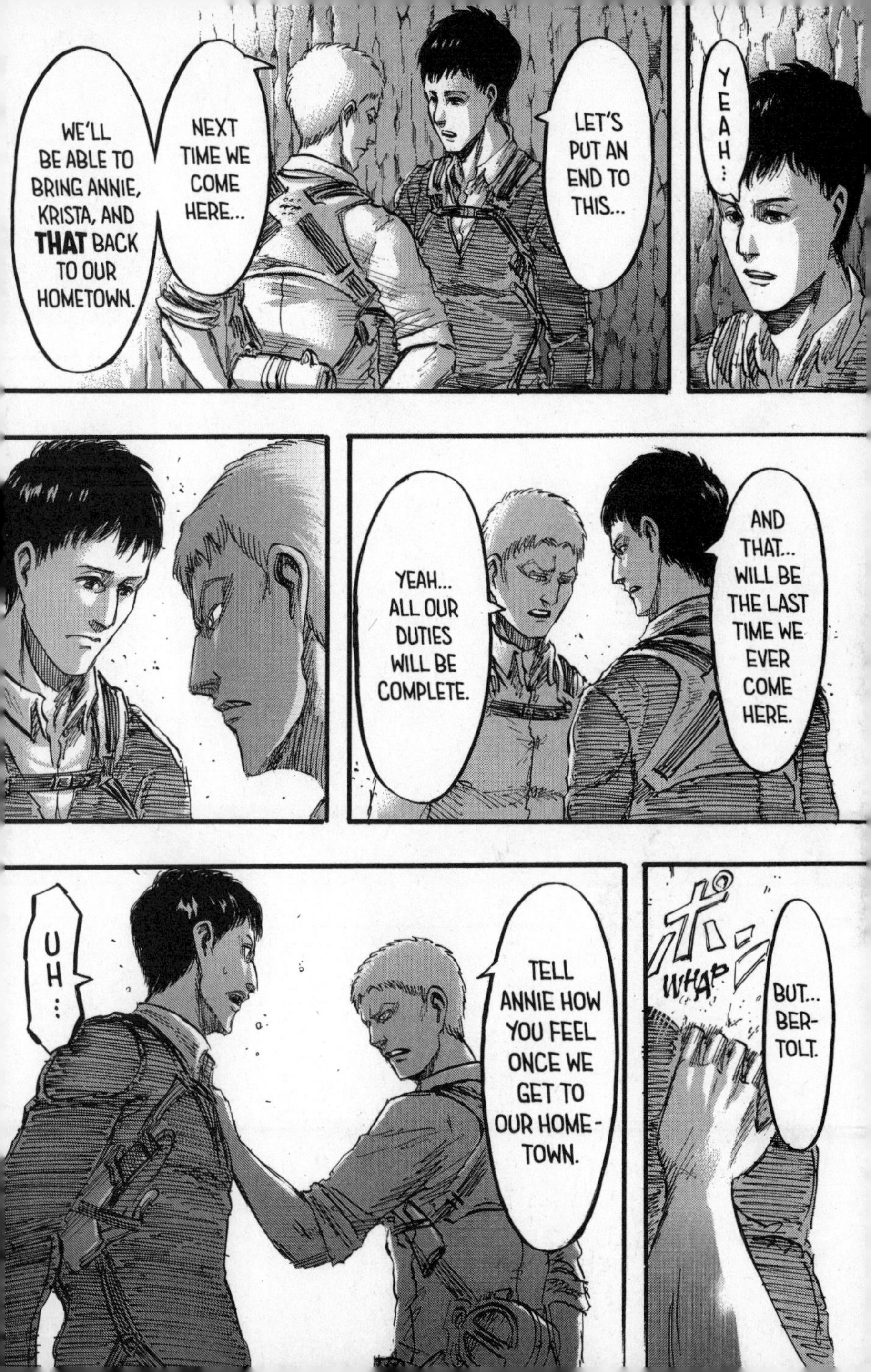
YEAH...
LET'S PUT AN END TO THIS...
NEXT TIME WE COME HERE...
WE'LL BE ABLE TO BRING ANNIE, KRISTA, AND THAT BACK TO OUR HOMETOWN.
AND THAT... WILL BE THE LAST TIME WE EVER COME HERE.
YEAH... ALL OUR DUTIES WILL BE COMPLETE.
WHAP
BUT... BER-TOLT.
TELL ANNIE HOW YOU FEEL ONCE WE GET TO OUR HOME-TOWN.
UH...

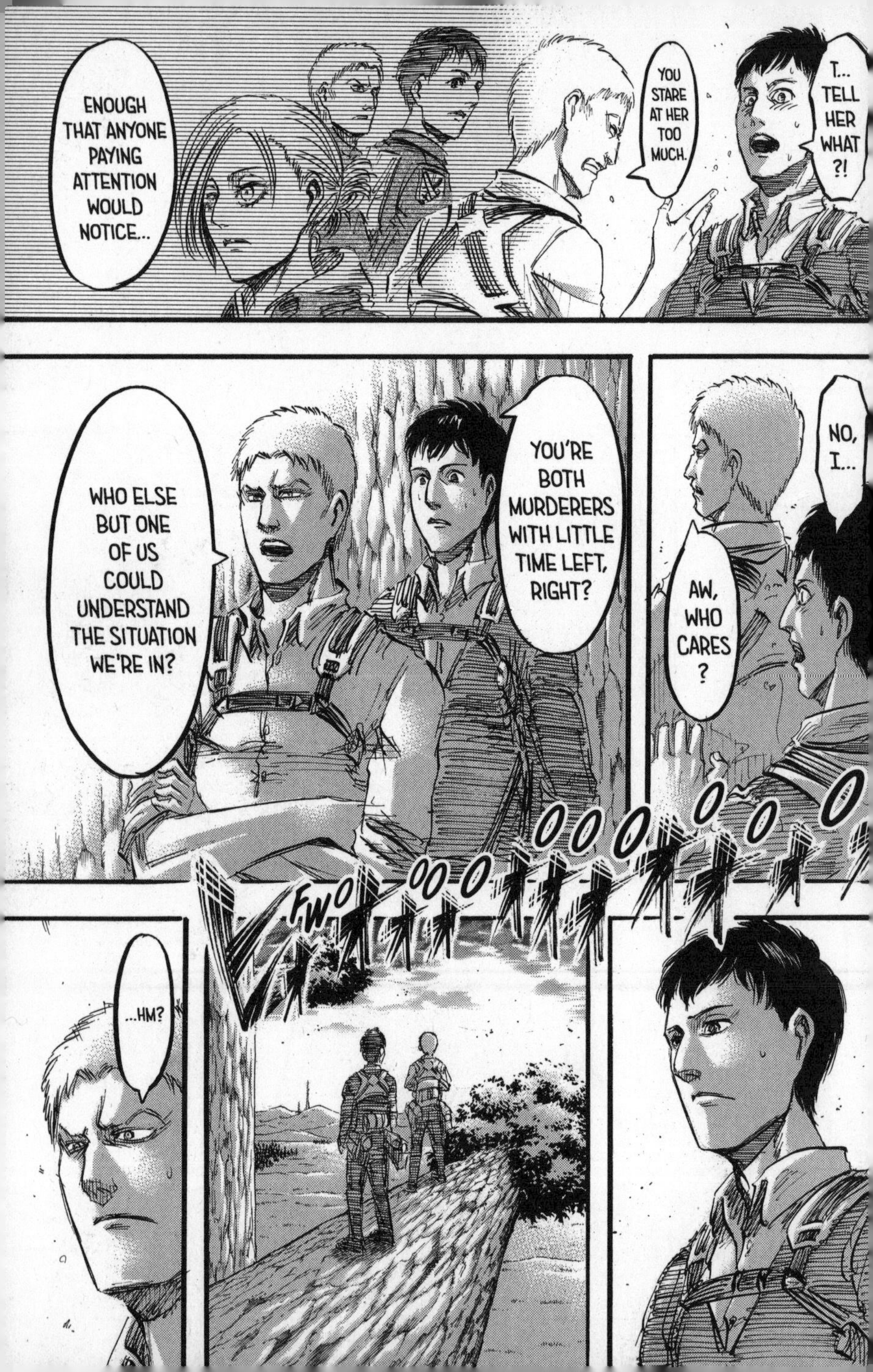
T... TELL HER WHAT?!
YOU STARE AT HER TOO MUCH.
ENOUGH THAT ANYONE PAYING ATTENTION WOULD NOTICE...
NO, I...
AW, WHO CARES?
YOU'RE BOTH MURDERERS WITH LITTLE TIME LEFT, RIGHT?
WHO ELSE BUT ONE OF US COULD UNDERSTAND THE SITUATION WE'RE IN?
FWOOOOOOOOOOOO
...HM?

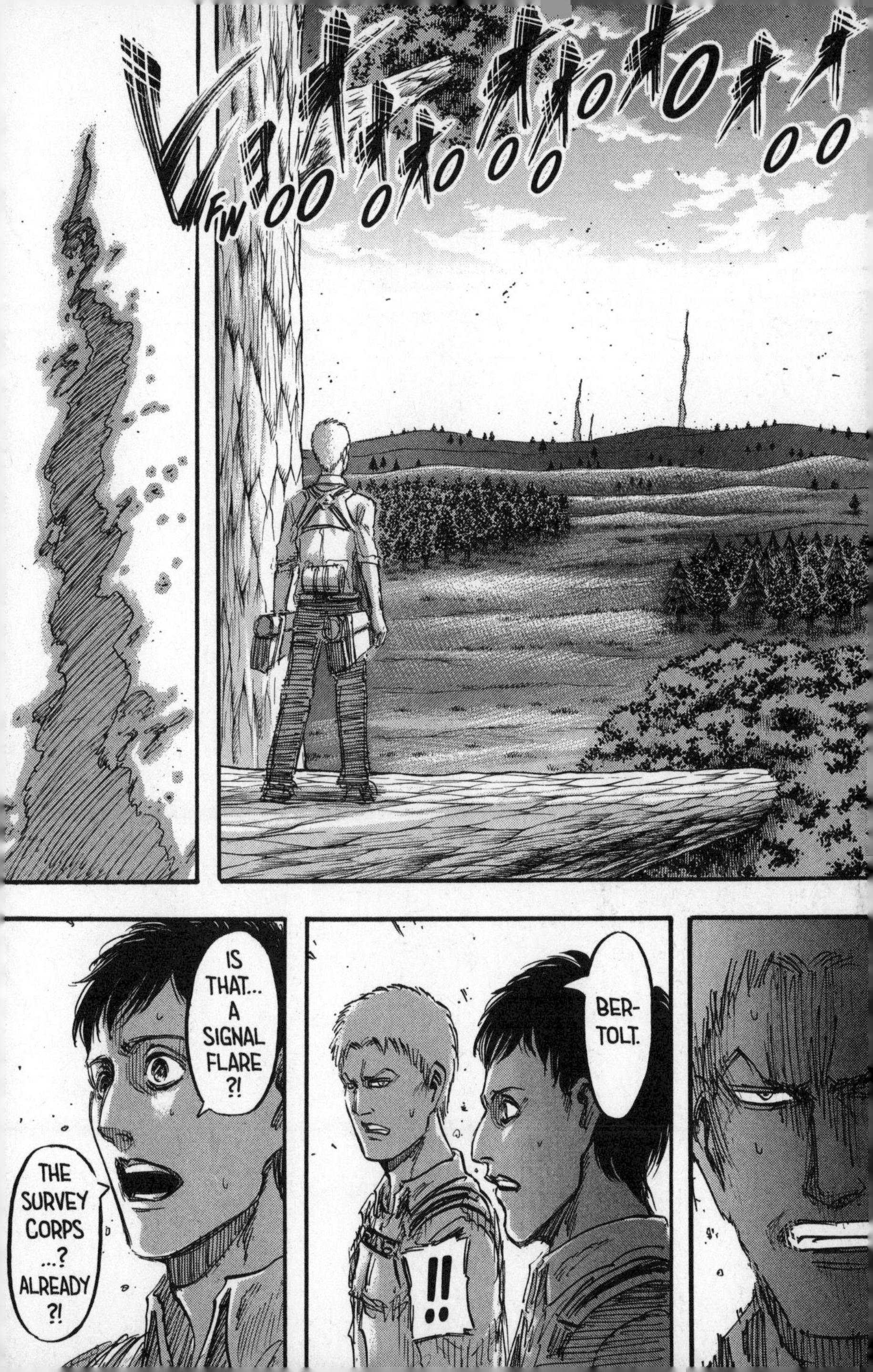
FWOOOOOOOOOOO
BER-TOLT.
!!
IS THAT... A SIGNAL FLARE?!
THE SURVEY CORPS...? ALREADY?!

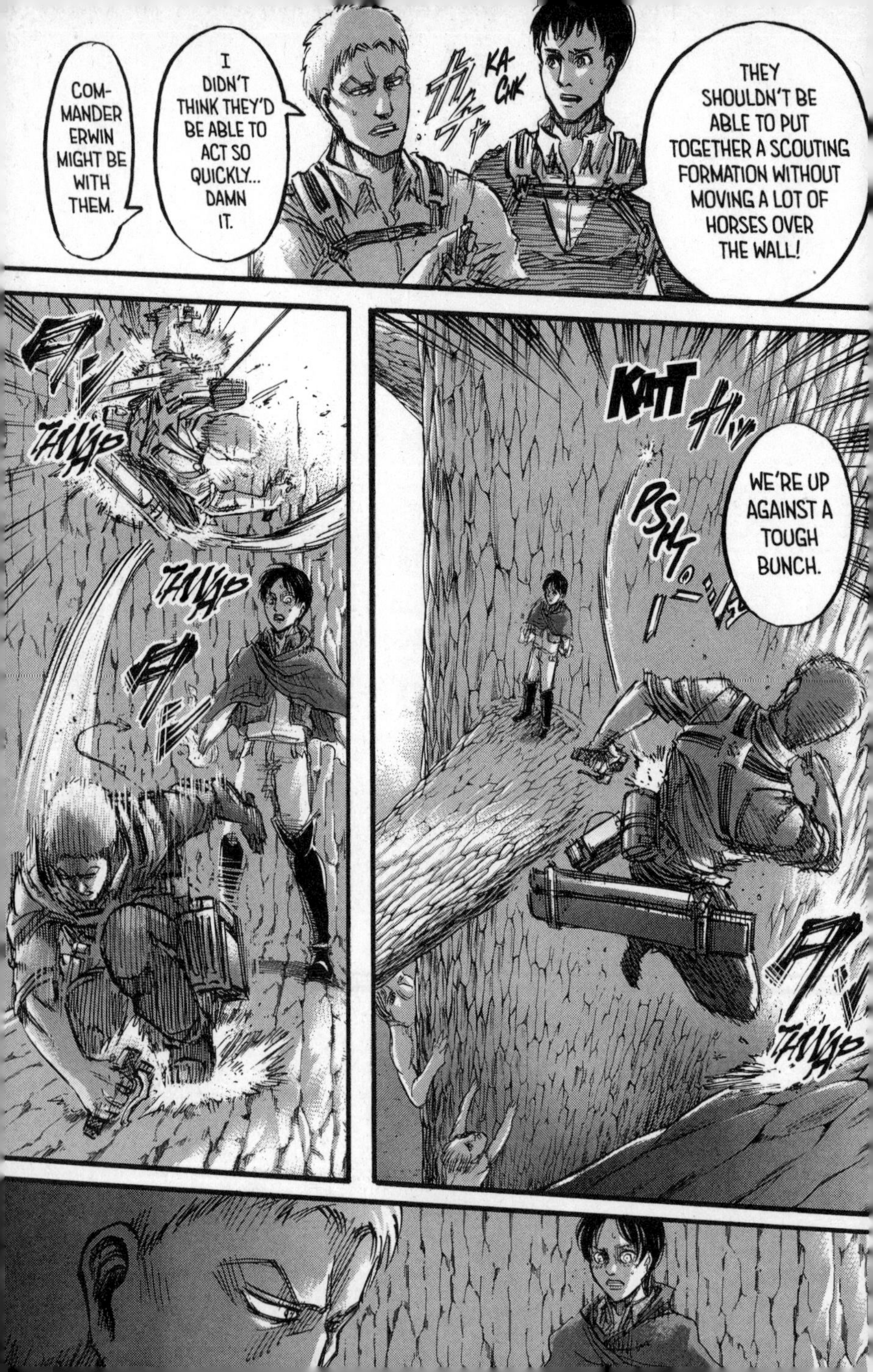
THEY SHOULDN'T BE ABLE TO PUT TOGETHER A SCOUTING FORMATION WITHOUT MOVING A LOT OF HORSES OVER THE WALL!
KA CHK
I DIDN'T THINK THEY'D BE ABLE TO ACT SO QUICKLY... DAMN IT.
COM-MANDER ERWIN MIGHT BE WITH THEM.
KATT
WE'RE UP AGAINST A TOUGH BUNCH.
PSHYU
THWAP
THWAP
THWAP

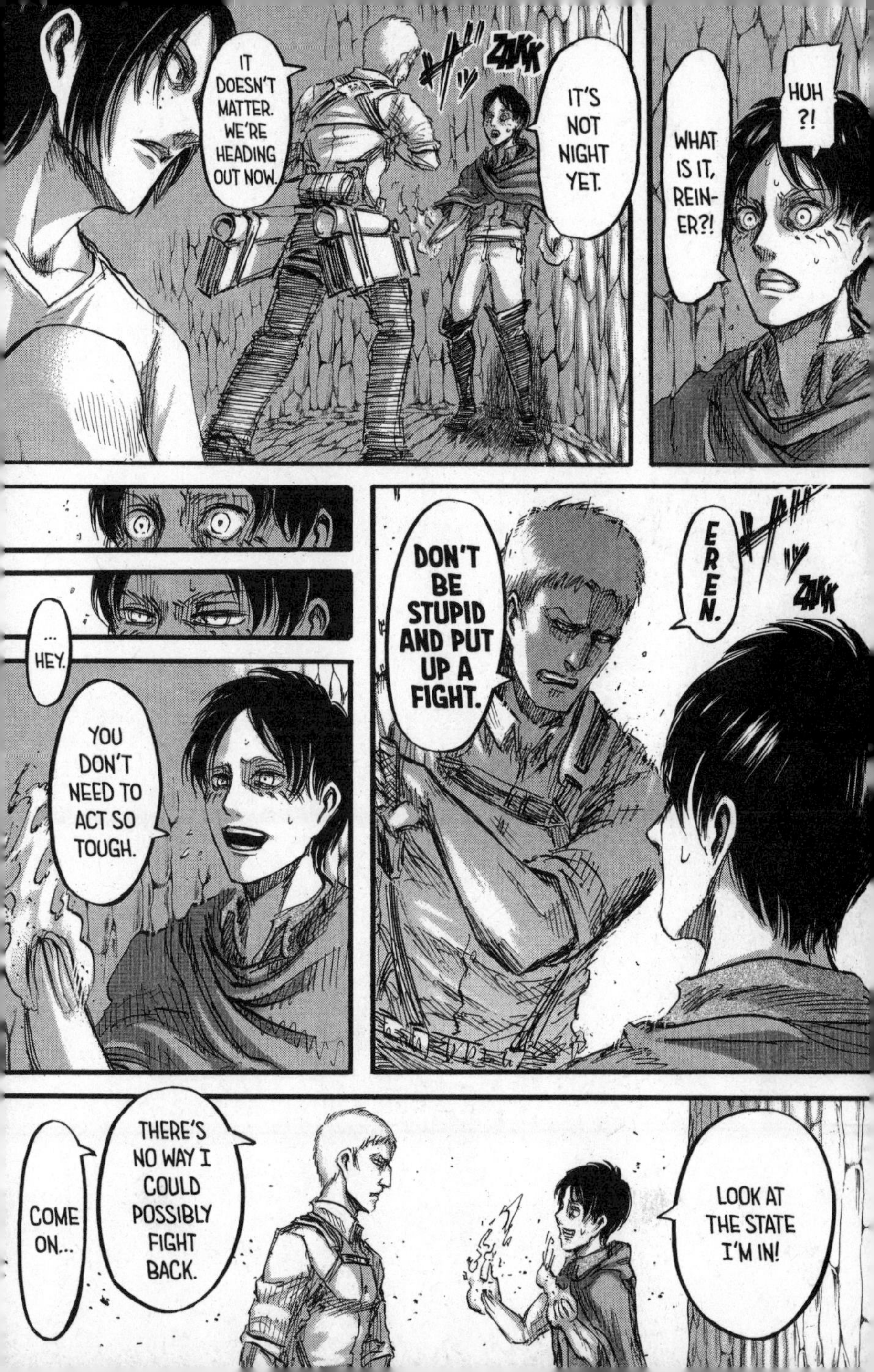

HUH ?!
WHAT IS IT, REINER?!
ZAKK
IT'S NOT NIGHT YET.
IT DOESN'T MATTER. WE'RE HEADING OUT NOW.
EREN.
ZAKK
DON'T BE STUPID AND PUT UP A FIGHT.
... HEY.
YOU DON'T NEED TO ACT SO TOUGH.
LOOK AT THE STATE I'M IN!
THERE'S NO WAY I COULD POSSIBLY FIGHT BACK.
COME ON...

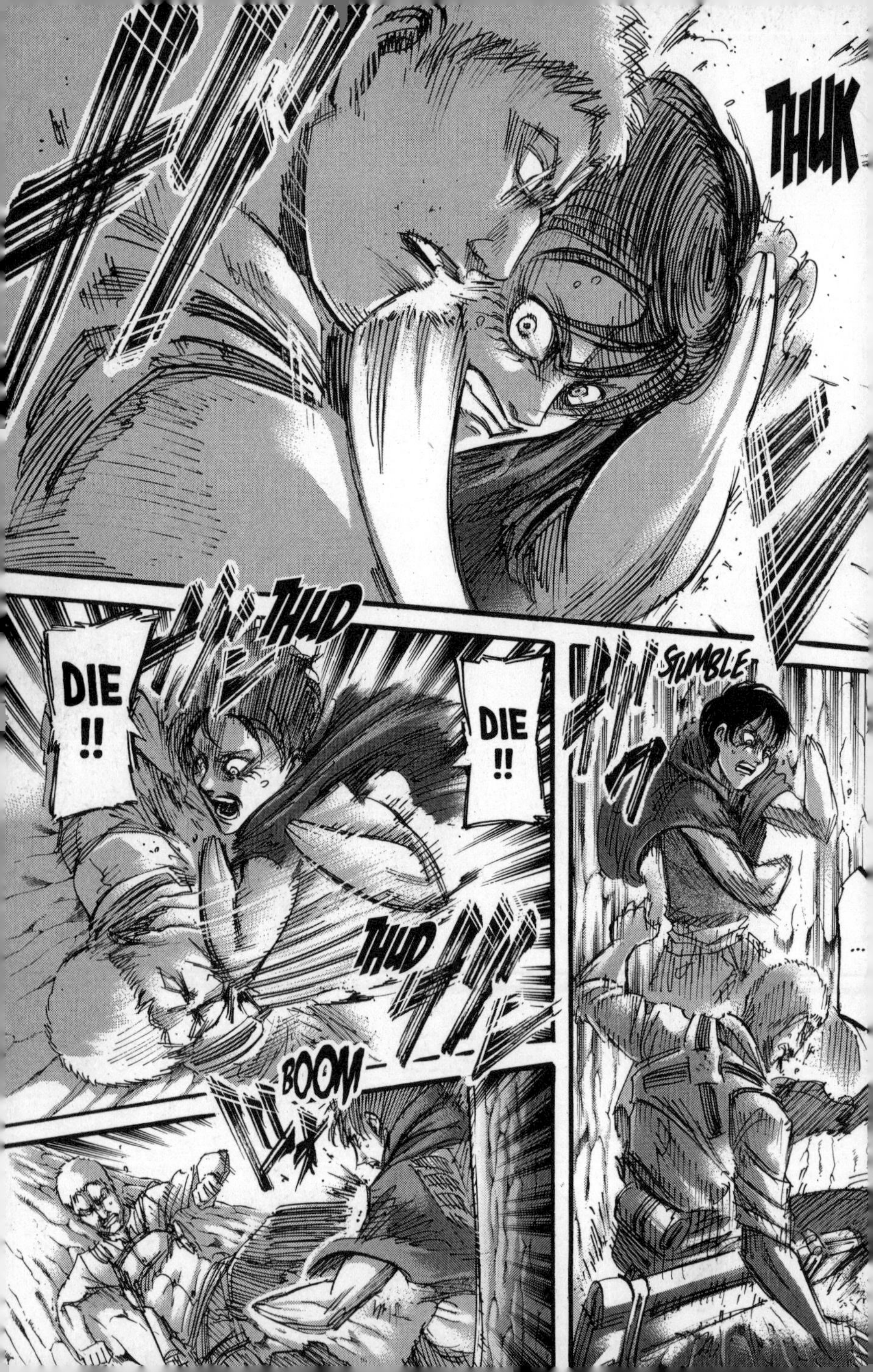

THUK
STUMBLE
...
THUD
DIE!!
DIE!!
THUD
BOOM

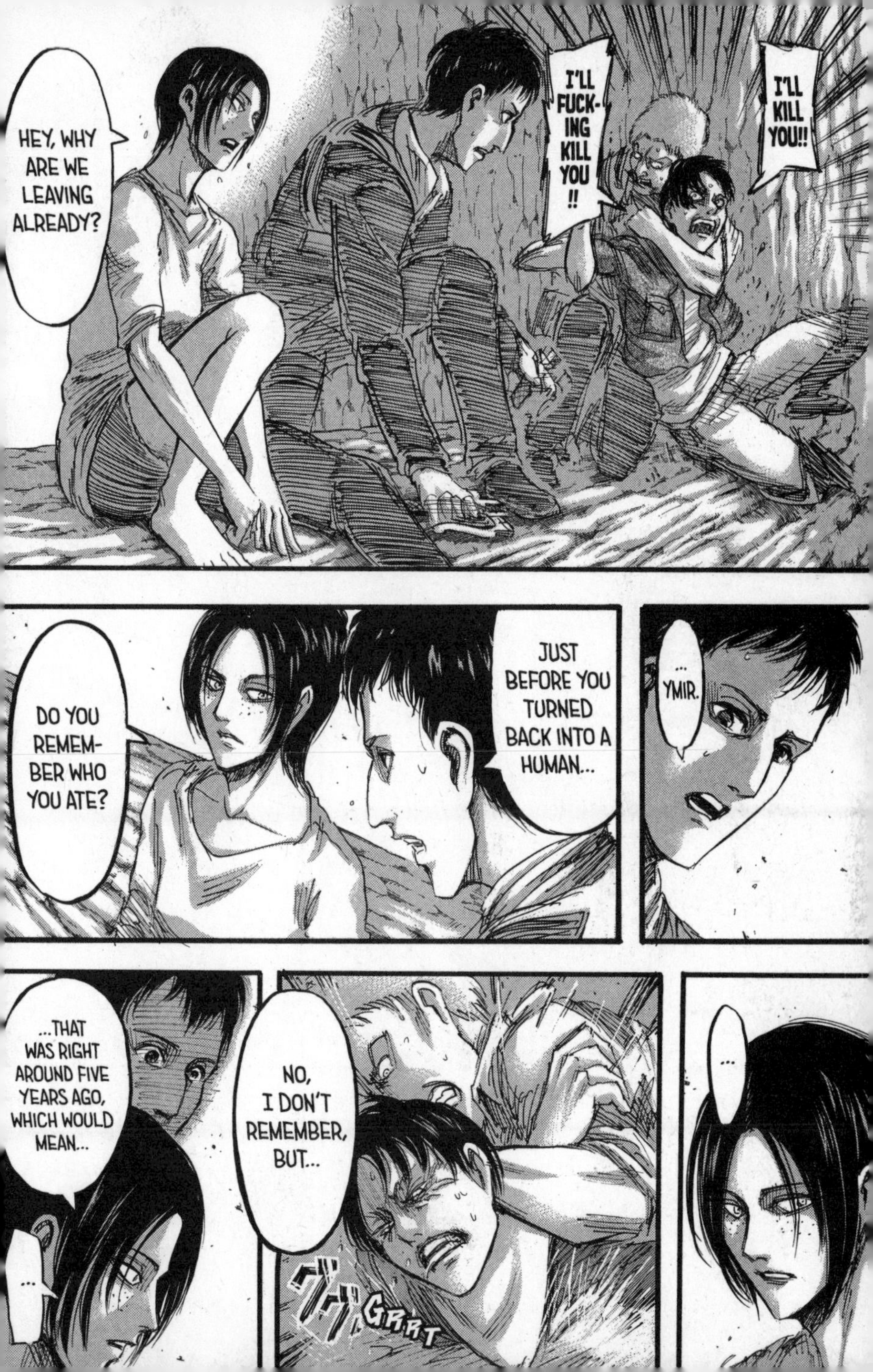
I'LL KILL YOU!!
I'LL FUCKING KILL YOU !!
HEY, WHY ARE WE LEAVING ALREADY?
... YMIR.
JUST BEFORE YOU TURNED BACK INTO A HUMAN...
DO YOU REMEMBER WHO YOU ATE?
...
NO, I DON'T REMEMBER, BUT...
GRRRT
...THAT WAS RIGHT AROUND FIVE YEARS AGO, WHICH WOULD MEAN...
...

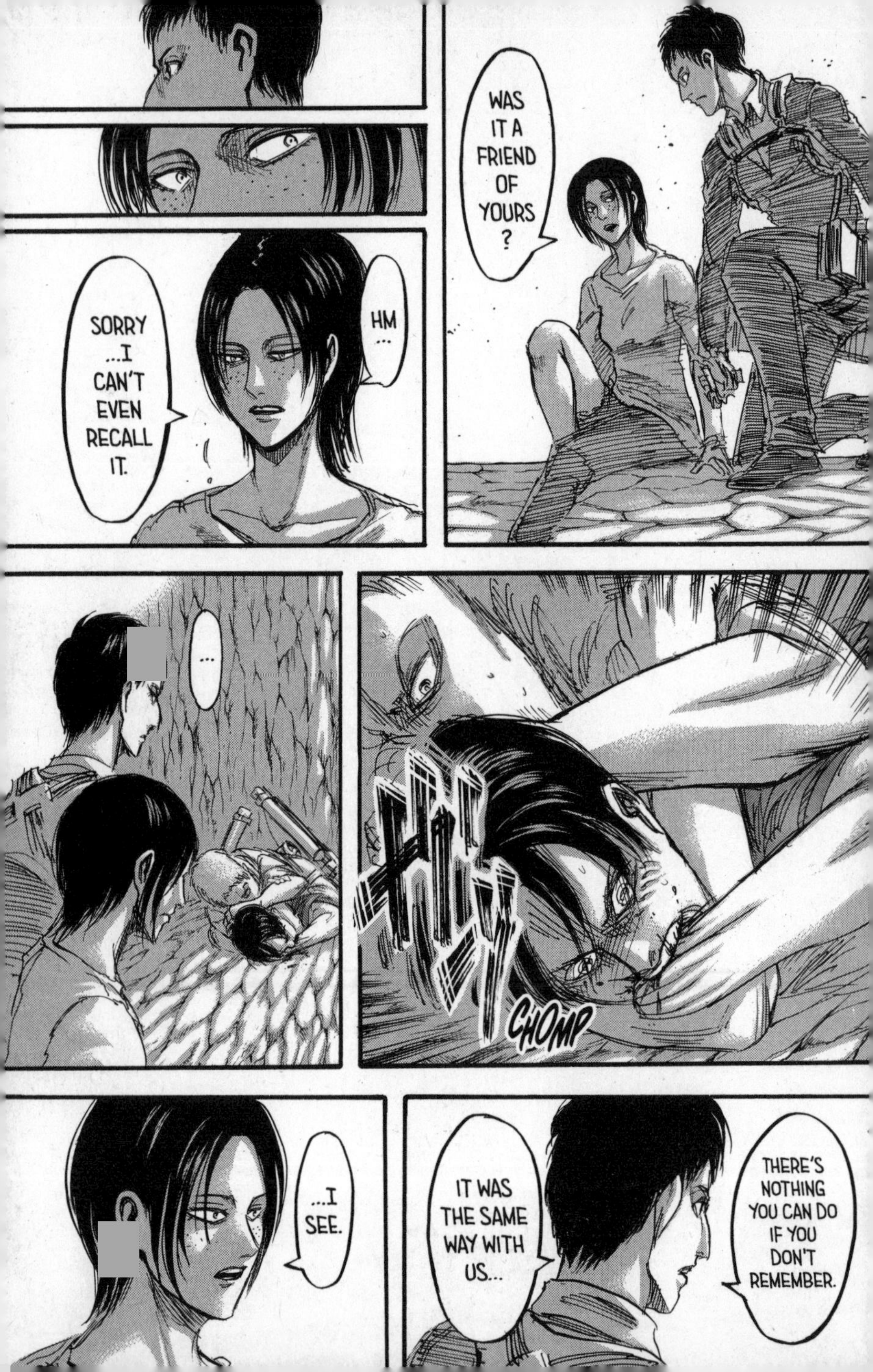
WAS IT A FRIEND OF YOURS?
HM...
SORRY ...I CAN'T EVEN RECALL IT.
CHOMP
...
THERE'S NOTHING YOU CAN DO IF YOU DON'T REMEMBER.
IT WAS THE SAME WAY WITH US...
...I SEE.

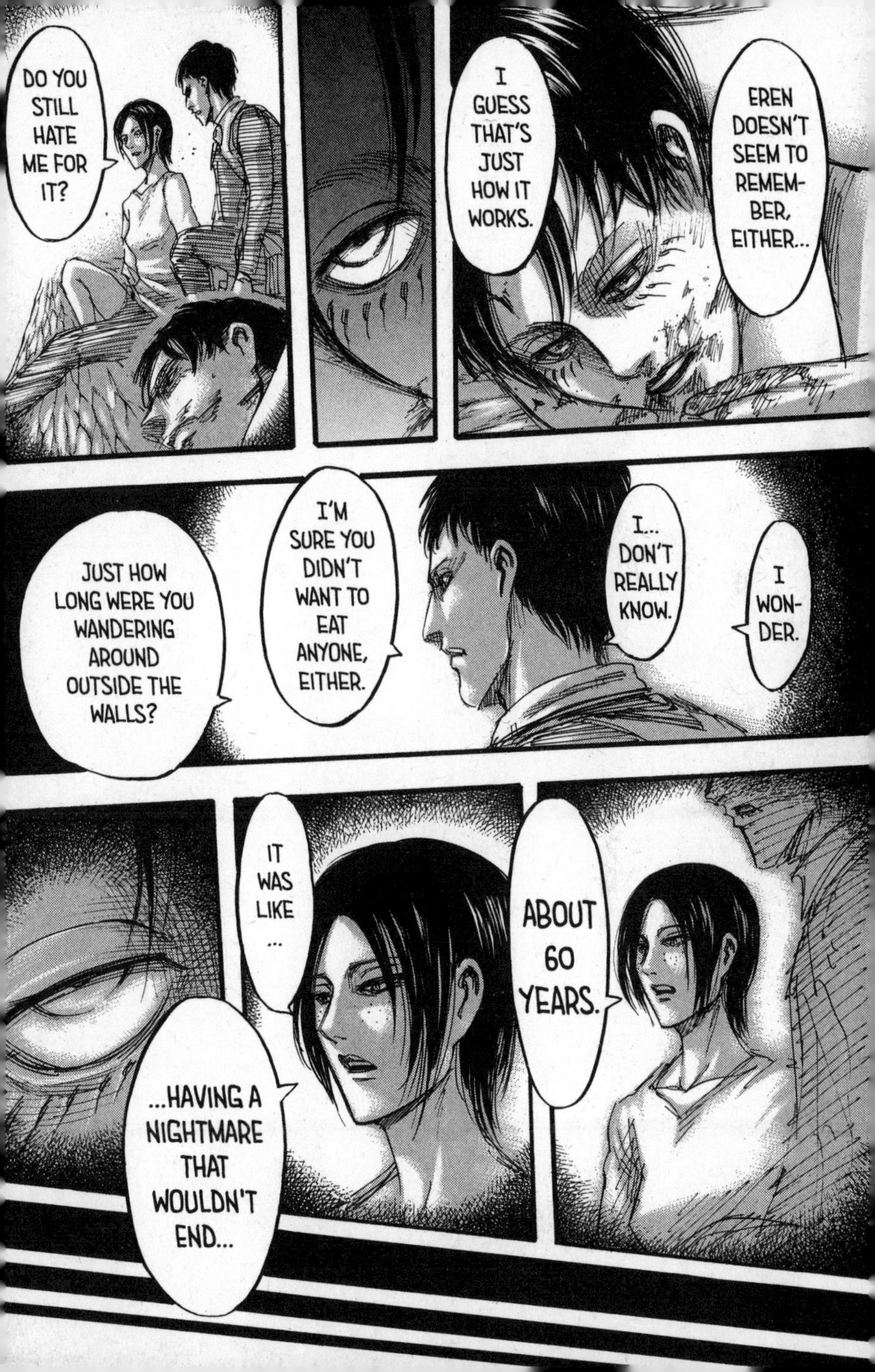
EREN DOESN'T SEEM TO REMEMBER, EITHER...
I GUESS THAT'S JUST HOW IT WORKS.
DO YOU STILL HATE ME FOR IT?
I WONDER.
I... DON'T REALLY KNOW.
I'M SURE YOU DIDN'T WANT TO EAT ANYONE, EITHER.
JUST HOW LONG WERE YOU WANDERING AROUND OUTSIDE THE WALLS?
ABOUT 60 YEARS.
IT WAS LIKE ...
...HAVING A NIGHTMARE THAT WOULDN'T END...

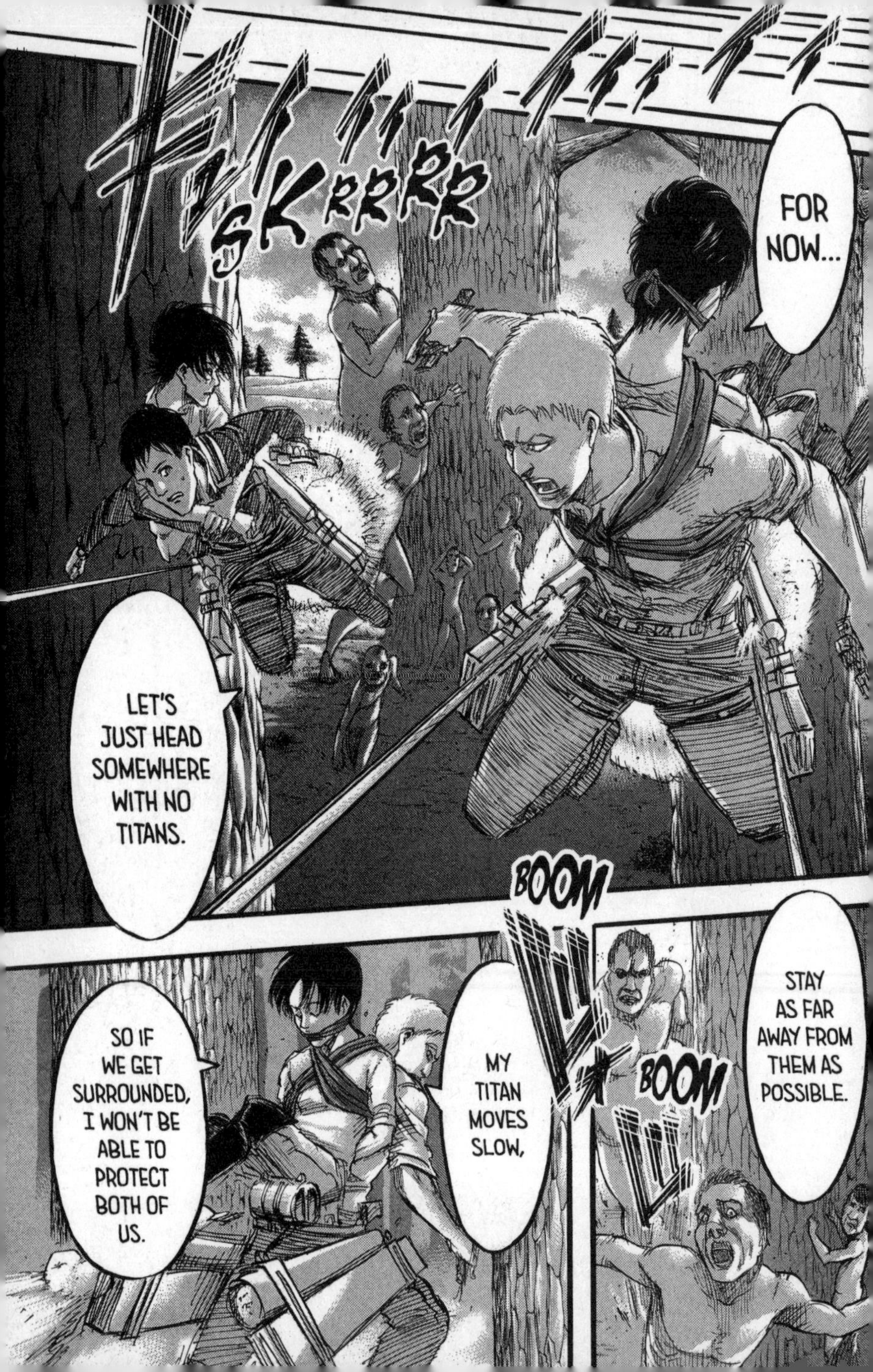
FOR NOW...
SKRRRR
LET'S JUST HEAD SOMEWHERE WITH NO TITANS.
BOOM
STAY AS FAR AWAY FROM THEM AS POSSIBLE.
BOOM
MY TITAN MOVES SLOW,
SO IF WE GET SURROUNDED, I WON'T BE ABLE TO PROTECT BOTH OF US.

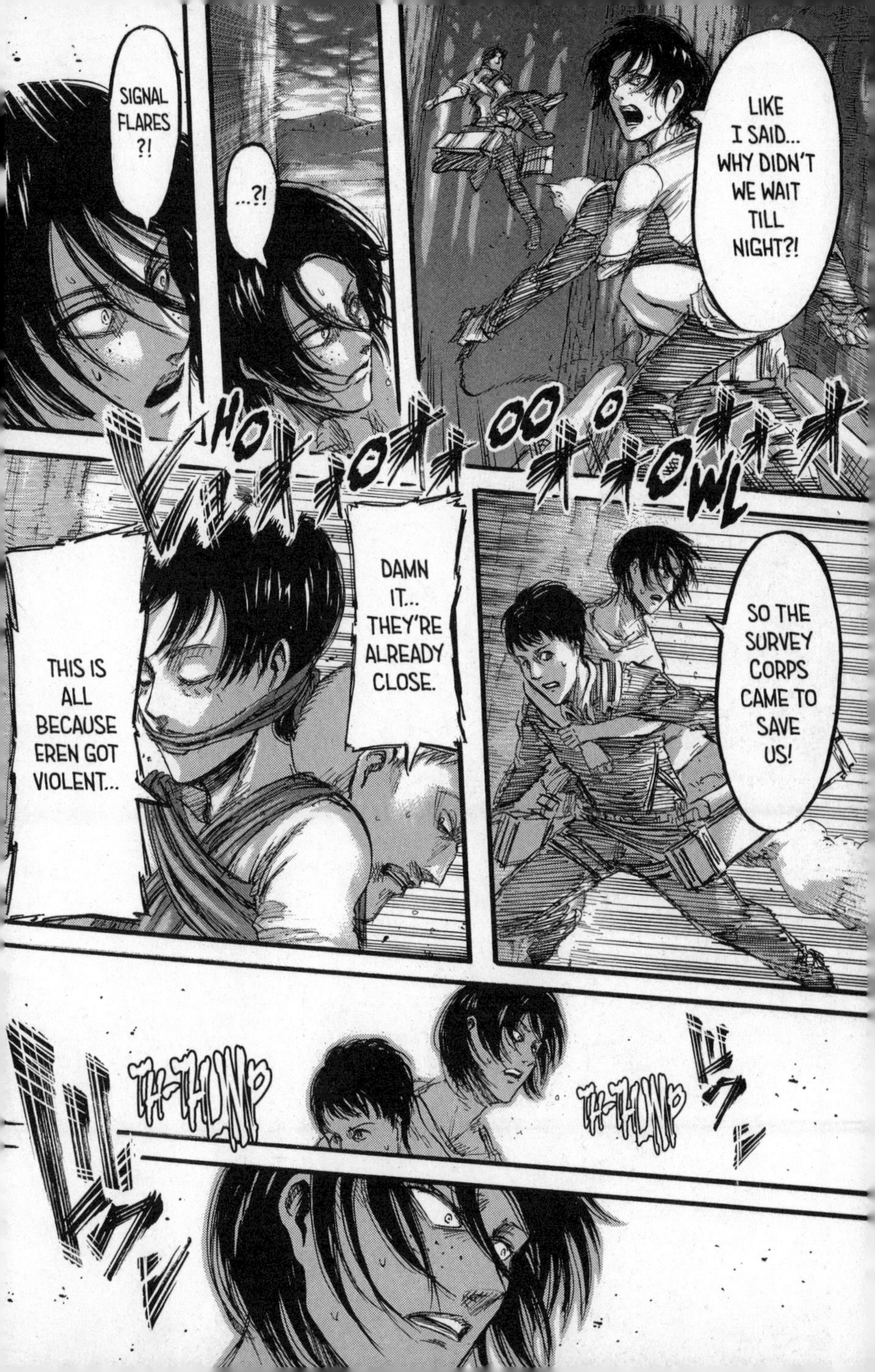
LIKE I SAID... WHY DIDN'T WE WAIT TILL NIGHT?!
...?!
SIGNAL FLARES ?!
HOOOOOWL
SO THE SURVEY CORPS CAME TO SAVE US!
DAMN IT... THEY'RE ALREADY CLOSE.
THIS IS ALL BECAUSE EREN GOT VIOLENT...
TH-THUMP
TH-THUMP

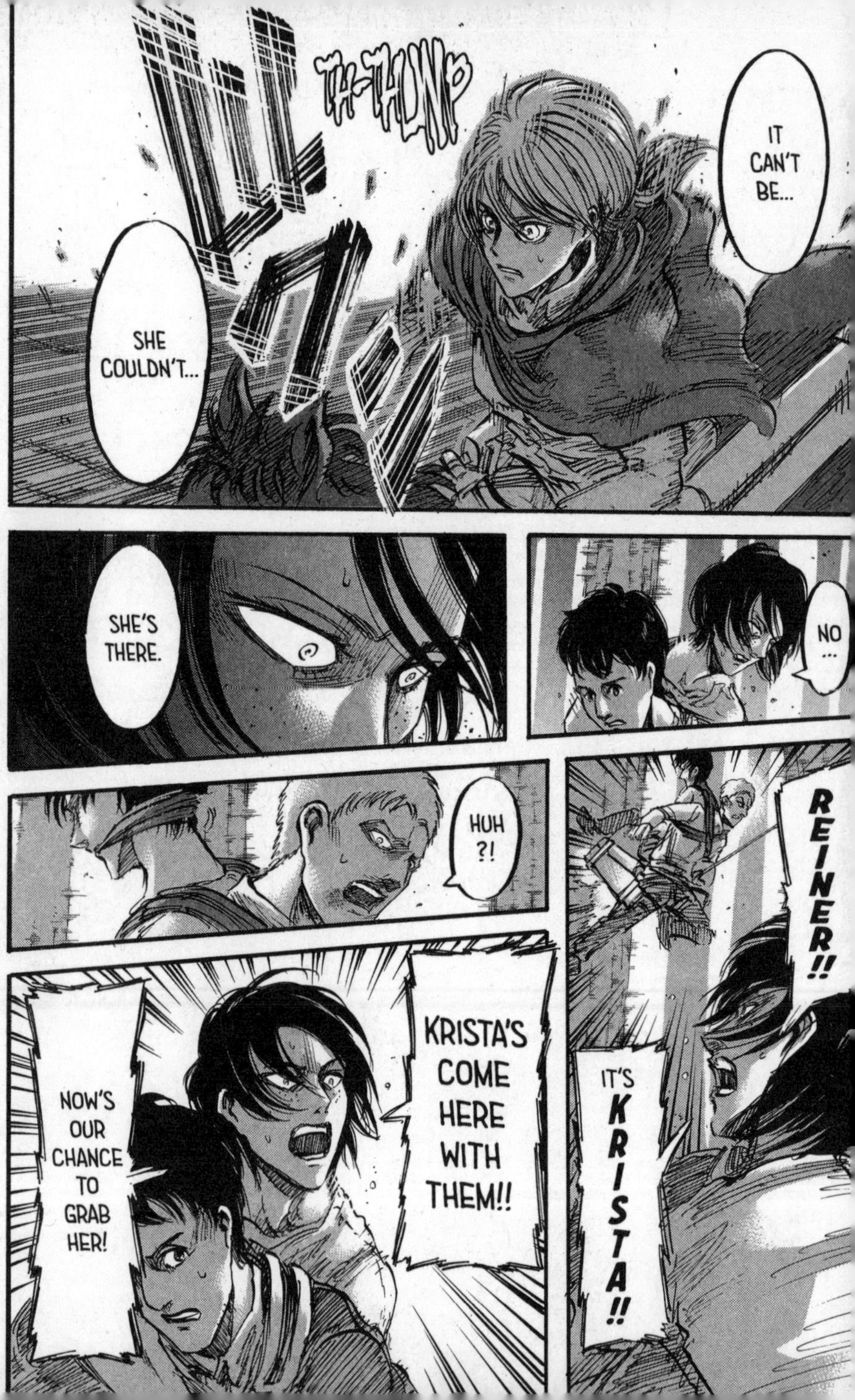
IT CAN'T BE...
TH-THUMP
SHE COULDN'T...
NO ...
SHE'S THERE.
REINER!!
IT'S KRISTA!!
HUH ?!
KRISTA'S COME HERE WITH THEM!!
NOW'S OUR CHANCE TO GRAB HER!

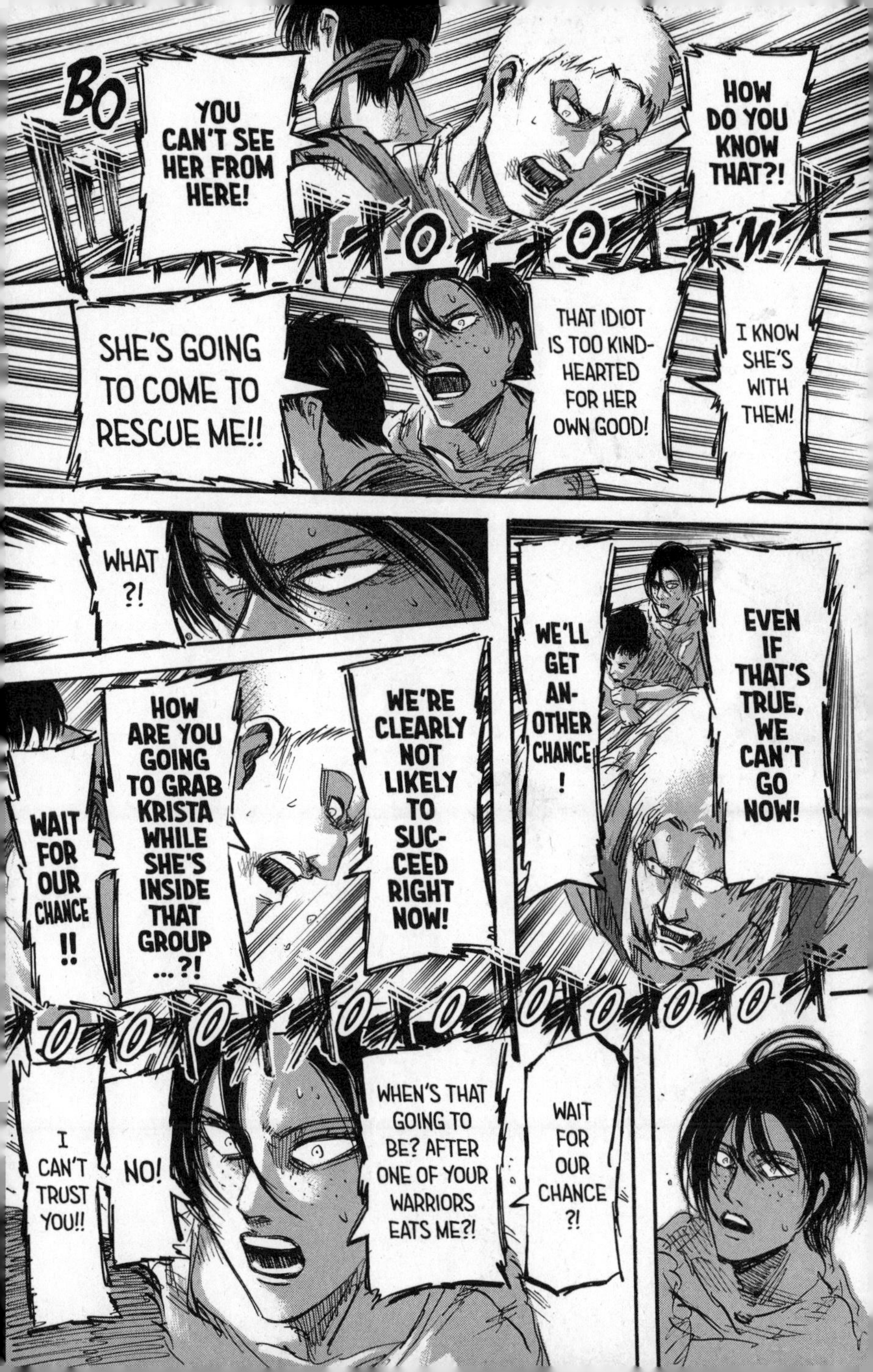
HOW DO YOU KNOW THAT?!
YOU CAN'T SEE HER FROM HERE!
BO
I KNOW SHE'S WITH THEM!
THAT IDIOT IS TOO KIND-HEARTED FOR HER OWN GOOD!
SHE'S GOING TO COME TO RESCUE ME!!
EVEN IF THAT'S TRUE, WE CAN'T GO NOW!
WE'LL GET AN-OTHER CHANCE!
WHAT ?!
WE'RE CLEARLY NOT LIKELY TO SUC-CEED RIGHT NOW!
HOW ARE YOU GOING TO GRAB KRISTA WHILE SHE'S INSIDE THAT GROUP ...?!
WAIT FOR OUR CHANCE !!
WAIT FOR OUR CHANCE ?!
WHEN'S THAT GOING TO BE? AFTER ONE OF YOUR WARRIORS EATS ME?!
NO!
I CAN'T TRUST YOU!!

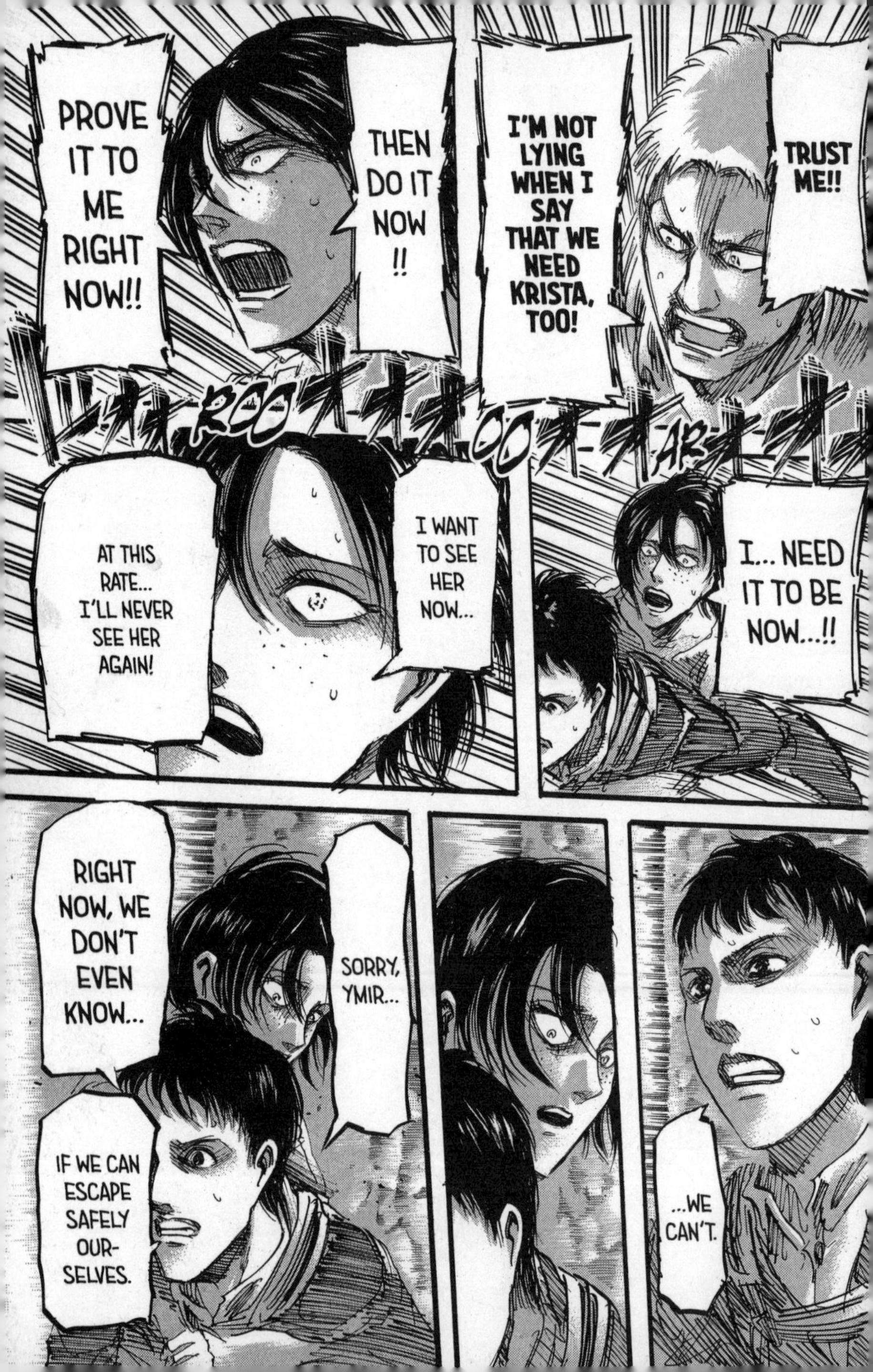
TRUST ME!!
I'M NOT LYING WHEN I SAY THAT WE NEED KRISTA, TOO!
THEN DO IT NOW !!
PROVE IT TO ME RIGHT NOW!!
ROO OO AR
I... NEED IT TO BE NOW...!!
I WANT TO SEE HER NOW...
AT THIS RATE... I'LL NEVER SEE HER AGAIN!
...WE CAN'T.
SORRY, YMIR...
RIGHT NOW, WE DON'T EVEN KNOW...
IF WE CAN ESCAPE SAFELY OUR-SELVES.

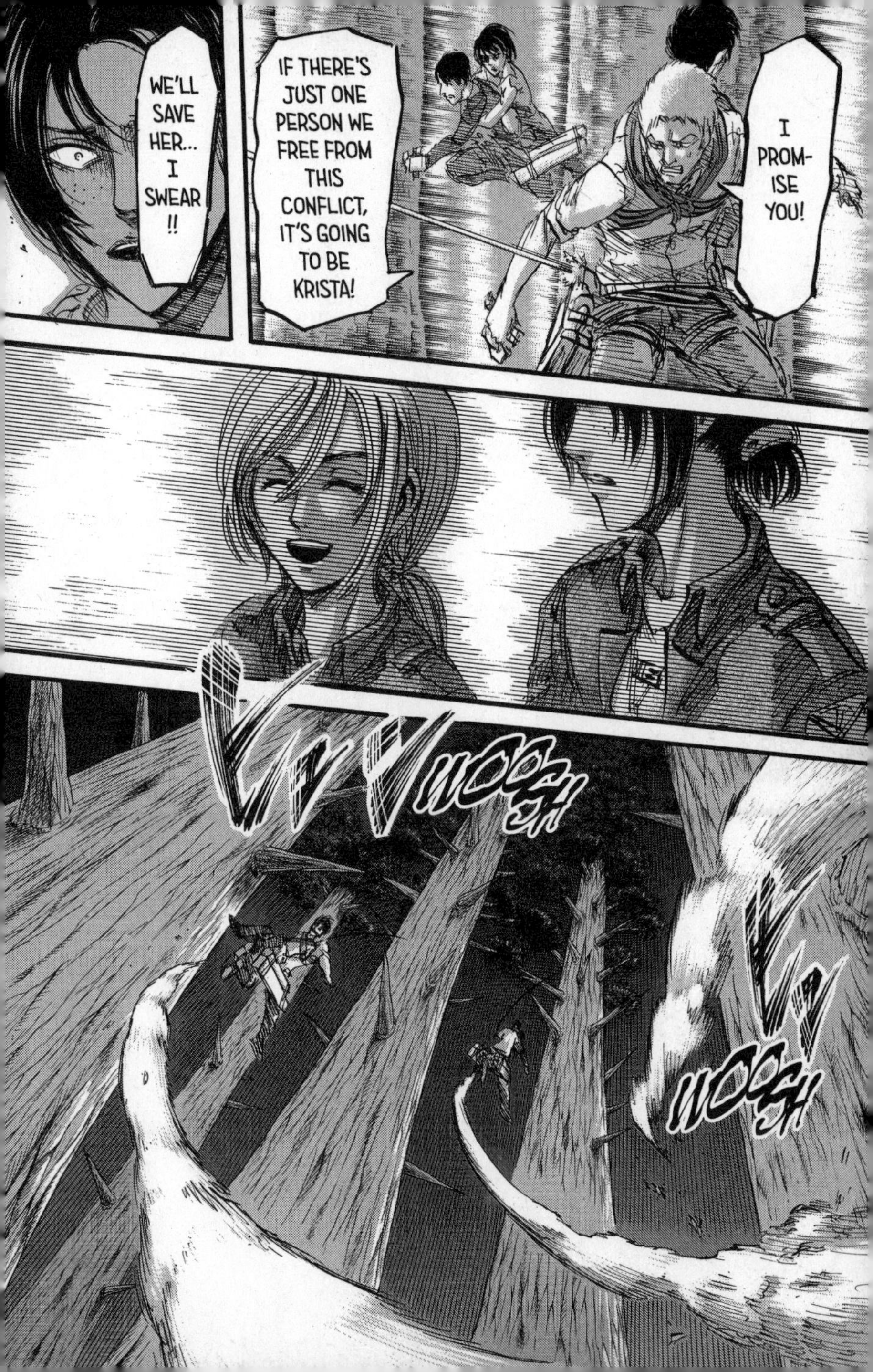
IF THERE'S JUST ONE PERSON WE FREE FROM THIS CONFLICT, IT'S GOING TO BE KRISTA!
I PROMISE YOU!
WE'LL SAVE HER... I SWEAR!!
VVWOOSH!
VVVWOOSH!

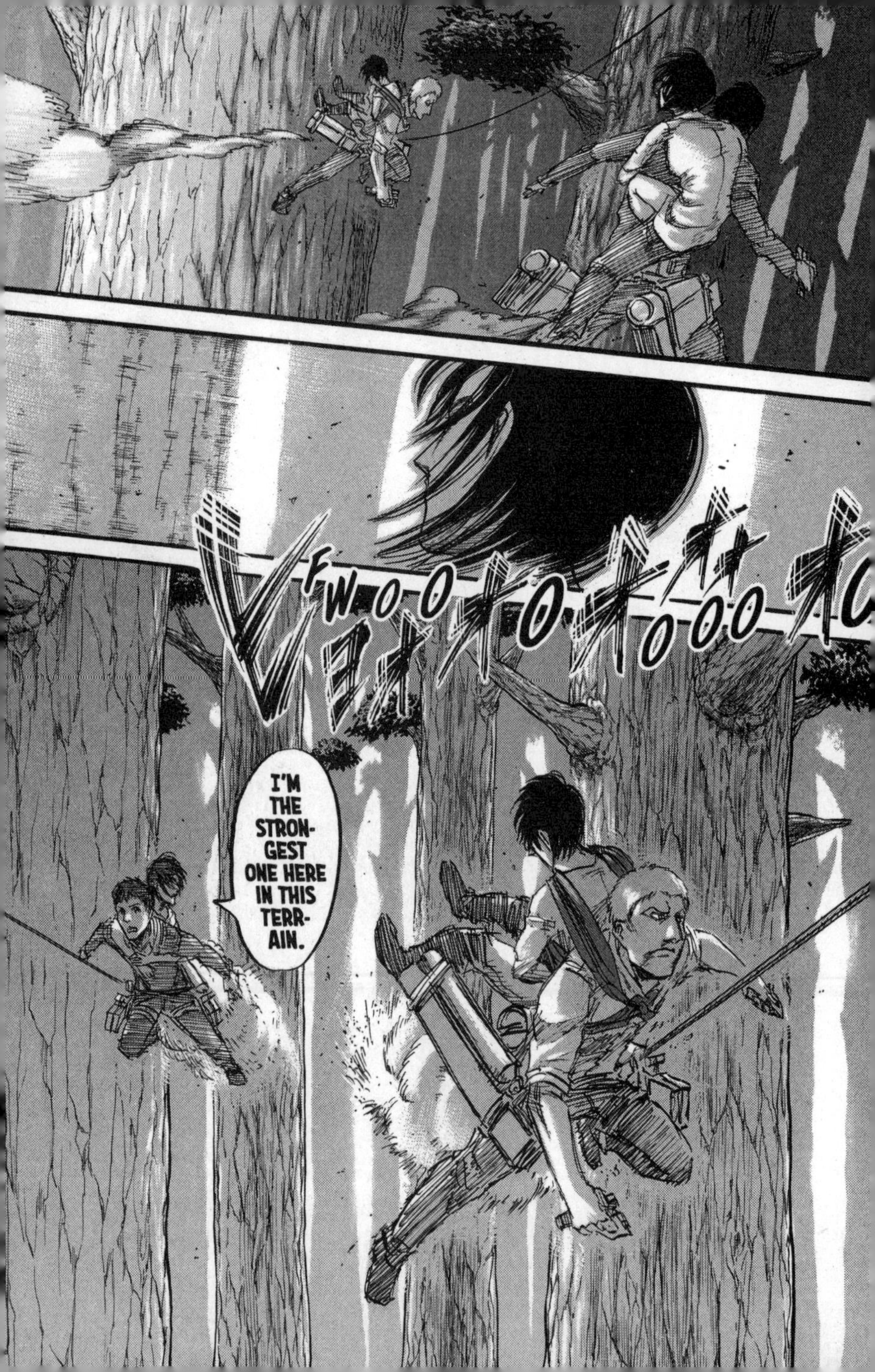
I'M THE STRONGEST ONE HERE IN THIS TERRAIN.

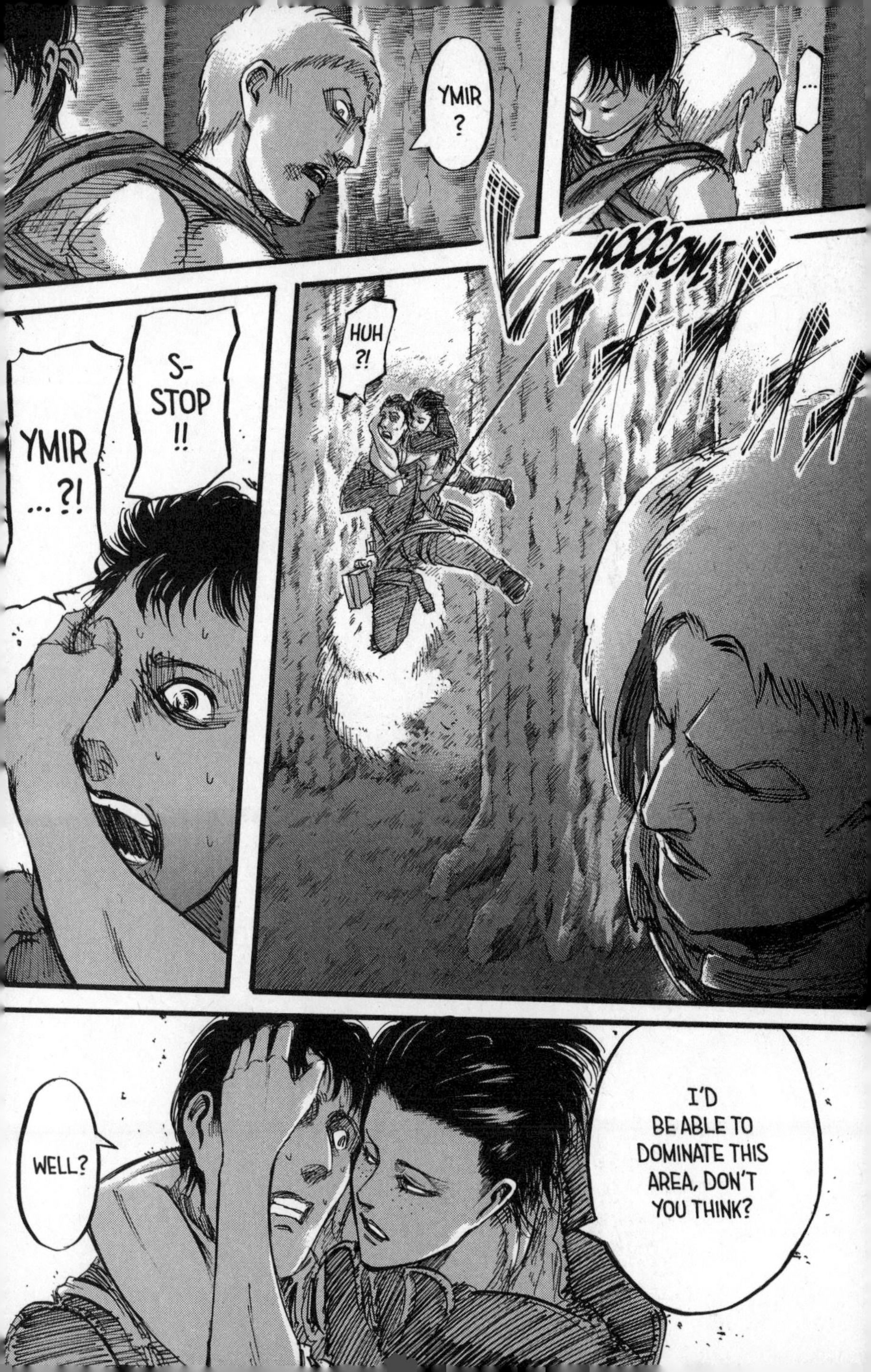
...
YMIR ?
HOOOOM
HUH ?!
S- STOP !!
YMIR ...?!
I'D BE ABLE TO DOMINATE THIS AREA, DON'T YOU THINK?
WELL?

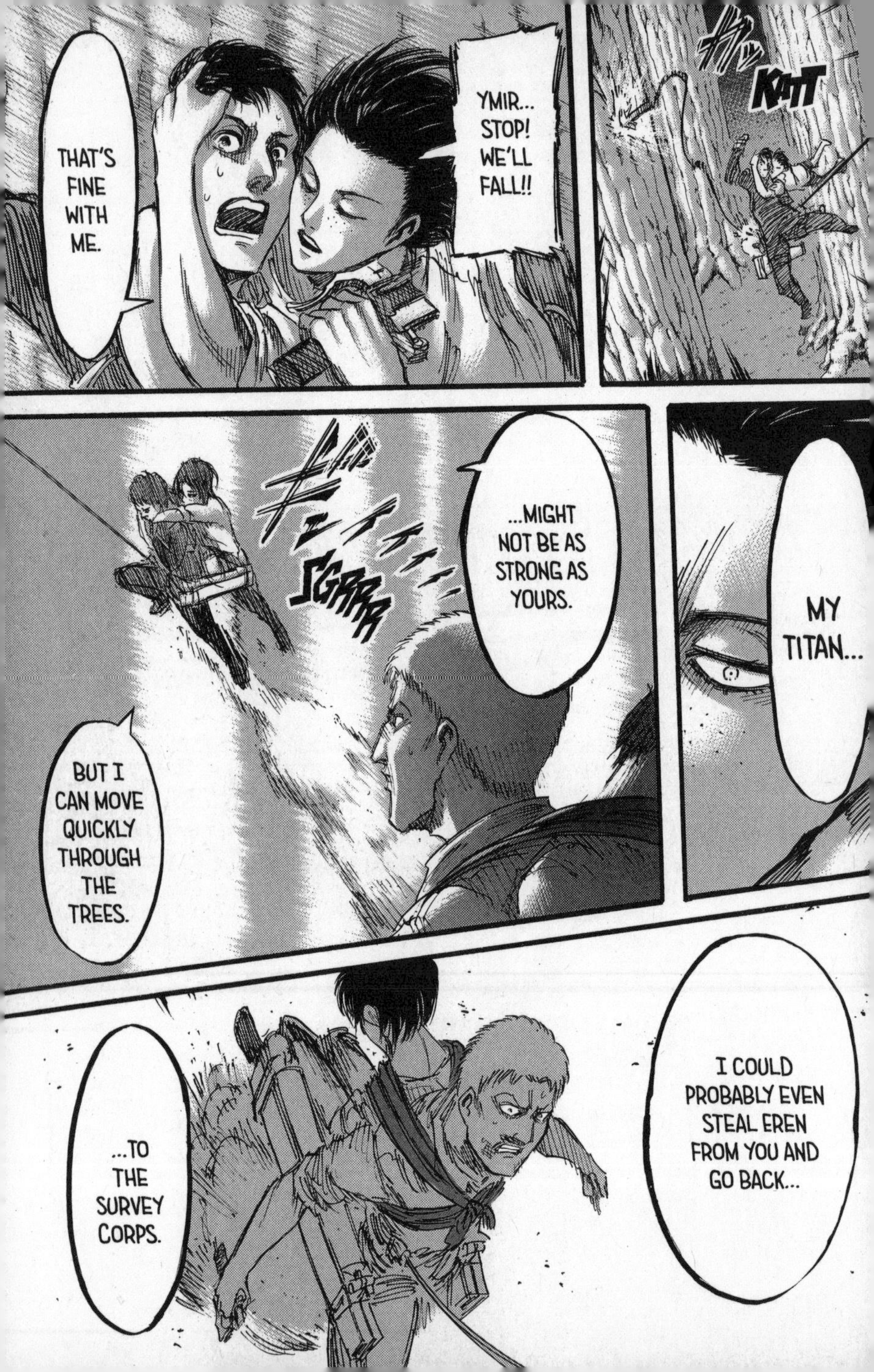
KATT
YMIR... STOP! WE'LL FALL!!
THAT'S FINE WITH ME.
MY TITAN...
...MIGHT NOT BE AS STRONG AS YOURS.
SGRRR
BUT I CAN MOVE QUICKLY THROUGH THE TREES.
I COULD PROBABLY EVEN STEAL EREN FROM YOU AND GO BACK...
...TO THE SURVEY CORPS.

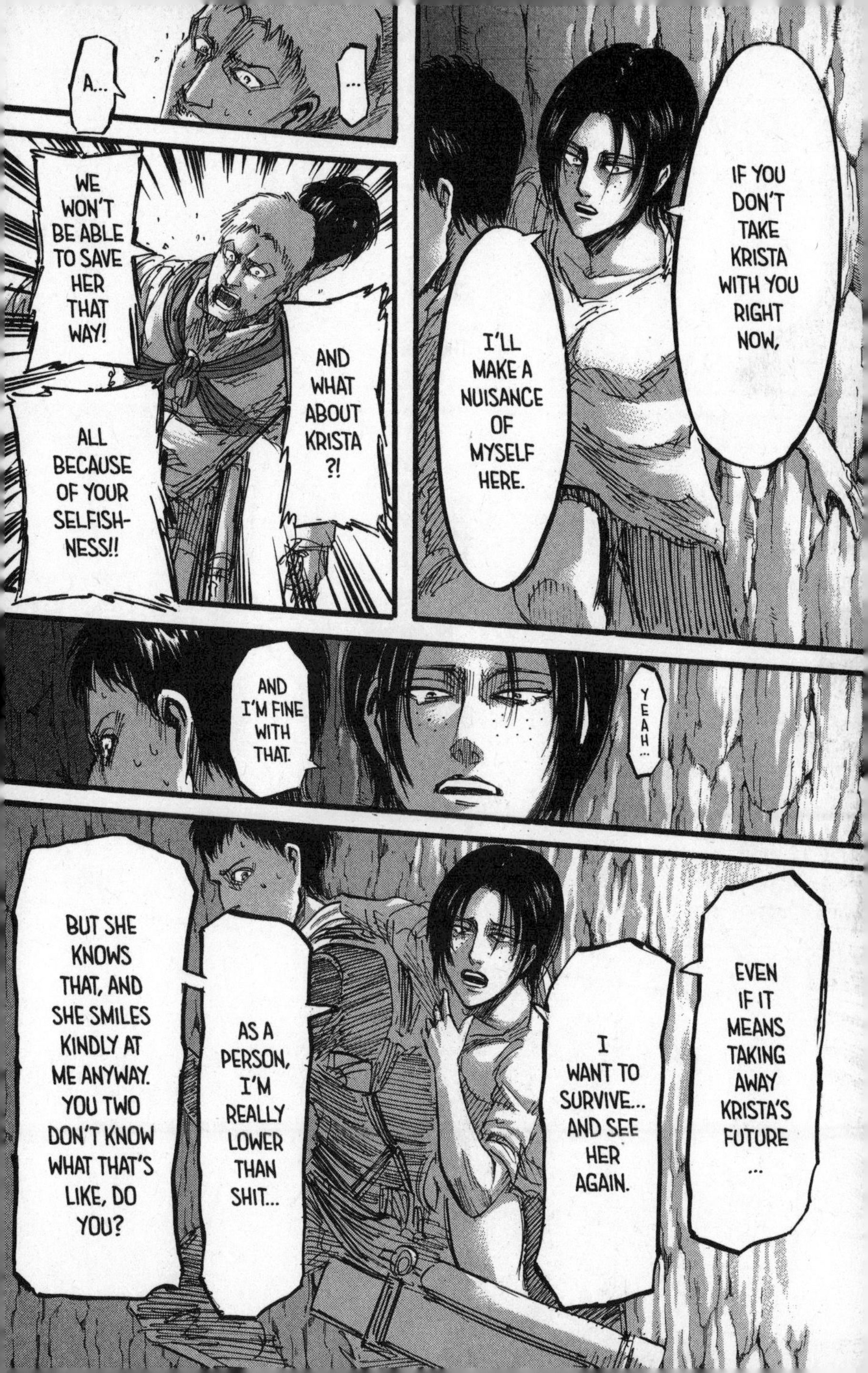
IF YOU DON'T TAKE KRISTA WITH YOU RIGHT NOW,
I'LL MAKE A NUISANCE OF MYSELF HERE.
...
A...
AND WHAT ABOUT KRISTA?!
WE WON'T BE ABLE TO SAVE HER THAT WAY!
ALL BECAUSE OF YOUR SELFISH-NESS!!
YEAH...
AND I'M FINE WITH THAT.
EVEN IF IT MEANS TAKING AWAY KRISTA'S FUTURE...
I WANT TO SURVIVE... AND SEE HER AGAIN.
AS A PERSON, I'M REALLY LOWER THAN SHIT...
BUT SHE KNOWS THAT, AND SHE SMILES KINDLY AT ME ANYWAY. YOU TWO DON'T KNOW WHAT THAT'S LIKE, DO YOU?

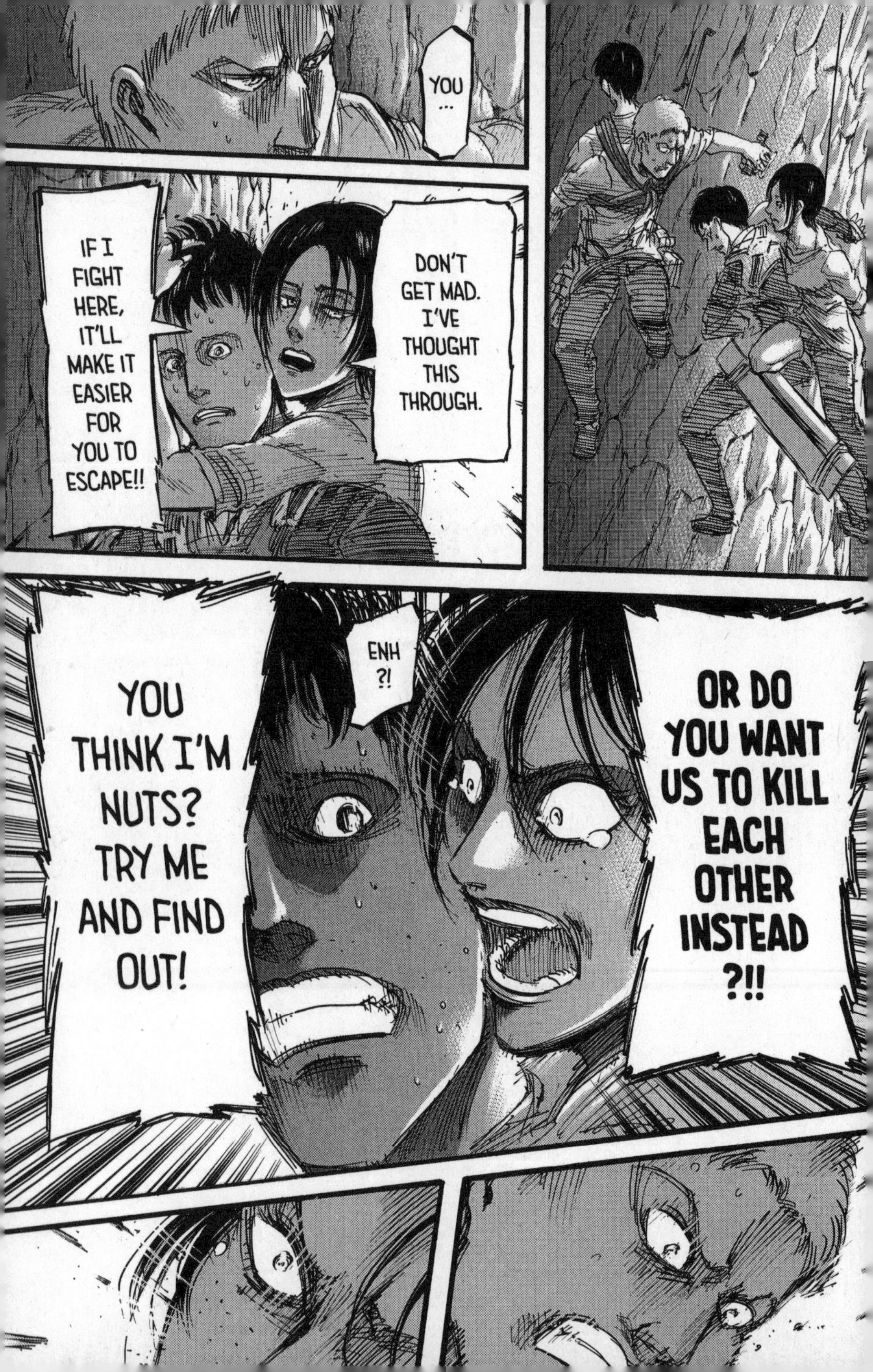
YOU ...
DON'T GET MAD. I'VE THOUGHT THIS THROUGH.
IF I FIGHT HERE, IT'LL MAKE IT EASIER FOR YOU TO ESCAPE!!
OR DO YOU WANT US TO KILL EACH OTHER INSTEAD ?!!
ENH ?!
YOU THINK I'M NUTS? TRY ME AND FIND OUT!

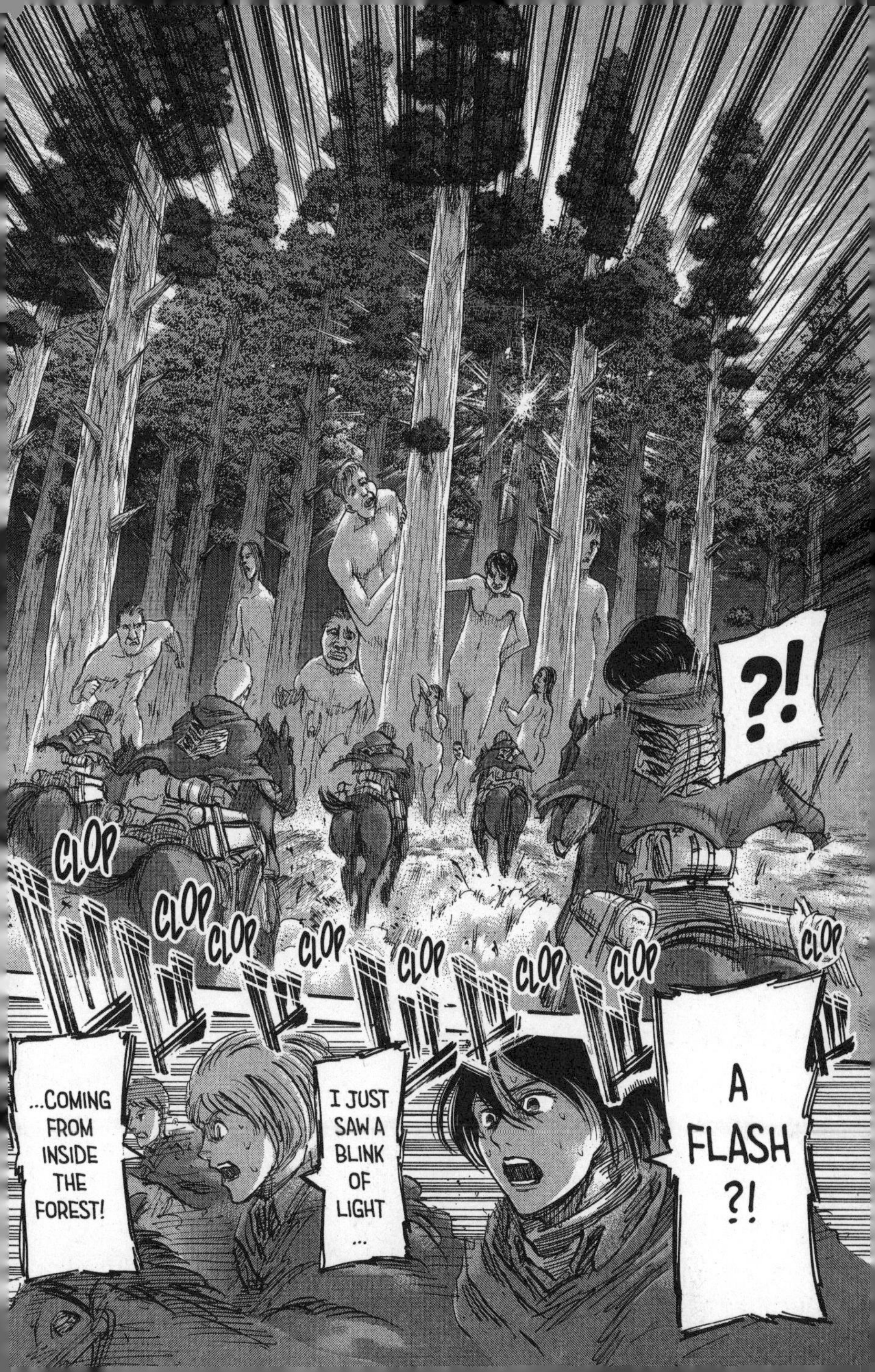
?!
CLOP
CLOP
CLOP
CLOP
CLOP
CLOP
CLOP
CLOP
CLOP
A FLASH ?!
I JUST SAW A BLINK OF LIGHT ...
...COMING FROM INSIDE THE FOREST!

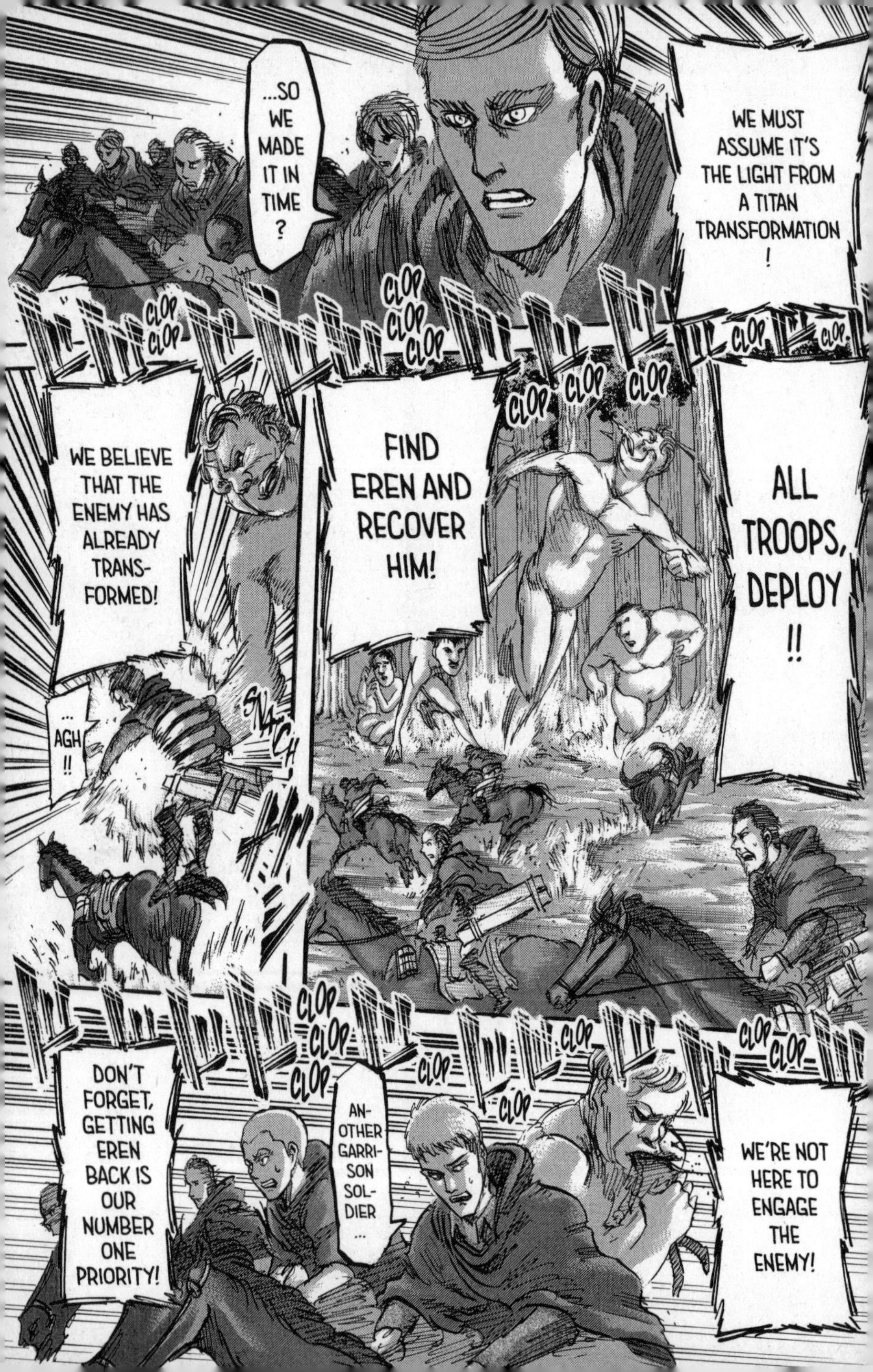
WE MUST ASSUME IT'S THE LIGHT FROM A TITAN TRANSFORMATION !
CLOP CLOP
...SO WE MADE IT IN TIME ?
CLOP CLOP CLOP
CLOP CLOP
ALL TROOPS, DEPLOY !!
CLOP CLOP CLOP
FIND EREN AND RECOVER HIM!
WE BELIEVE THAT THE ENEMY HAS ALREADY TRANS-FORMED!
SNATCH
... AGH !!
CLOP CLOP
WE'RE NOT HERE TO ENGAGE THE ENEMY!
CLOP CLOP CLOP
AN-OTHER GARRI-SON SOL-DIER ...
CLOP CLOP CLOP
DON'T FORGET, GETTING EREN BACK IS OUR NUMBER ONE PRIORITY!

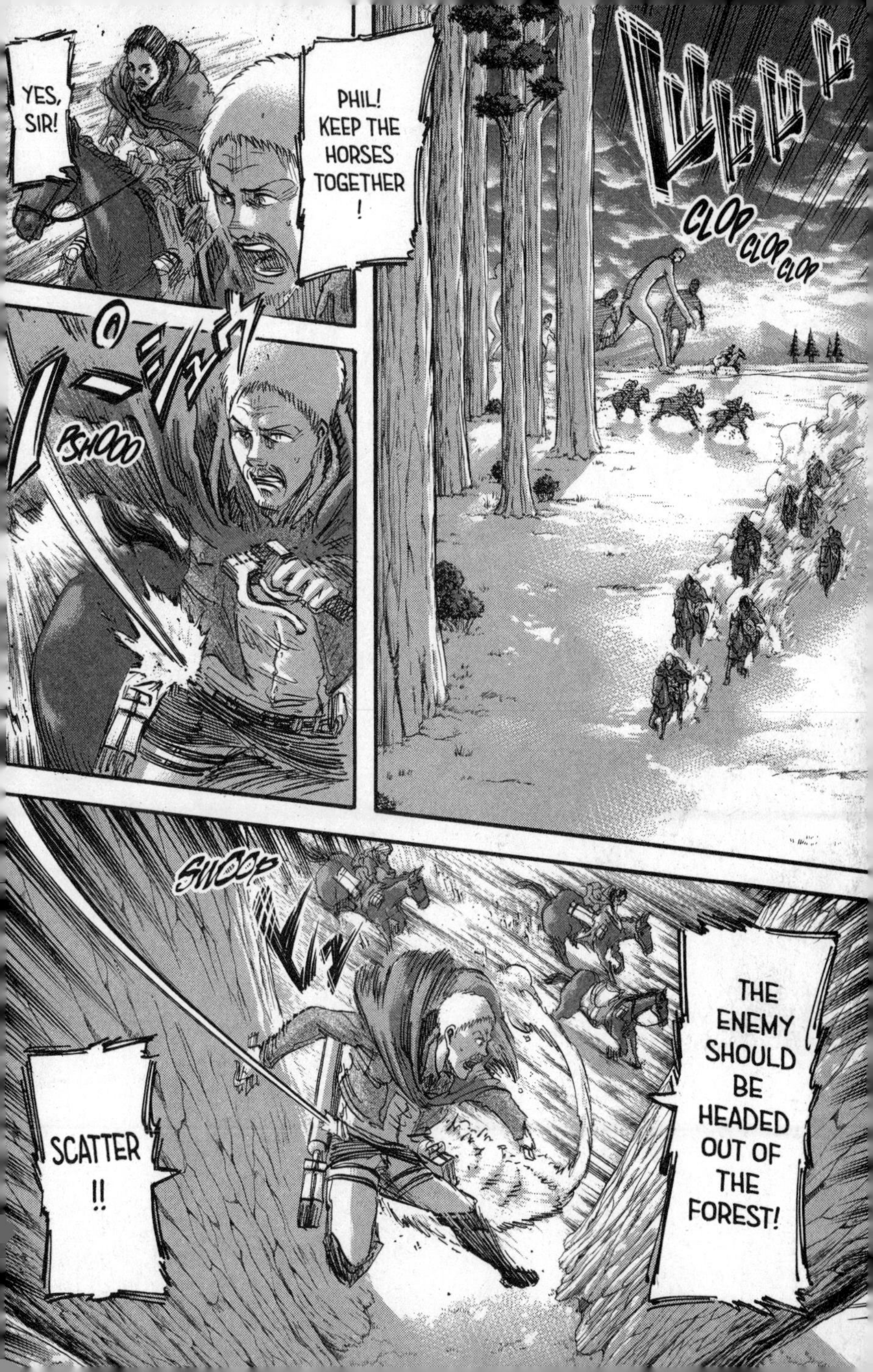
CLOP CLOP CLOP
PHIL! KEEP THE HORSES TOGETHER!
YES, SIR!
PSHOOO
THE ENEMY SHOULD BE HEADED OUT OF THE FOREST!
SWOOP
SCATTER!!

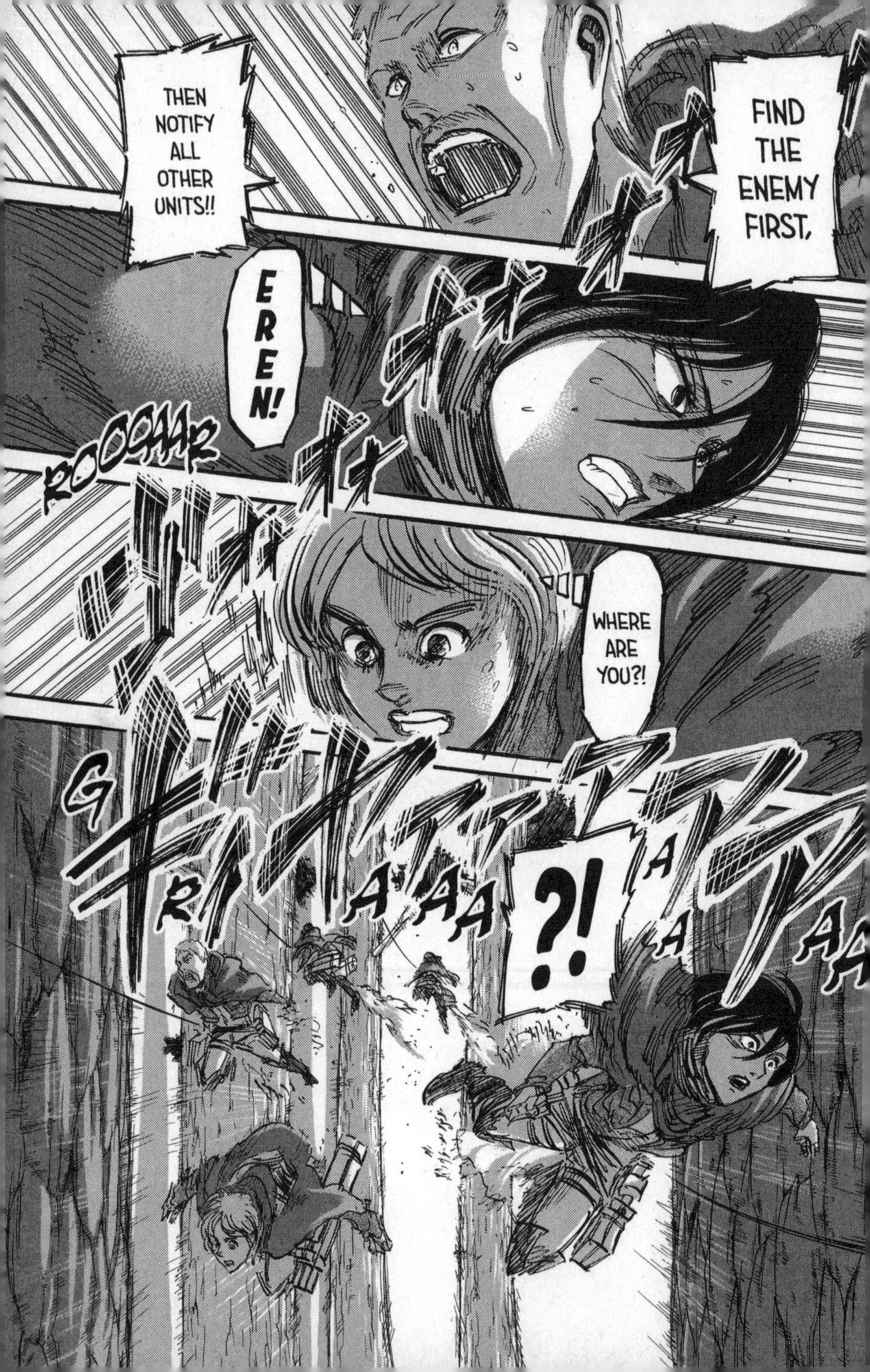
FIND THE ENEMY FIRST,
THEN NOTIFY ALL OTHER UNITS!!
EREN!
ROOOAAR
WHERE ARE YOU?!
GRAAAAAAA
?!

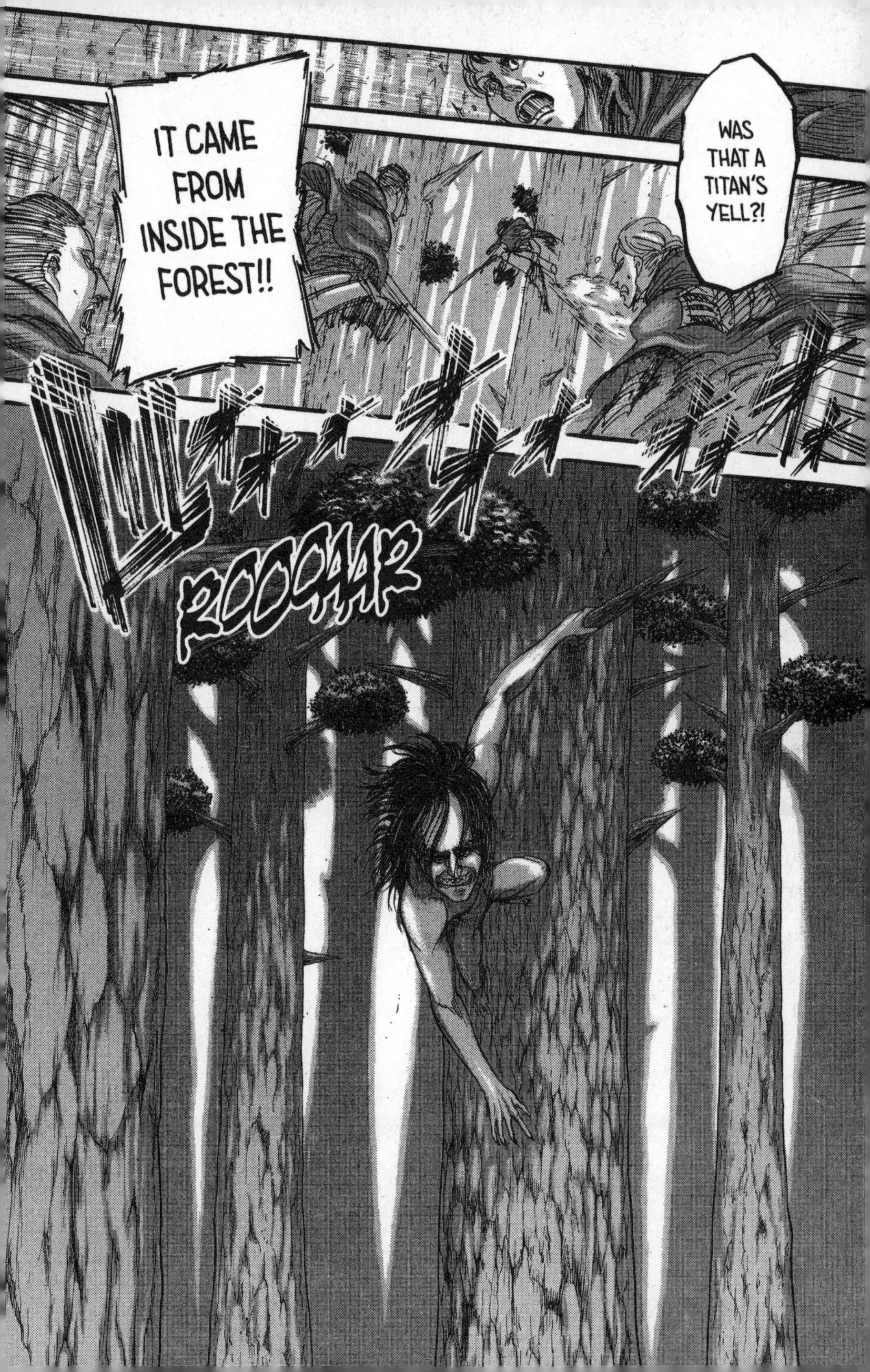
WAS THAT A TITAN'S YELL?!
IT CAME FROM INSIDE THE FOREST!!
ROOOAAR

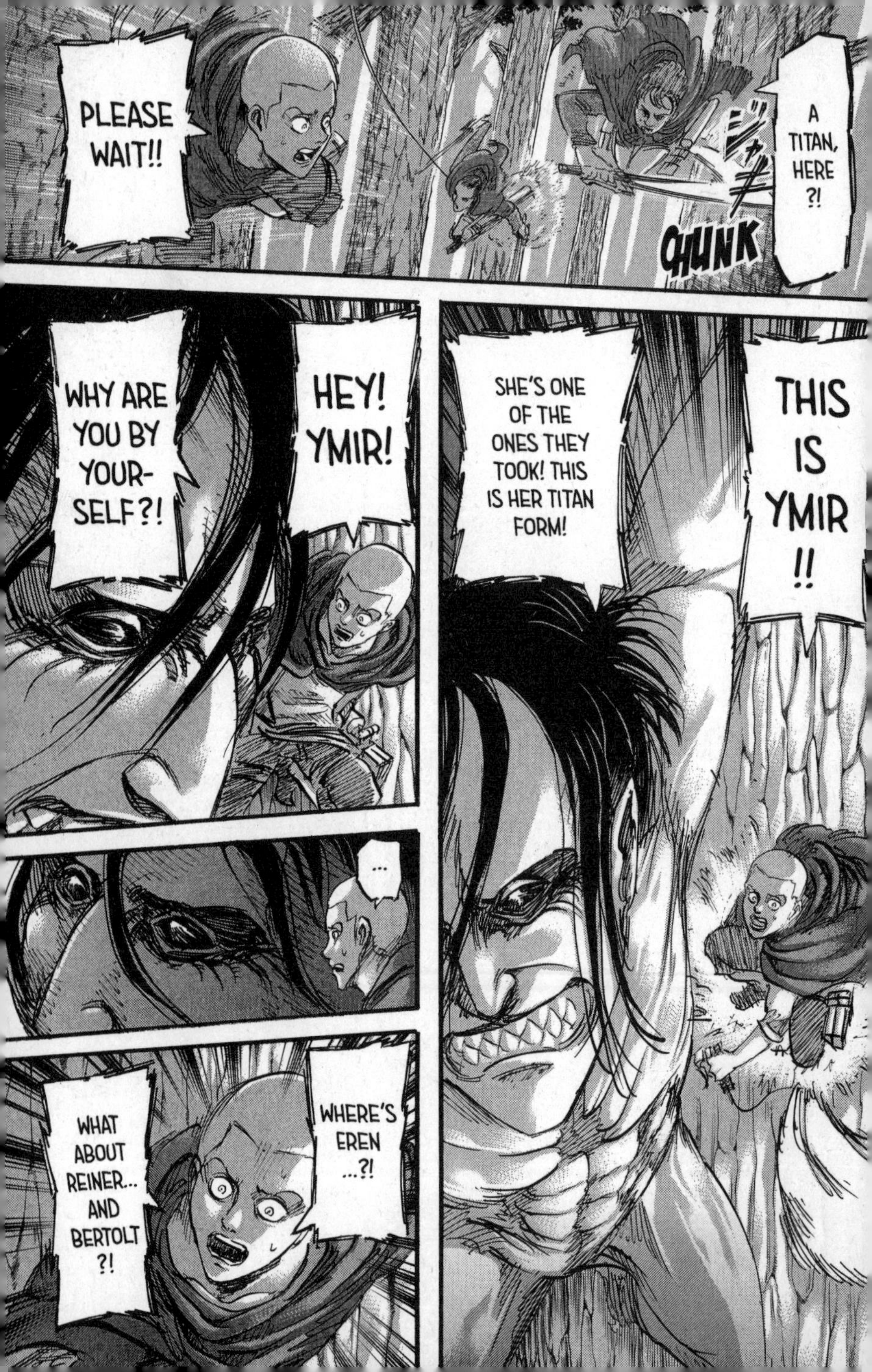
A TITAN, HERE ?!
CHUNK
PLEASE WAIT!!
THIS IS YMIR !!
SHE'S ONE OF THE ONES THEY TOOK! THIS IS HER TITAN FORM!
HEY! YMIR!
WHY ARE YOU BY YOUR-SELF?!
...
WHERE'S EREN ...?!
WHAT ABOUT REINER... AND BERTOLT ?!

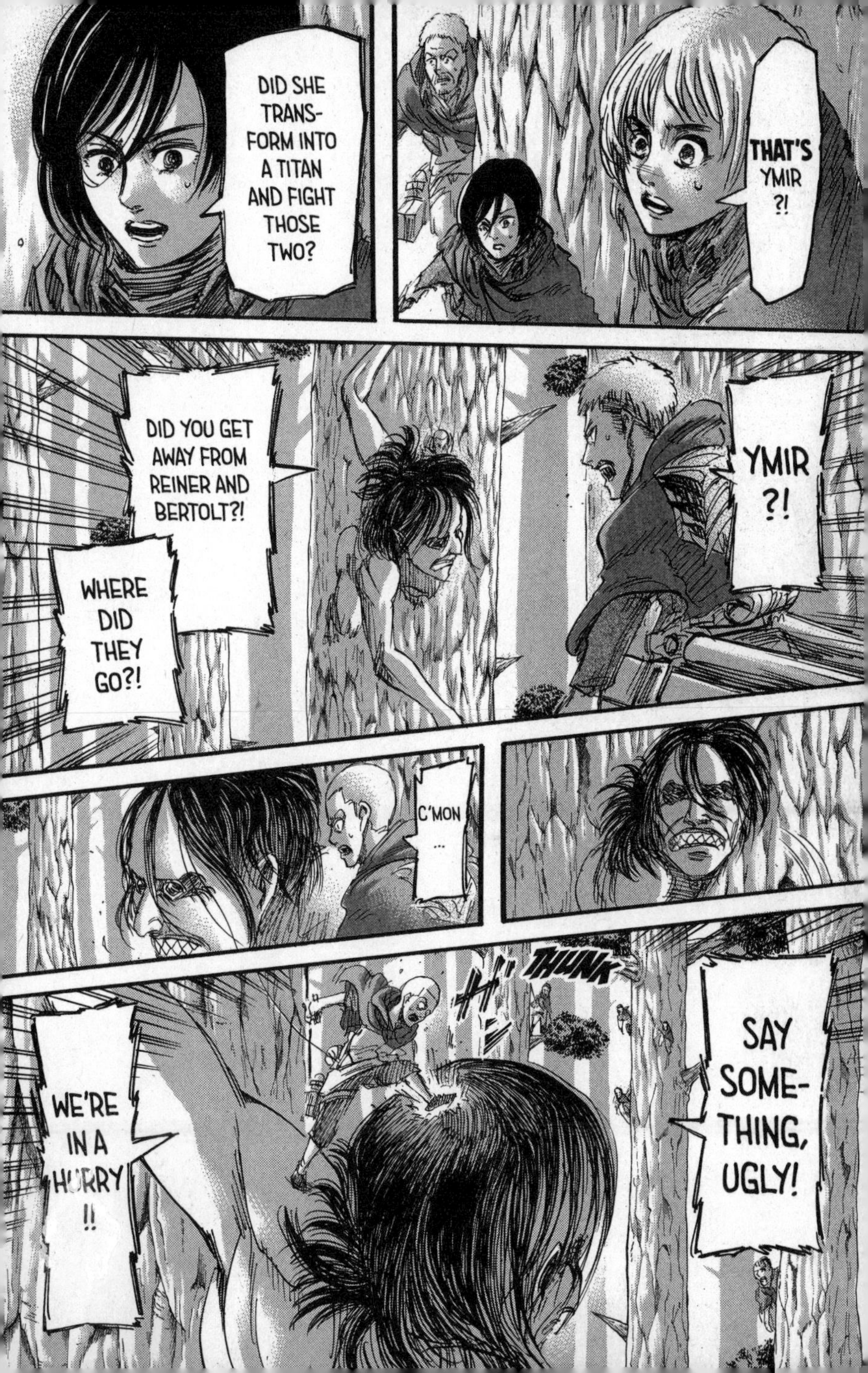
THAT'S YMIR ?!
DID SHE TRANS-FORM INTO A TITAN AND FIGHT THOSE TWO?
YMIR ?!
DID YOU GET AWAY FROM REINER AND BERTOLT?!
WHERE DID THEY GO?!
C'MON ...
THUNK
SAY SOME-THING, UGLY!
WE'RE IN A HURRY !!

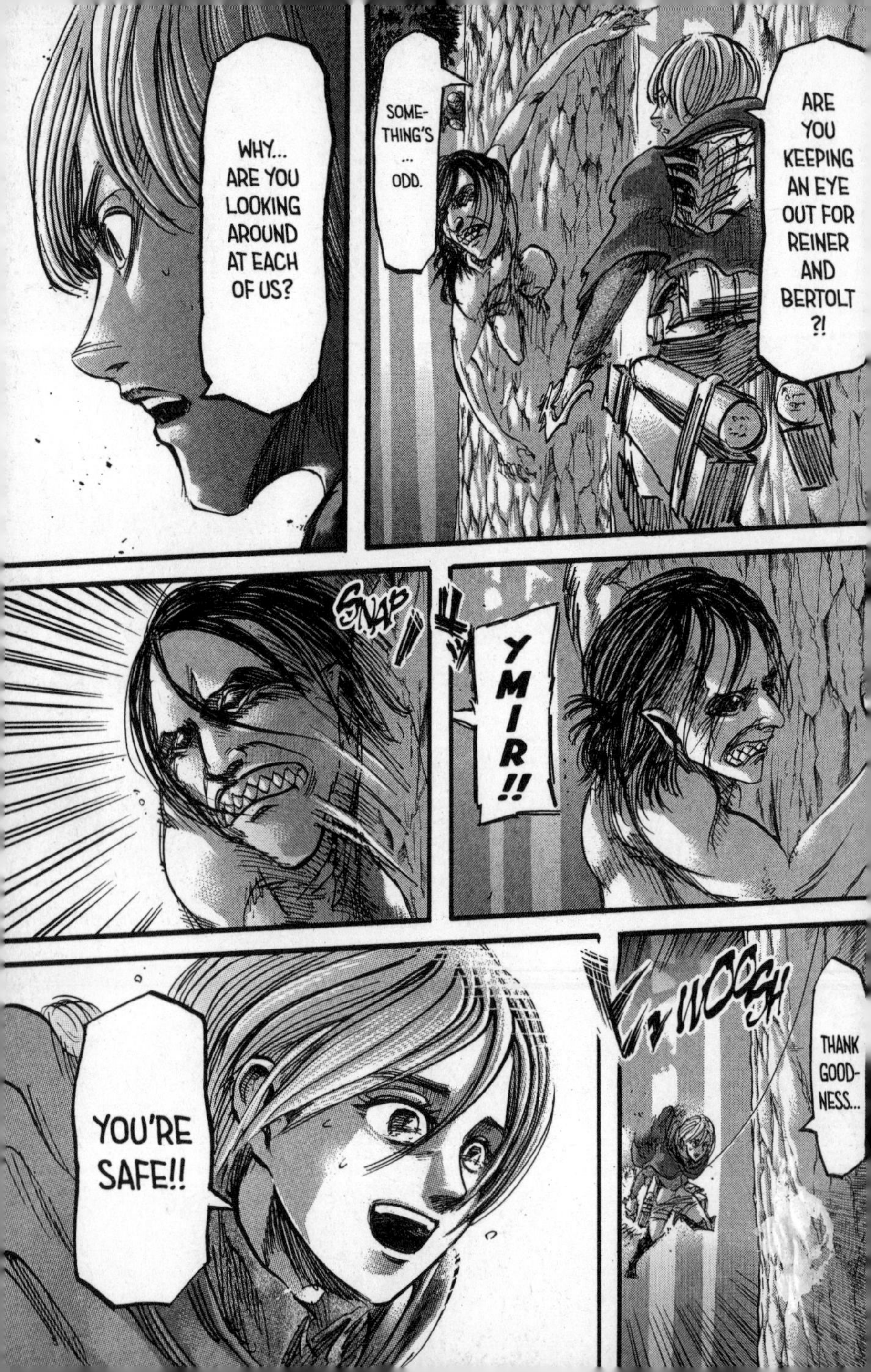
ARE YOU KEEPING AN EYE OUT FOR REINER AND BERTOLT ?!
SOME-THING'S ... ODD.
WHY... ARE YOU LOOKING AROUND AT EACH OF US?
SNAP
YMIR!!
WHOOSH
THANK GOOD-NESS...
YOU'RE SAFE!!

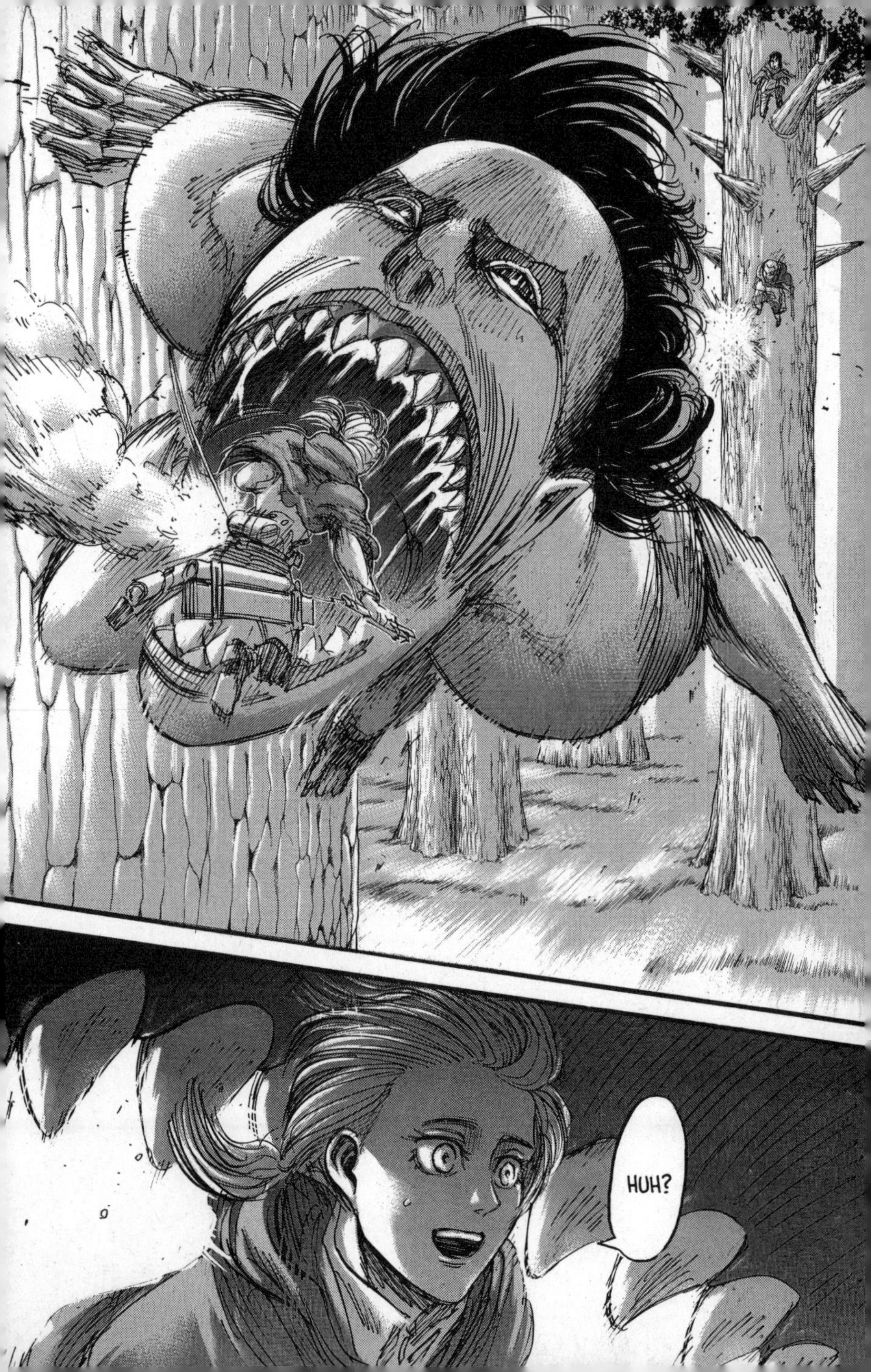
HUH?

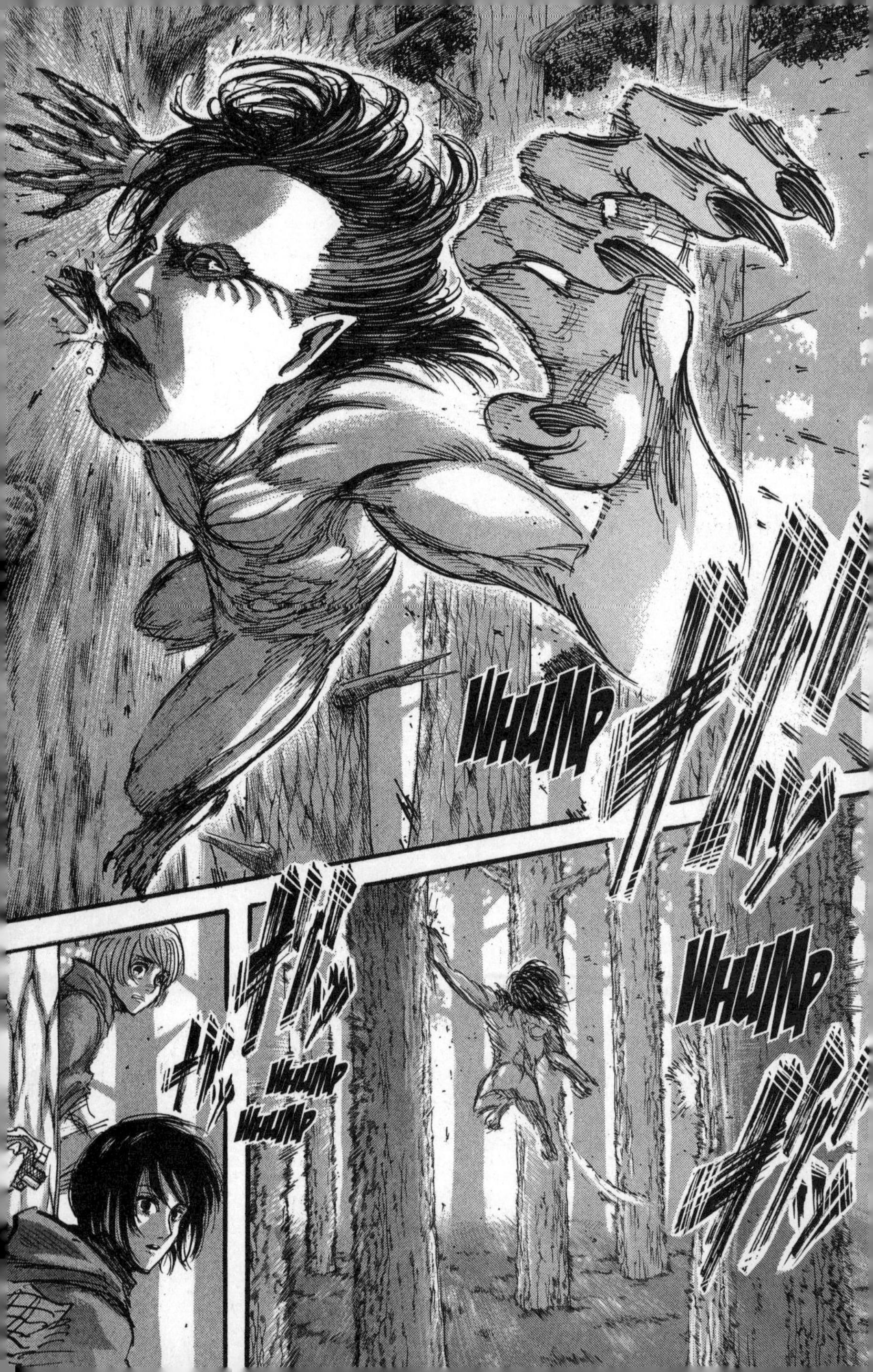
WHUMP
WHUMP
WHUMP
WHUMP

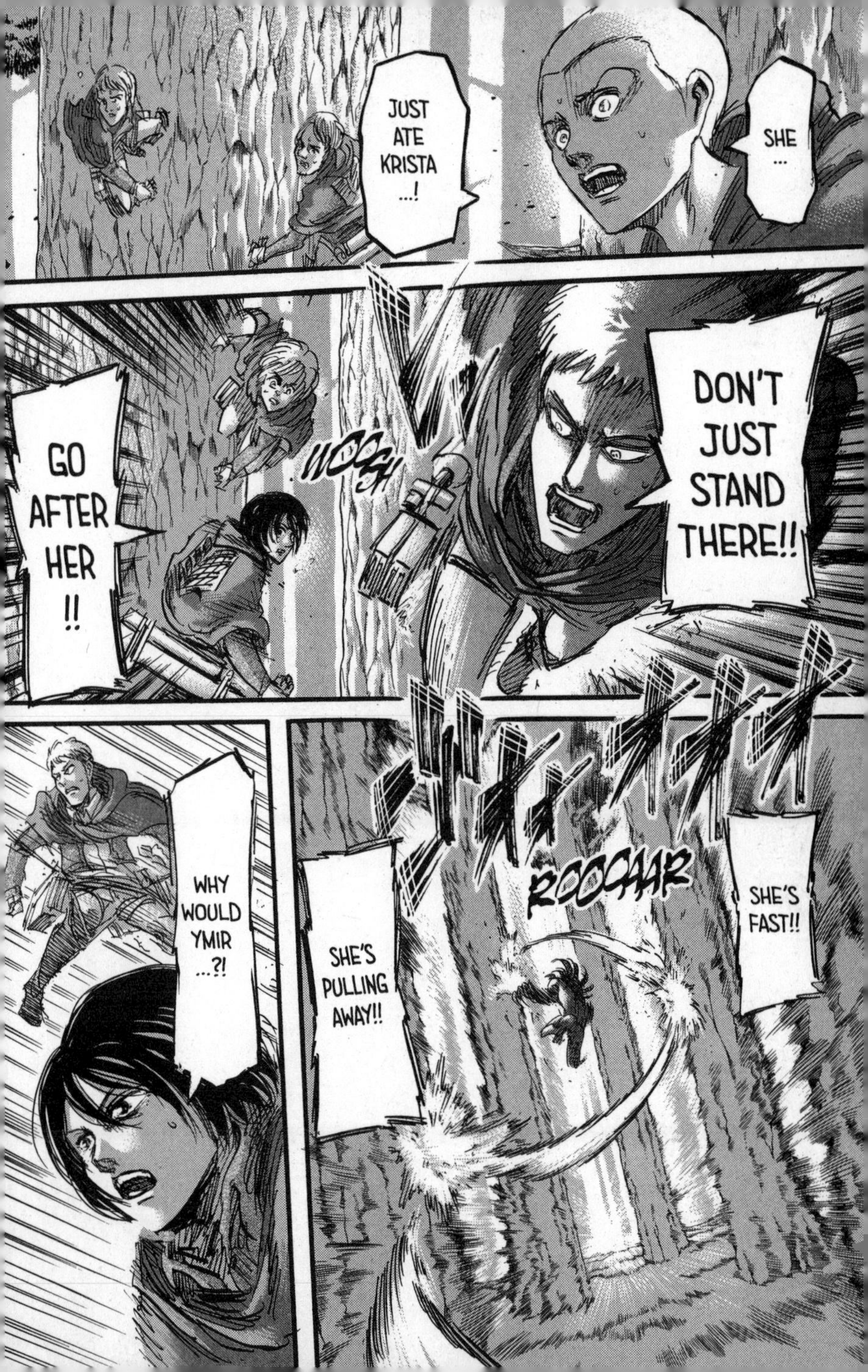
SHE ...
JUST ATE KRISTA ...!
DON'T JUST STAND THERE!!
WOOSH
GO AFTER HER !!
SHE'S FAST!!
ROOOAAR
SHE'S PULLING AWAY!!
WHY WOULD YMIR ...?!

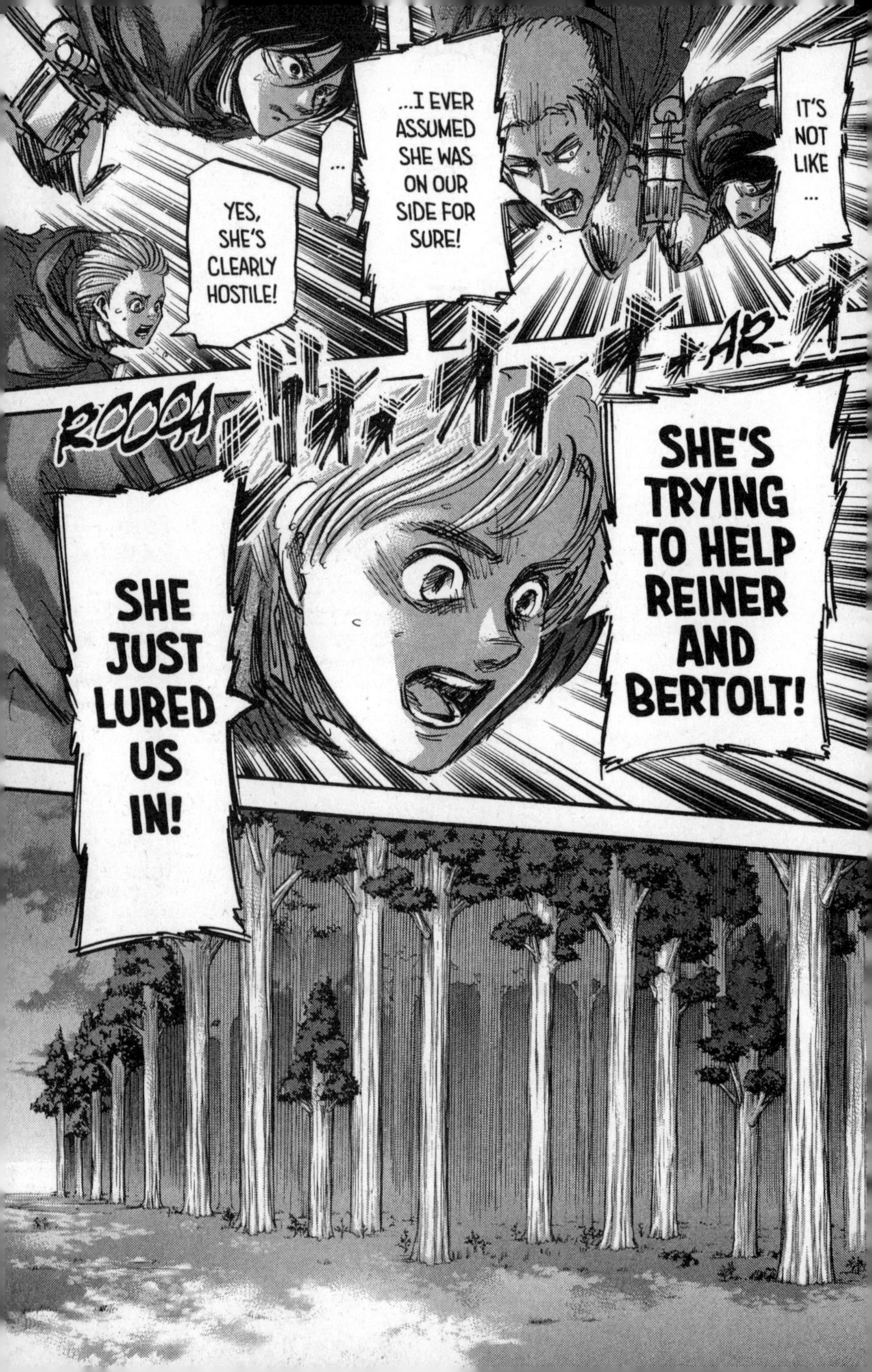
IT'S NOT LIKE ...
...I EVER ASSUMED SHE WAS ON OUR SIDE FOR SURE!
...
YES, SHE'S CLEARLY HOSTILE!
ROOOA
AR
SHE'S TRYING TO HELP REINER AND BERTOLT!
SHE JUST LURED US IN!

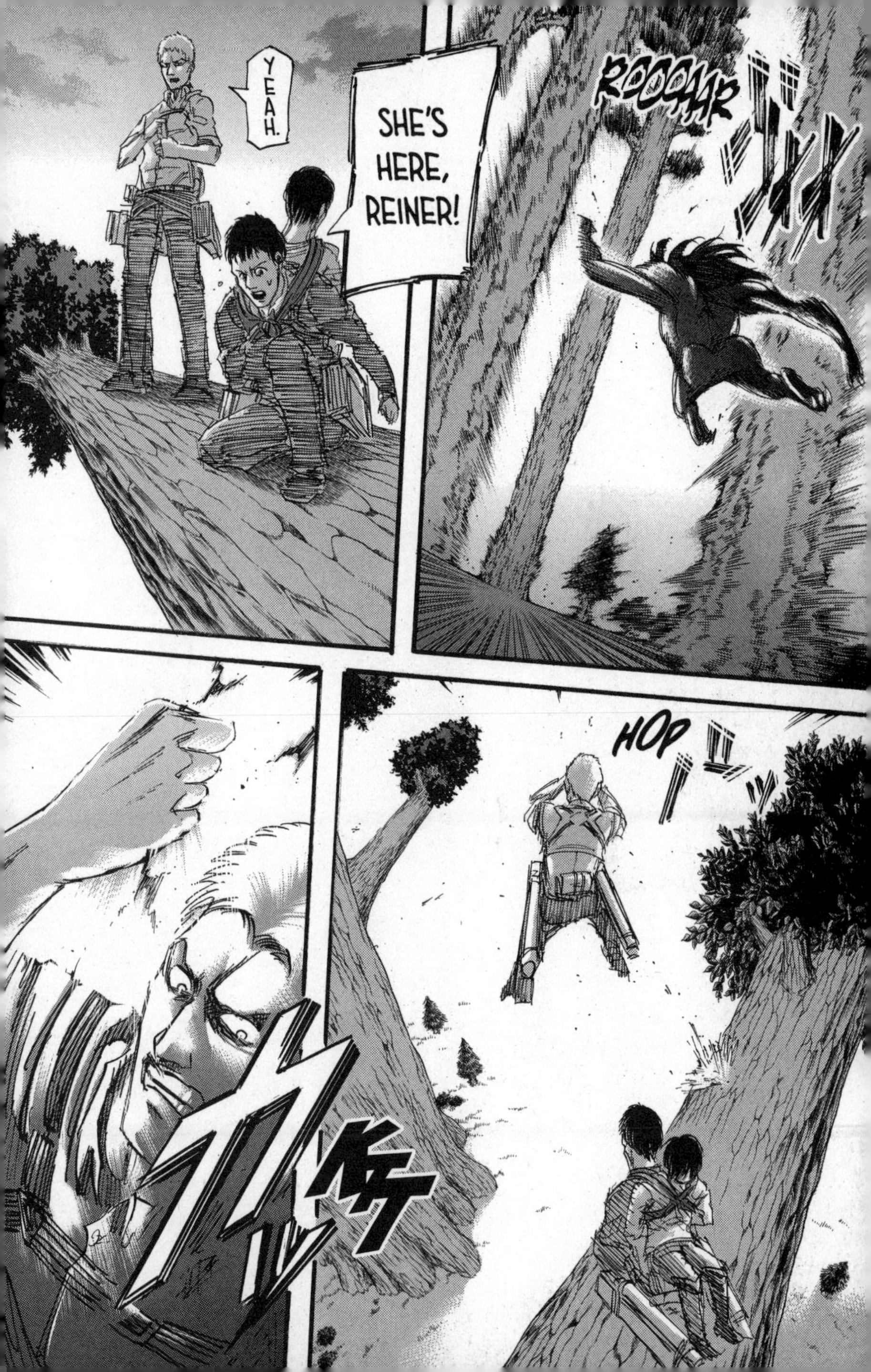
ROOOAAR
SHE'S HERE, REINER!
YEAH.
HOP

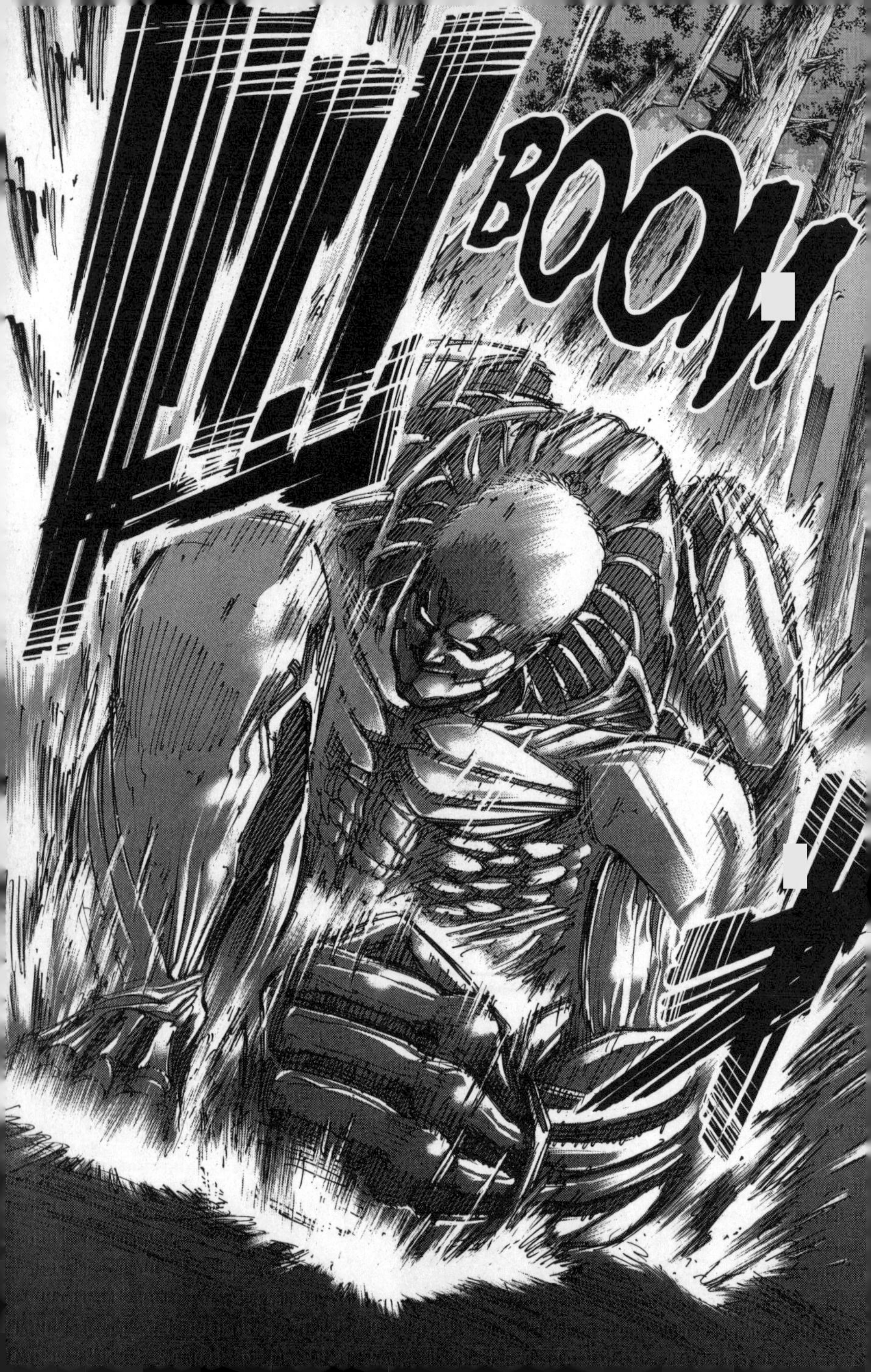
BOOM

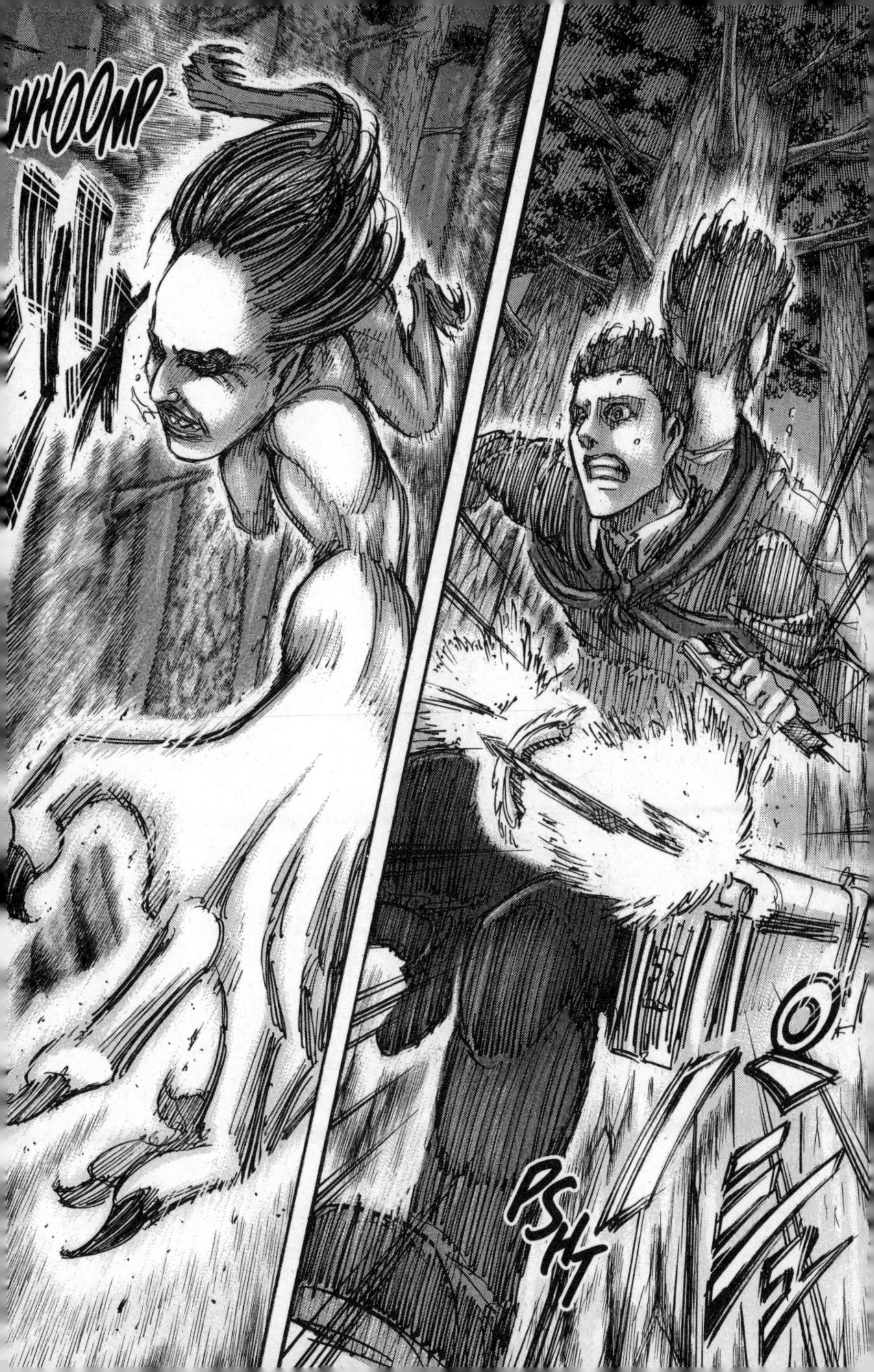
PSHT
WHOOMP

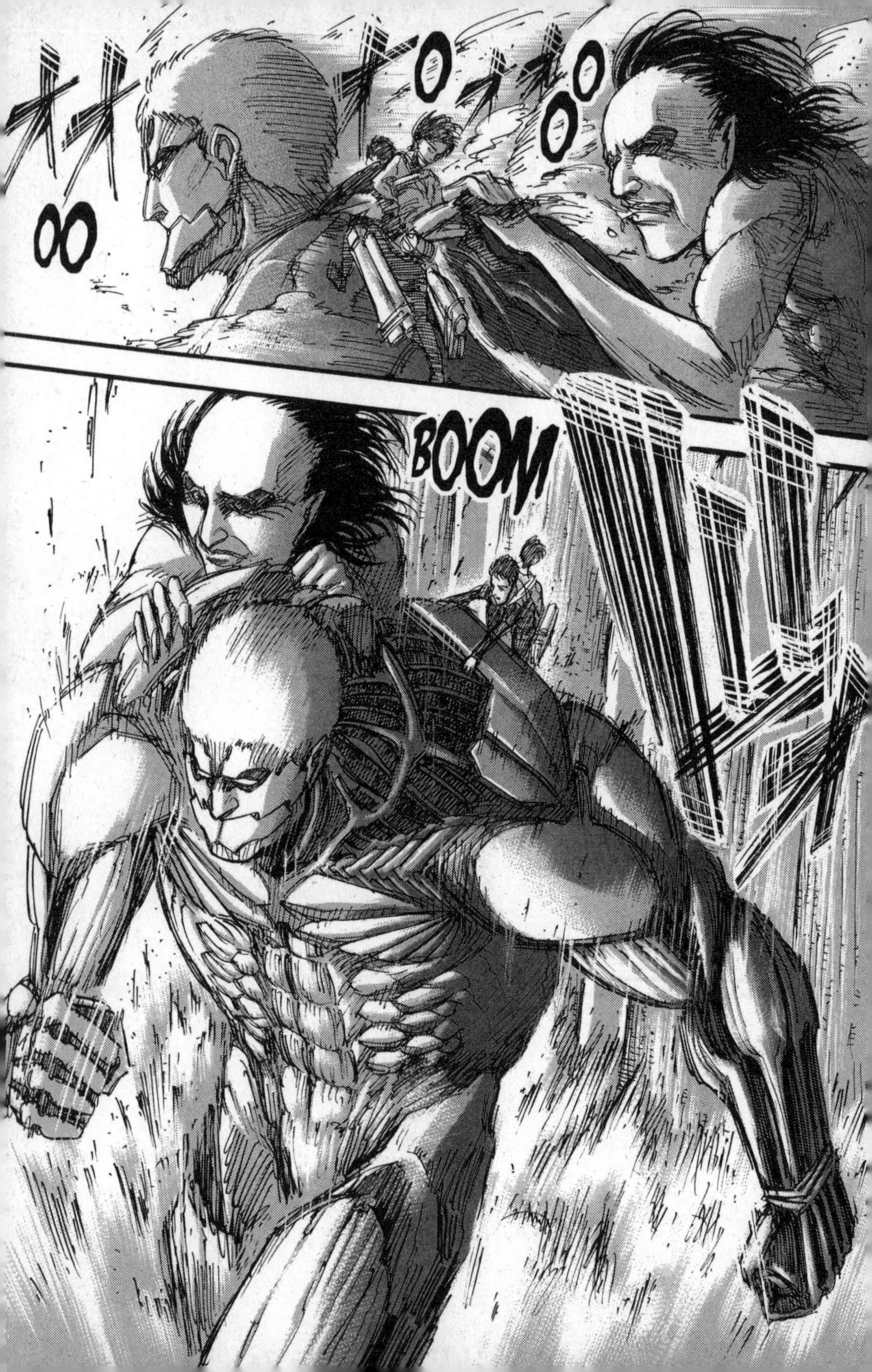
OO
BOOM

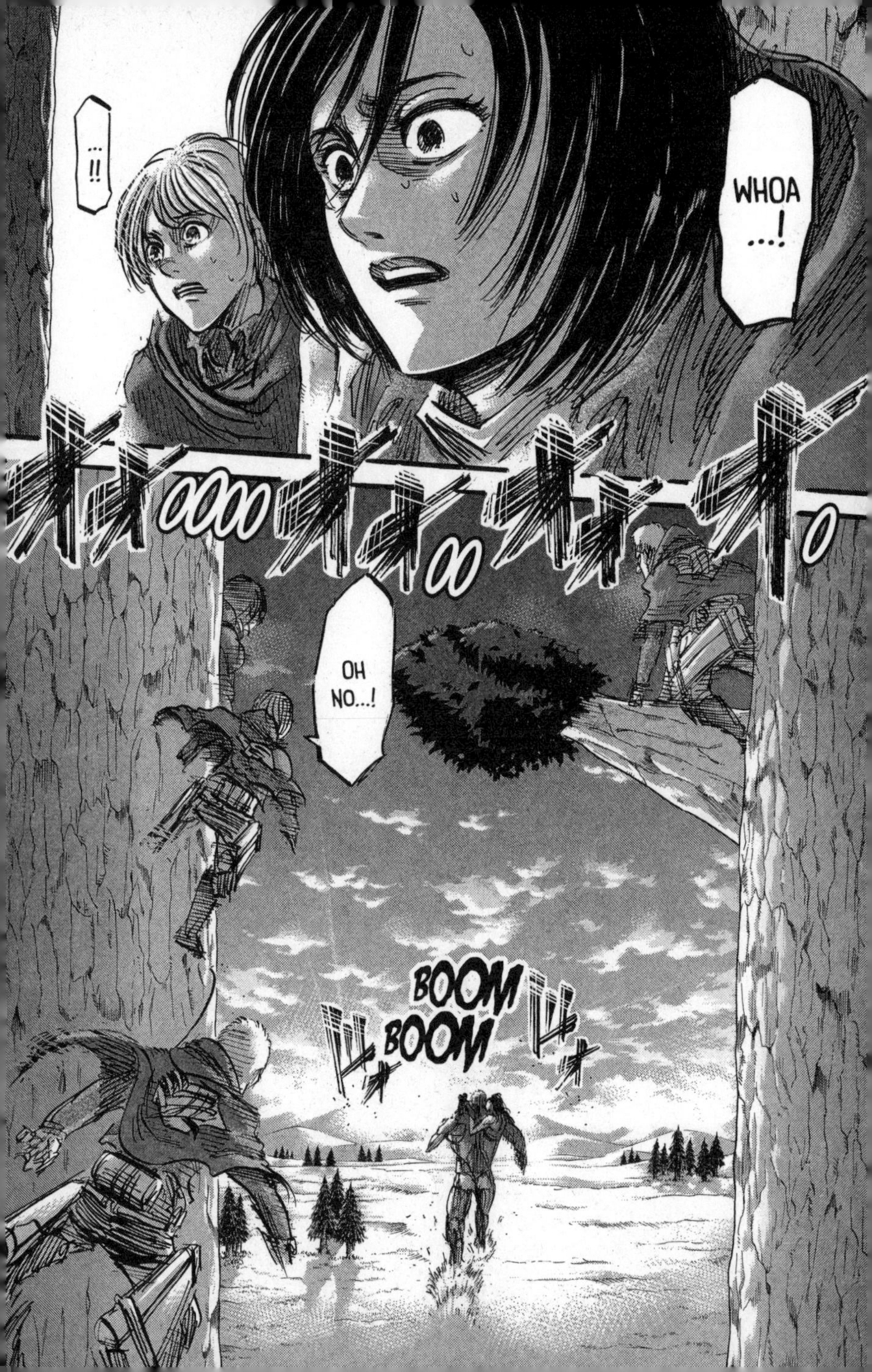

WHOA ...!
...!!
OOOO OO O
OH NO...!
BOOM BOOM

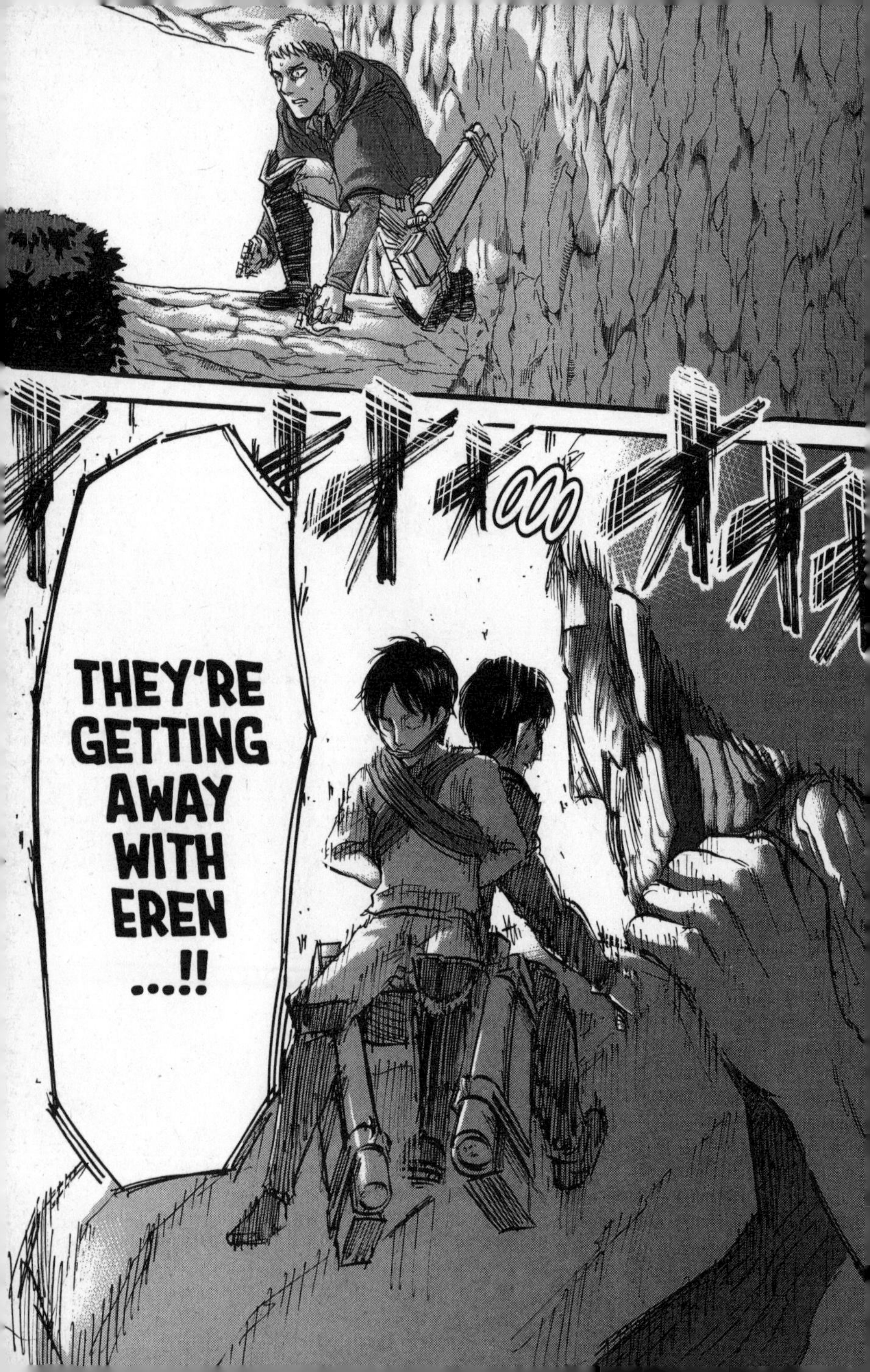
THEY'RE GETTING AWAY WITH EREN ...!!

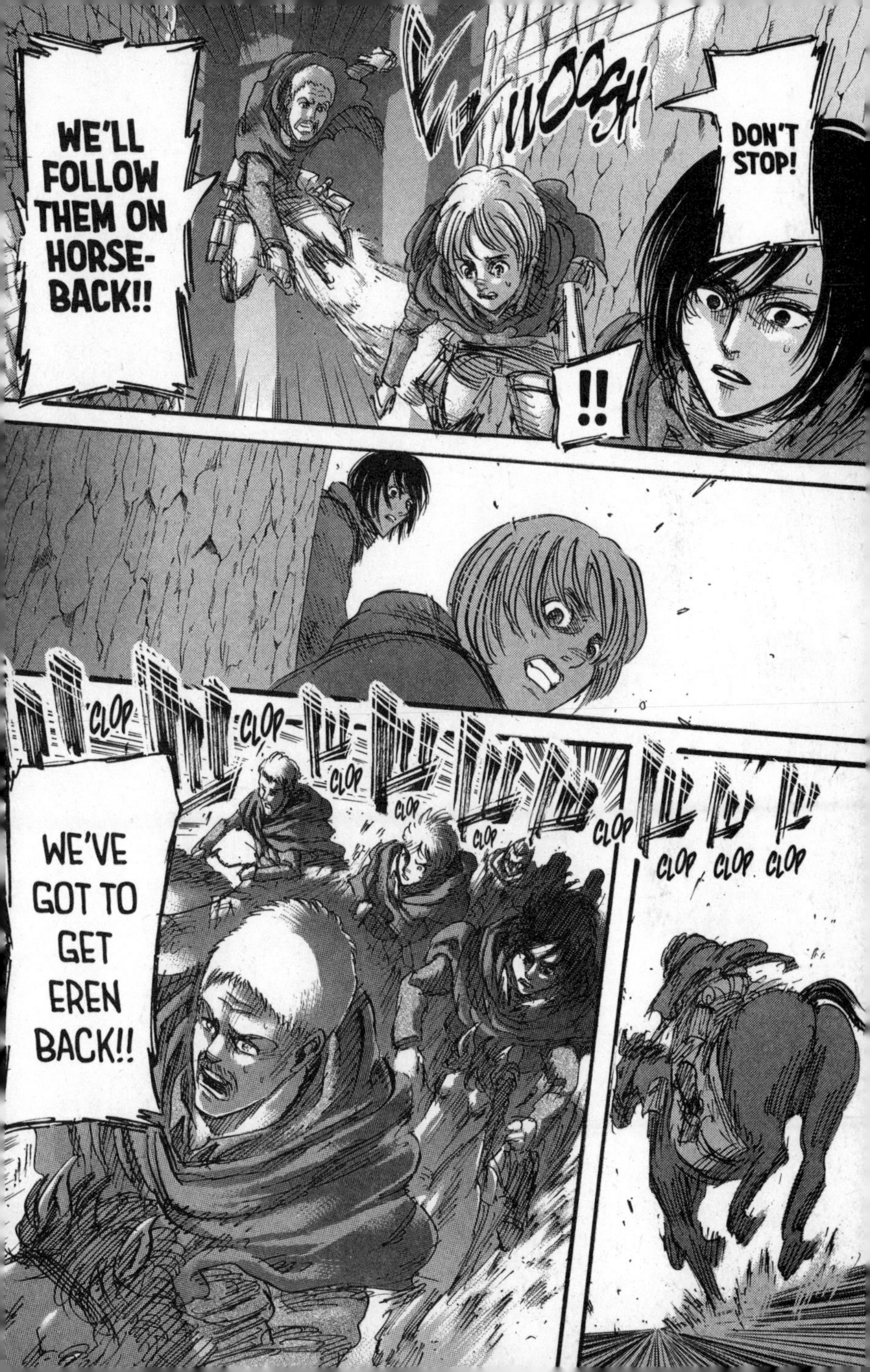
DON'T STOP!
WHOOSH
WE'LL FOLLOW THEM ON HORSE-BACK!!
!!
CLOP CLOP CLOP
CLOP CLOP CLOP CLOP CLOP CLOP
WE'VE GOT TO GET EREN BACK!!

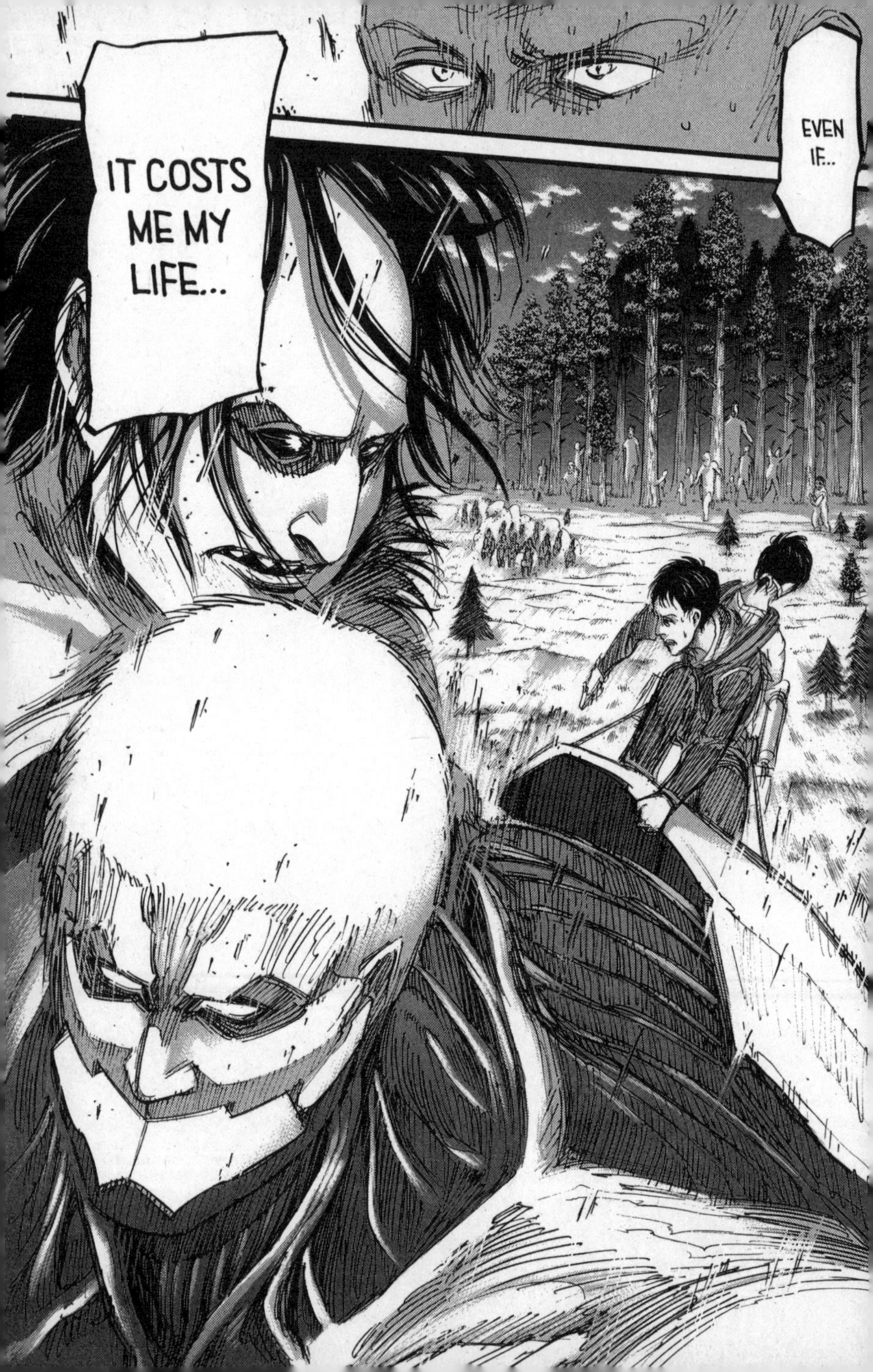
EVEN IF...
IT COSTS ME MY LIFE...

ATTACK on TITAN

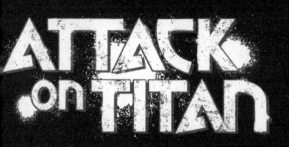

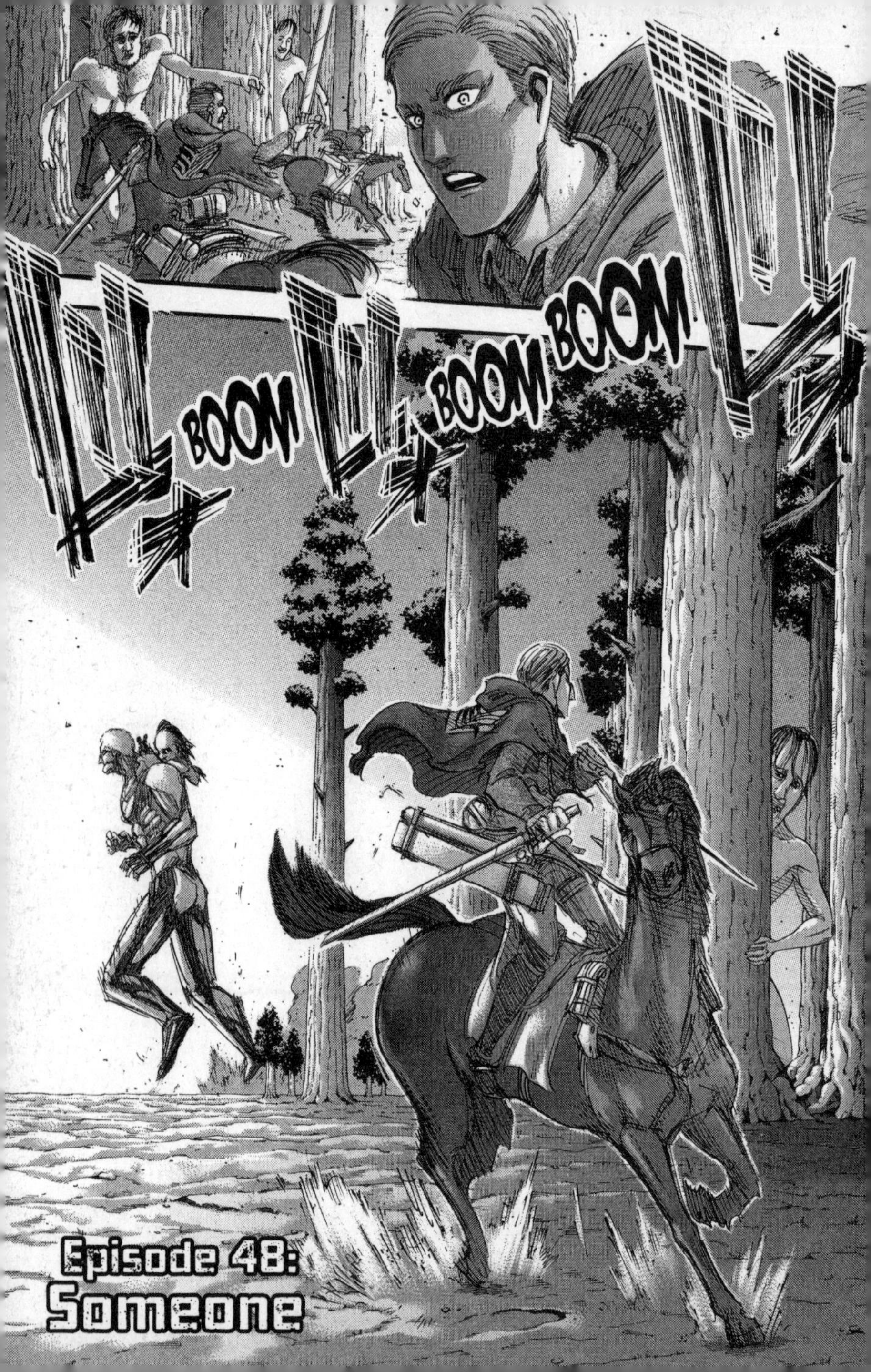
BOOM
BOOM BOOM
Episode 48:
Someone

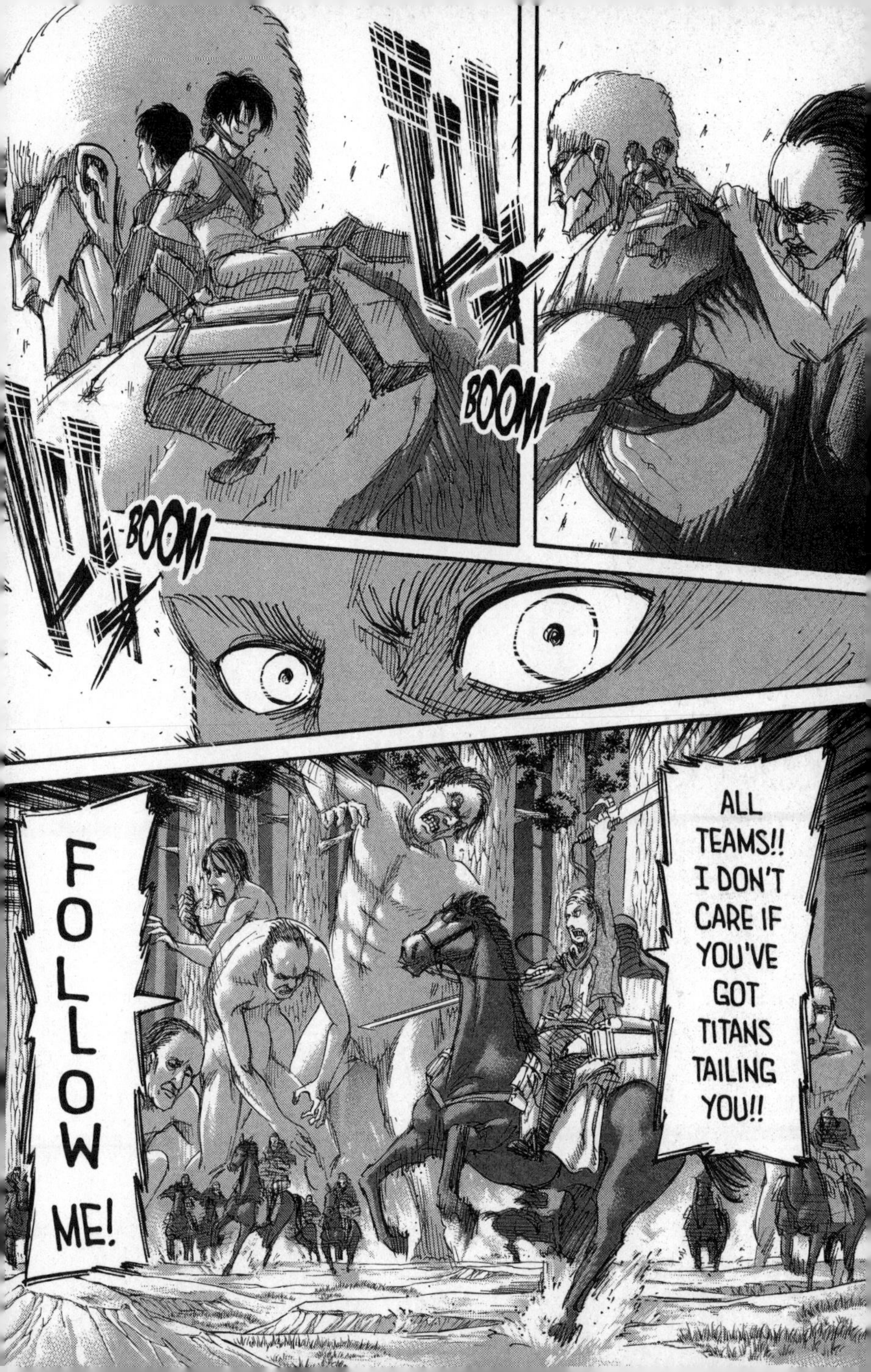
BOOM
BOOM
ALL TEAMS!! I DON'T CARE IF YOU'VE GOT TITANS TAILING YOU!!
FOLLOW ME!

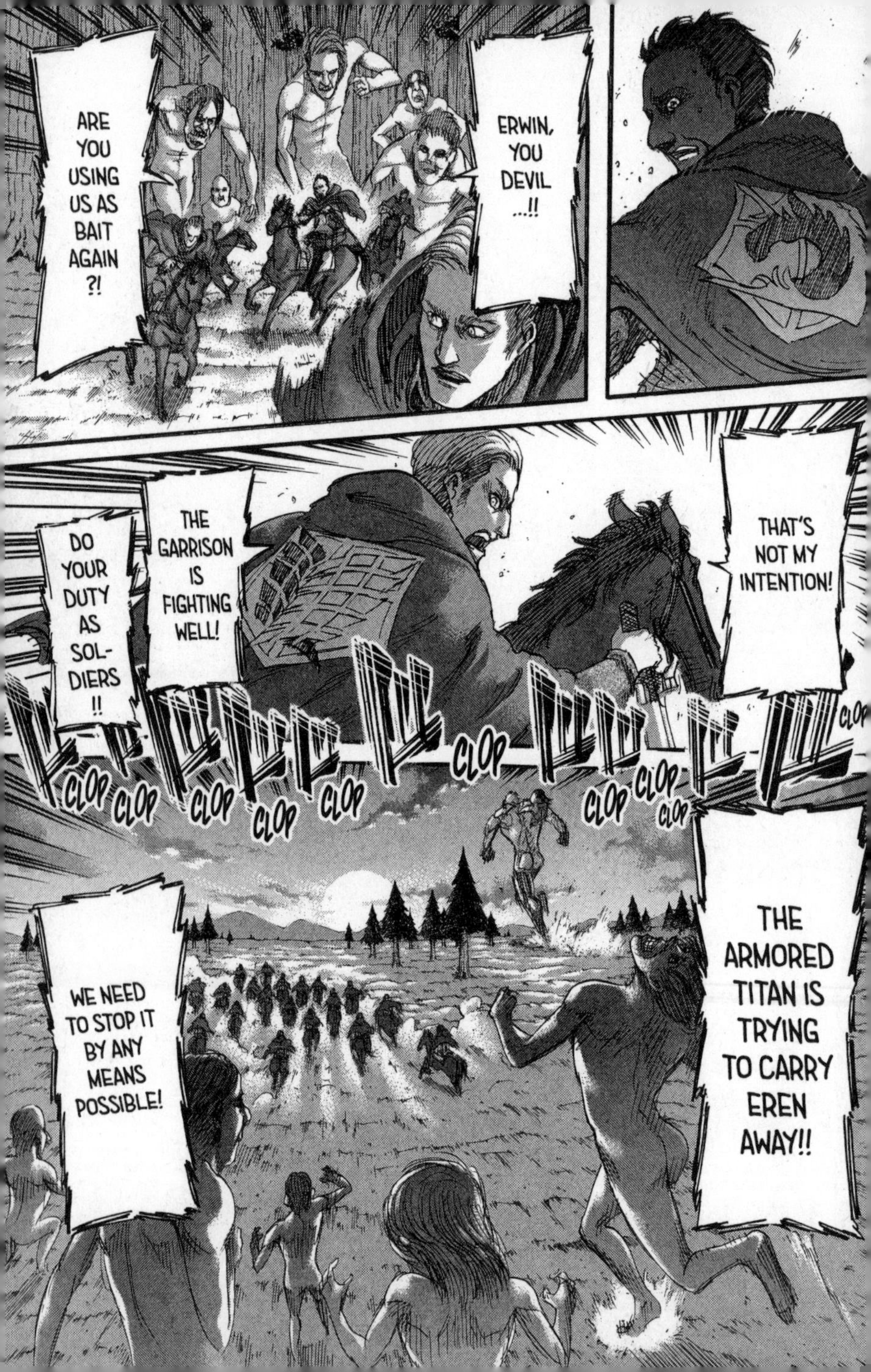
ERWIN, YOU DEVIL ...!!
ARE YOU USING US AS BAIT AGAIN ?!
THAT'S NOT MY INTENTION!
THE GARRISON IS FIGHTING WELL!
DO YOUR DUTY AS SOL-DIERS!!
CLOP
CLOP
CLOP
CLOP
CLOP
CLOP
CLOP
CLOP
CLOP
CLOP
CLOP
THE ARMORED TITAN IS TRYING TO CARRY EREN AWAY!!
WE NEED TO STOP IT BY ANY MEANS POSSIBLE!

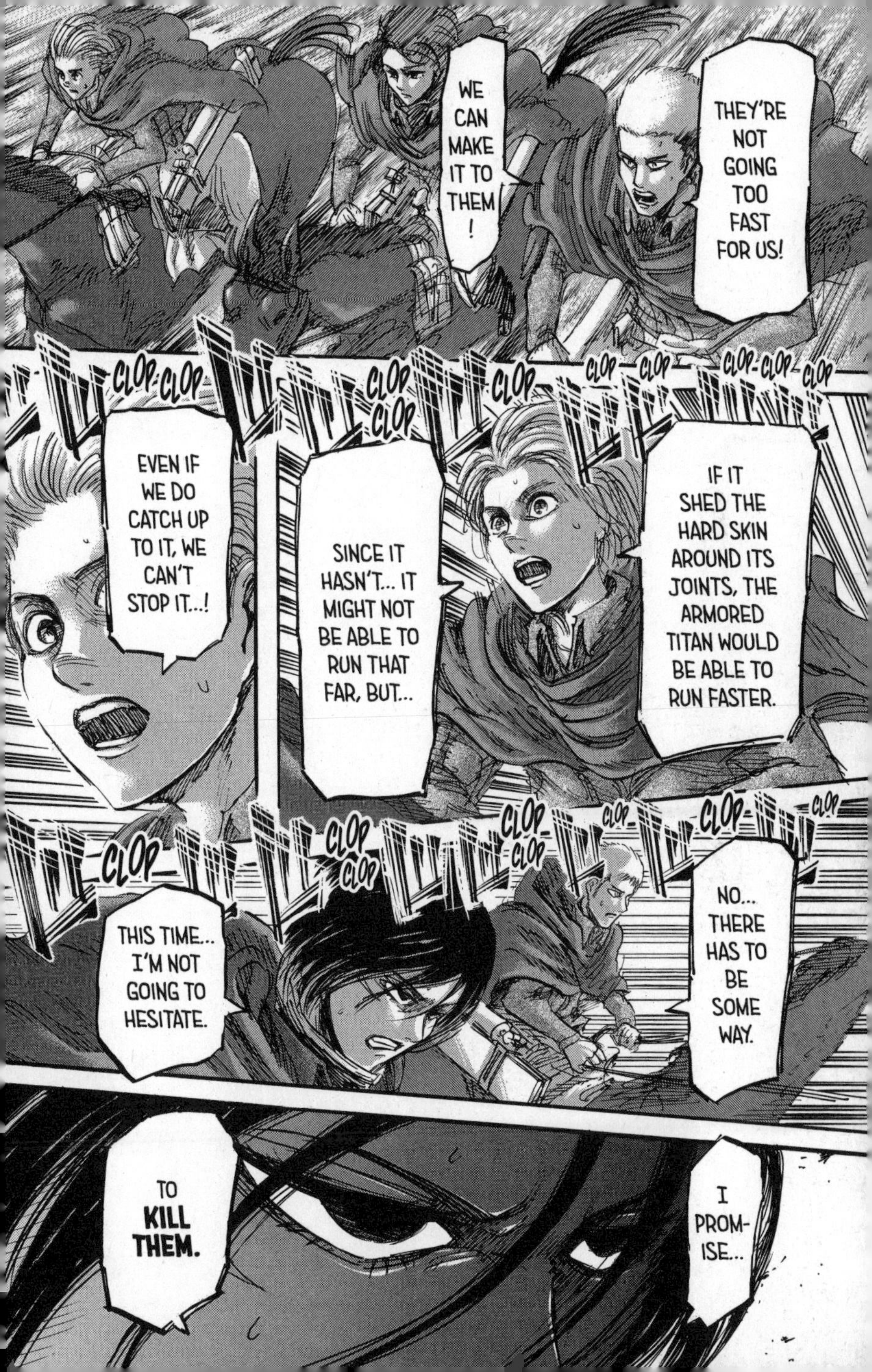
THEY'RE NOT GOING TOO FAST FOR US!
WE CAN MAKE IT TO THEM!
CLOP CLOP CLOP CLOP CLOP CLOP CLOP CLOP CLOP
IF IT SHED THE HARD SKIN AROUND ITS JOINTS, THE ARMORED TITAN WOULD BE ABLE TO RUN FASTER.
SINCE IT HASN'T... IT MIGHT NOT BE ABLE TO RUN THAT FAR, BUT...
EVEN IF WE DO CATCH UP TO IT, WE CAN'T STOP IT...!
CLOP CLOP CLOP CLOP CLOP CLOP CLOP
NO... THERE HAS TO BE SOME WAY.
THIS TIME... I'M NOT GOING TO HESITATE.
I PROMISE...
TO **KILL THEM.**

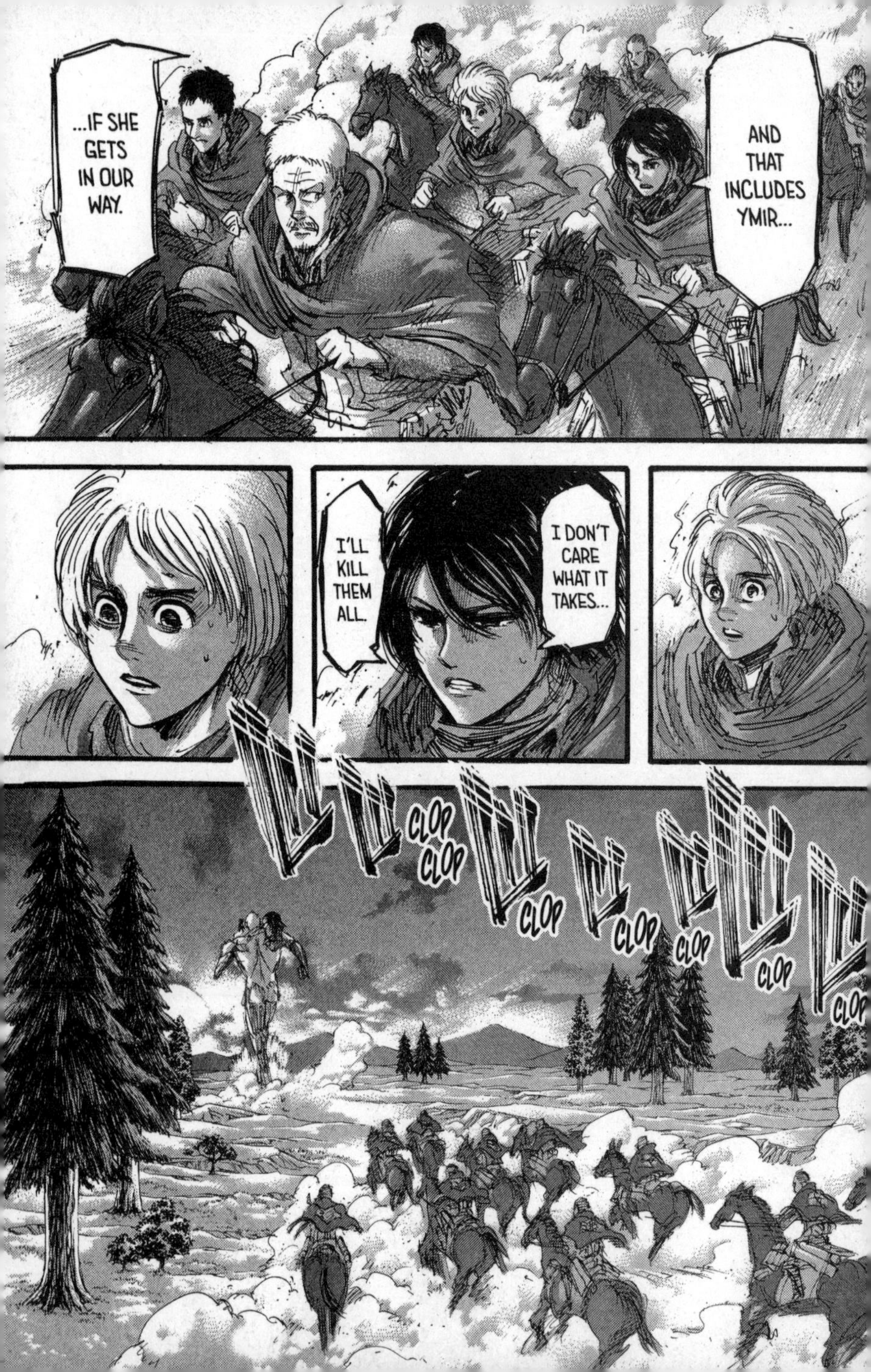
AND THAT INCLUDES YMIR...
...IF SHE GETS IN OUR WAY.
I DON'T CARE WHAT IT TAKES...
I'LL KILL THEM ALL.
CLOP
CLOP
CLOP
CLOP
CLOP
CLOP
CLOP CLOP

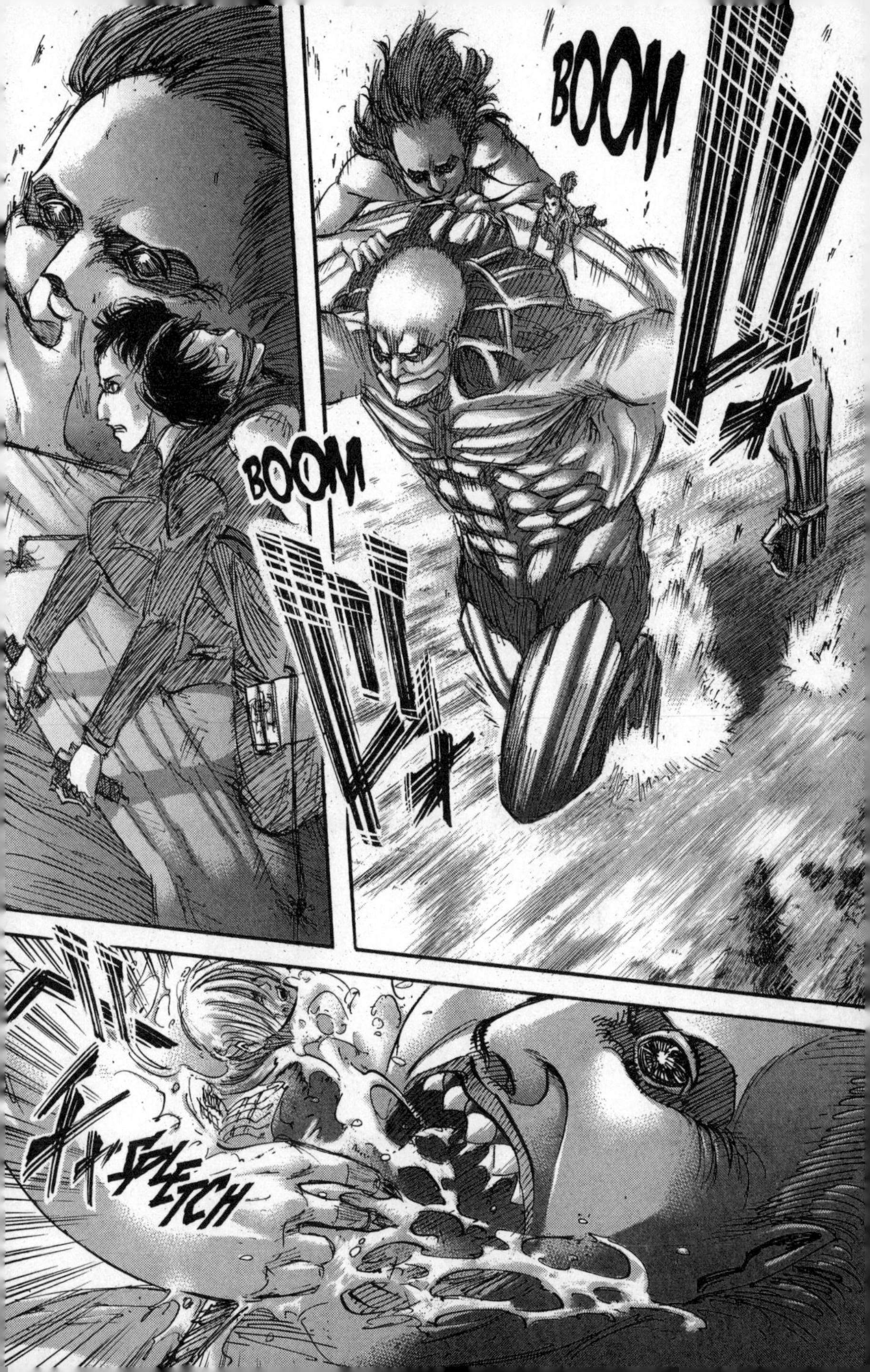
BOOM
BOOM
SPLETCH

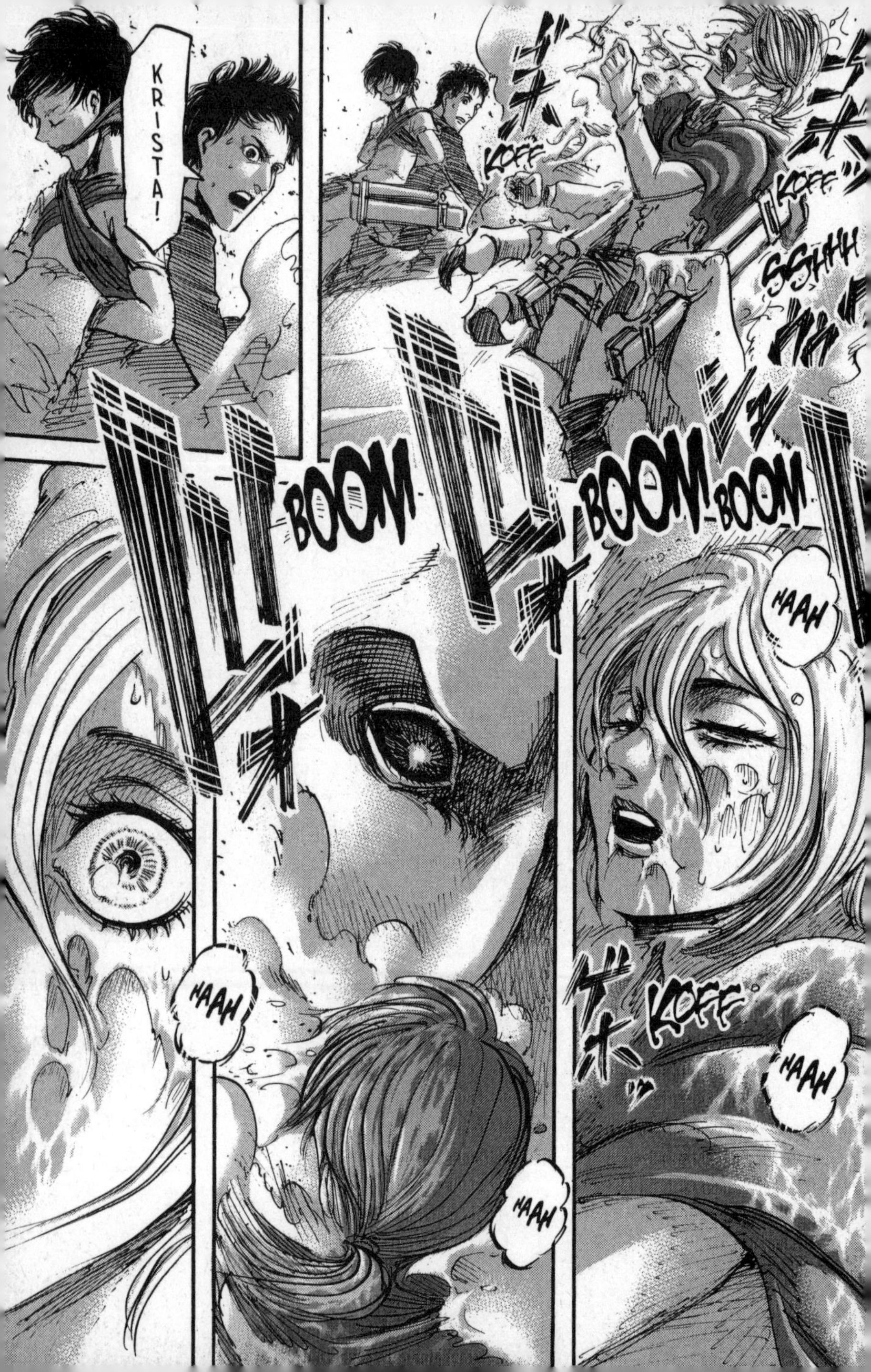
KOFF
KOFF
SSHHH
KRISTA!
BOOM
BOOM
BOOM
HAAH
KOFF
HAAH
HAAH
HAAH

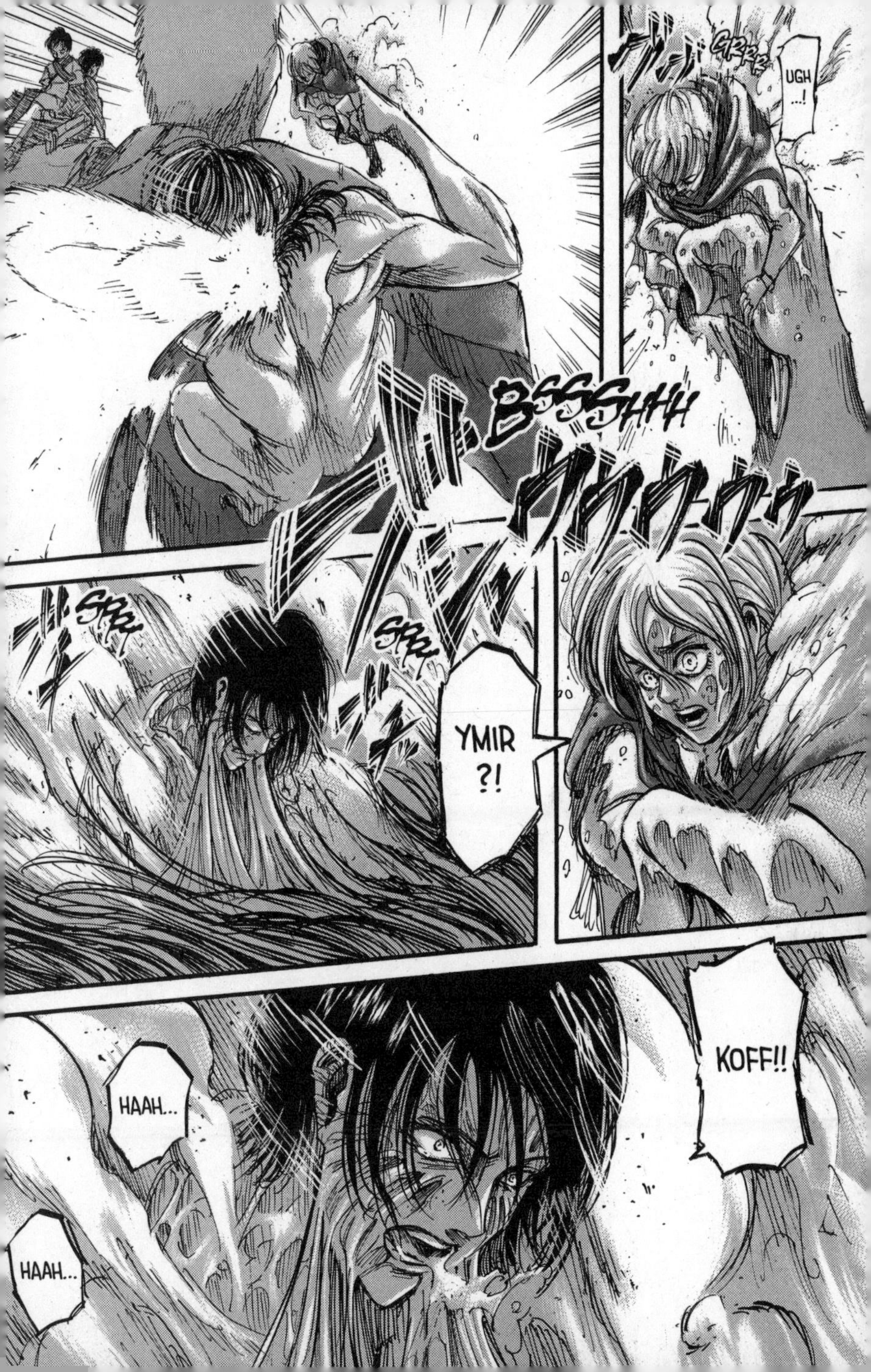
GRRR
UGH ...!
BSSSHHH
YMIR ?!
KOFF!!
HAAH...
HAAH...

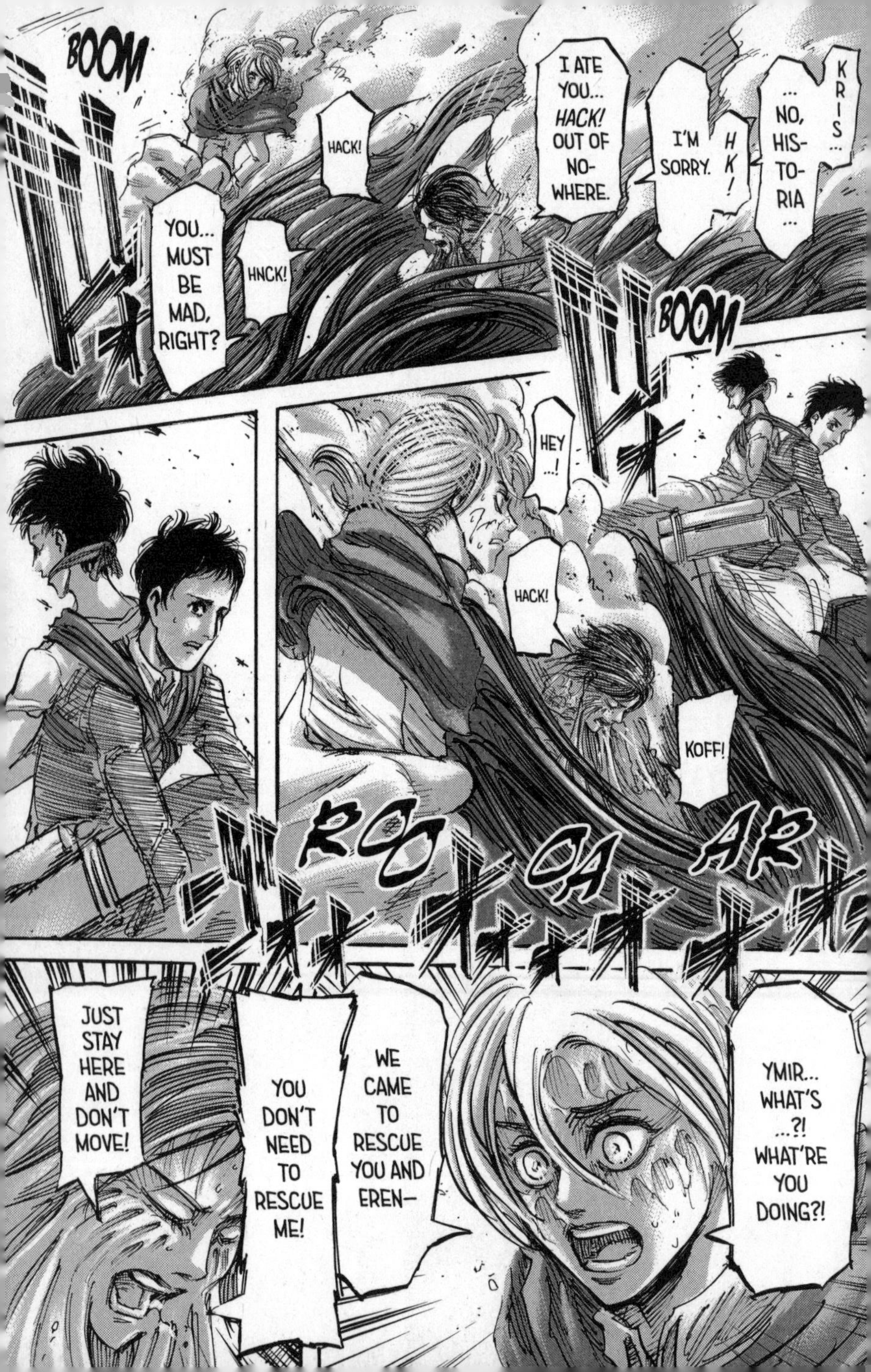
KRIS...
...NO, HIS-TO-RIA...
HK!
I'M SORRY.
I ATE YOU... HACK! OUT OF NO-WHERE.
HACK!
BOOM
HNCK!
YOU... MUST BE MAD, RIGHT?
BOOM
HEY...!
HACK!
KOFF!
ROOOAAR
YMIR... WHAT'S ...?! WHAT'RE YOU DOING?!
WE CAME TO RESCUE YOU AND EREN—
YOU DON'T NEED TO RESCUE ME!
JUST STAY HERE AND DON'T MOVE!

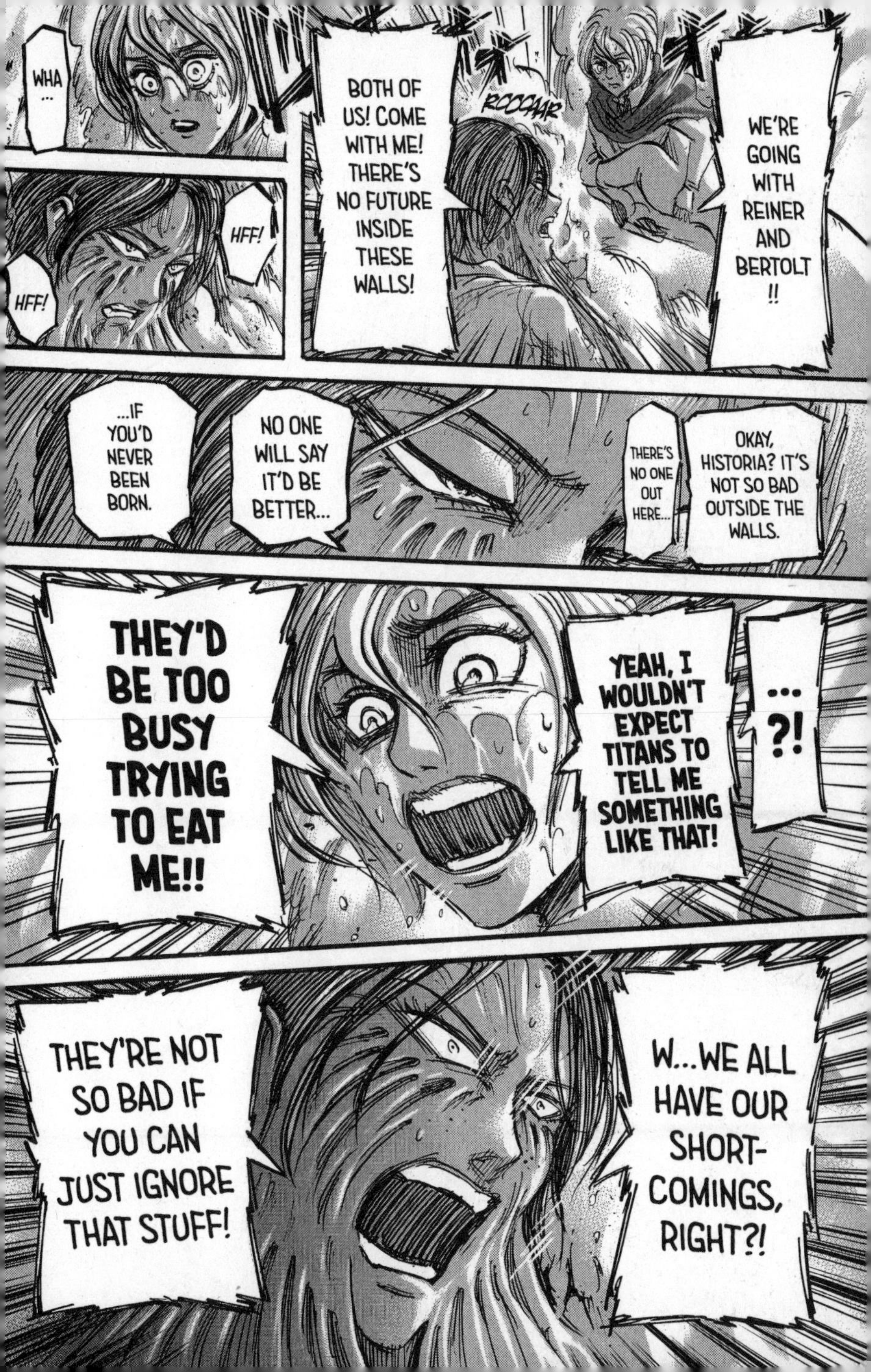
WE'RE GOING WITH REINER AND BERTOLT !!
ROOOAAR
BOTH OF US! COME WITH ME! THERE'S NO FUTURE INSIDE THESE WALLS!
WHA ...
HFF!
HFF!
OKAY, HISTORIA? IT'S NOT SO BAD OUTSIDE THE WALLS.
THERE'S NO ONE OUT HERE...
NO ONE WILL SAY IT'D BE BETTER...
...IF YOU'D NEVER BEEN BORN.
... ?!
YEAH, I WOULDN'T EXPECT TITANS TO TELL ME SOMETHING LIKE THAT!
THEY'D BE TOO BUSY TRYING TO EAT ME!!
W...WE ALL HAVE OUR SHORT-COMINGS, RIGHT?!
THEY'RE NOT SO BAD IF YOU CAN JUST IGNORE THAT STUFF!

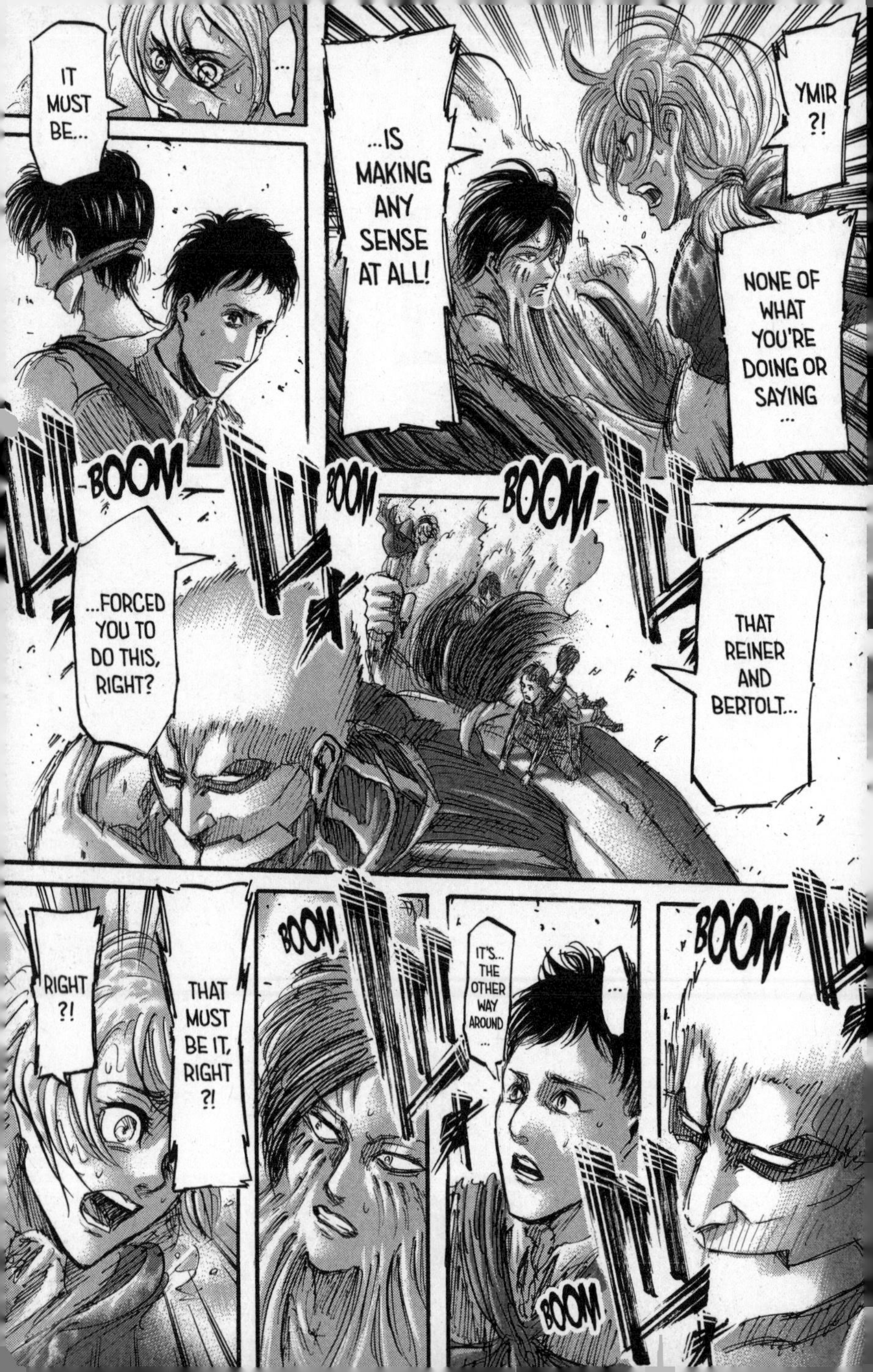

YMIR ?!
NONE OF WHAT YOU'RE DOING OR SAYING ...
...IS MAKING ANY SENSE AT ALL!
...
IT MUST BE...
BOOM
BOOM
BOOM
THAT REINER AND BERTOLT...
...FORCED YOU TO DO THIS, RIGHT?
BOOM
...
IT'S... THE OTHER WAY AROUND ...
BOOM
BOOM
THAT MUST BE IT, RIGHT ?!
RIGHT ?!

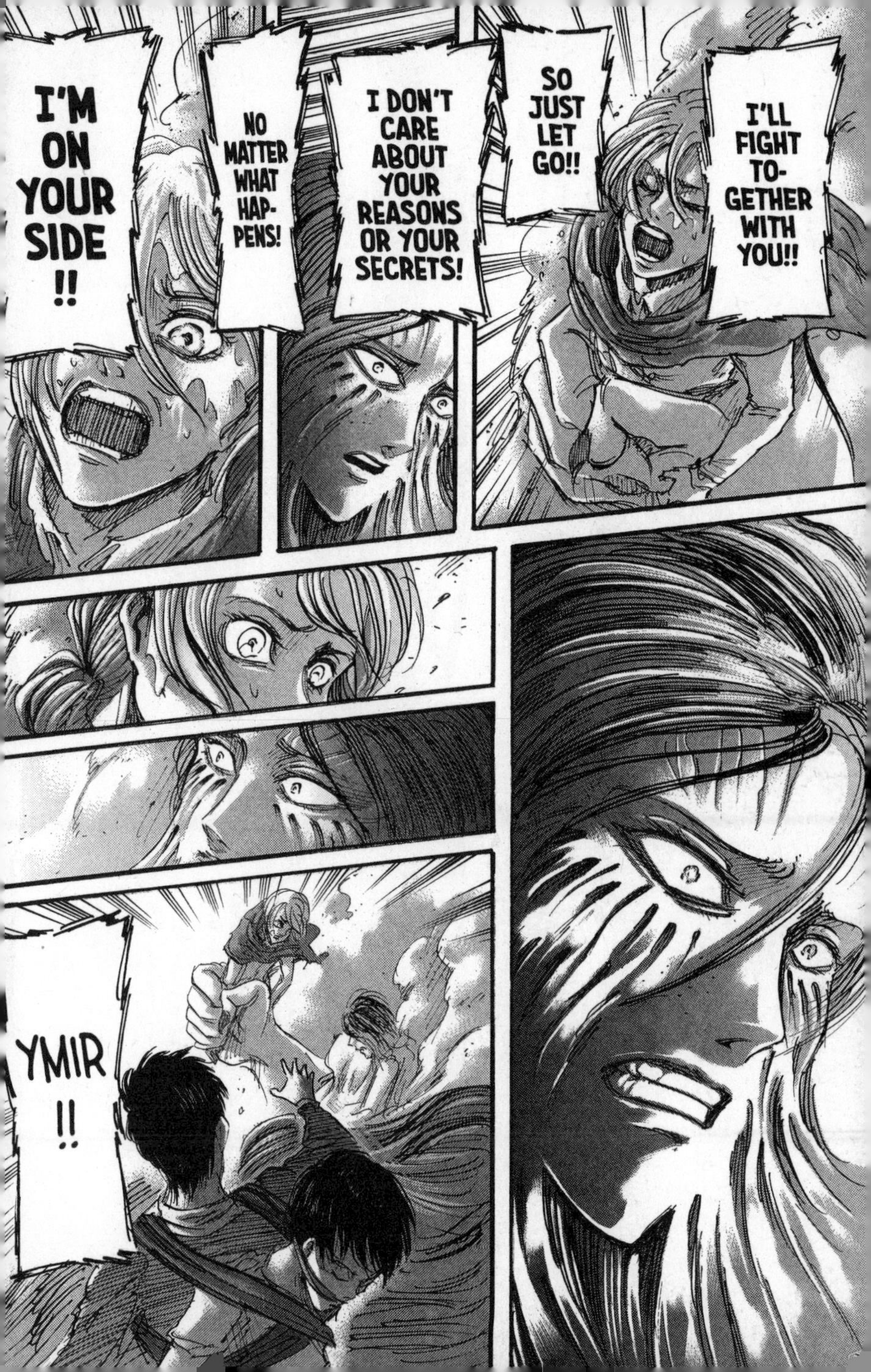
I'LL FIGHT TO-GETHER WITH YOU!!
SO JUST LET GO!!
I DON'T CARE ABOUT YOUR REASONS OR YOUR SECRETS!
NO MATTER WHAT HAP-PENS!
I'M ON YOUR SIDE !!
YMIR !!

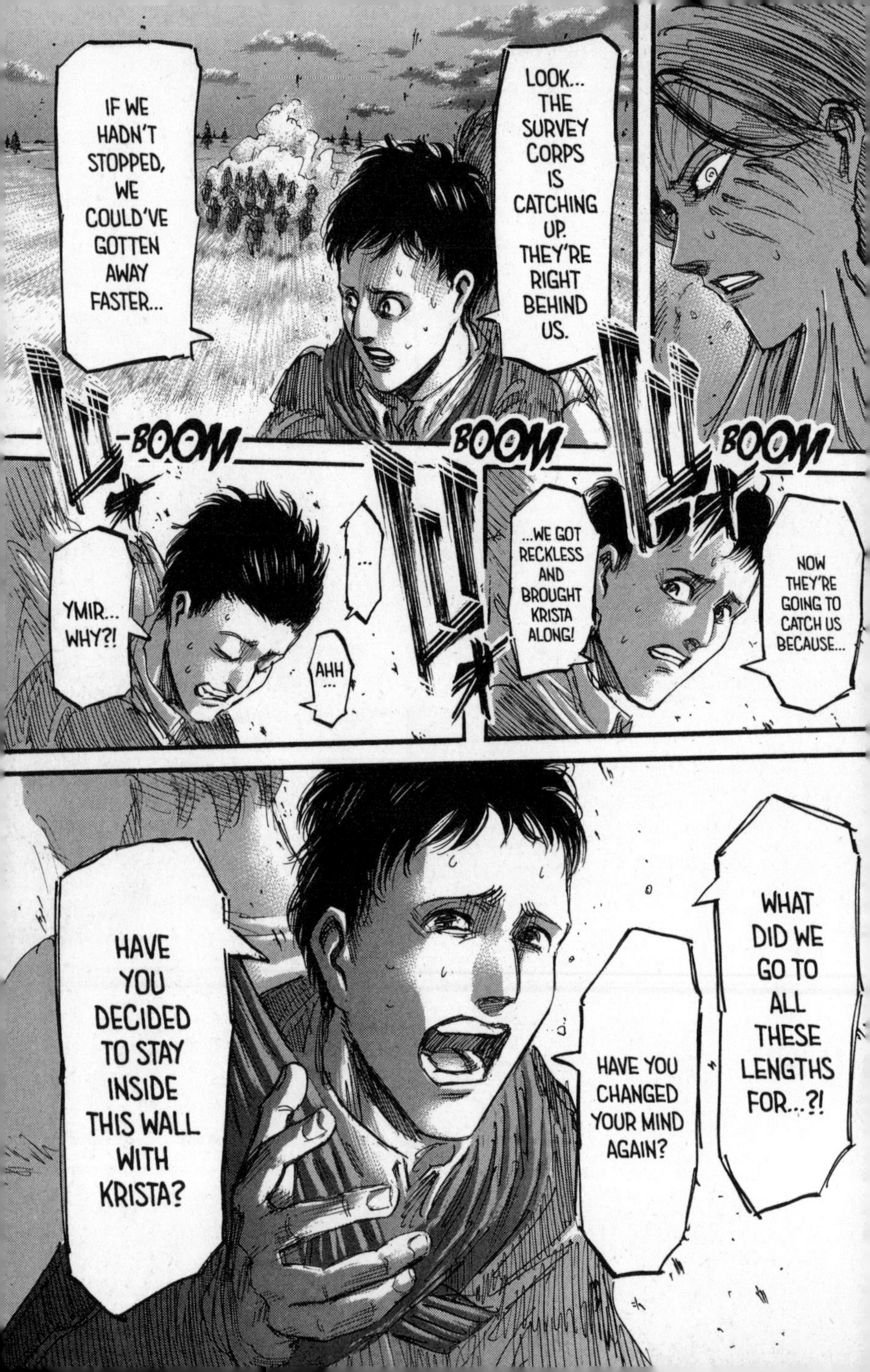
LOOK... THE SURVEY CORPS IS CATCHING UP. THEY'RE RIGHT BEHIND US.
IF WE HADN'T STOPPED, WE COULD'VE GOTTEN AWAY FASTER...
BOOM
NOW THEY'RE GOING TO CATCH US BECAUSE...
...WE GOT RECKLESS AND BROUGHT KRISTA ALONG!
BOOM
...
AHH ...
BOOM
YMIR... WHY?!
WHAT DID WE GO TO ALL THESE LENGTHS FOR...?!
HAVE YOU CHANGED YOUR MIND AGAIN?
HAVE YOU DECIDED TO STAY INSIDE THIS WALL WITH KRISTA?

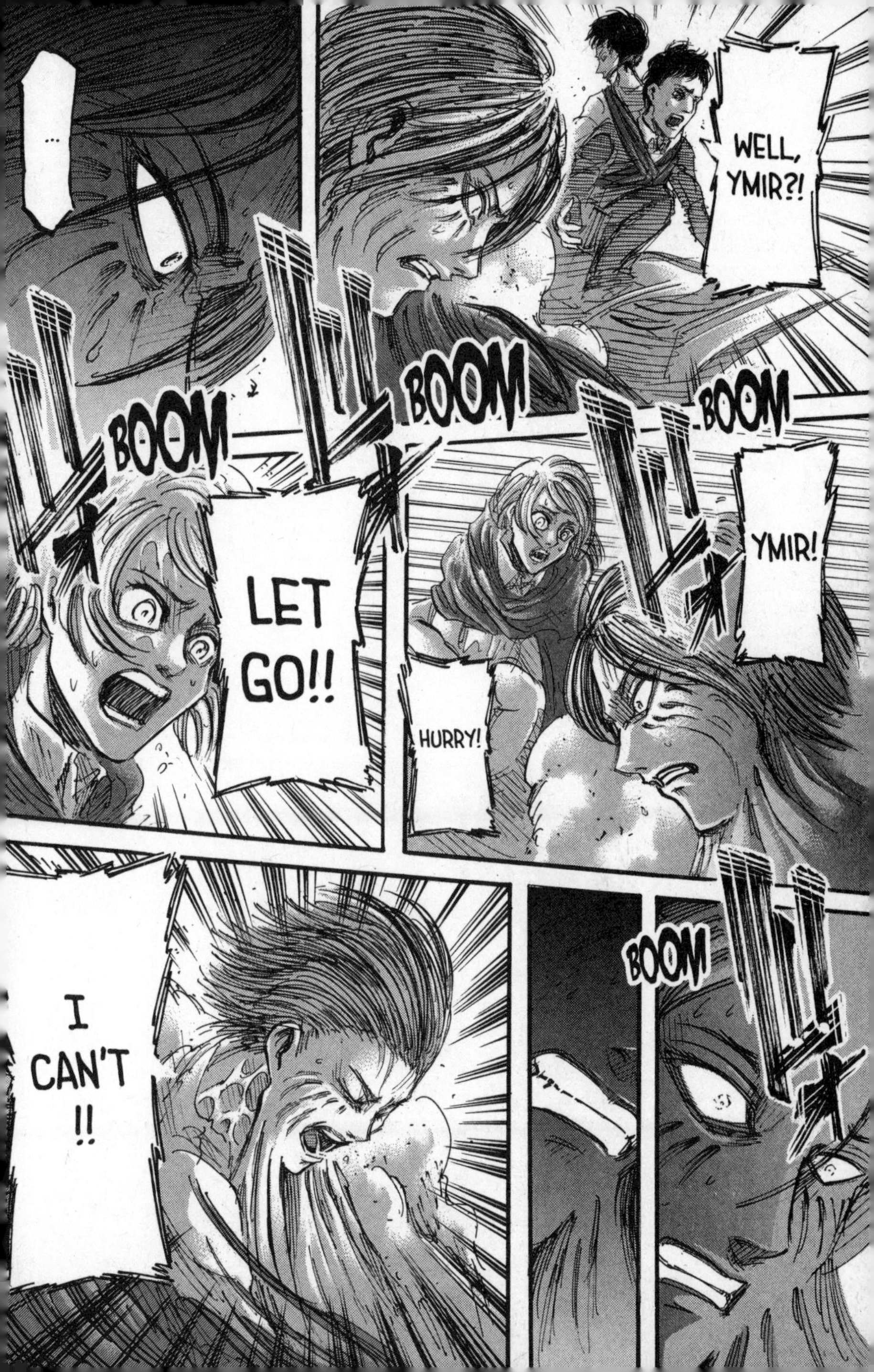
WELL, YMIR?!
BOOM
BOOM
...
BOOM
YMIR!
HURRY!
LET GO!!
BOOM
I CAN'T!!

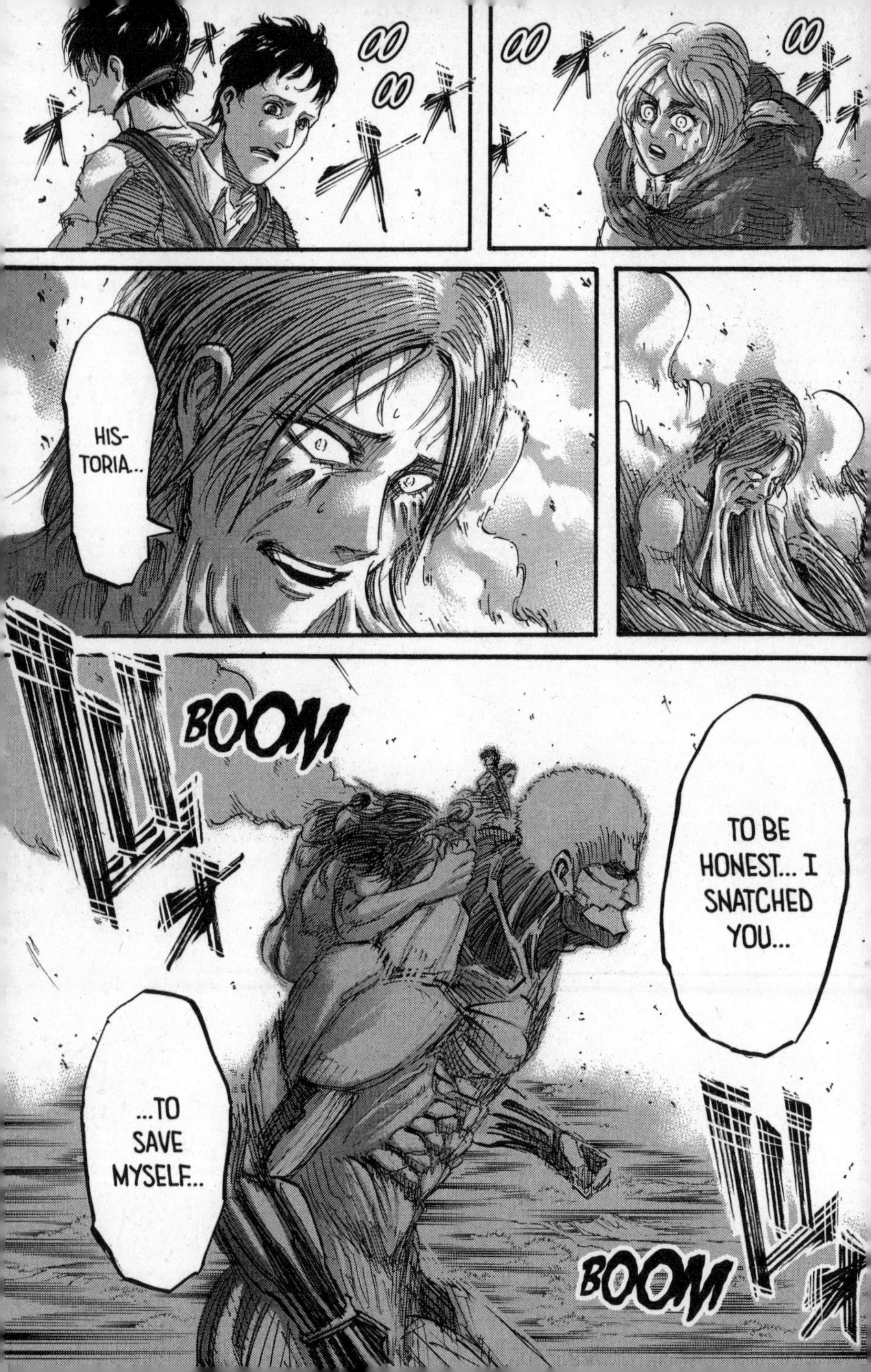
HIS-TORIA...
BOOM
TO BE HONEST... I SNATCHED YOU...
...TO SAVE MYSELF...
BOOM

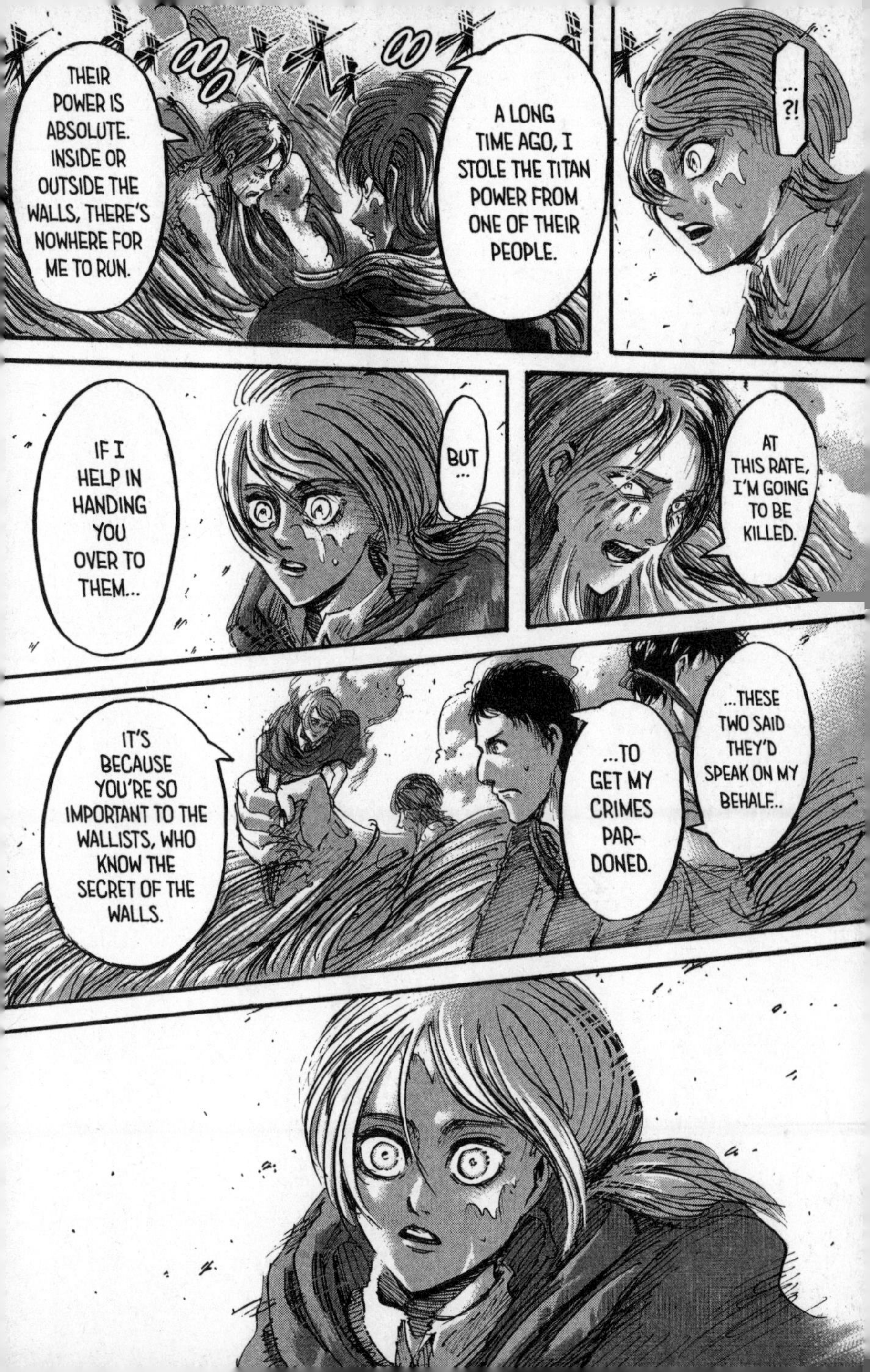
...?!
A LONG TIME AGO, I STOLE THE TITAN POWER FROM ONE OF THEIR PEOPLE.
THEIR POWER IS ABSOLUTE. INSIDE OR OUTSIDE THE WALLS, THERE'S NOWHERE FOR ME TO RUN.
AT THIS RATE, I'M GOING TO BE KILLED.
BUT ...
IF I HELP IN HANDING YOU OVER TO THEM...
...THESE TWO SAID THEY'D SPEAK ON MY BEHALF..
...TO GET MY CRIMES PAR-DONED.
IT'S BECAUSE YOU'RE SO IMPORTANT TO THE WALLISTS, WHO KNOW THE SECRET OF THE WALLS.

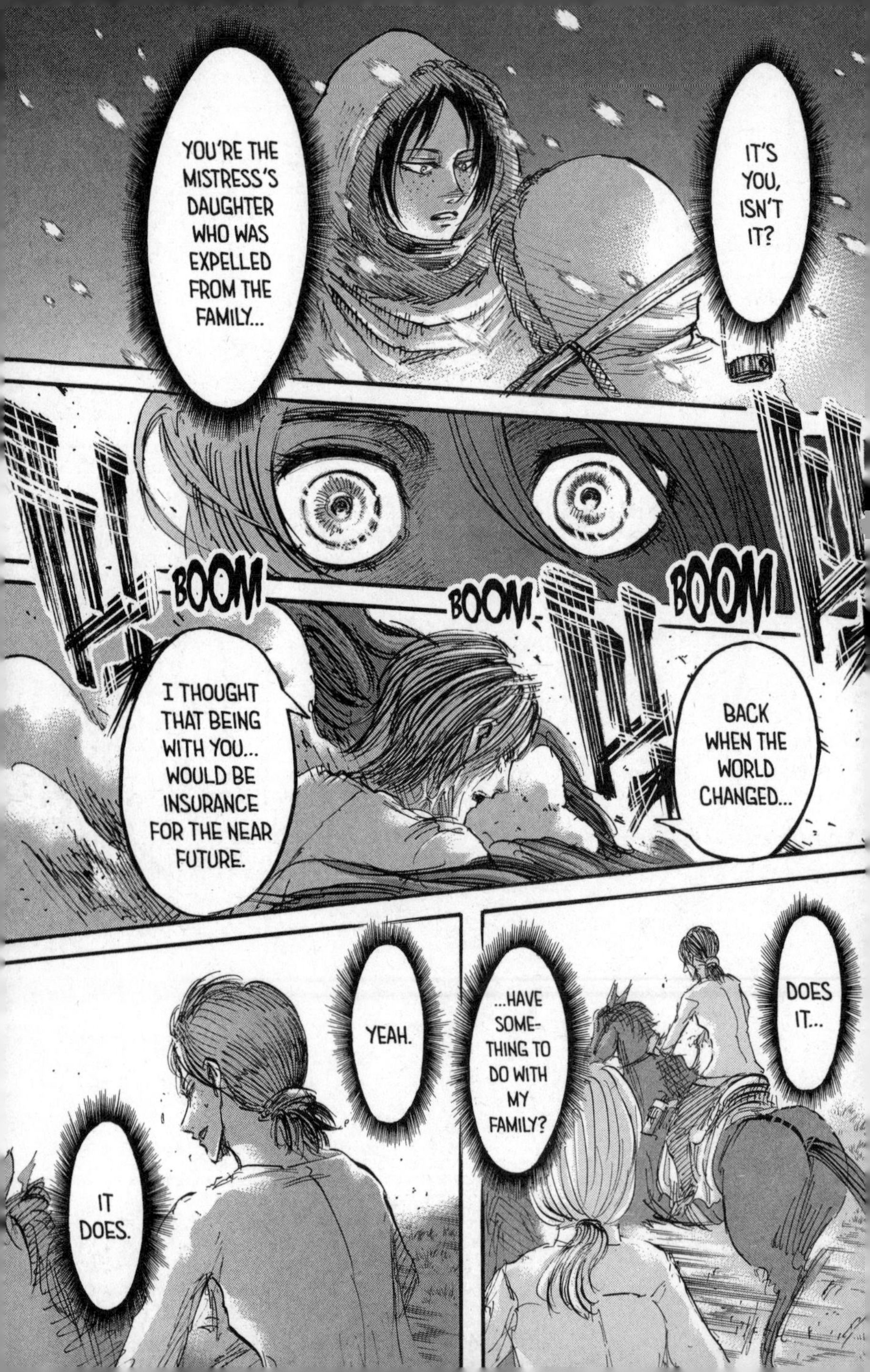
IT'S YOU, ISN'T IT?
YOU'RE THE MISTRESS'S DAUGHTER WHO WAS EXPELLED FROM THE FAMILY...
BOOM
BOOM
BOOM
BACK WHEN THE WORLD CHANGED...
I THOUGHT THAT BEING WITH YOU... WOULD BE INSURANCE FOR THE NEAR FUTURE.
DOES IT...
...HAVE SOME-THING TO DO WITH MY FAMILY?
YEAH.
IT DOES.

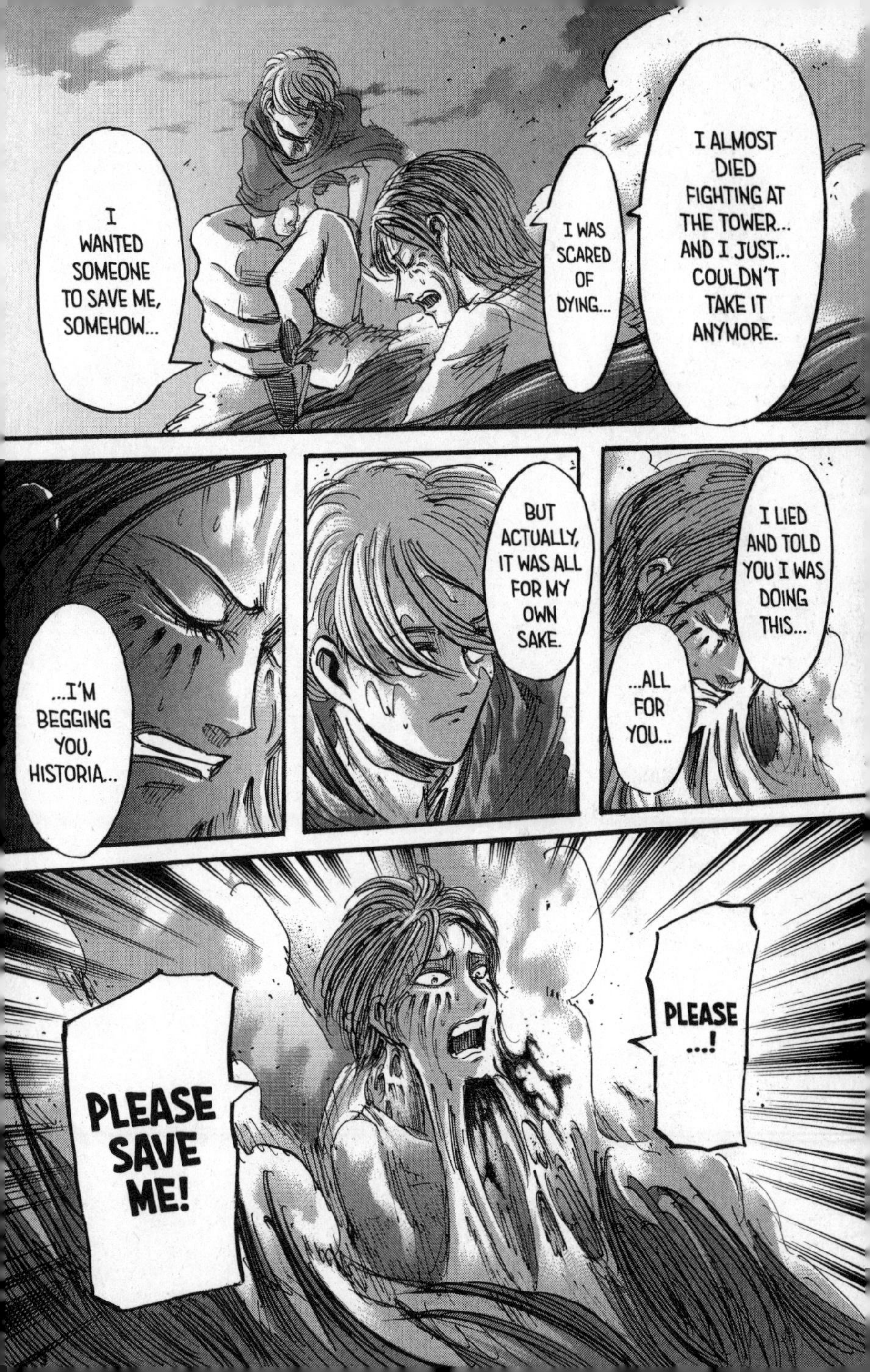
I ALMOST DIED FIGHTING AT THE TOWER... AND I JUST... COULDN'T TAKE IT ANYMORE.
I WAS SCARED OF DYING...
I WANTED SOMEONE TO SAVE ME, SOMEHOW...
I LIED AND TOLD YOU I WAS DOING THIS...
...ALL FOR YOU...
BUT ACTUALLY, IT WAS ALL FOR MY OWN SAKE.
...I'M BEGGING YOU, HISTORIA...
PLEASE ...!
PLEASE SAVE ME!

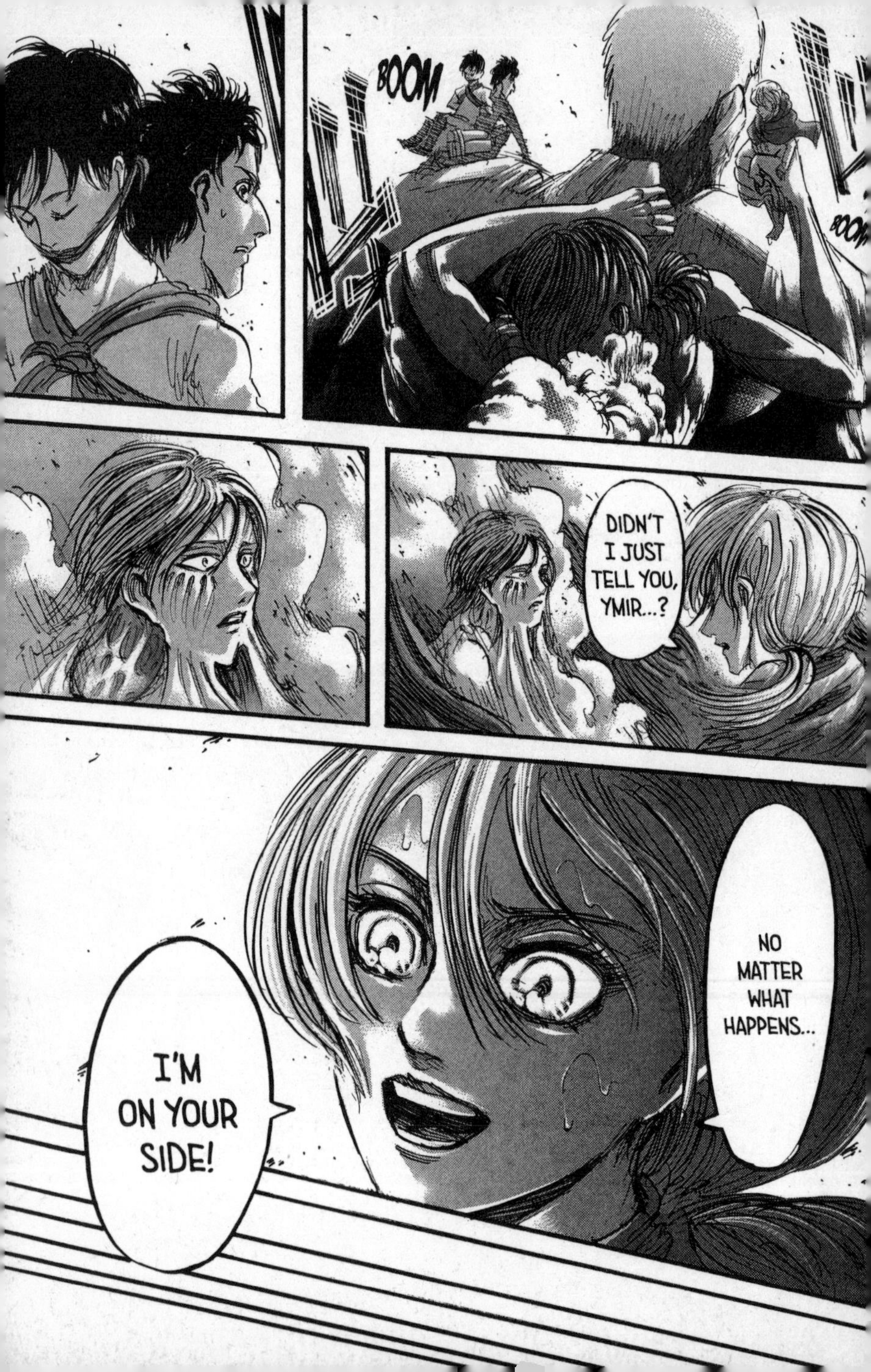
BOOM
BOOM
DIDN'T I JUST TELL YOU, YMIR...?
NO MATTER WHAT HAPPENS...
I'M ON YOUR SIDE!

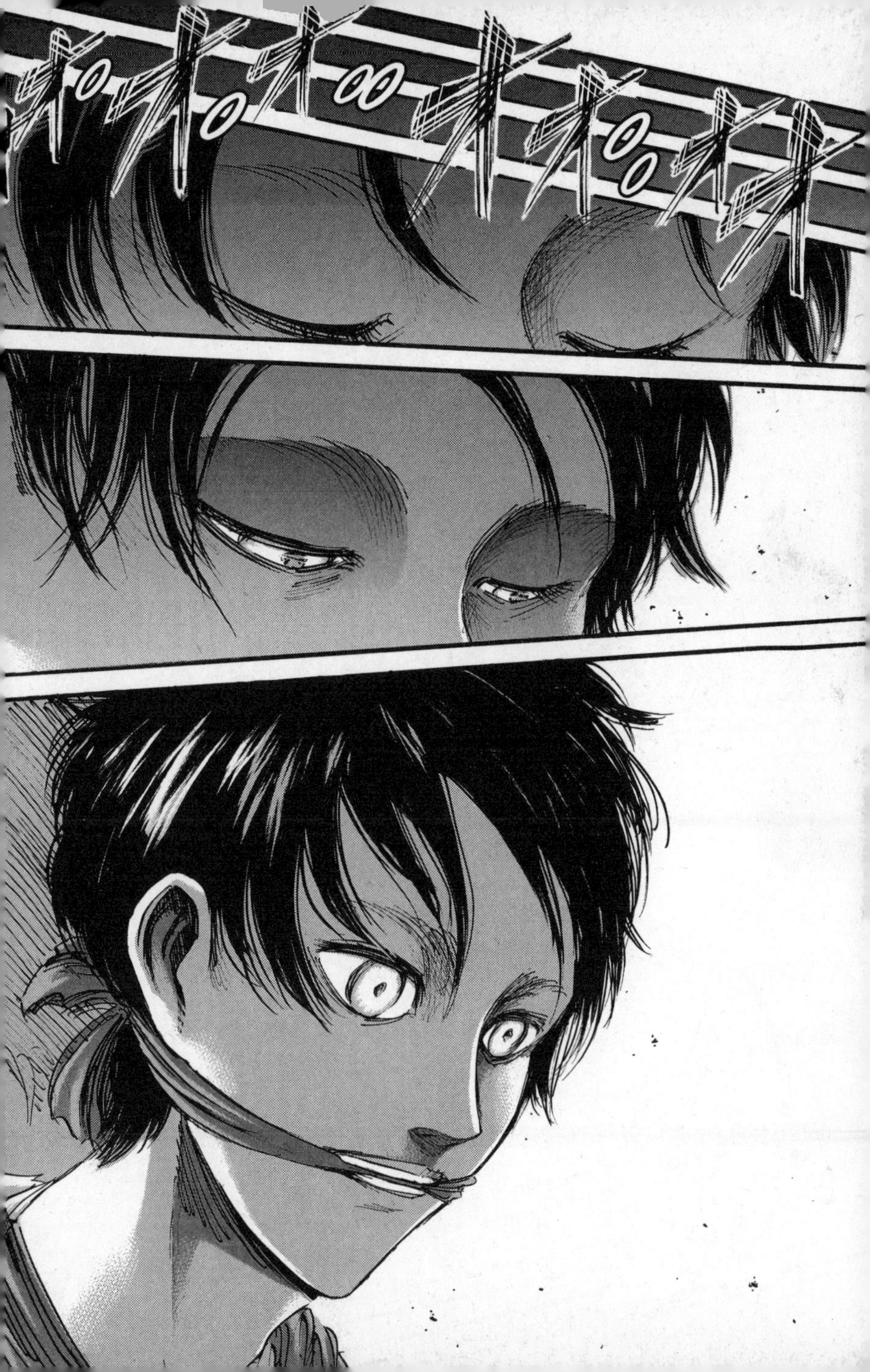

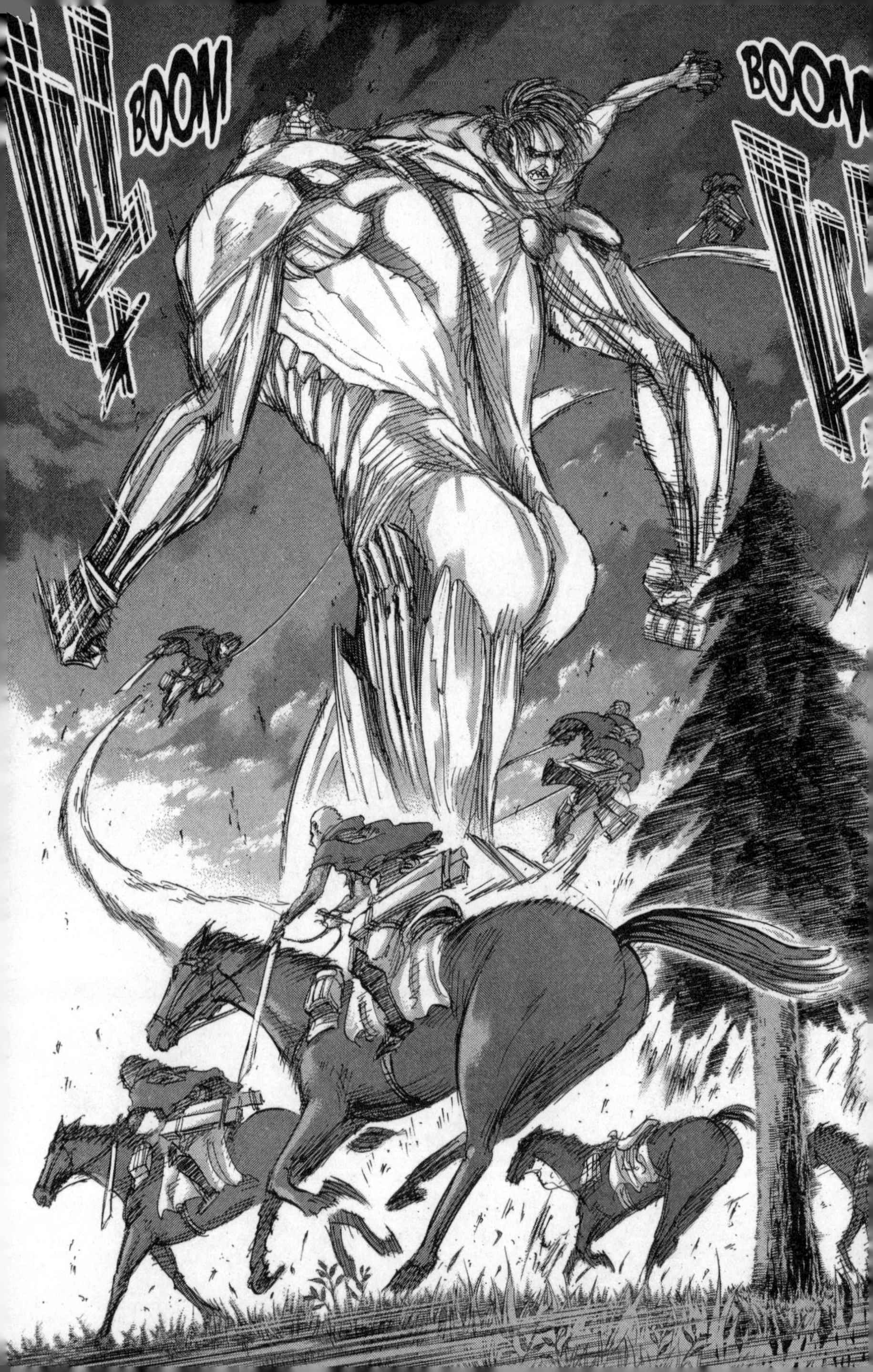
BOOM
BOOM

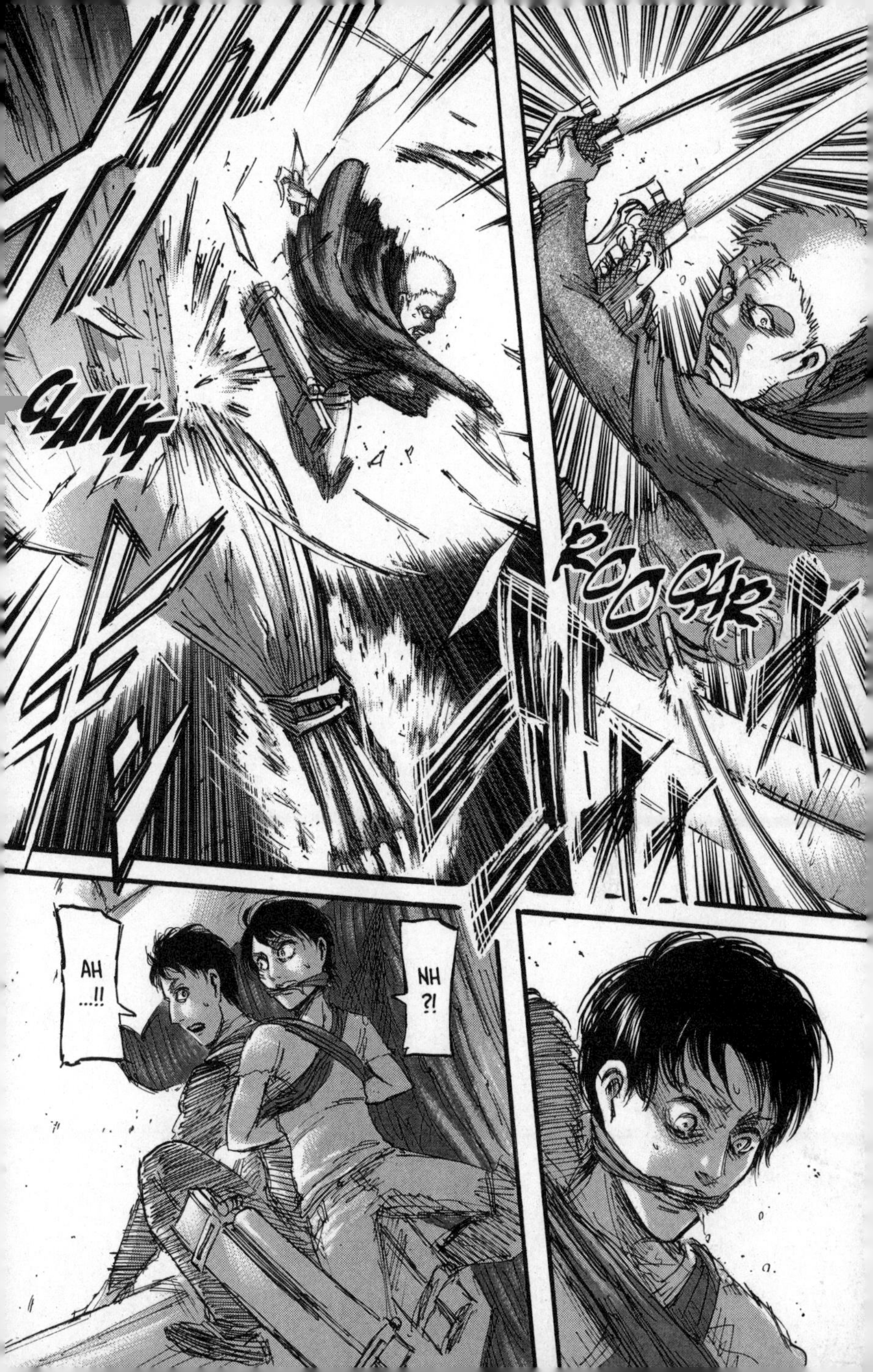

ROOOAR
CLANK!
NH ?!
AH ...!!

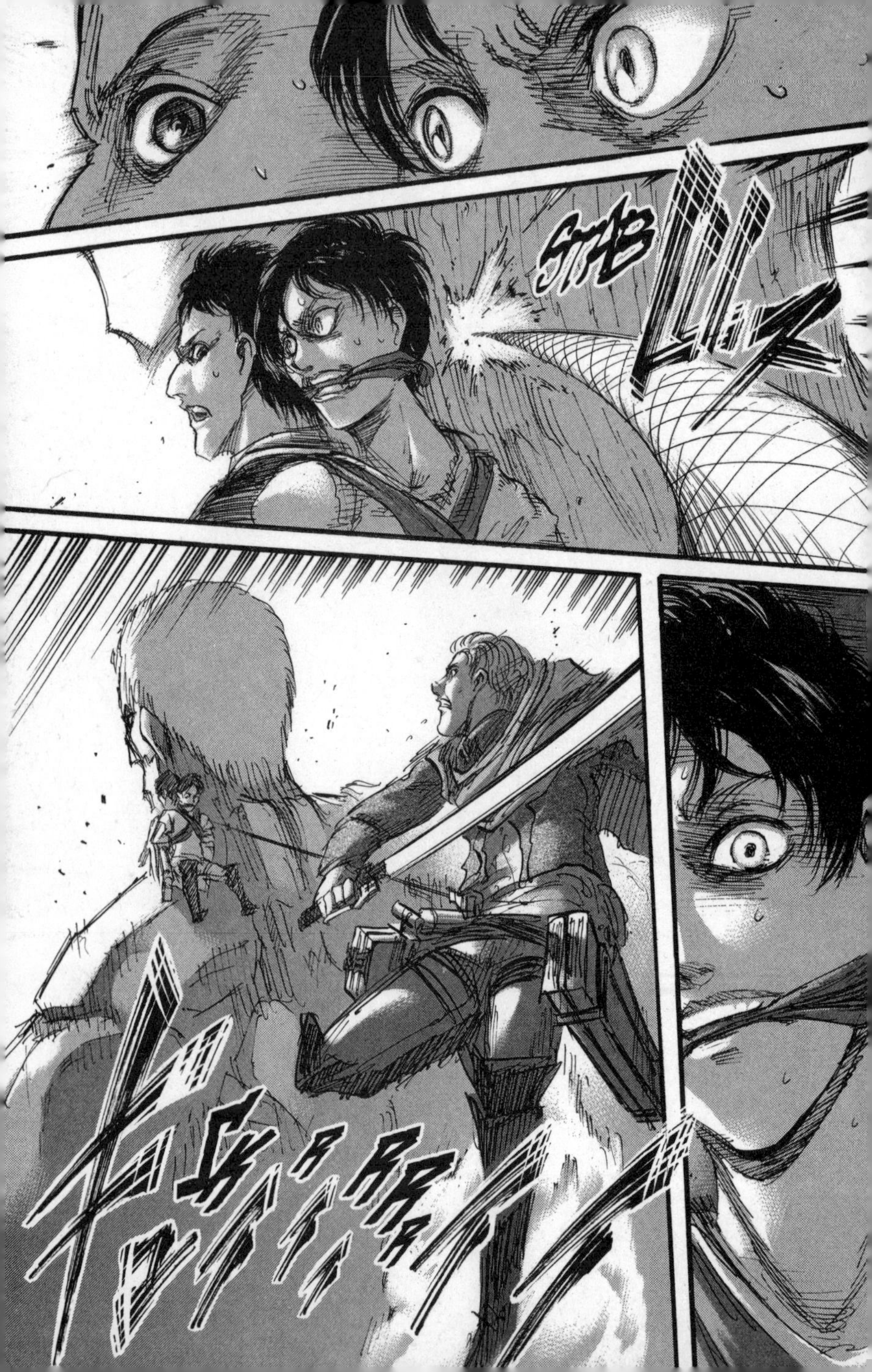
STAB
SKRRRR

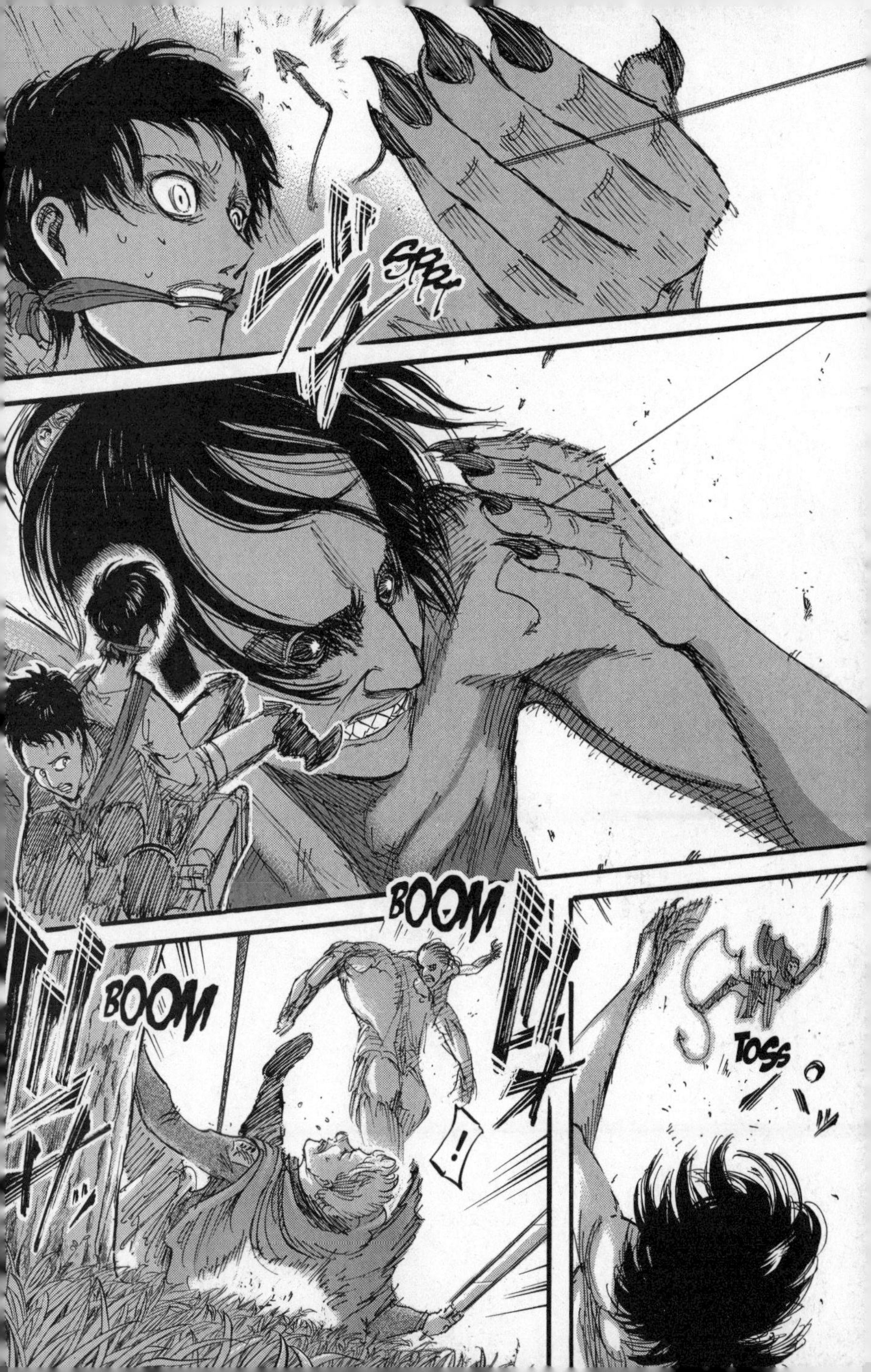
SPPY
TOSS
BOOM
BOOM
!

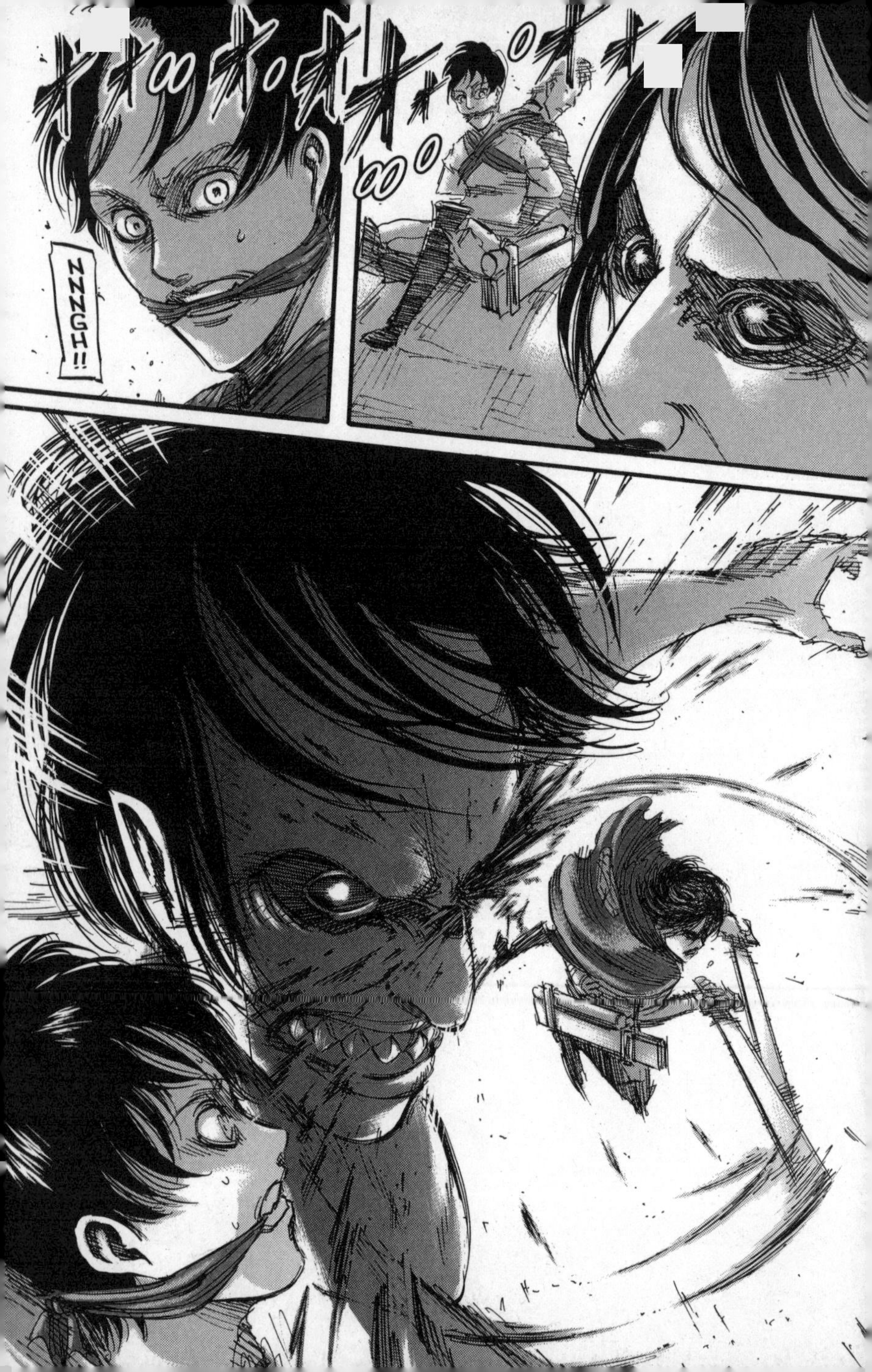
NNNGH!!

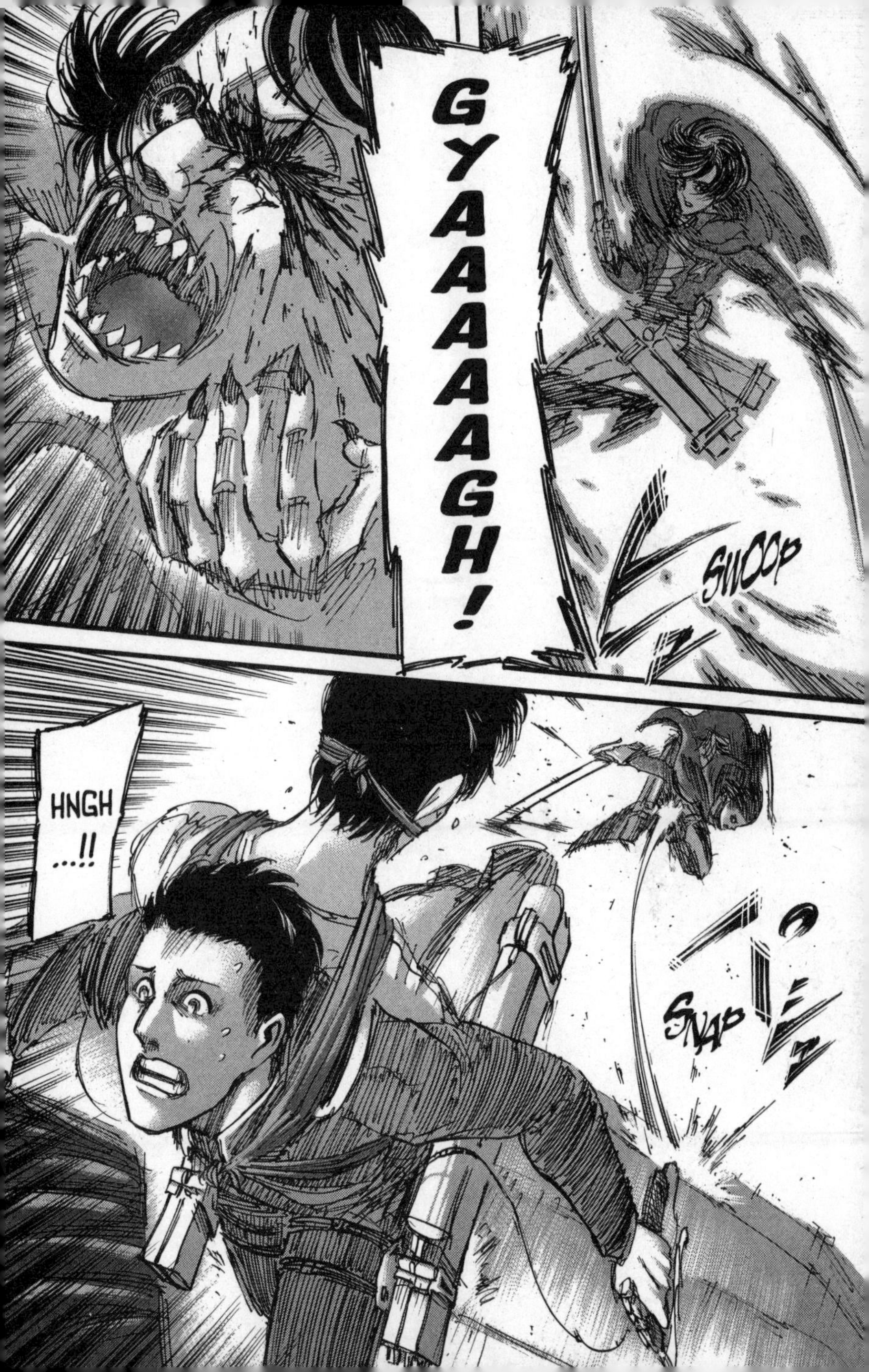
SWOOP
GYAAAAAGH!
SNAP
HNGH ...!!

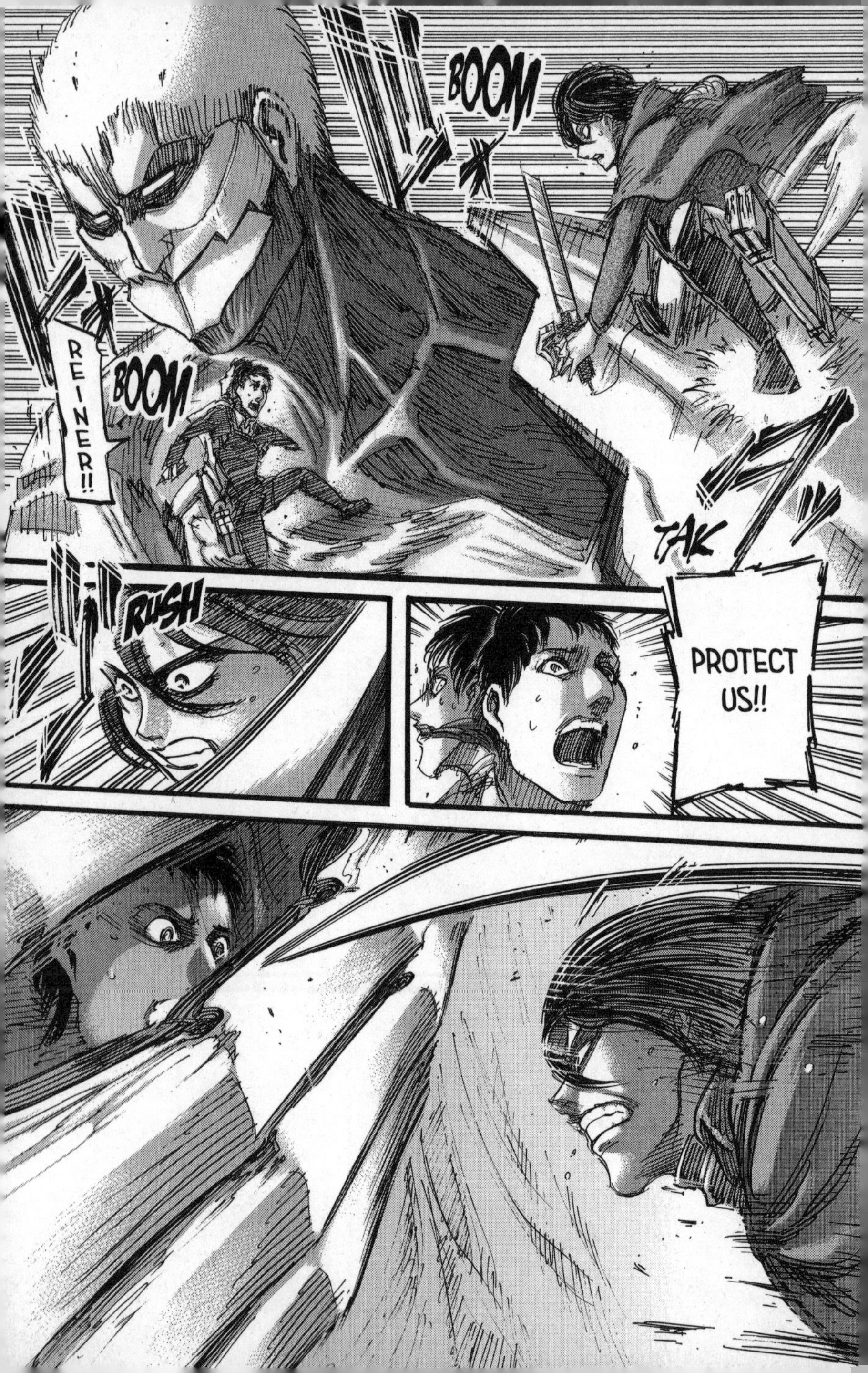
BOOM
REINER!!
BOOM
TAK
PROTECT US!!
RUSH

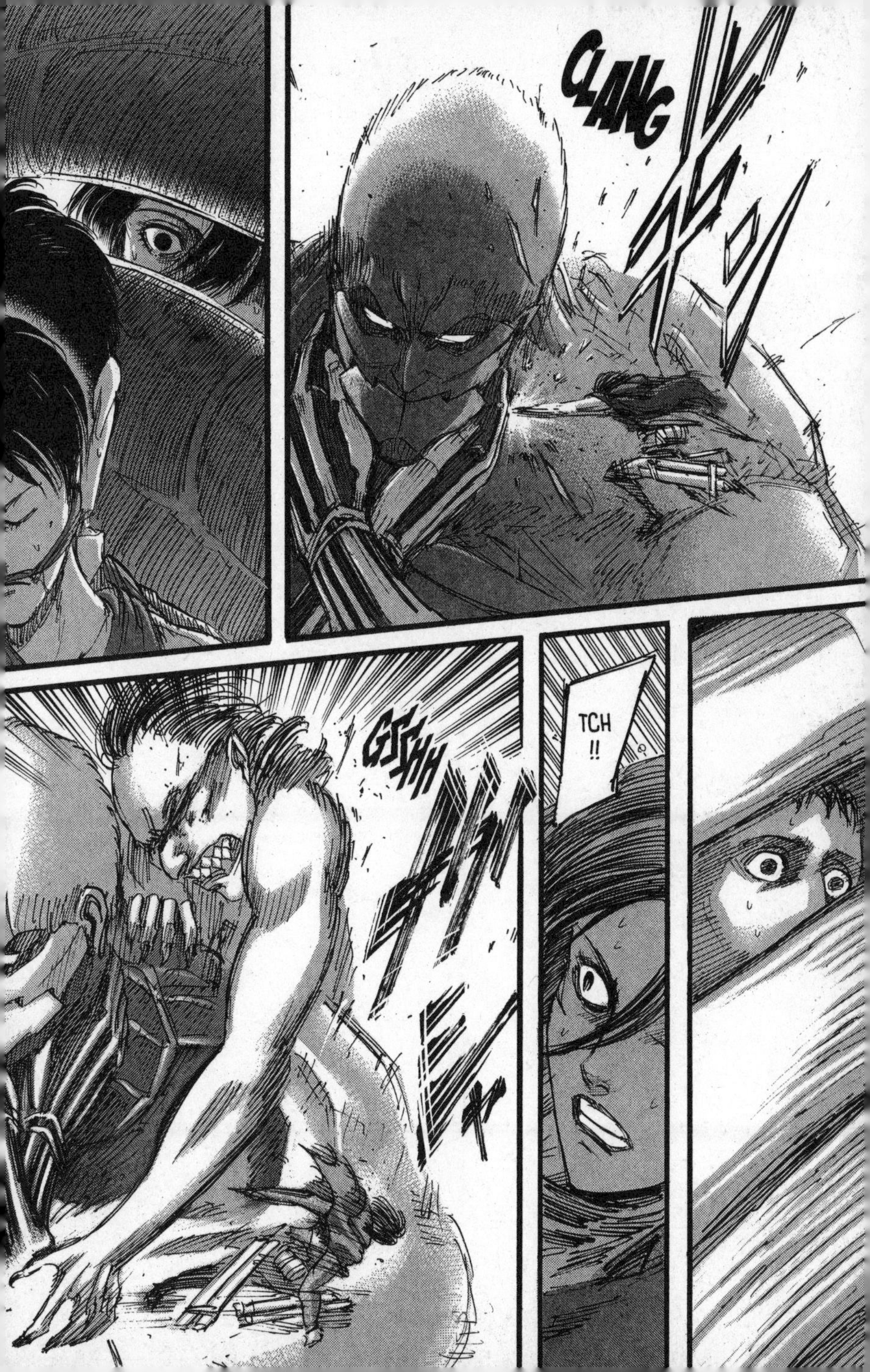
CLANG
TCH !!
GSSHH

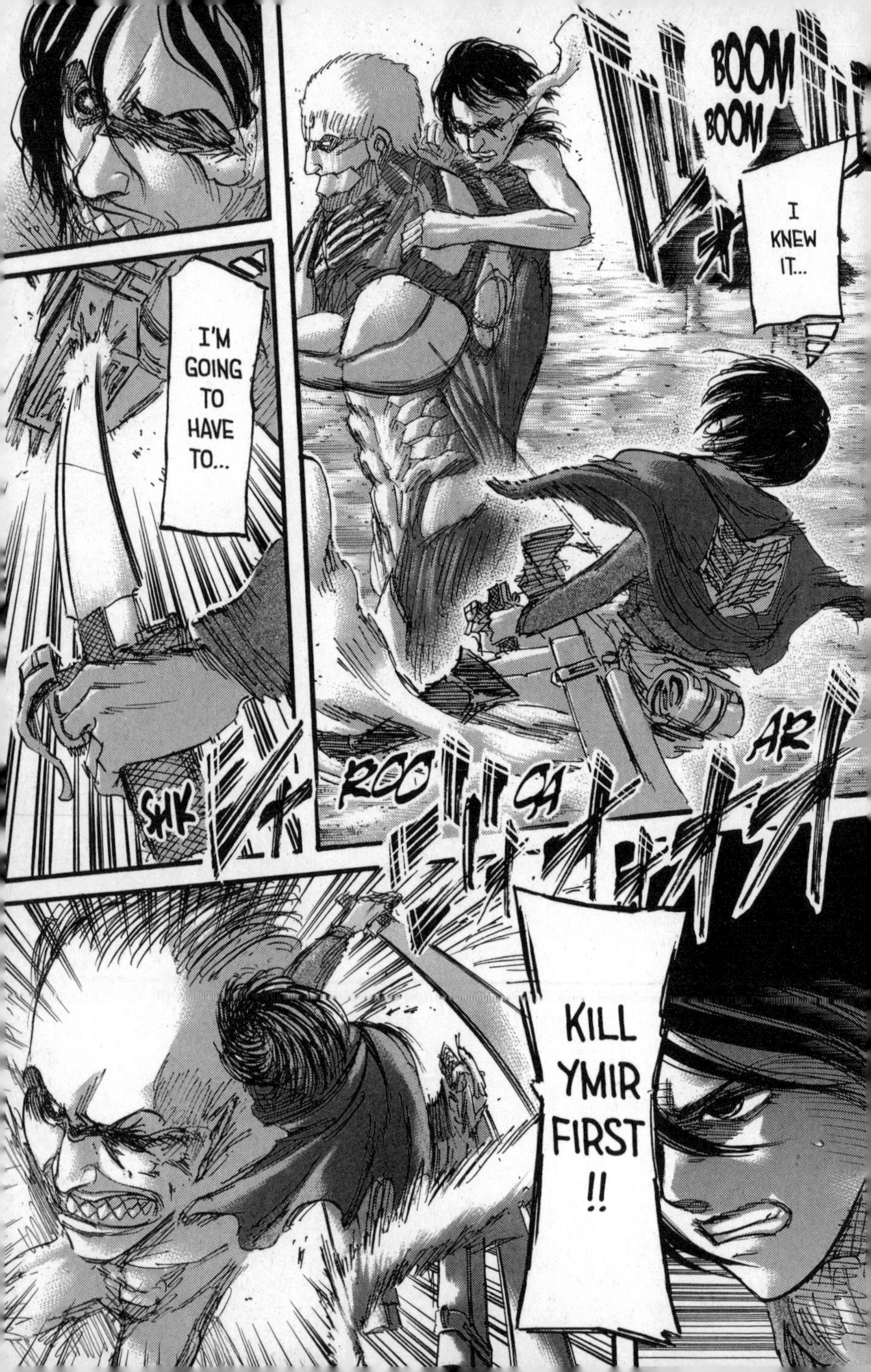
BOOM
BOOM
I KNEW IT...
ROO
OA
AR
I'M GOING TO HAVE TO...
SHK
KILL YMIR FIRST !!

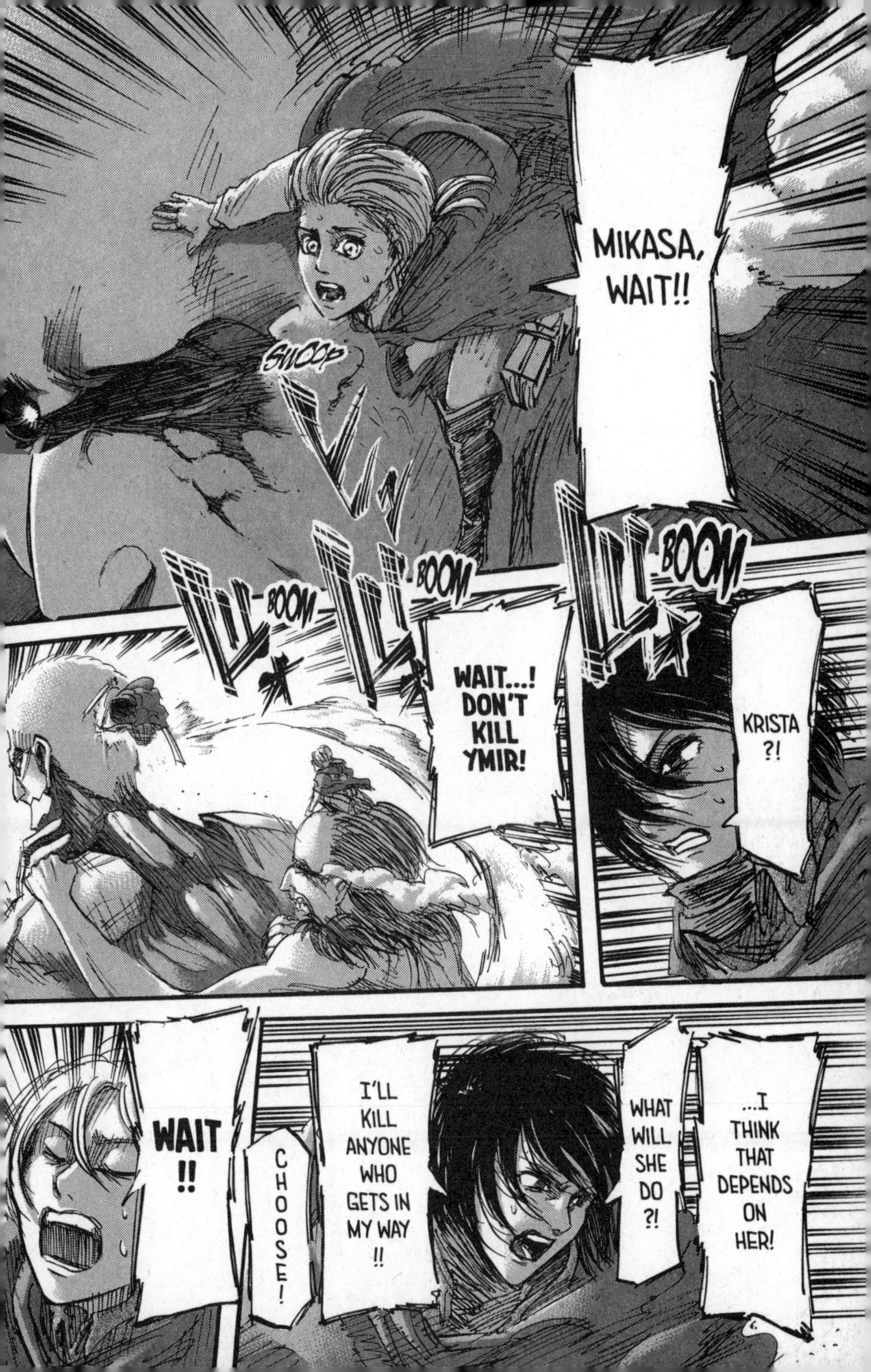
MIKASA, WAIT!!
SWOOP
BOOM
KRISTA ?!
WAIT...! DON'T KILL YMIR!
BOOM
BOOM
...I THINK THAT DEPENDS ON HER!
WHAT WILL SHE DO ?!
I'LL KILL ANYONE WHO GETS IN MY WAY !!
CHOOSE!
WAIT !!

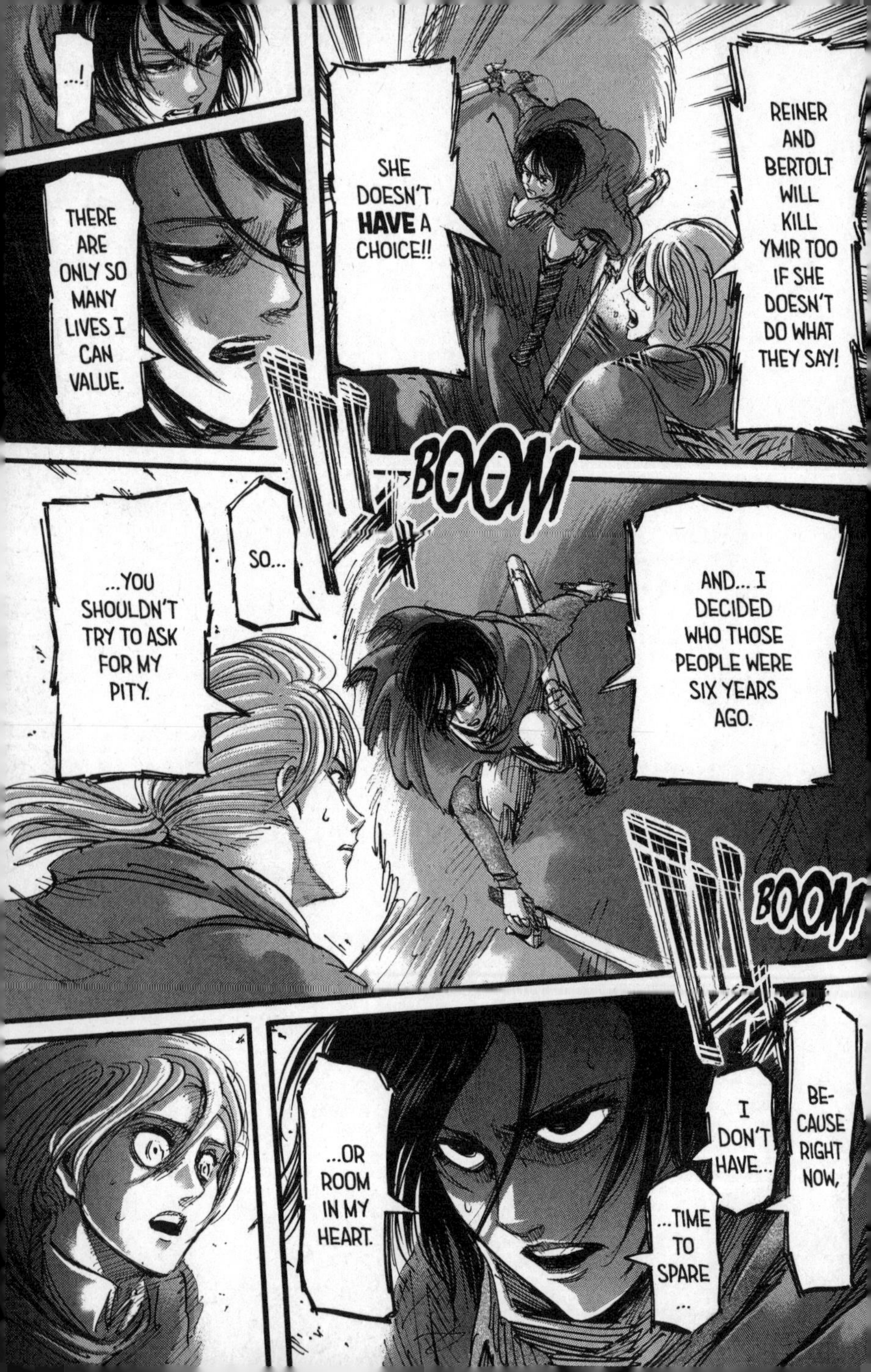
REINER AND BERTOLT WILL KILL YMIR TOO IF SHE DOESN'T DO WHAT THEY SAY!
SHE DOESN'T **HAVE** A CHOICE!!
...!
THERE ARE ONLY SO MANY LIVES I CAN VALUE.
BOOM
AND... I DECIDED WHO THOSE PEOPLE WERE SIX YEARS AGO.
SO...
...YOU SHOULDN'T TRY TO ASK FOR MY PITY.
BOOM
BE-CAUSE RIGHT NOW,
I DON'T HAVE...
...TIME TO SPARE ...
...OR ROOM IN MY HEART.

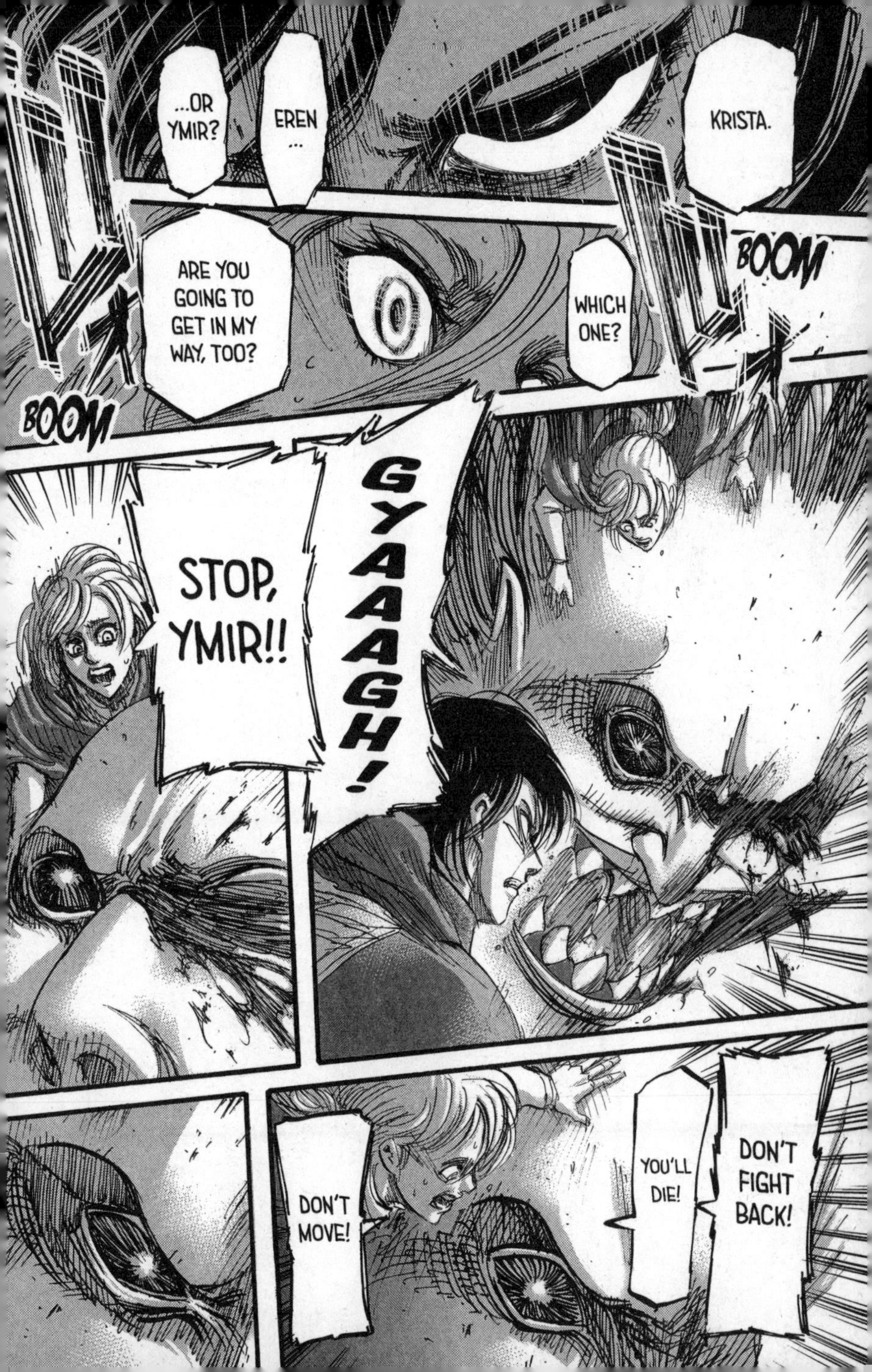
KRISTA.
EREN ...
...OR YMIR?
BOOM
WHICH ONE?
ARE YOU GOING TO GET IN MY WAY, TOO?
BOOM
GYAAAAGH!
STOP, YMIR!!
DON'T FIGHT BACK!
YOU'LL DIE!
DON'T MOVE!

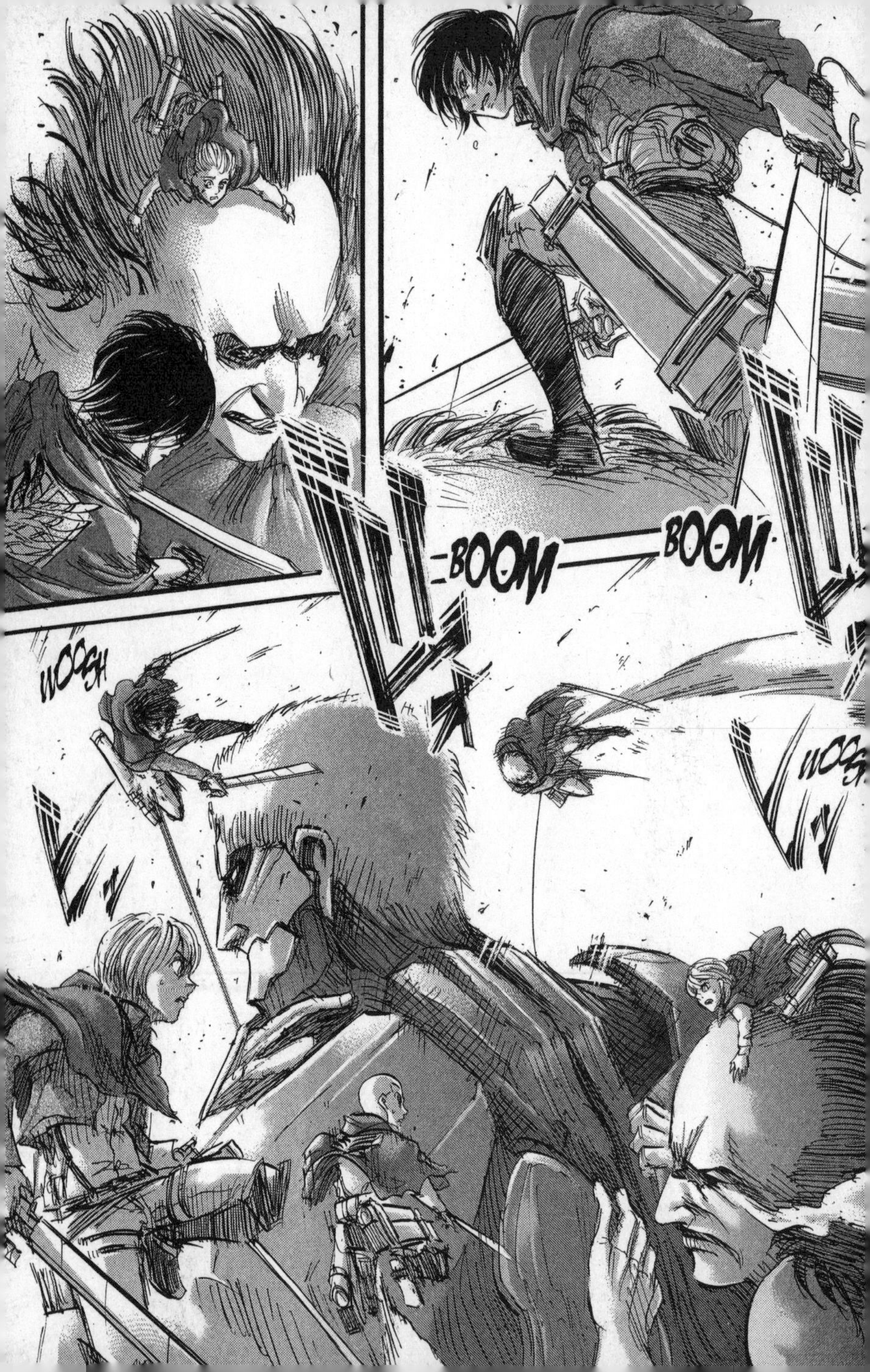
BOOM
BOOM
WOOSH
WOOSH

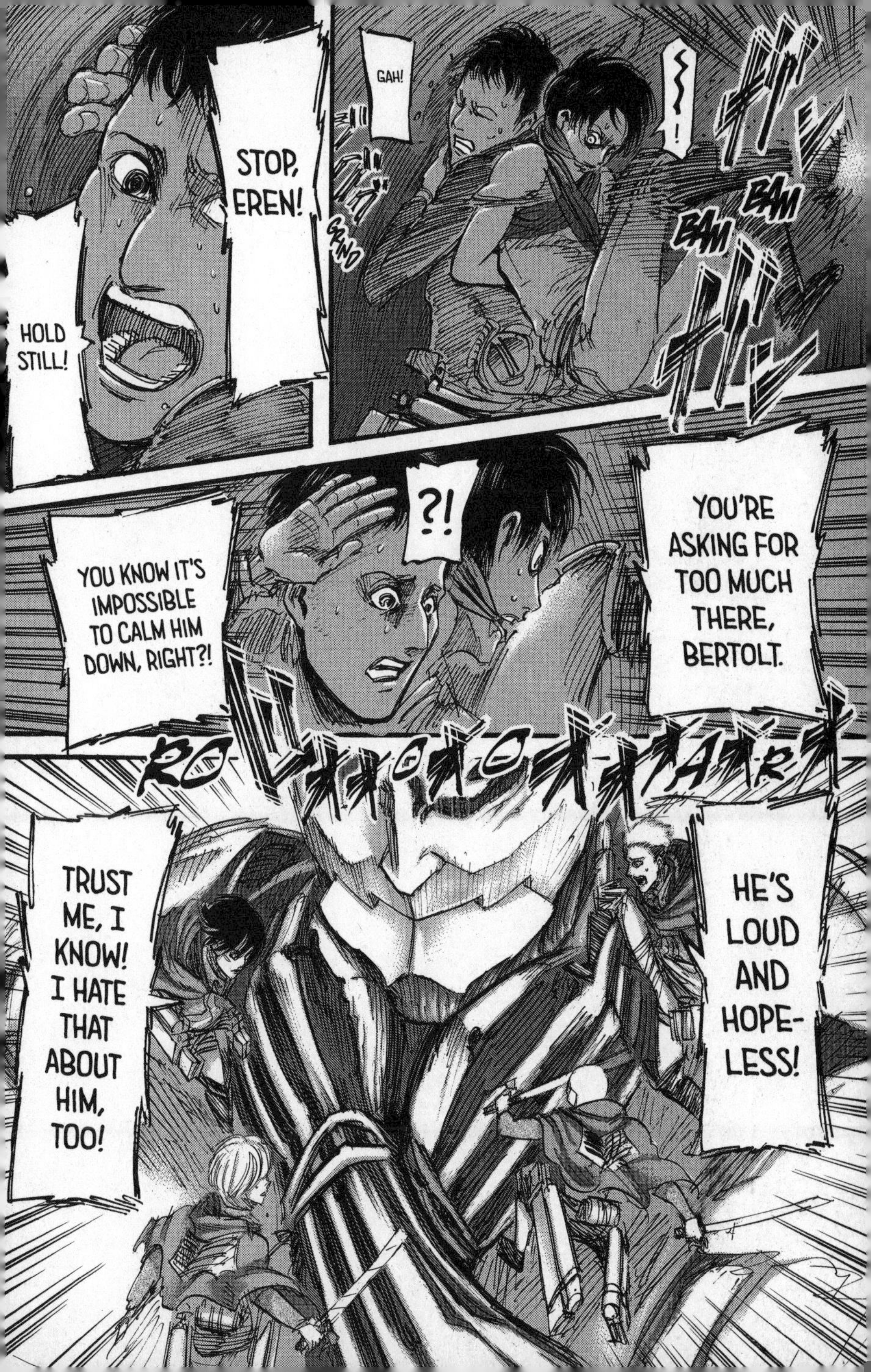
!
GAH!
BAM
BAM
GRIND
STOP, EREN!
HOLD STILL!
YOU'RE ASKING FOR TOO MUCH THERE, BERTOLT.
?!
YOU KNOW IT'S IMPOSSIBLE TO CALM HIM DOWN, RIGHT?!
HE'S LOUD AND HOPE-LESS!
TRUST ME, I KNOW! I HATE THAT ABOUT HIM, TOO!

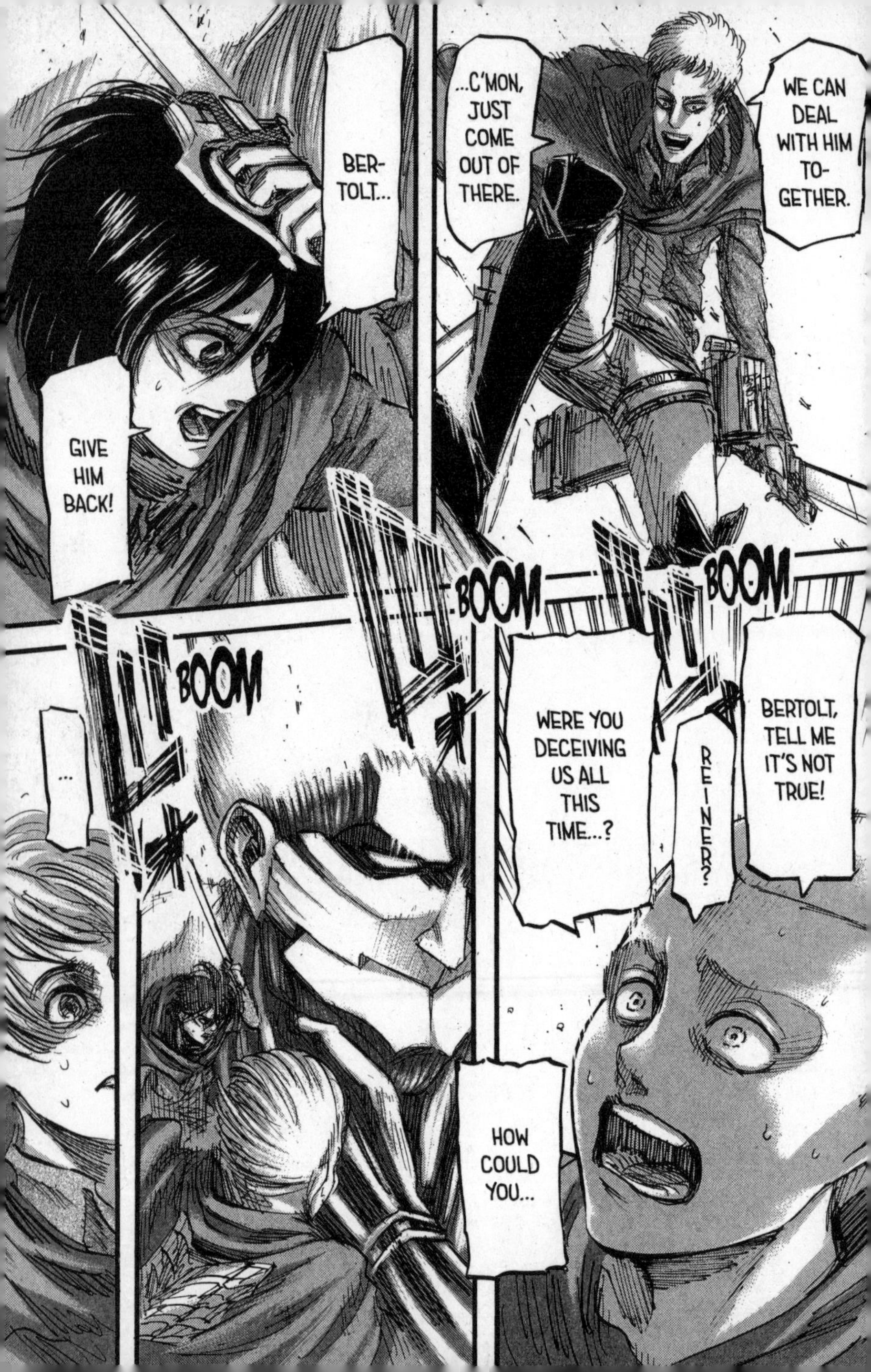
WE CAN DEAL WITH HIM TO-GETHER.
...C'MON, JUST COME OUT OF THERE.
BER-TOLT...
GIVE HIM BACK!
BOOM
BOOM
BERTOLT, TELL ME IT'S NOT TRUE!
REINER?
WERE YOU DECEIVING US ALL THIS TIME...?
HOW COULD YOU...
BOOM
...

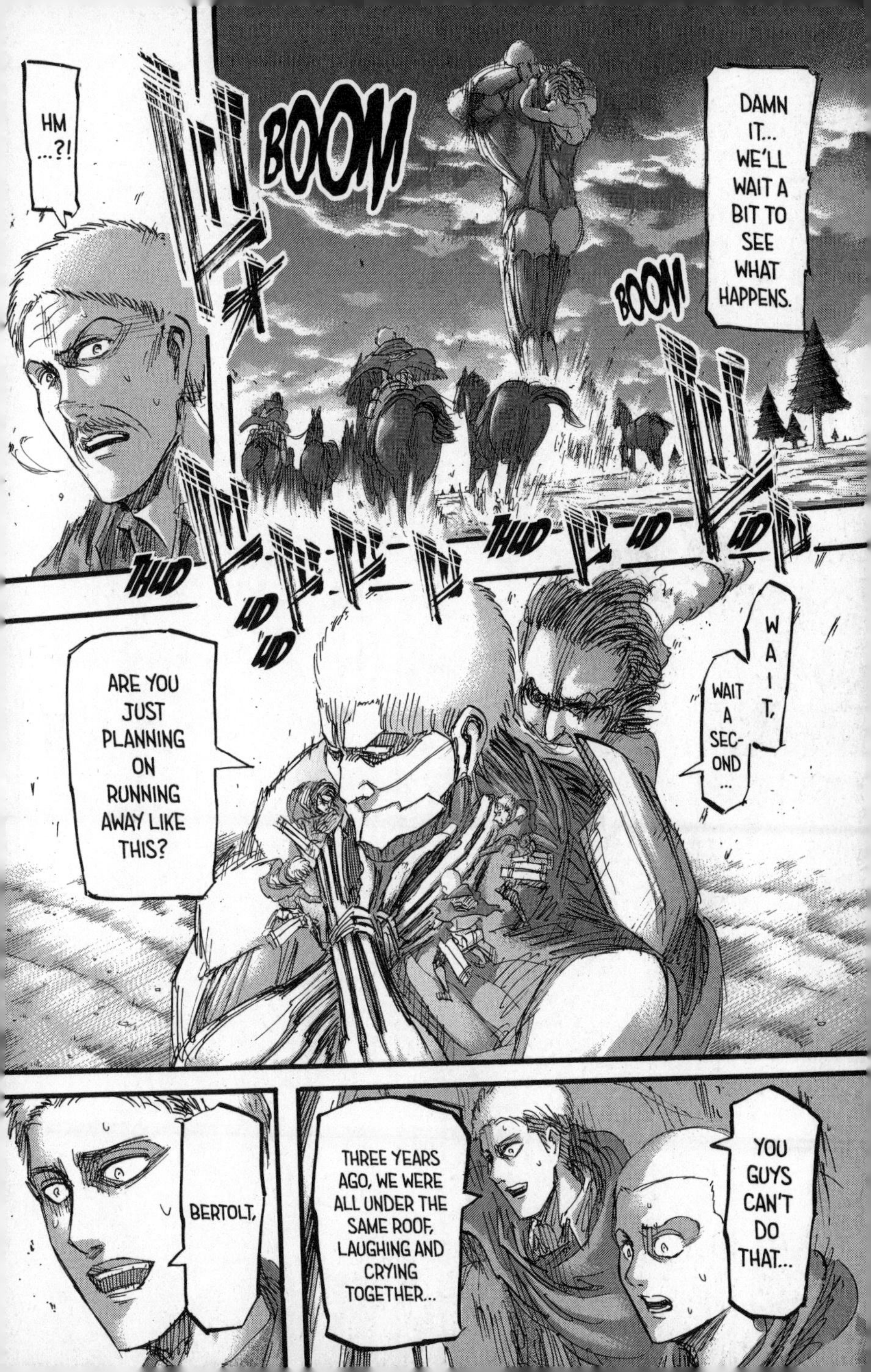
DAMN IT... WE'LL WAIT A BIT TO SEE WHAT HAPPENS.
BOOM
BOOM
HM ...?!
UD
THUD
THUD
UD
UD
WAIT, WAIT A SECOND...
ARE YOU JUST PLANNING ON RUNNING AWAY LIKE THIS?
YOU GUYS CAN'T DO THAT...
THREE YEARS AGO, WE WERE ALL UNDER THE SAME ROOF, LAUGHING AND CRYING TOGETHER...
BERTOLT,

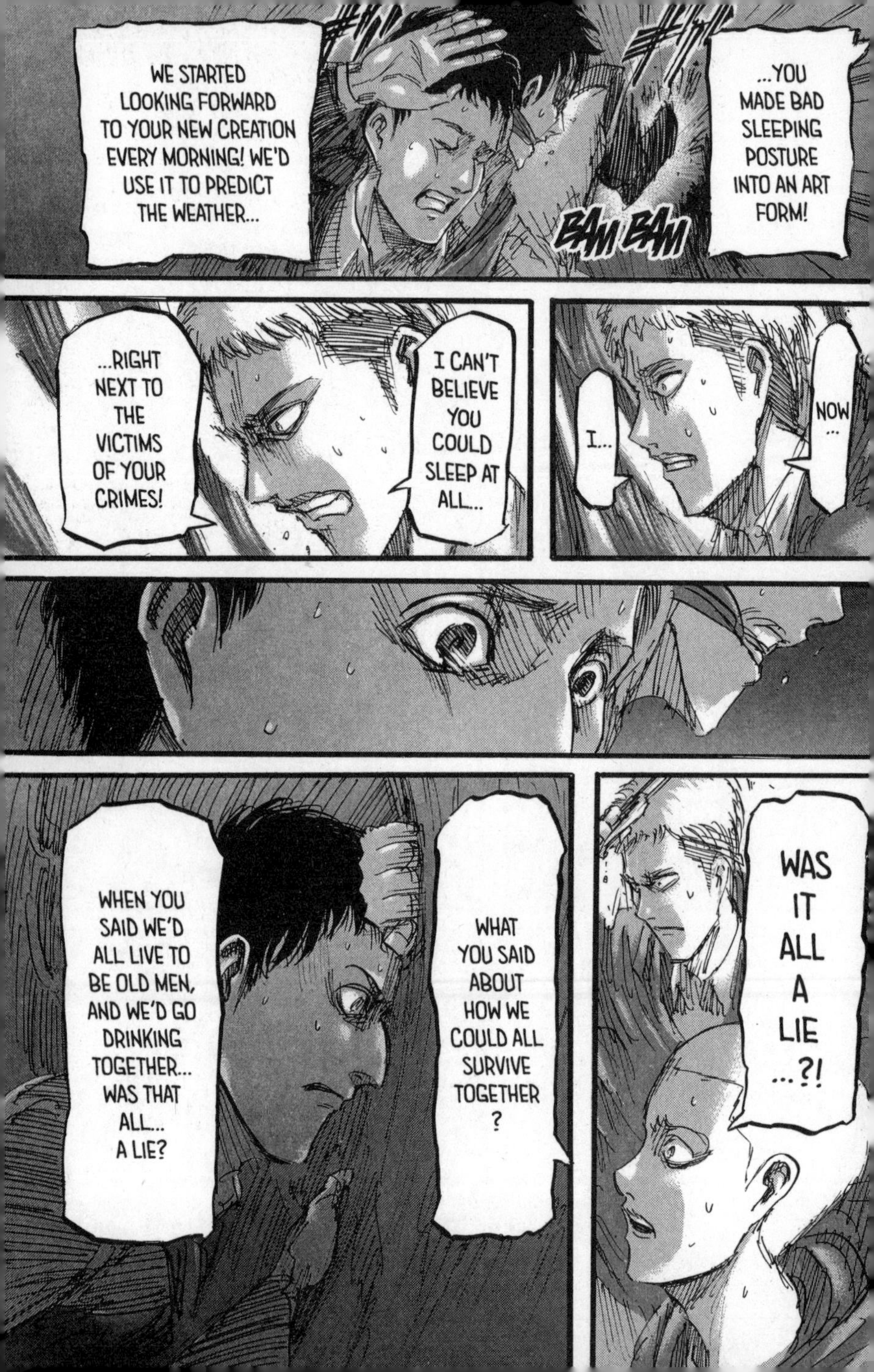
...YOU MADE BAD SLEEPING POSTURE INTO AN ART FORM!
BAM BAM
WE STARTED LOOKING FORWARD TO YOUR NEW CREATION EVERY MORNING! WE'D USE IT TO PREDICT THE WEATHER...
NOW...
I...
I CAN'T BELIEVE YOU COULD SLEEP AT ALL...
...RIGHT NEXT TO THE VICTIMS OF YOUR CRIMES!
WAS IT ALL A LIE...?!
WHAT YOU SAID ABOUT HOW WE COULD ALL SURVIVE TOGETHER?
WHEN YOU SAID WE'D ALL LIVE TO BE OLD MEN, AND WE'D GO DRINKING TOGETHER... WAS THAT ALL... A LIE?

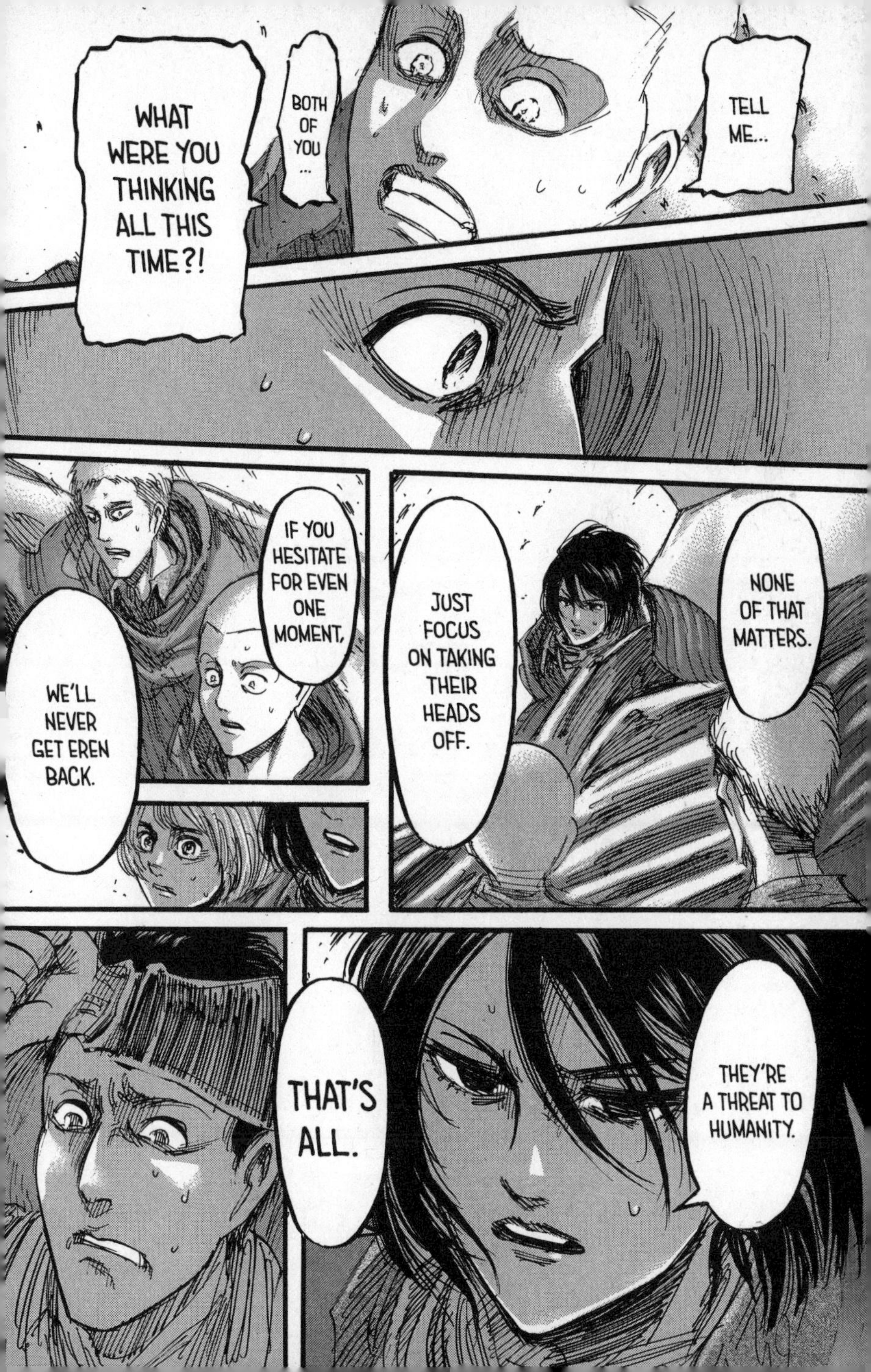
TELL ME...
BOTH OF YOU...
WHAT WERE YOU THINKING ALL THIS TIME?!
NONE OF THAT MATTERS.
JUST FOCUS ON TAKING THEIR HEADS OFF.
IF YOU HESITATE FOR EVEN ONE MOMENT,
WE'LL NEVER GET EREN BACK.
THEY'RE A THREAT TO HUMANITY.
THAT'S ALL.

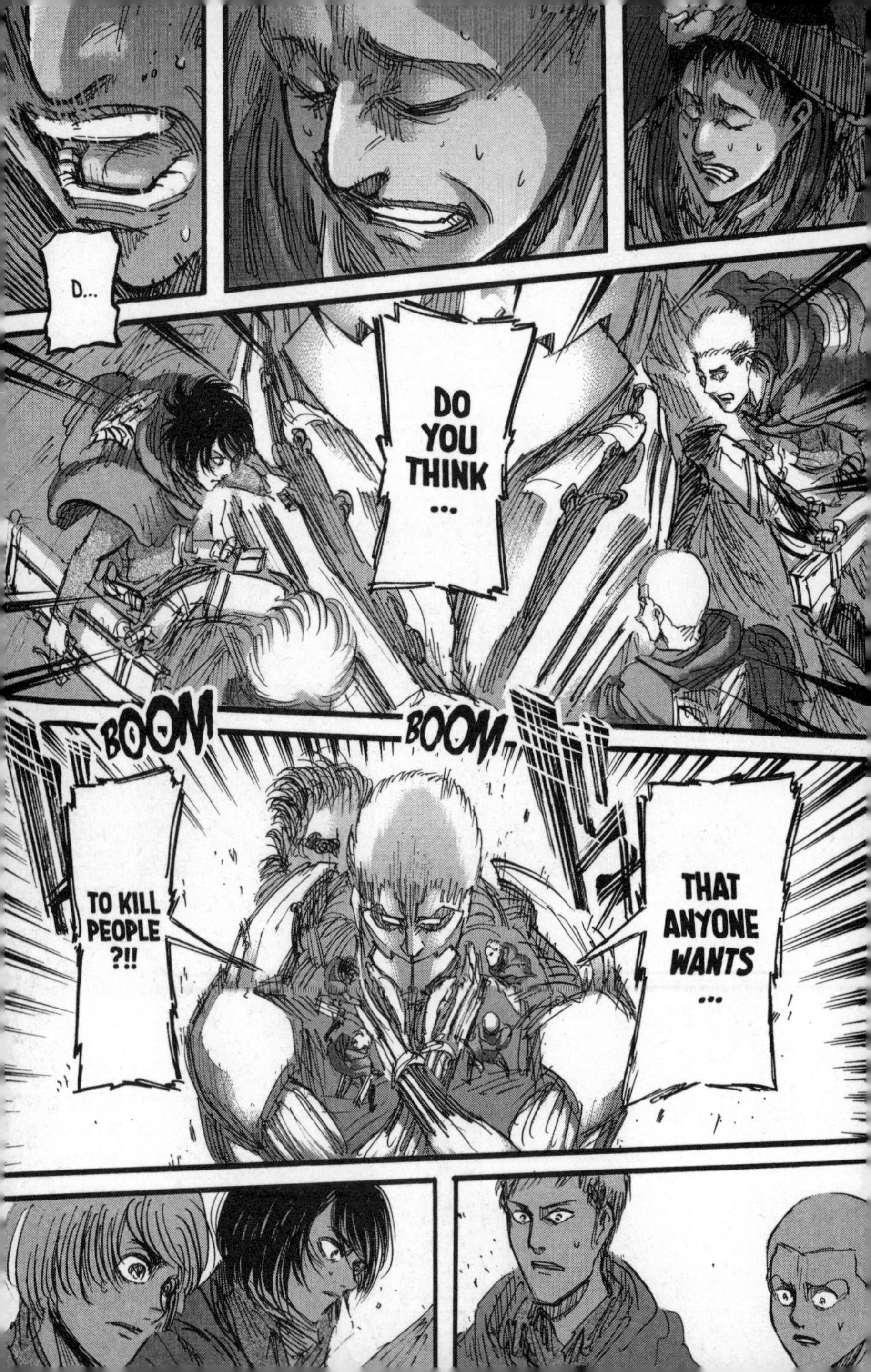

D...
DO YOU THINK ...
BOOM
BOOM
THAT ANYONE WANTS ...
TO KILL PEOPLE ?!!

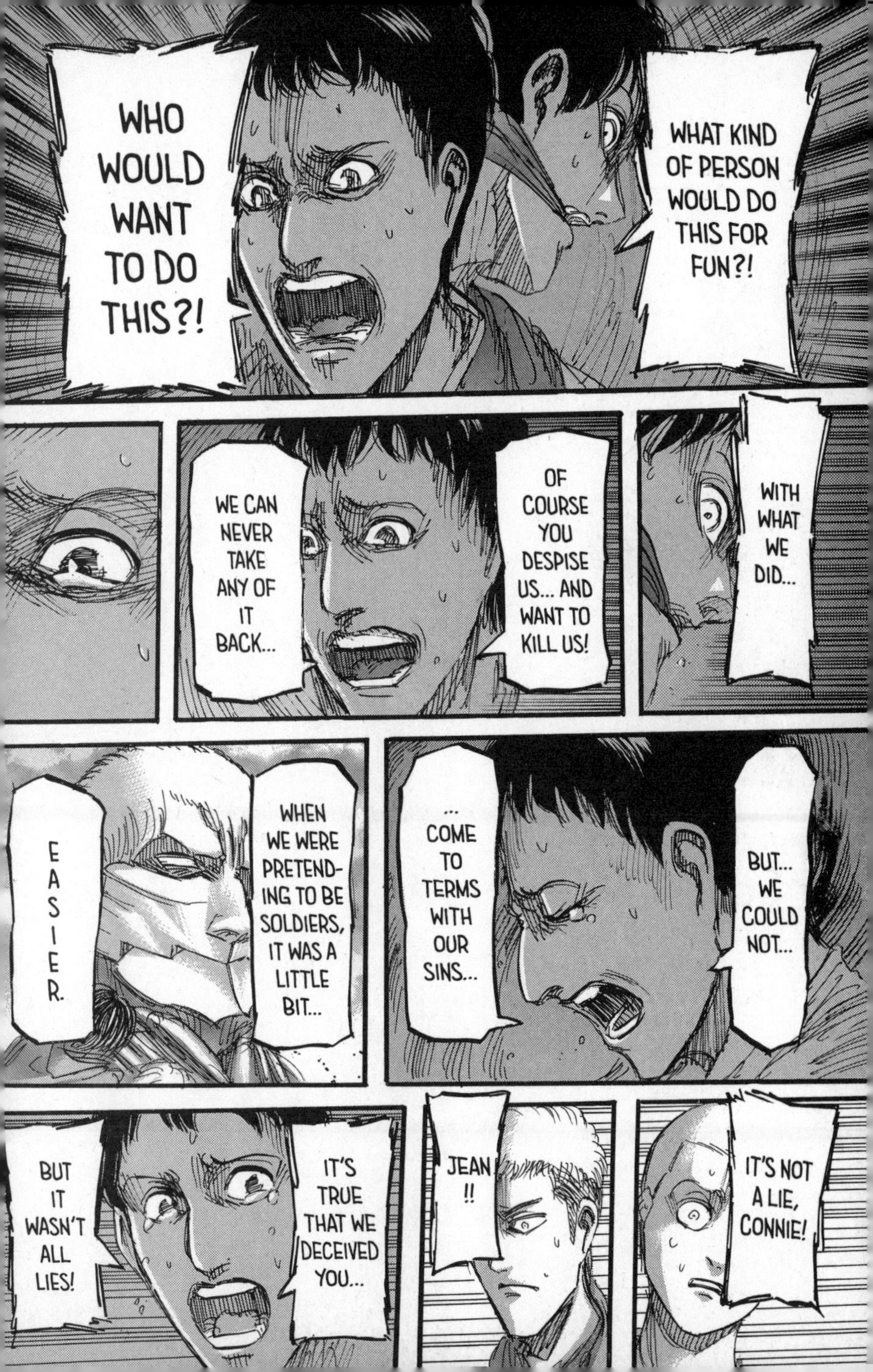

WHAT KIND OF PERSON WOULD DO THIS FOR FUN?!
WHO WOULD WANT TO DO THIS?!
WITH WHAT WE DID...
OF COURSE YOU DESPISE US... AND WANT TO KILL US!
WE CAN NEVER TAKE ANY OF IT BACK...
BUT... WE COULD NOT...
...COME TO TERMS WITH OUR SINS...
WHEN WE WERE PRETEND-ING TO BE SOLDIERS, IT WAS A LITTLE BIT...
EASIER.
IT'S NOT A LIE, CONNIE!
JEAN !!
IT'S TRUE THAT WE DECEIVED YOU...
BUT IT WASN'T ALL LIES!

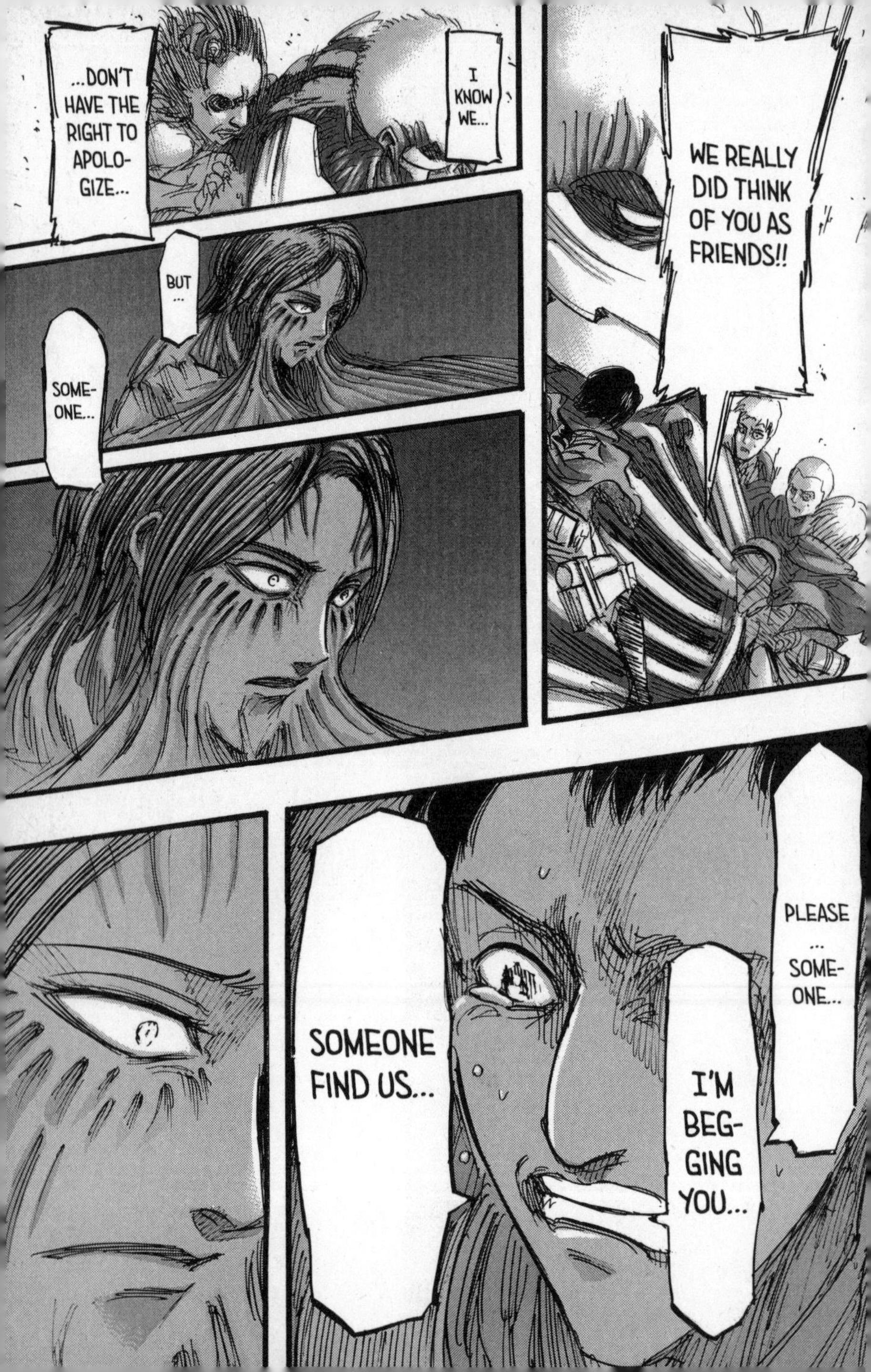
WE REALLY DID THINK OF YOU AS FRIENDS!!
I KNOW WE...
...DON'T HAVE THE RIGHT TO APOLO-GIZE...
BUT...
SOME-ONE...
PLEASE... SOME-ONE...
I'M BEG-GING YOU...
SOMEONE FIND US...

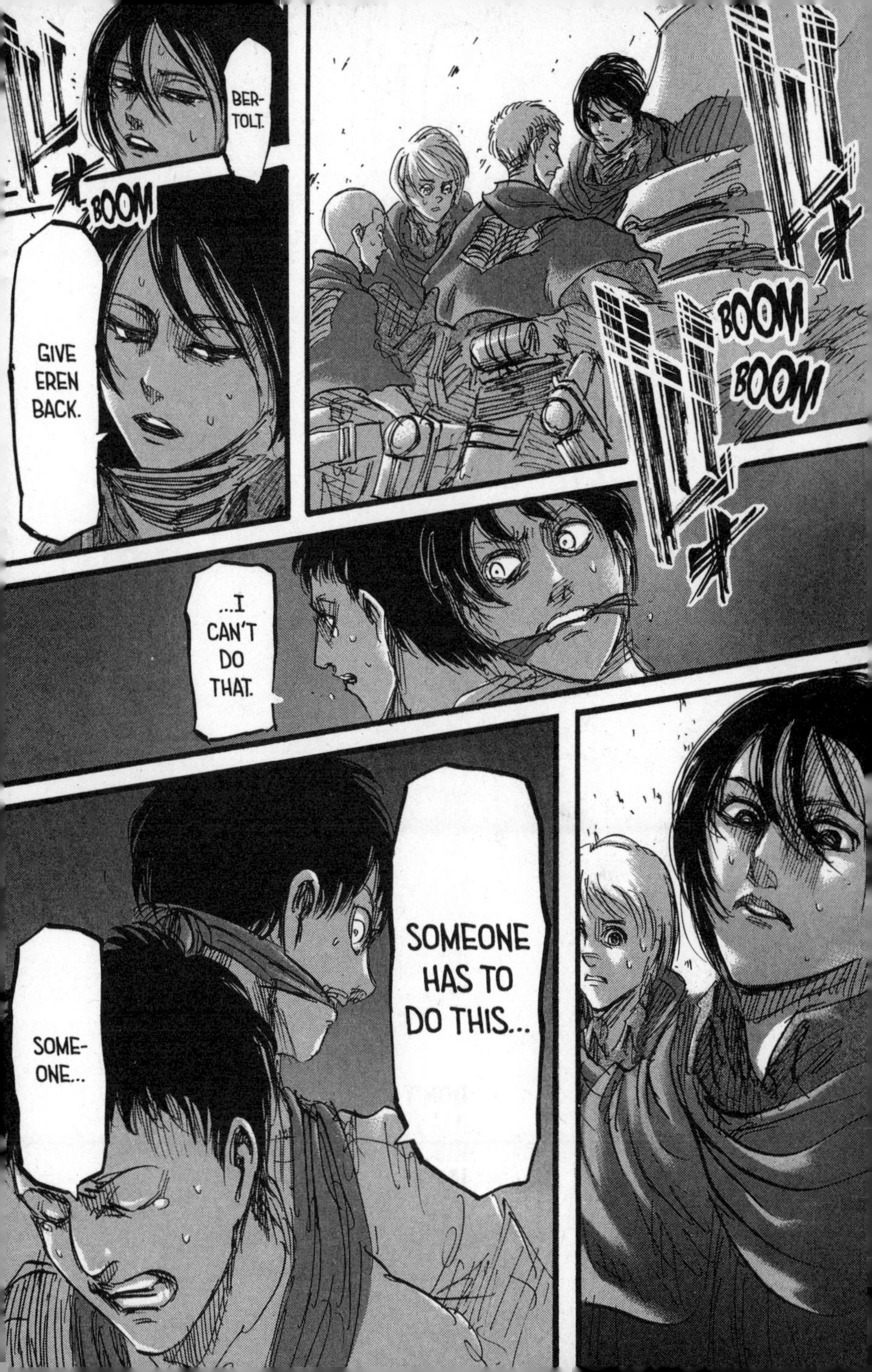
BOOM
BOOM
BER-TOLT.
BOOM
GIVE EREN BACK.
...I CAN'T DO THAT.
SOMEONE HAS TO DO THIS...
SOME-ONE...

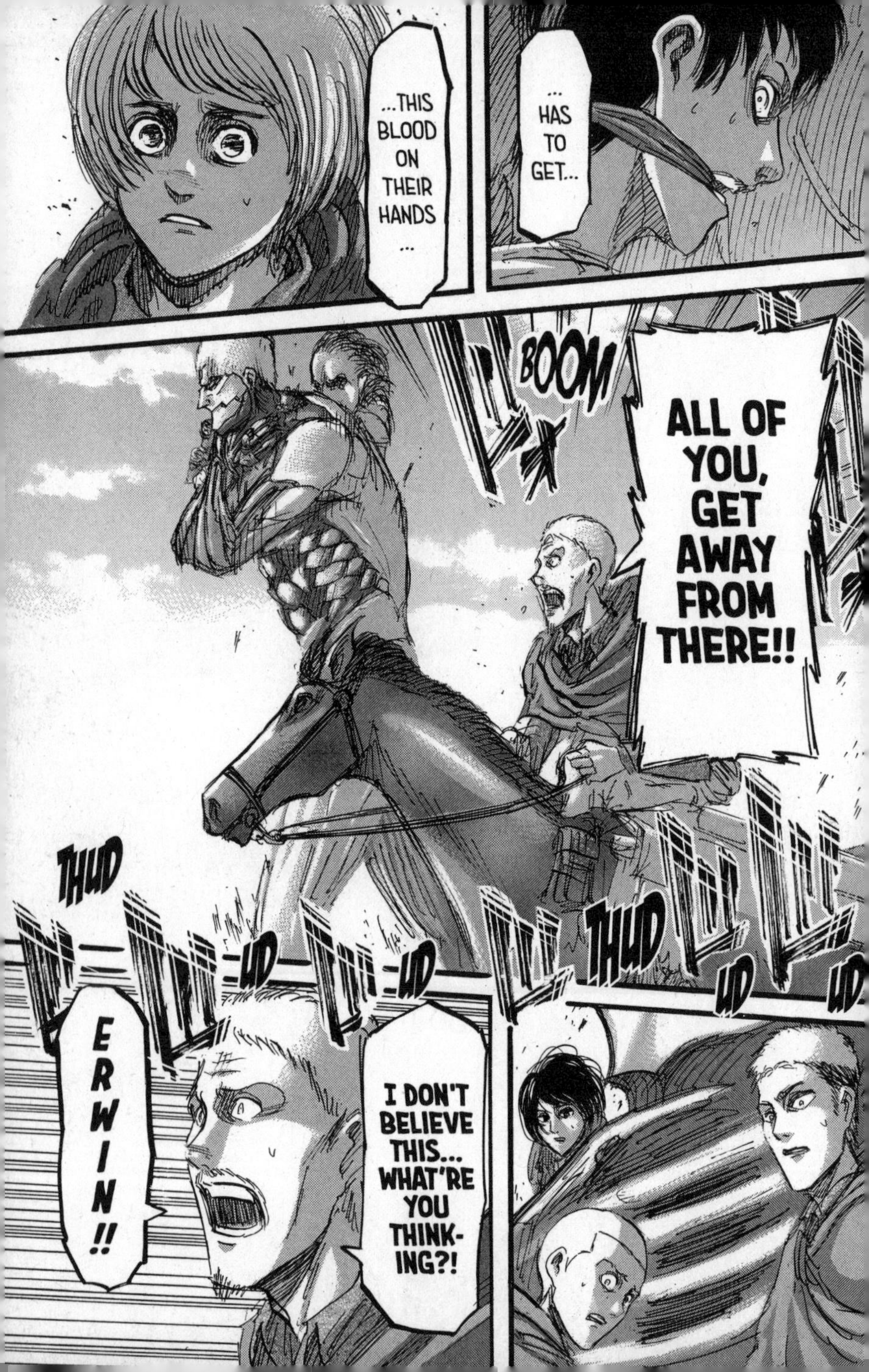
... HAS TO GET...
...THIS BLOOD ON THEIR HANDS ...
BOOM
ALL OF YOU, GET AWAY FROM THERE!!
THUD
THUD
I DON'T BELIEVE THIS... WHAT'RE YOU THINKING?!
ERWIN!!

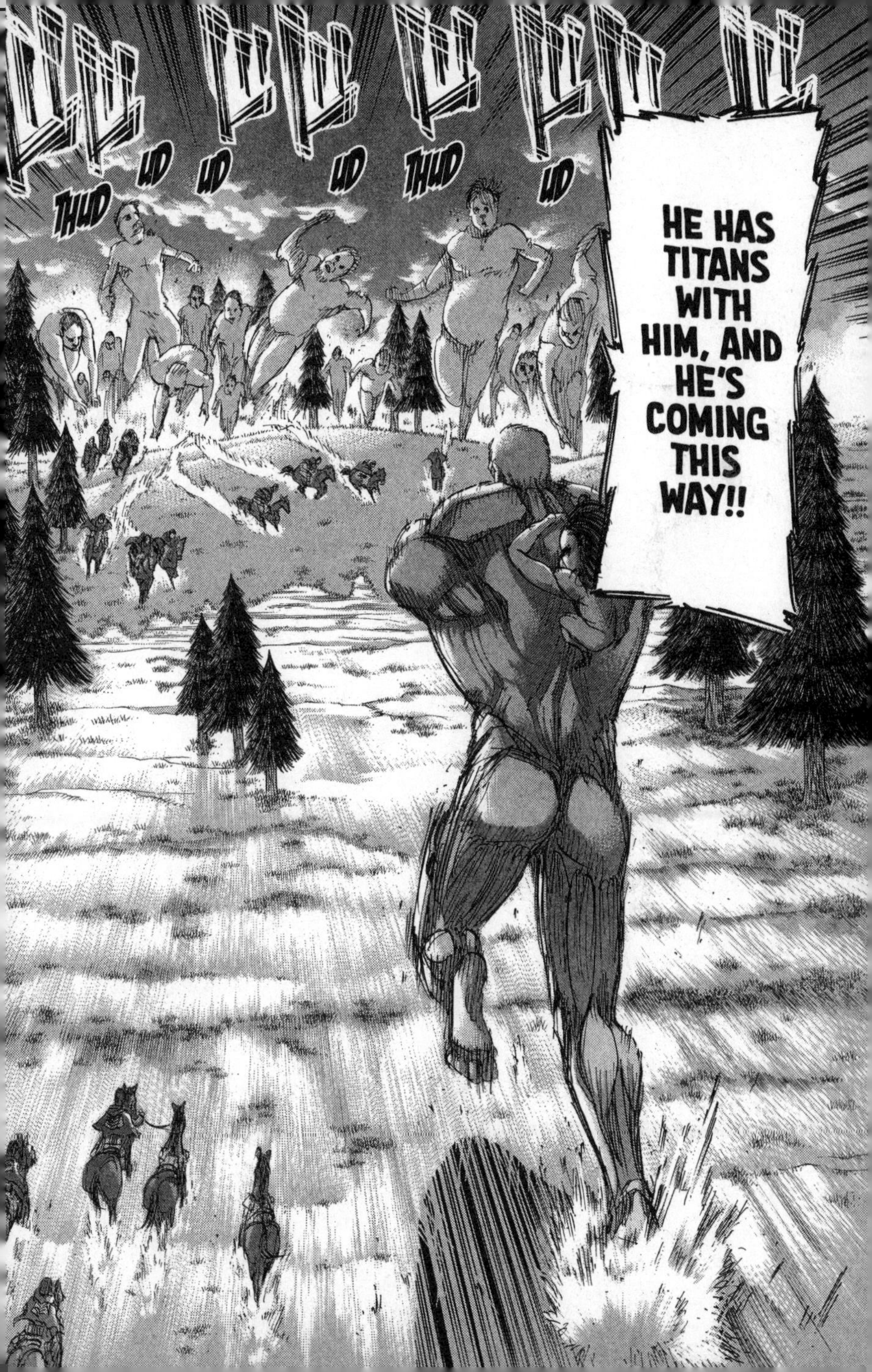
HE HAS TITANS WITH HIM, AND HE'S COMING THIS WAY!!
UD
THUD
UD
UD
UD
THUD

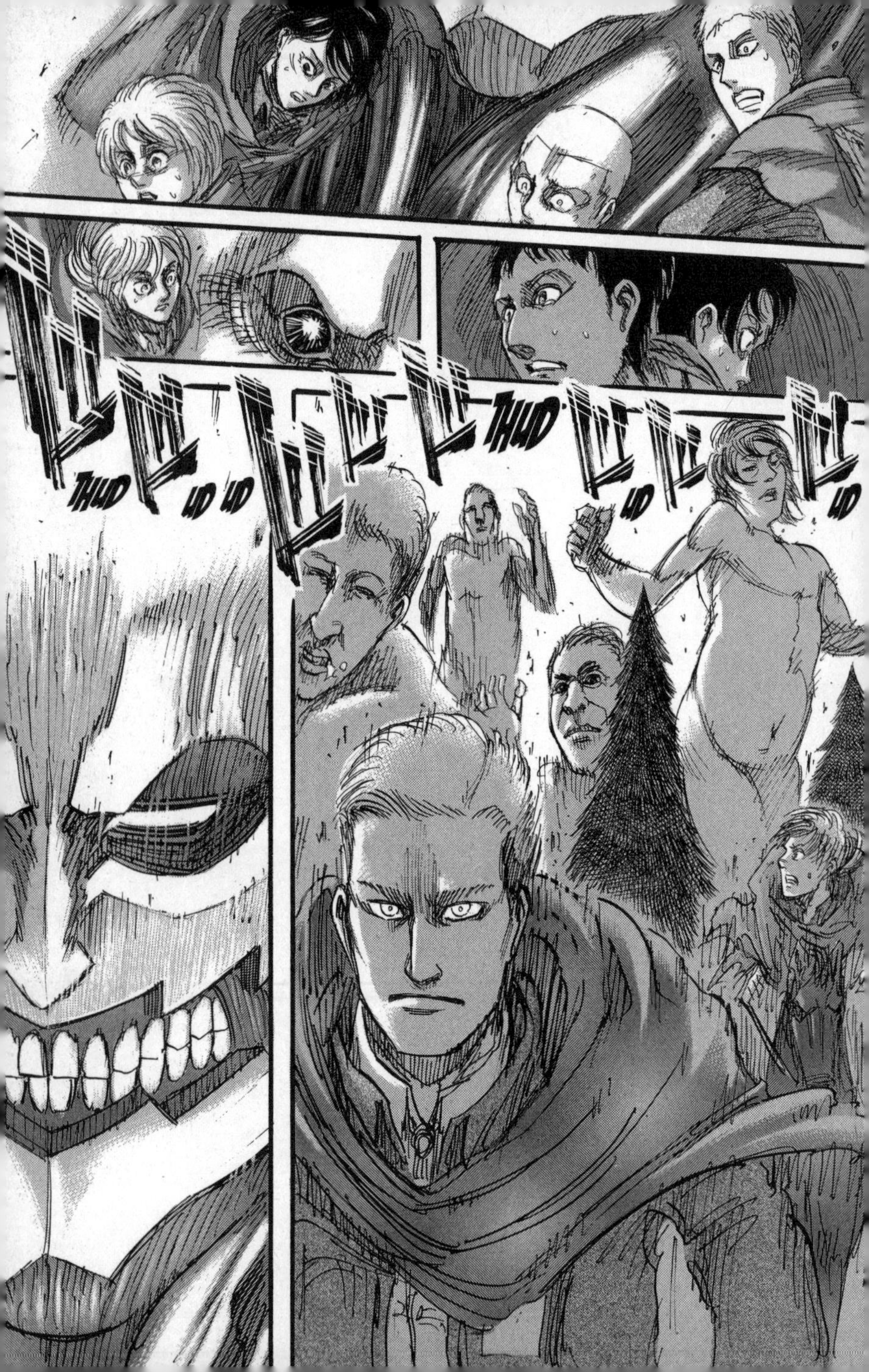
UD
UD
THUD
UD UD
THUD

ATTACK on TITAN

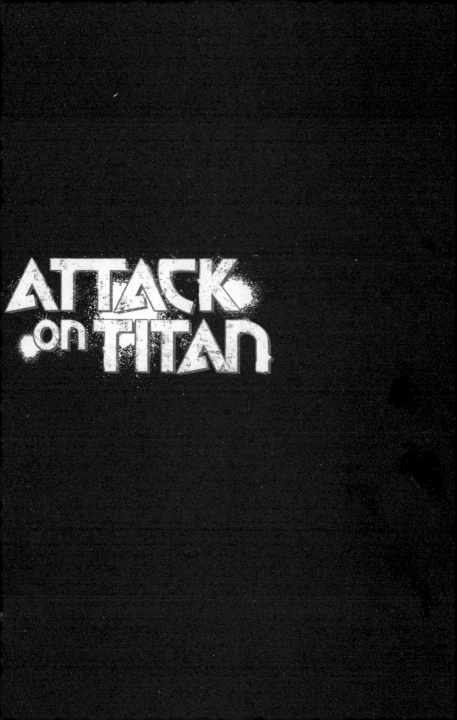

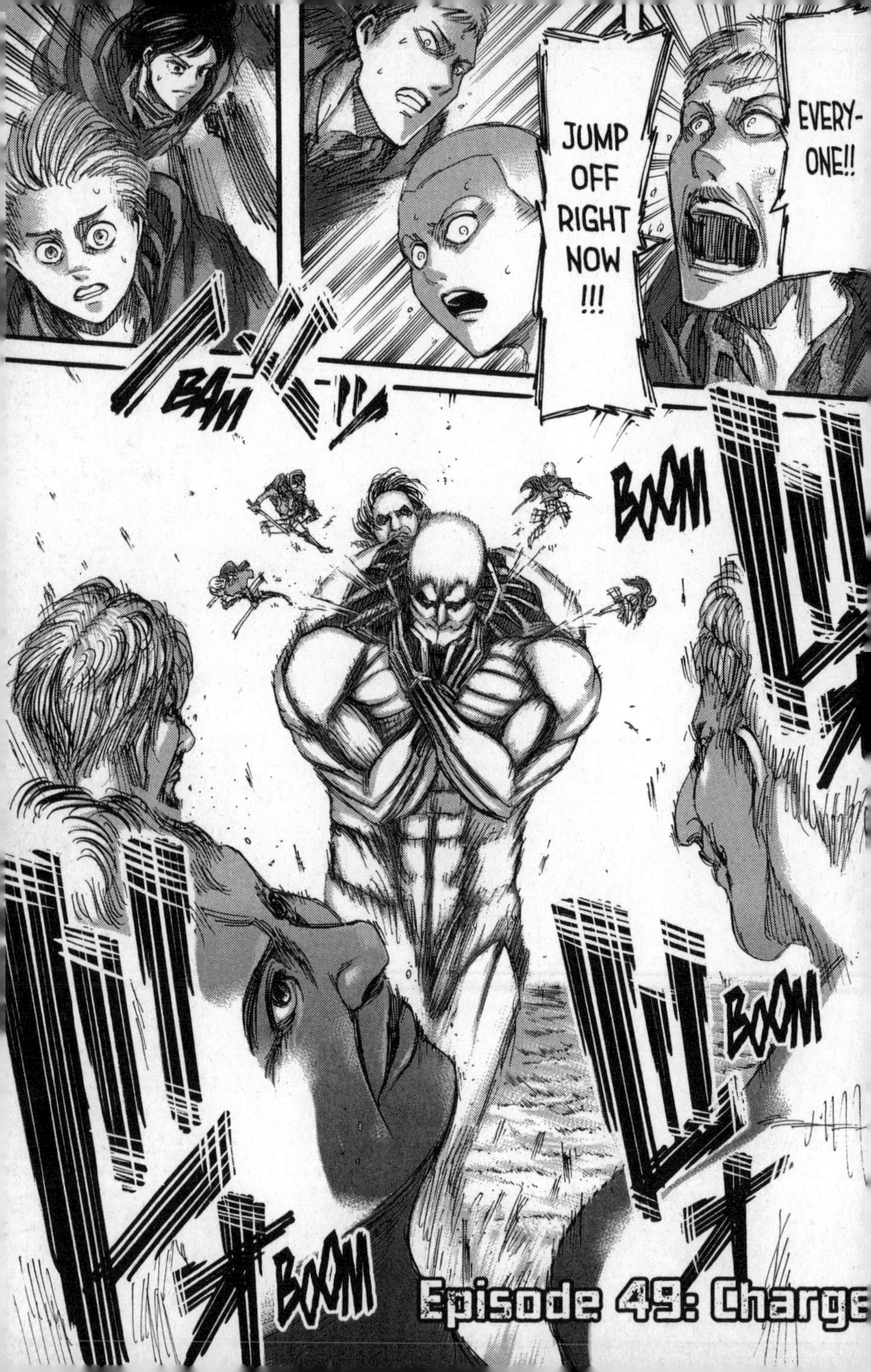
EVERY-ONE!!
JUMP OFF RIGHT NOW !!!
BAM
BOOM
BOOM
BOOM
Episode 49: Charge

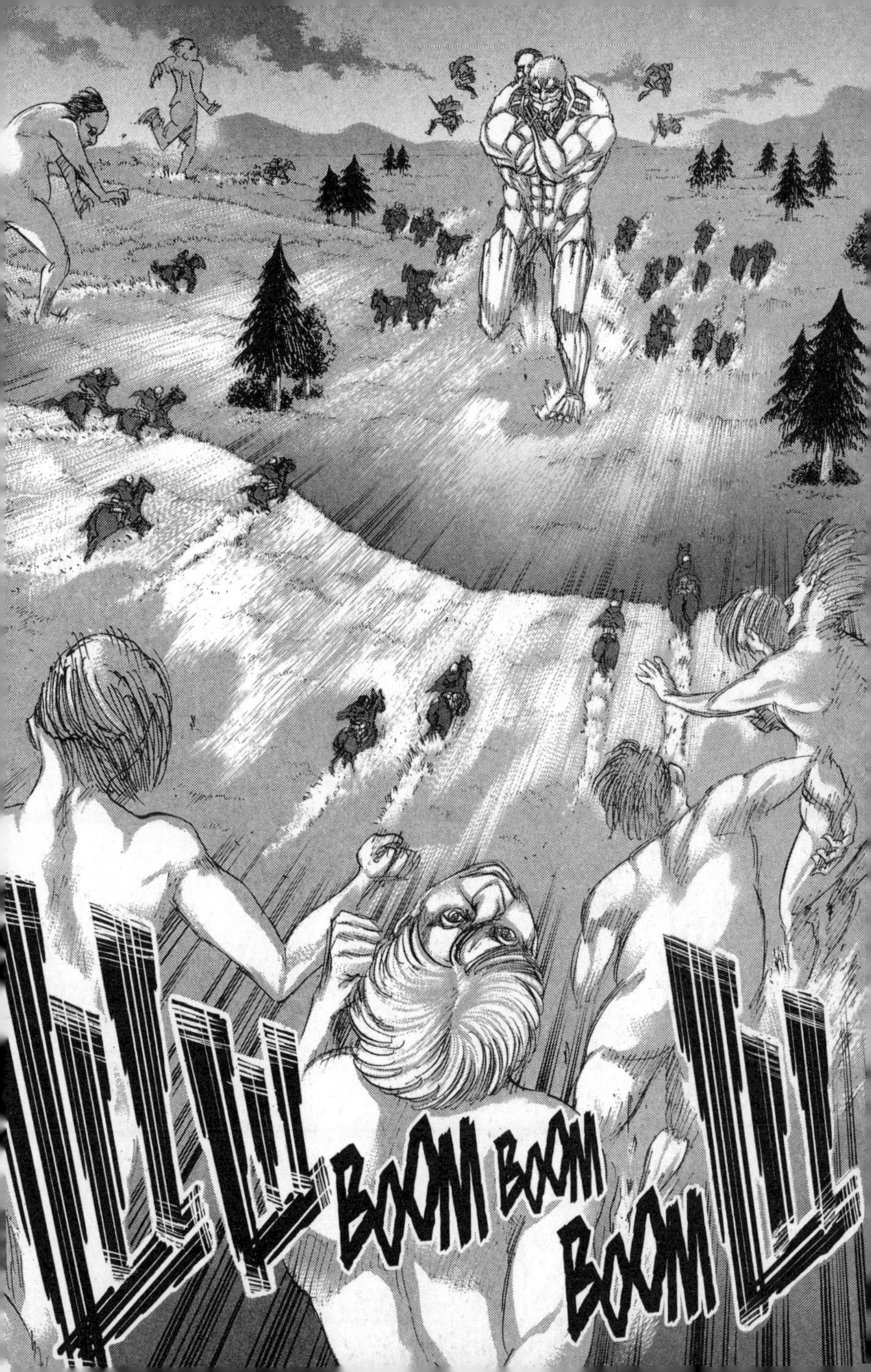
BOOM BOOM
BOOM BOOM

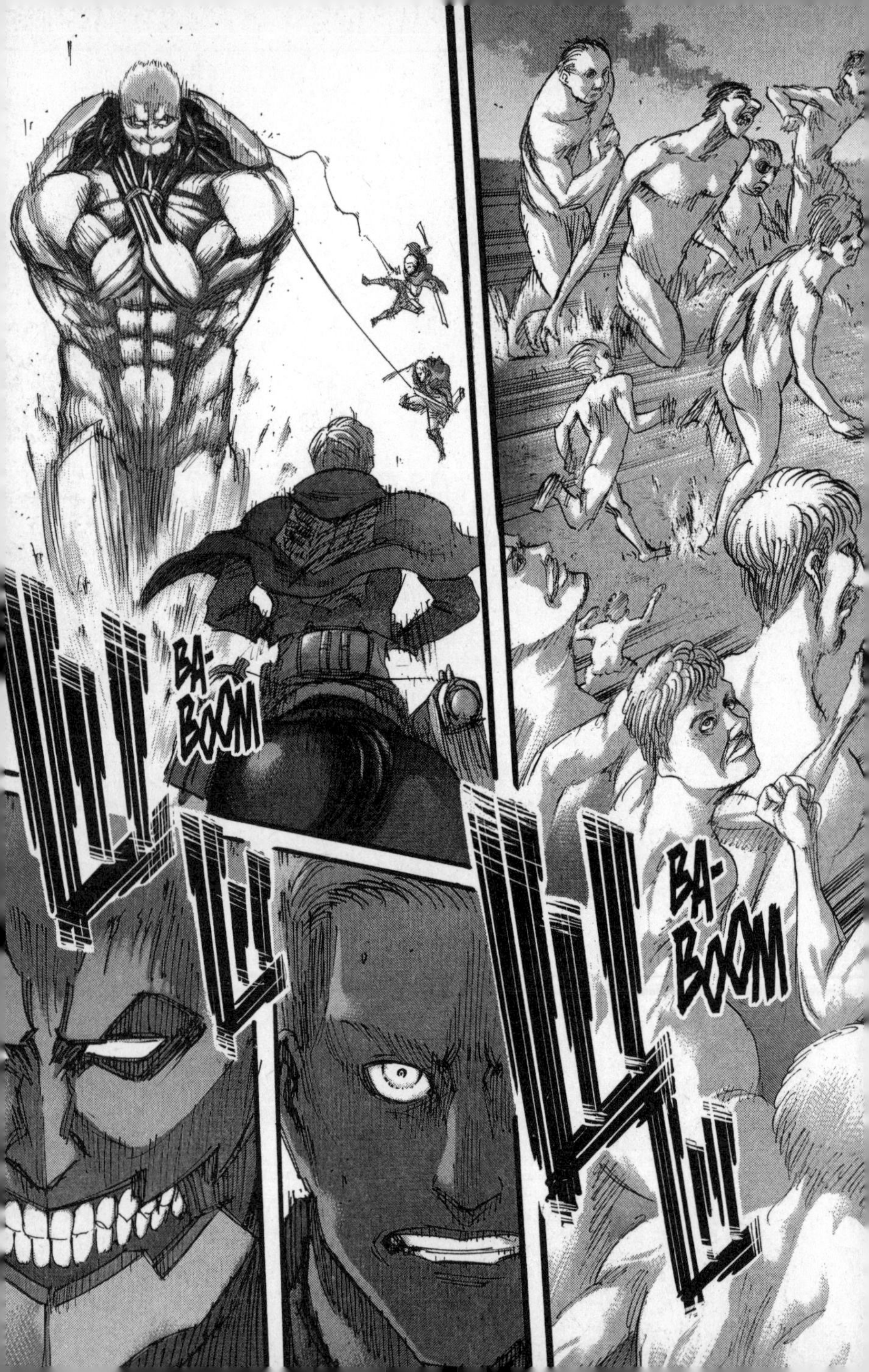
BA-BOOM
BA-BOOM

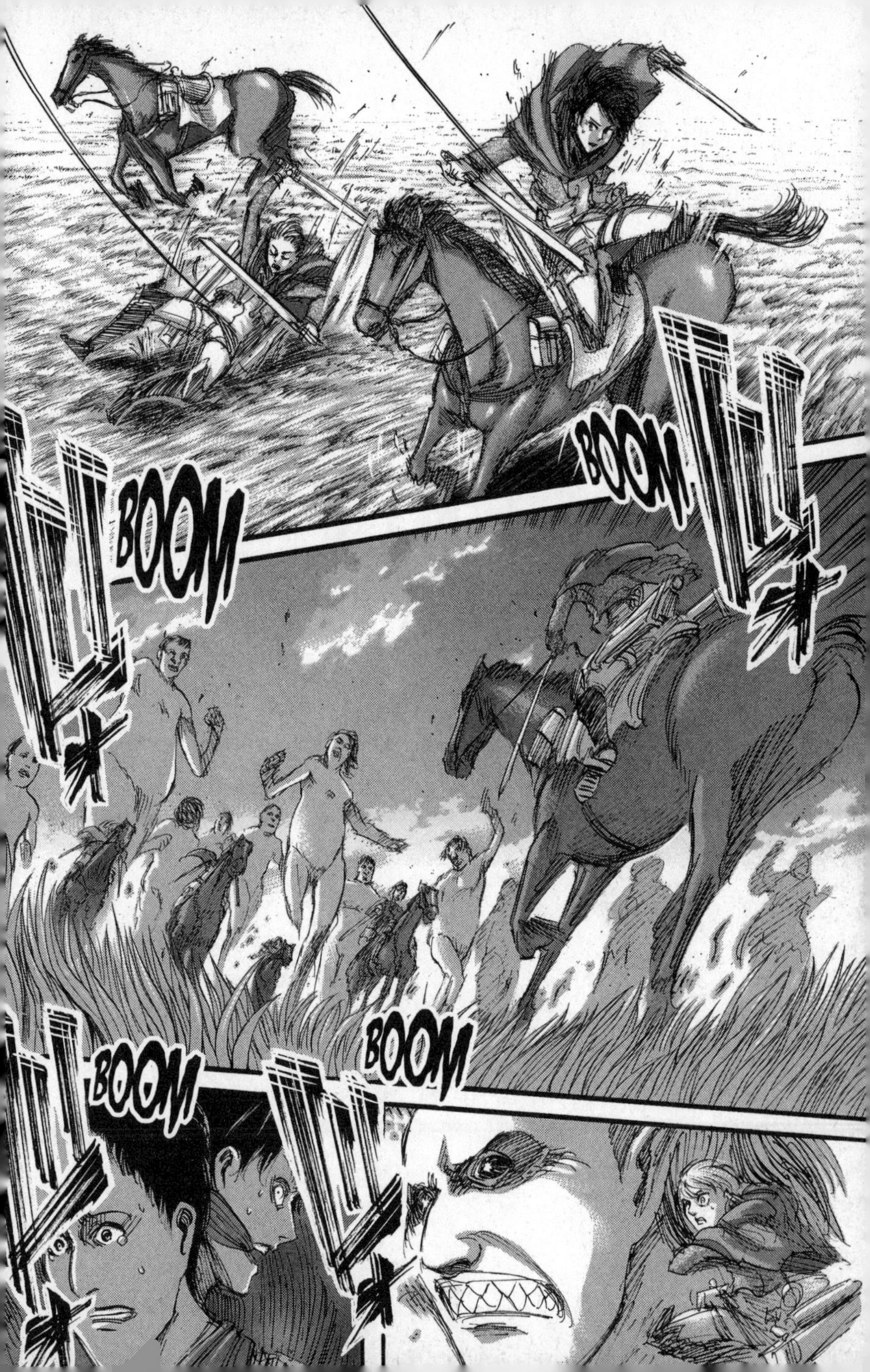
BOOM
BOOM
BOOM
BOOM

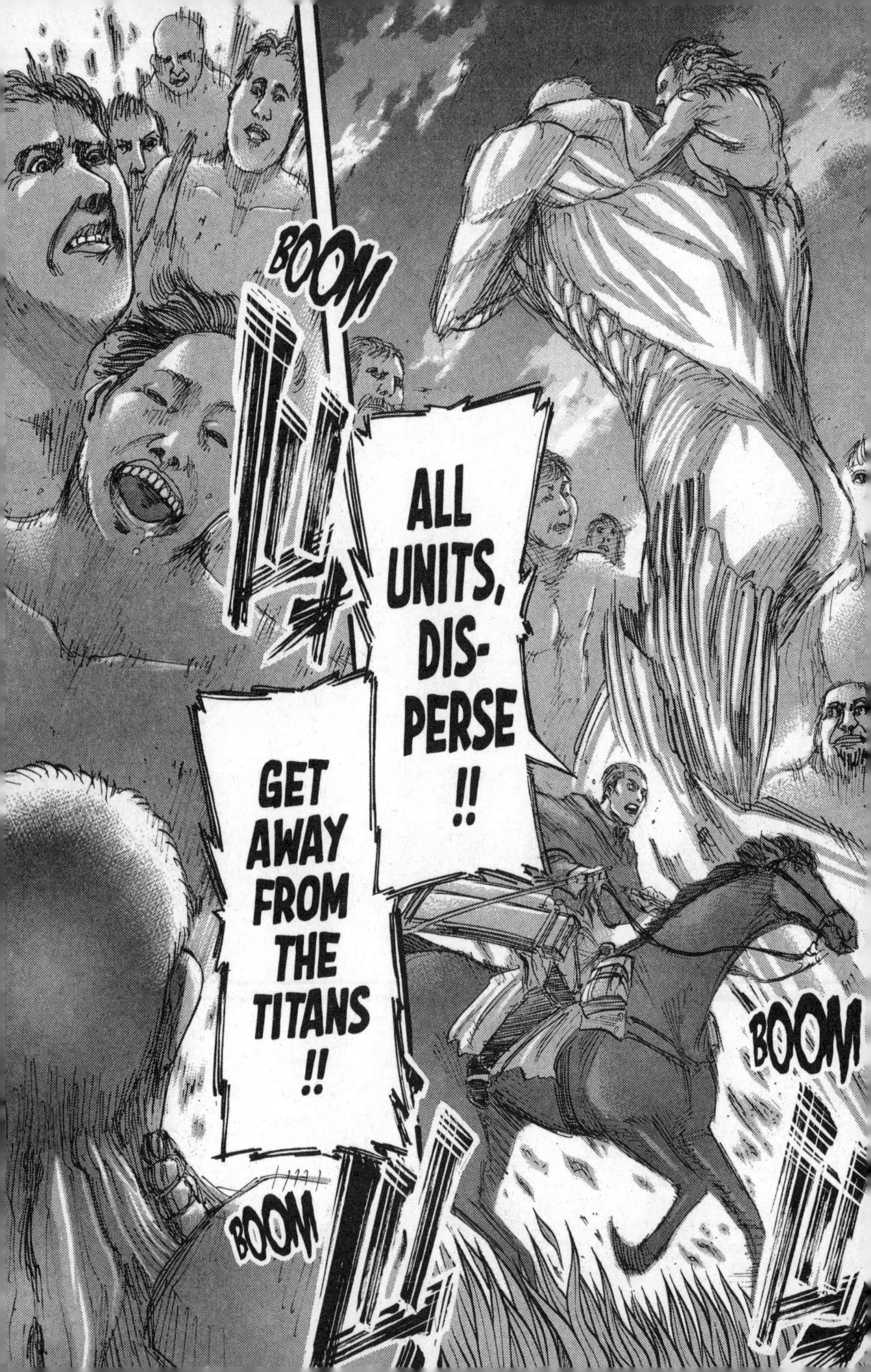
BOOM
ALL UNITS, DISPERSE!!
GET AWAY FROM THE TITANS!!
BOOM
BOOM

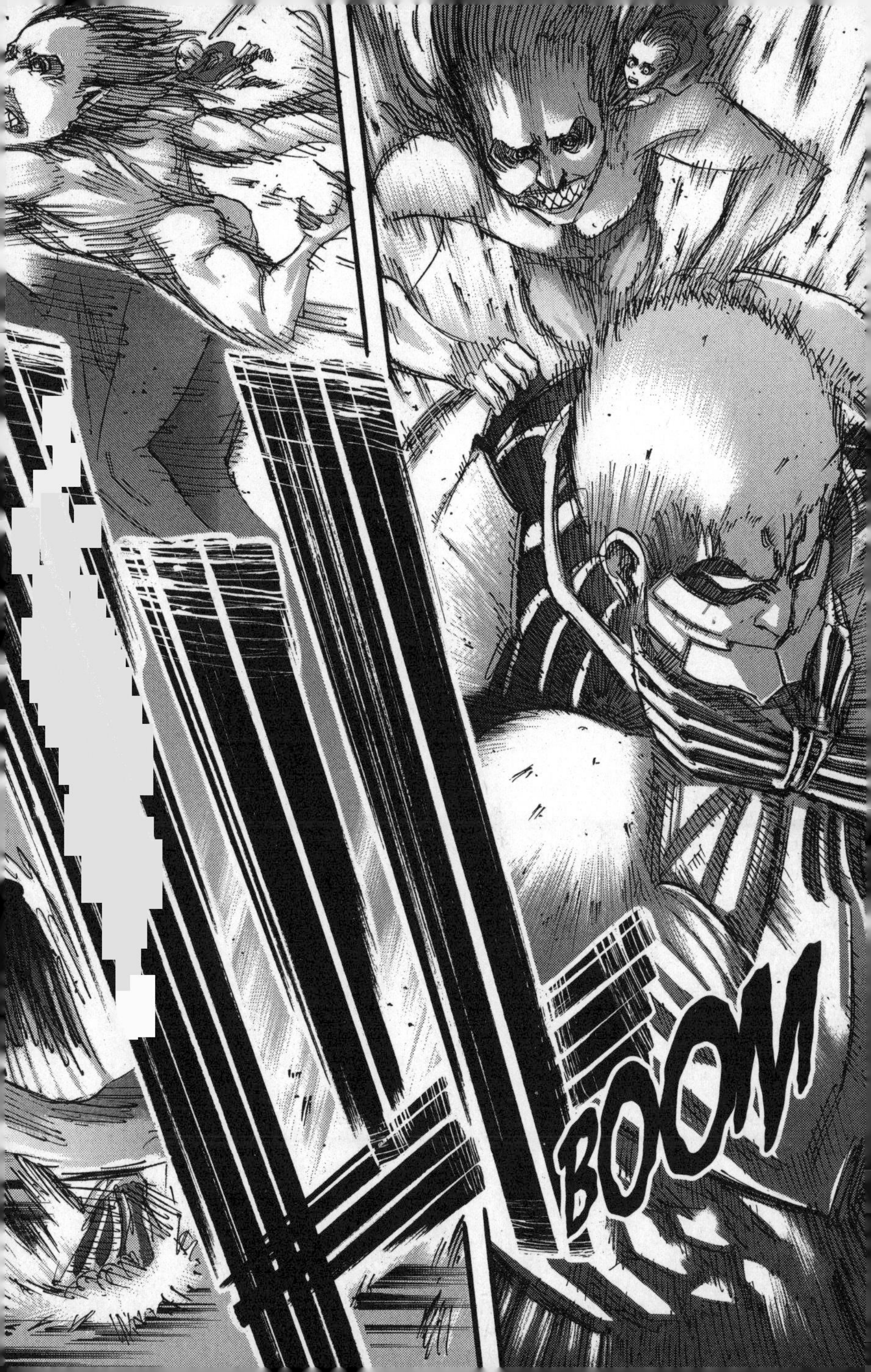
BOOM

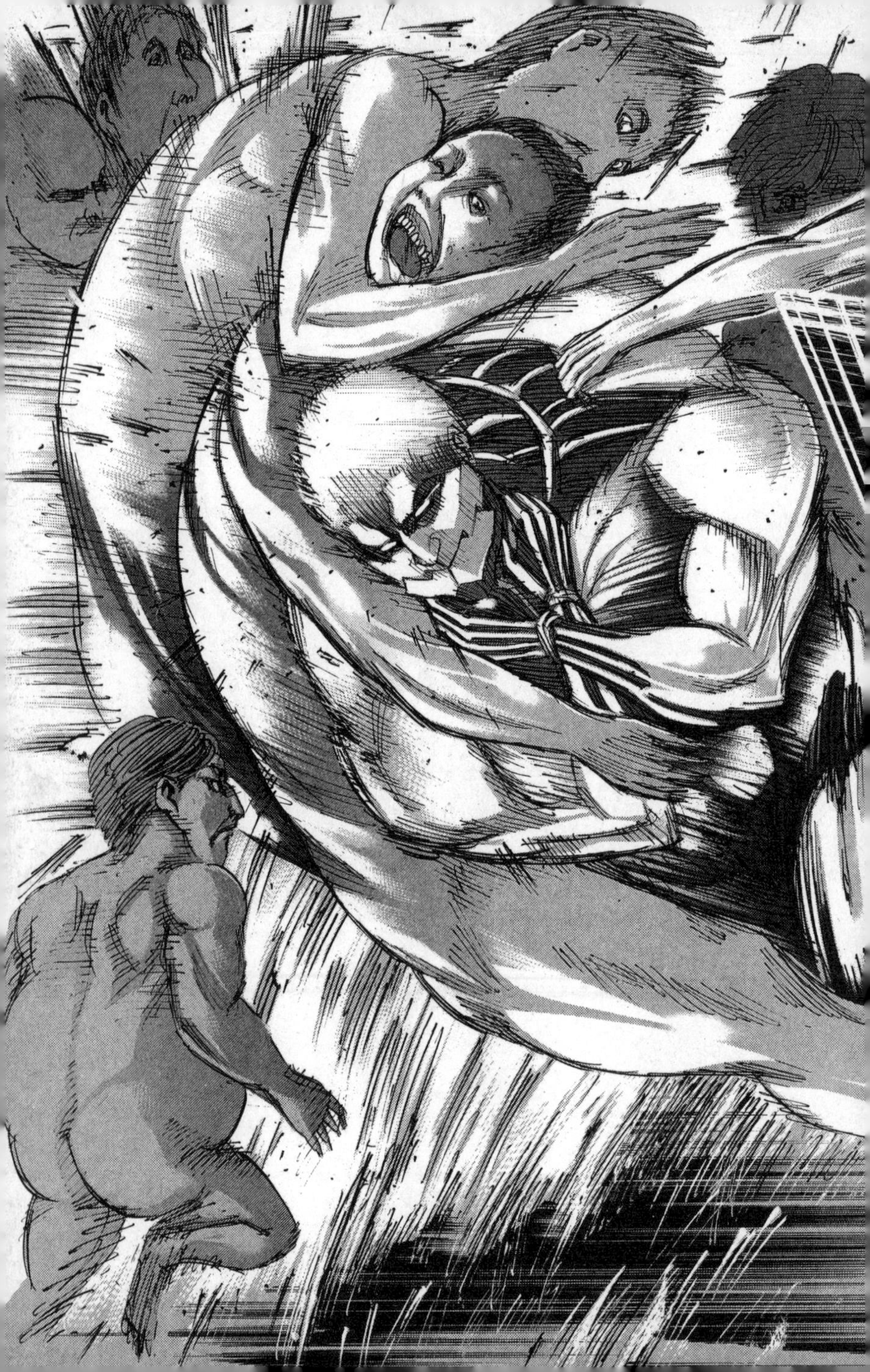

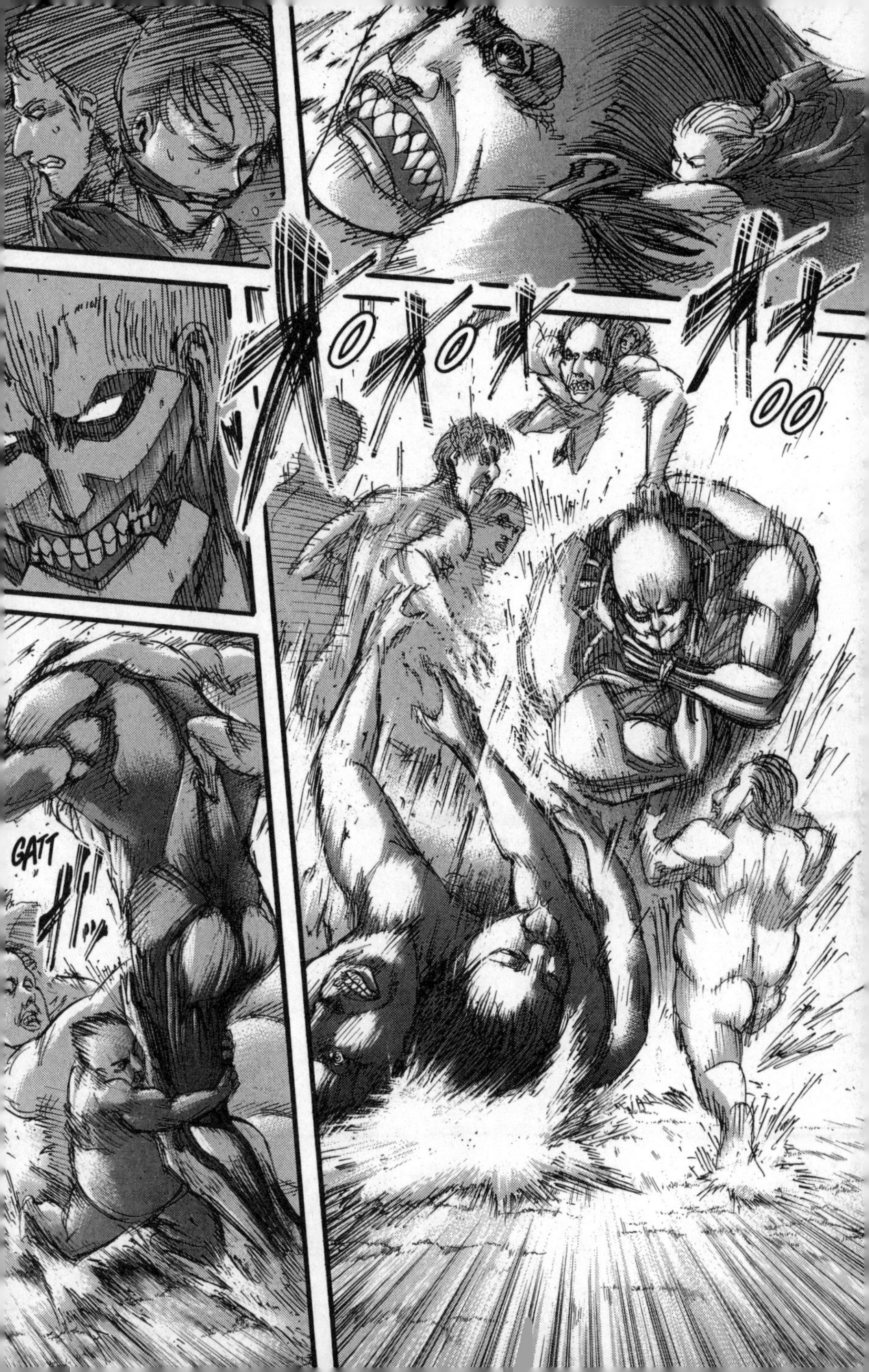
GATT

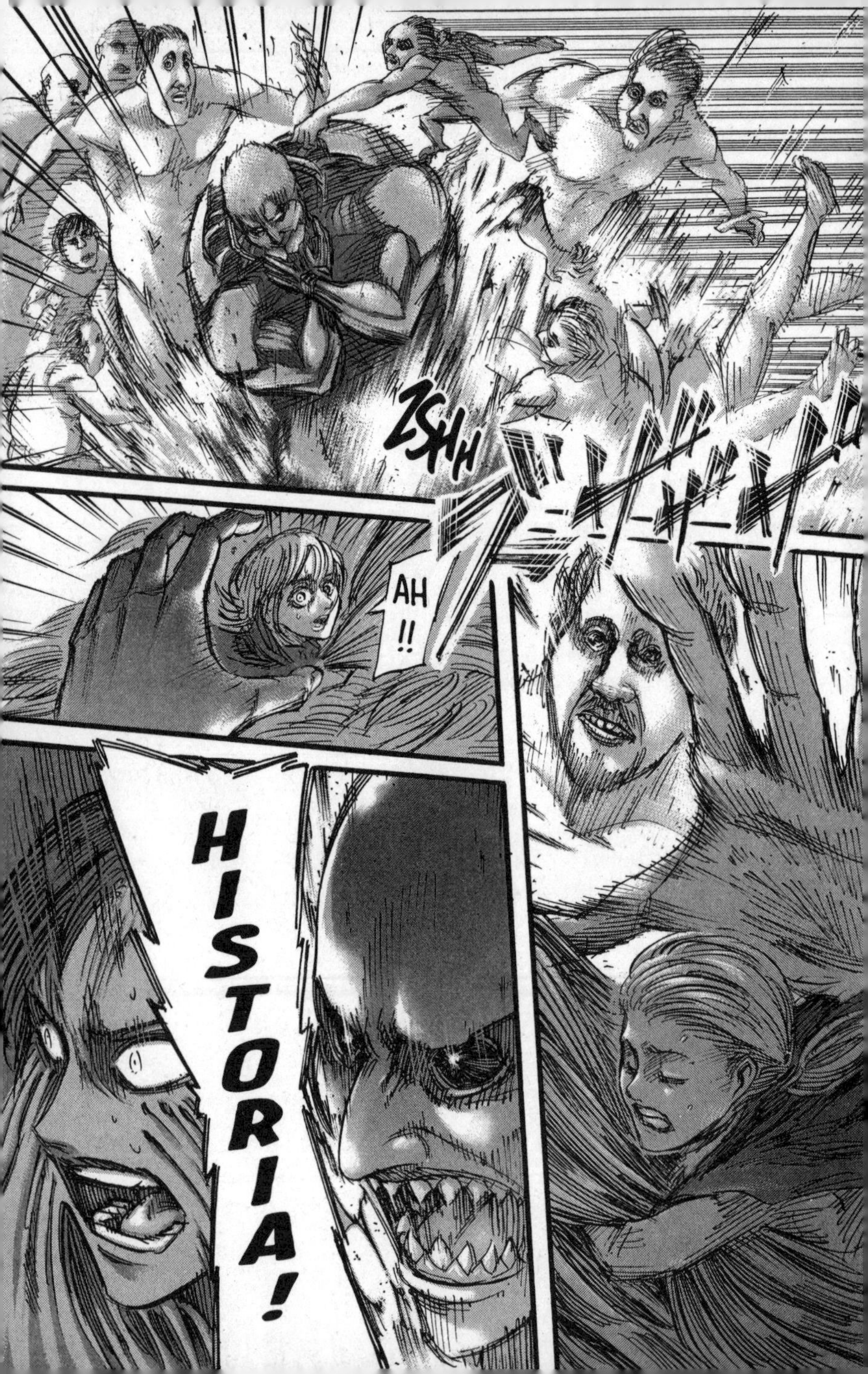
ZSHH
AH !!
HISTORIA!

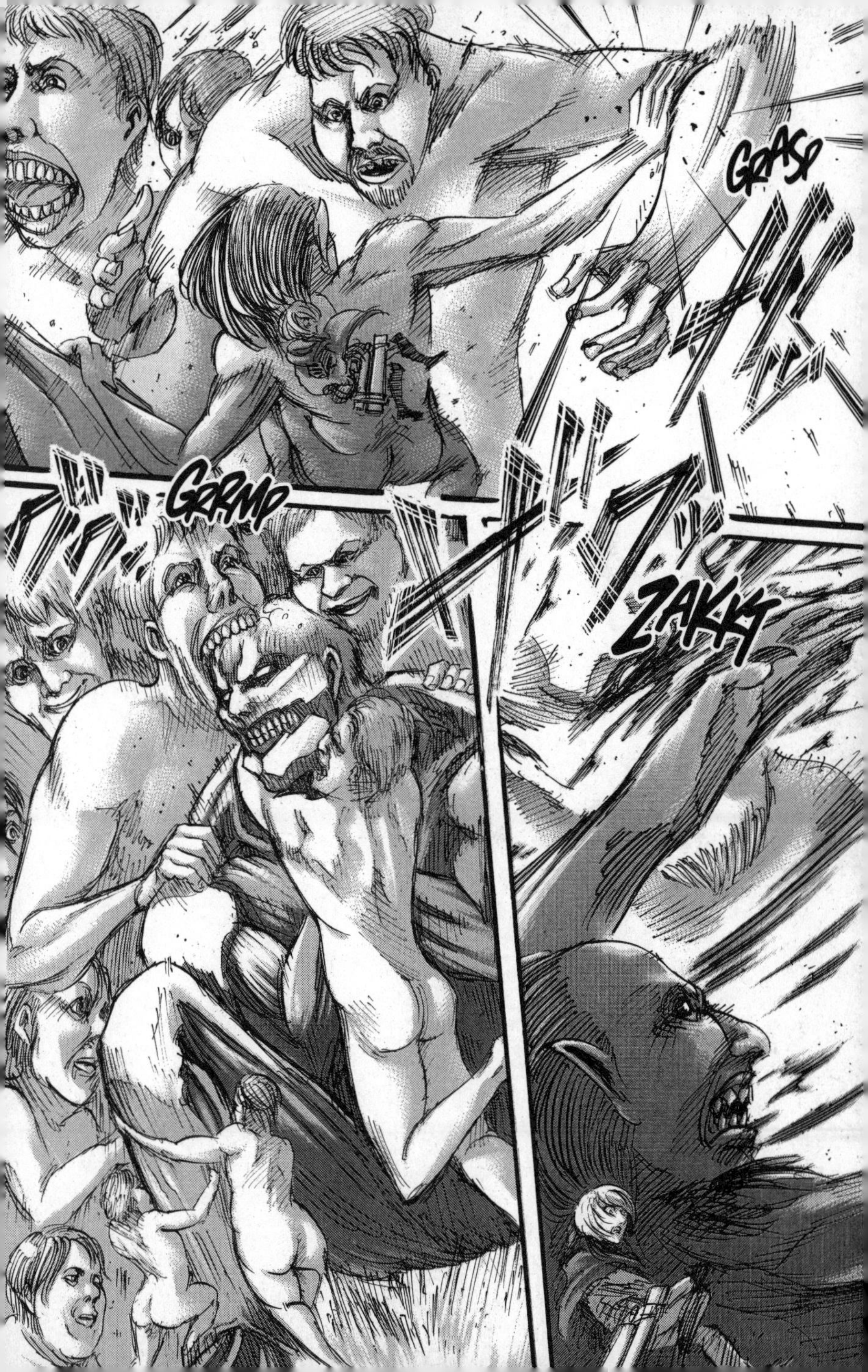
GRASP
ZAKK
GRRMP

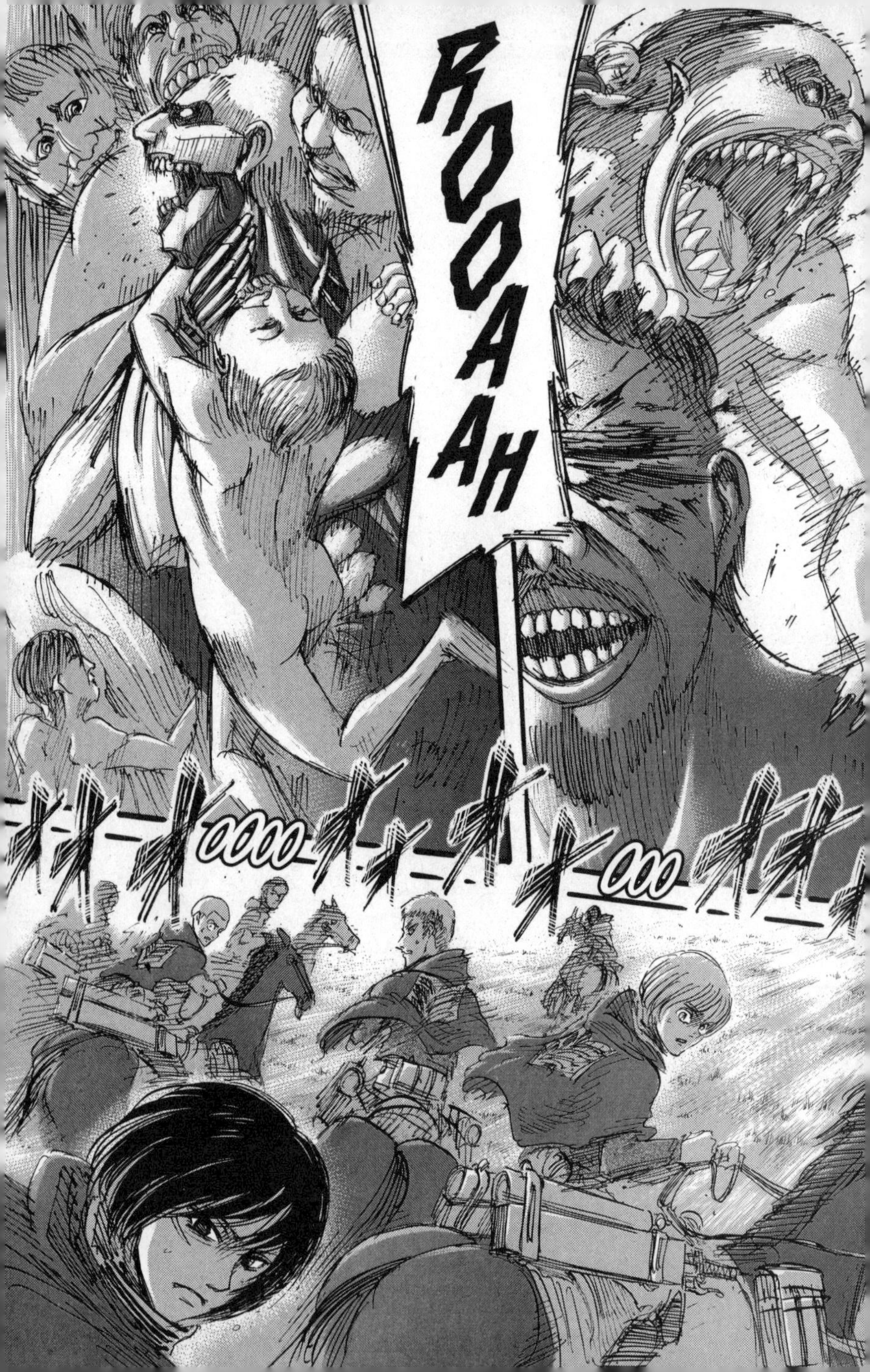
ROOAAH
OOOO
OOO

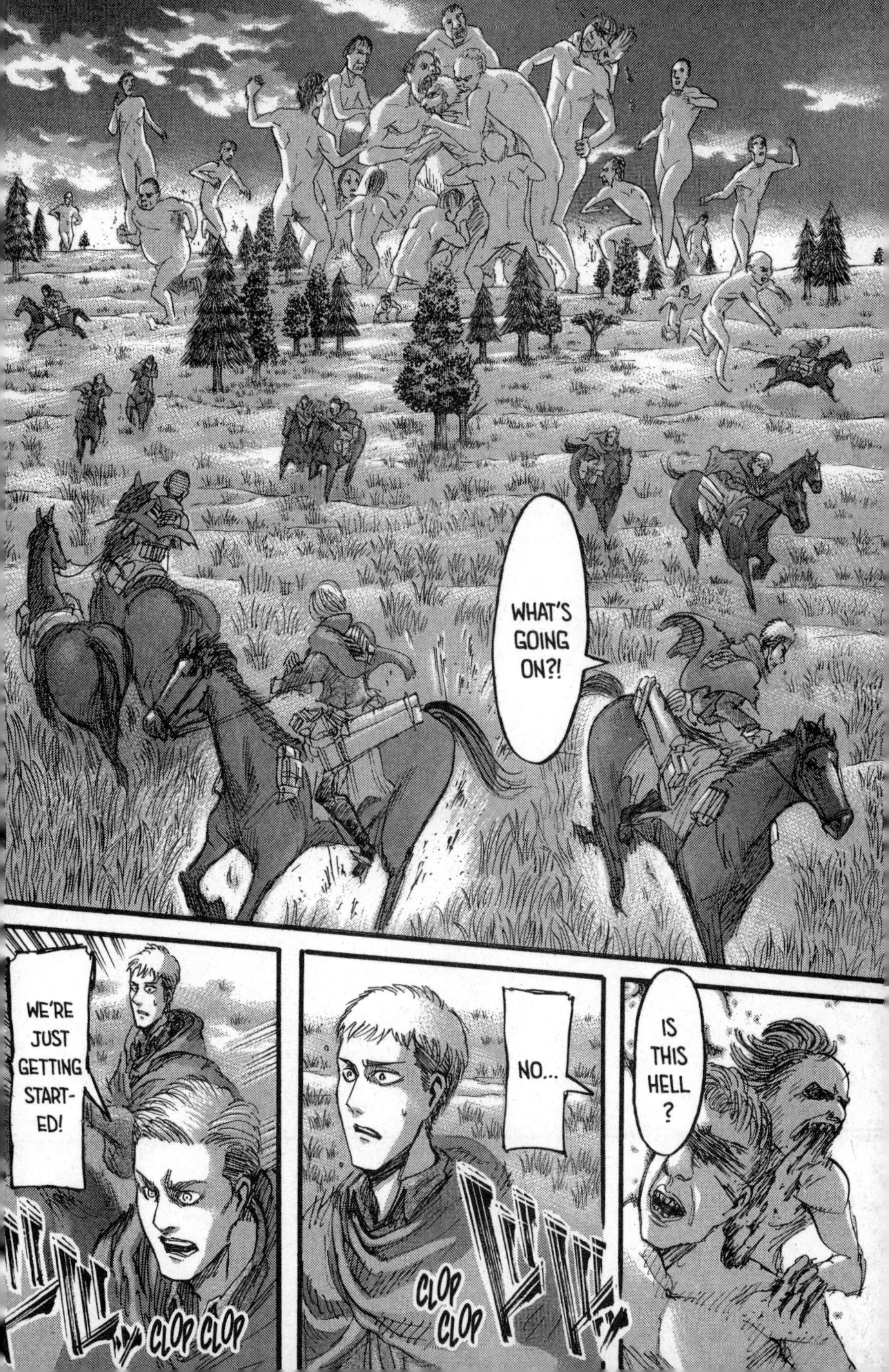
WHAT'S GOING ON?!
IS THIS HELL ?
NO...
CLOP CLOP
WE'RE JUST GETTING START-ED!
CLOP CLOP

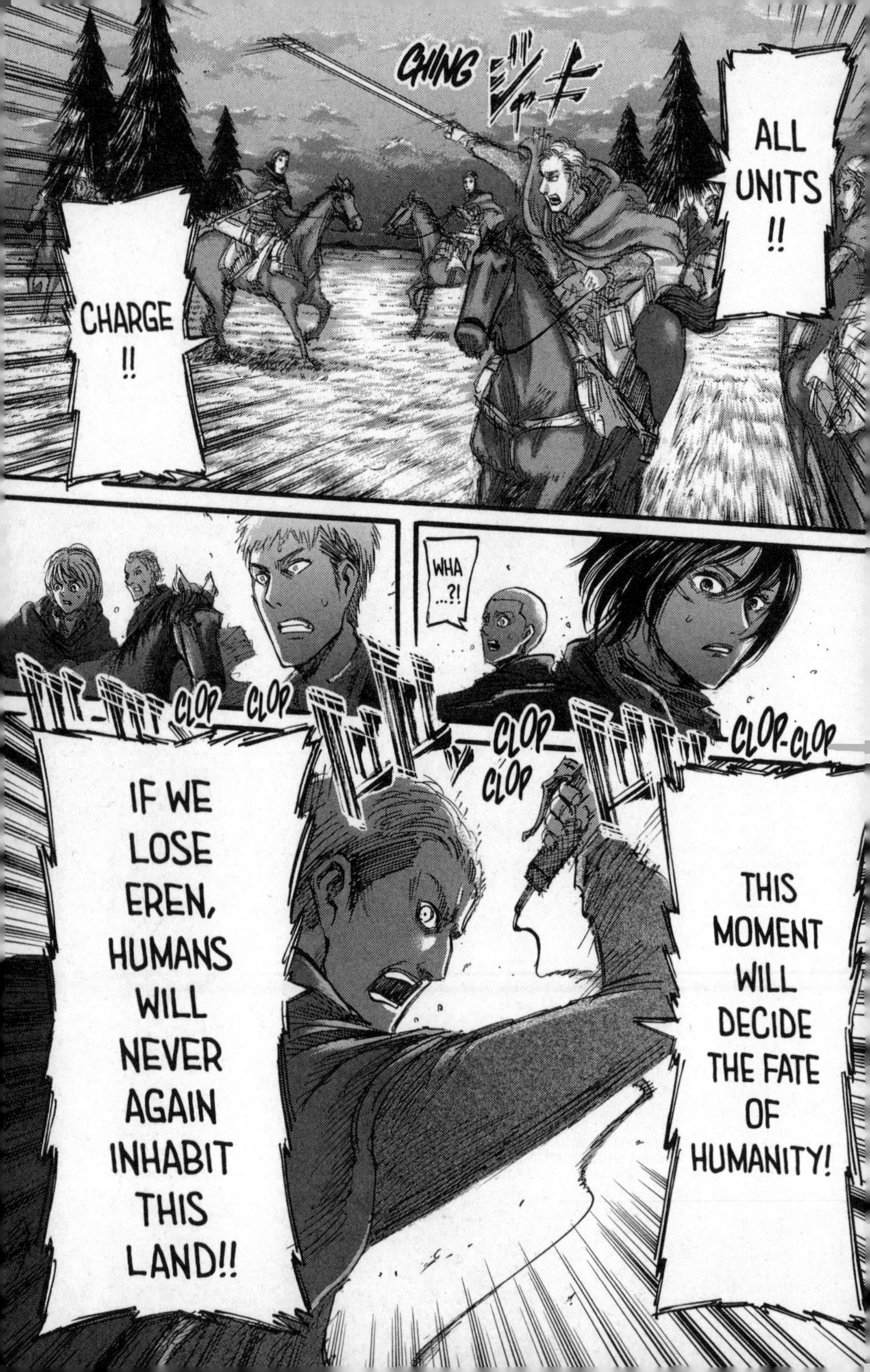
CHING
ALL UNITS !!
CHARGE !!
WHA ...?!
CLOP CLOP
CLOP CLOP
CLOP-CLOP
THIS MOMENT WILL DECIDE THE FATE OF HUMANITY!
IF WE LOSE EREN, HUMANS WILL NEVER AGAIN INHABIT THIS LAND!!

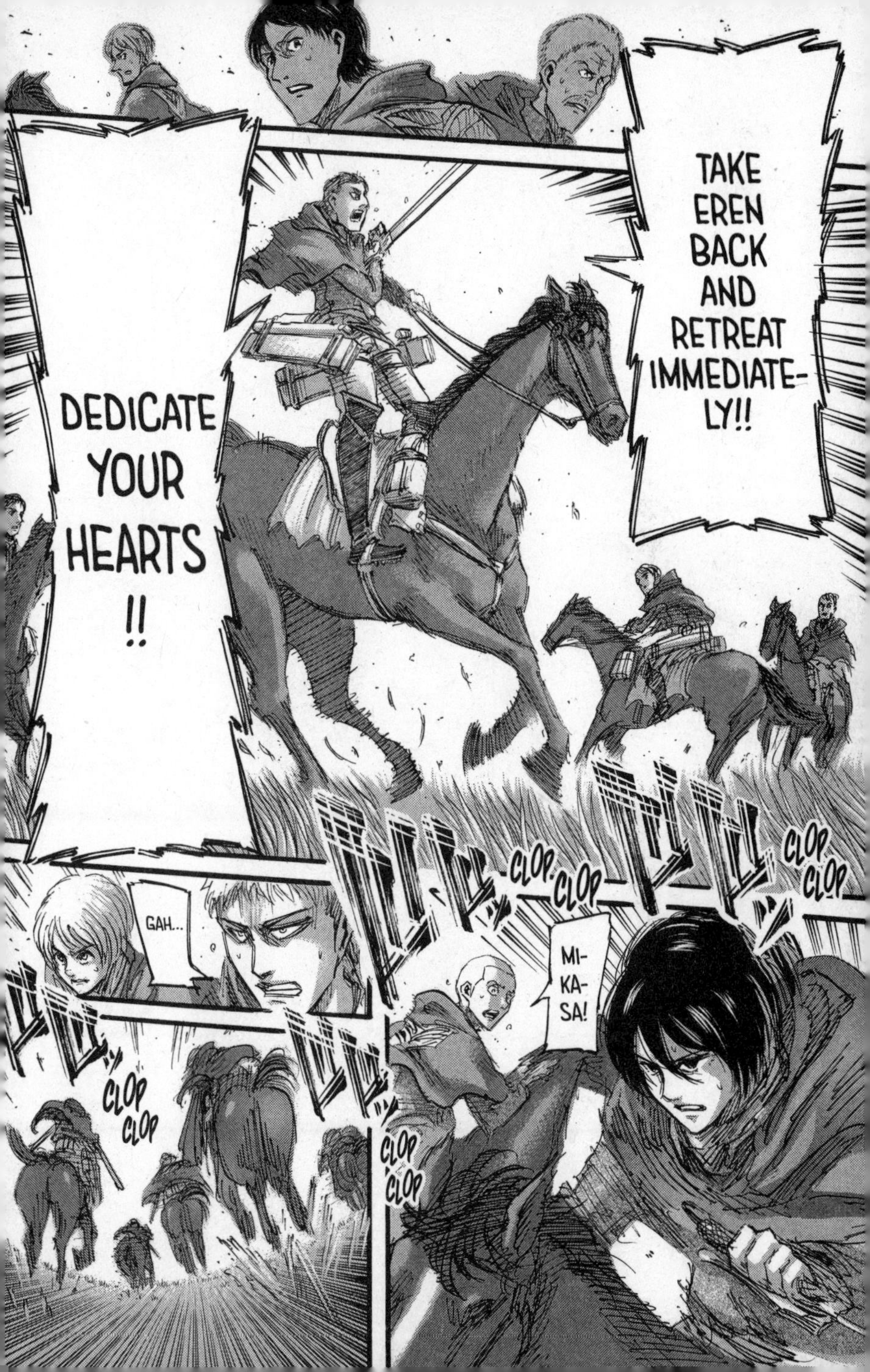
TAKE EREN BACK AND RETREAT IMMEDIATE-LY!!
DEDICATE YOUR HEARTS !!
CLOP CLOP
CLOP CLOP
MI-KA-SA!
GAH...
CLOP CLOP
CLOP CLOP

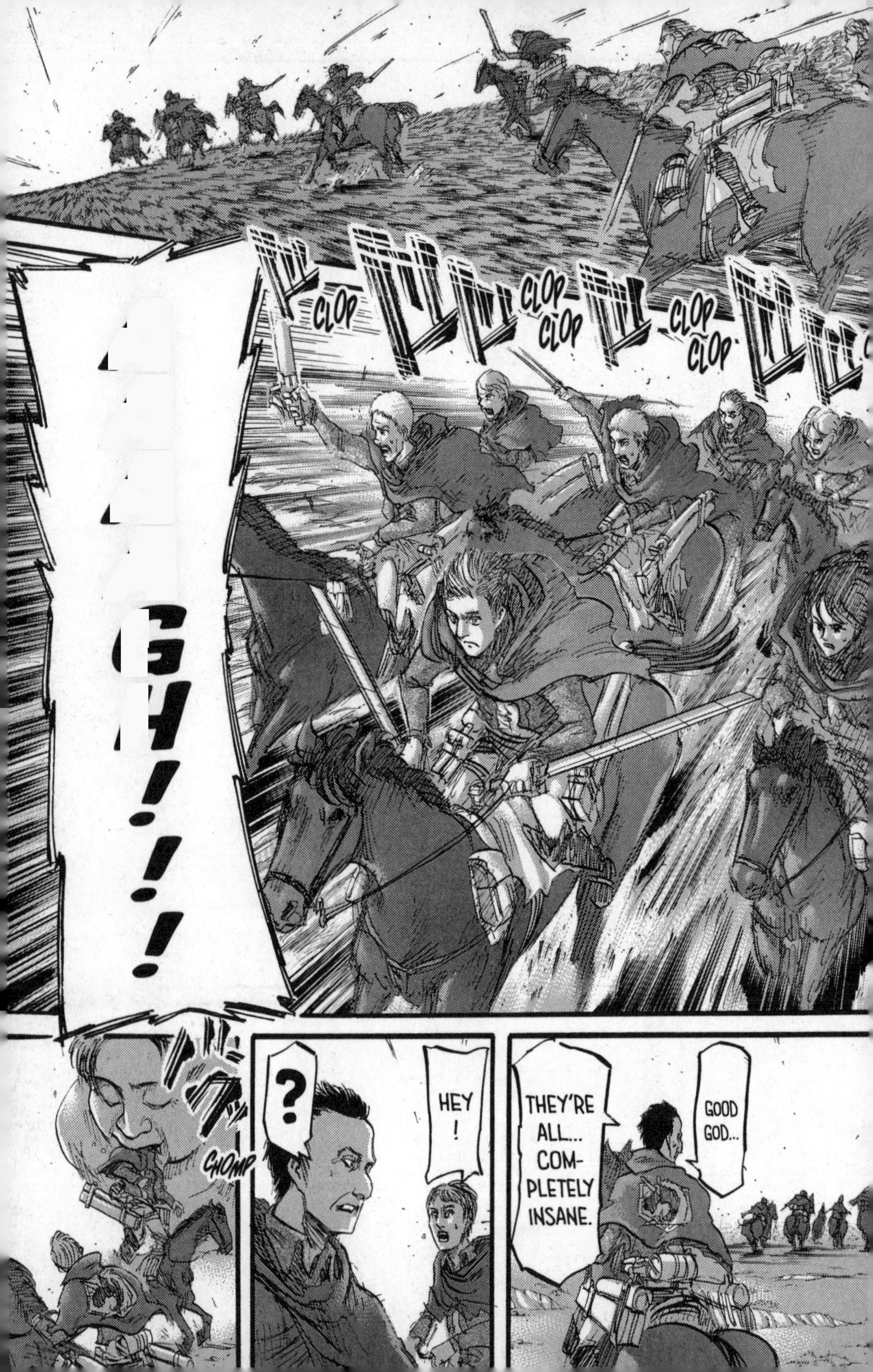
CLOP
CLOP
CLOP
CLOP
CLOP
GH!!!!
GOOD GOD...
THEY'RE ALL... COMPLETELY INSANE.
HEY!
?
CHOMP

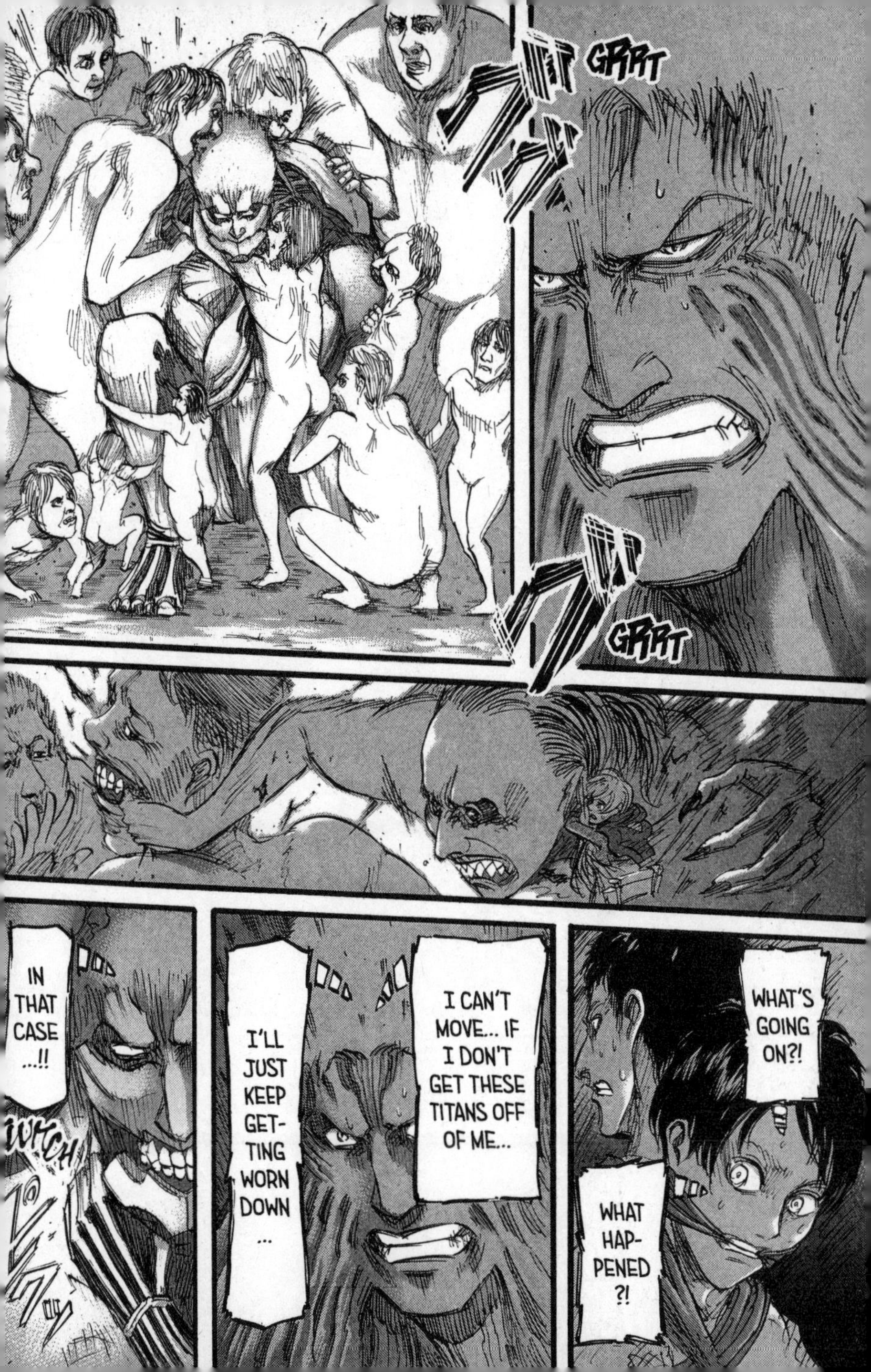
GRRT
GRRT
WHAT'S GOING ON?!
WHAT HAPPENED?!
I CAN'T MOVE... IF I DON'T GET THESE TITANS OFF OF ME...
I'LL JUST KEEP GETTING WORN DOWN...
IN THAT CASE ...!!

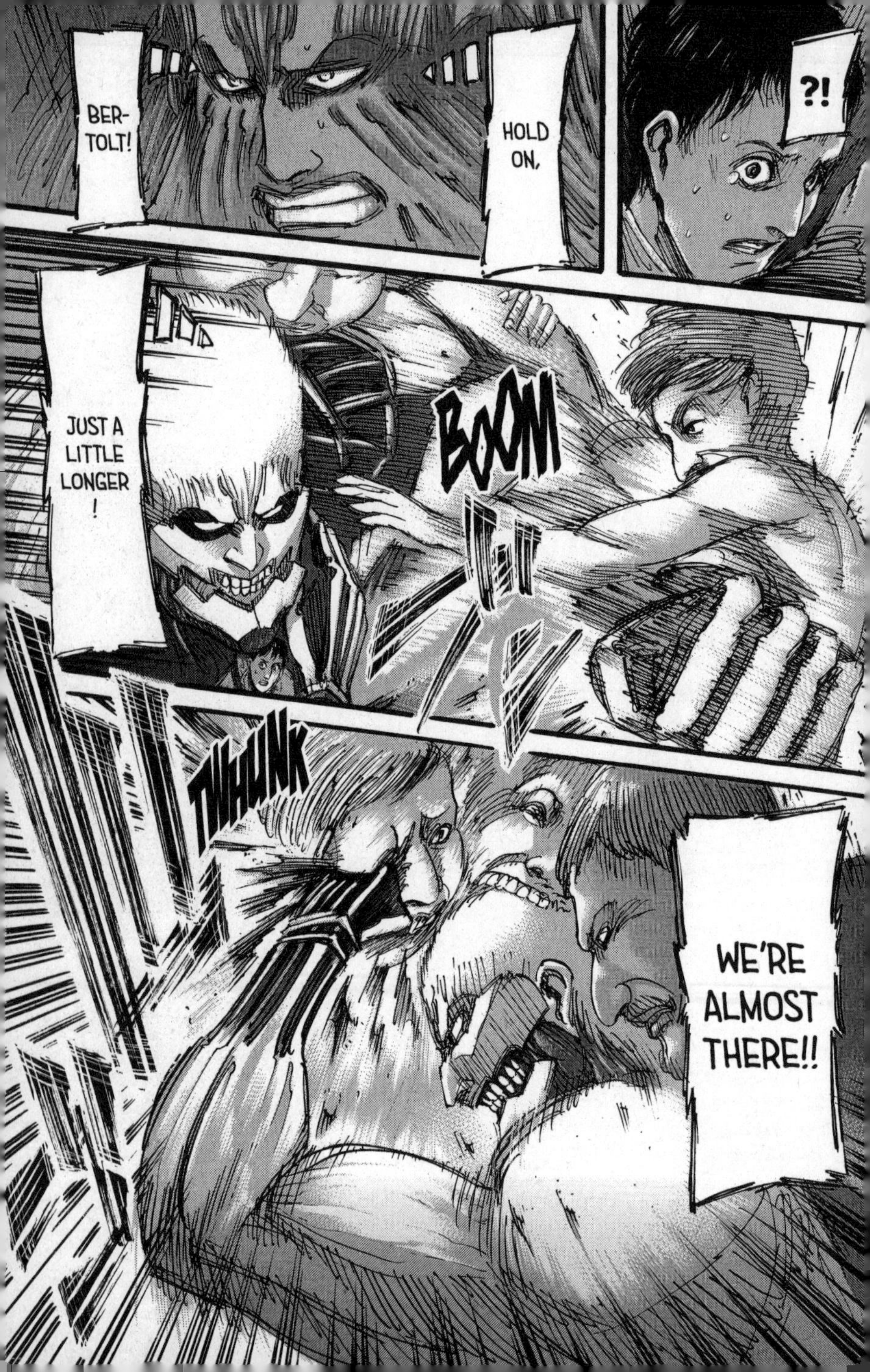
?!
HOLD ON,
BER-TOLT!
BOOM
JUST A LITTLE LONGER!
THWUNK
WE'RE ALMOST THERE!!

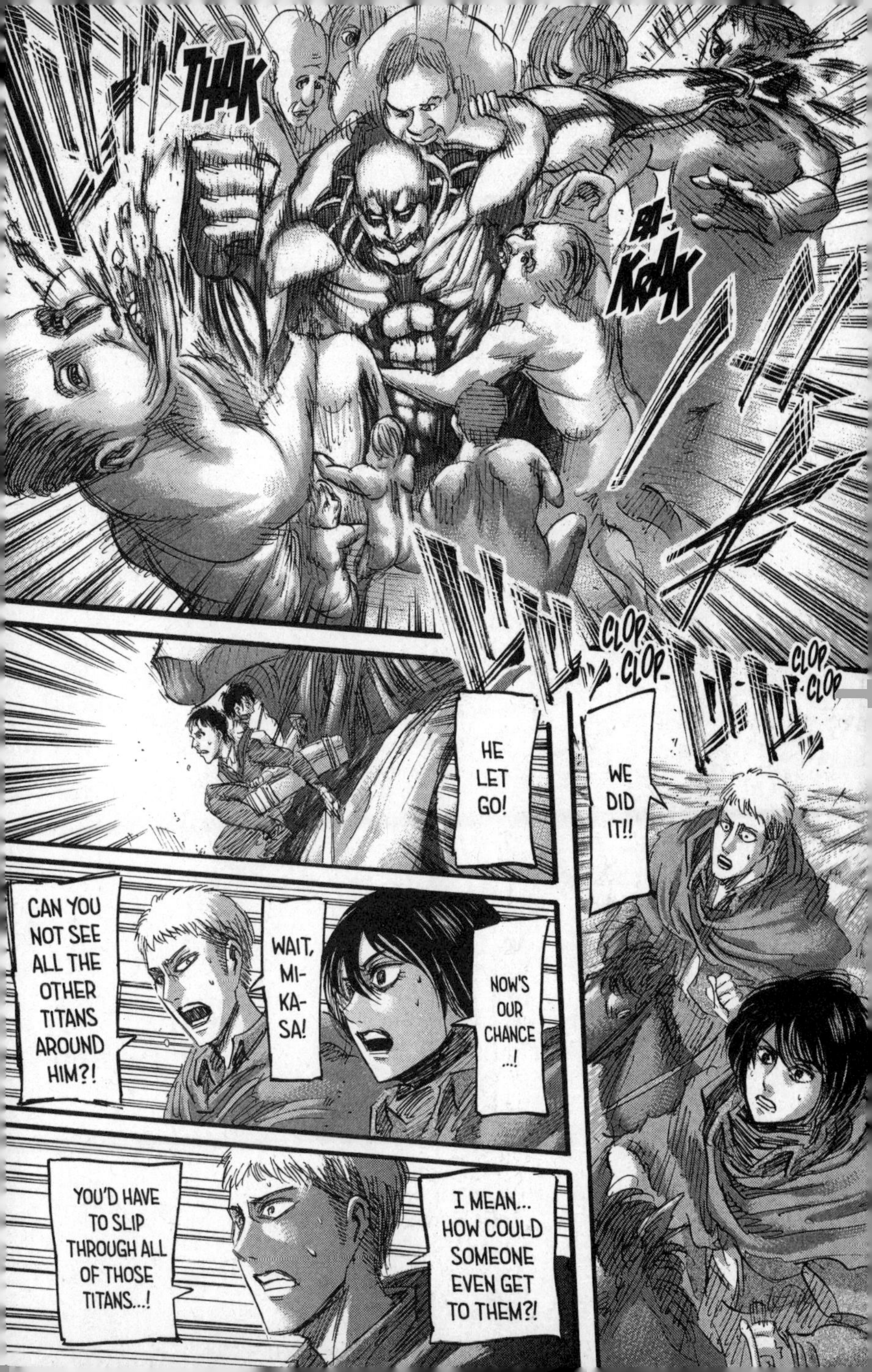
BA-KRAK
THAK
CLOP CLOP
CLOP CLOP
WE DID IT!!
HE LET GO!
NOW'S OUR CHANCE...!
WAIT, MI-KA-SA!
CAN YOU NOT SEE ALL THE OTHER TITANS AROUND HIM?!
I MEAN... HOW COULD SOMEONE EVEN GET TO THEM?!
YOU'D HAVE TO SLIP THROUGH ALL OF THOSE TITANS...!

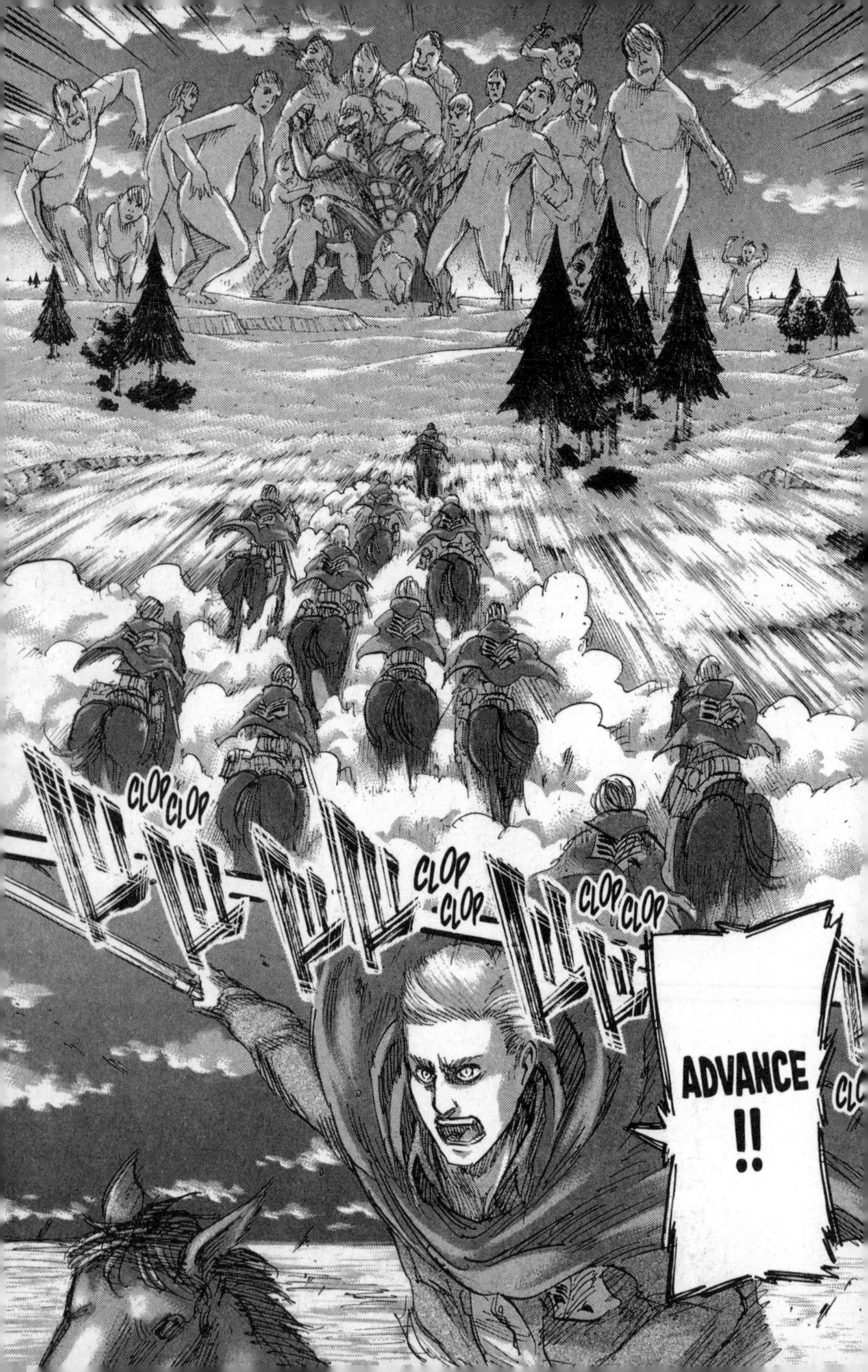
ADVANCE !!
CLOP CLOP
CLOP CLOP
CLOP -CLOP-
CLOP CLOP

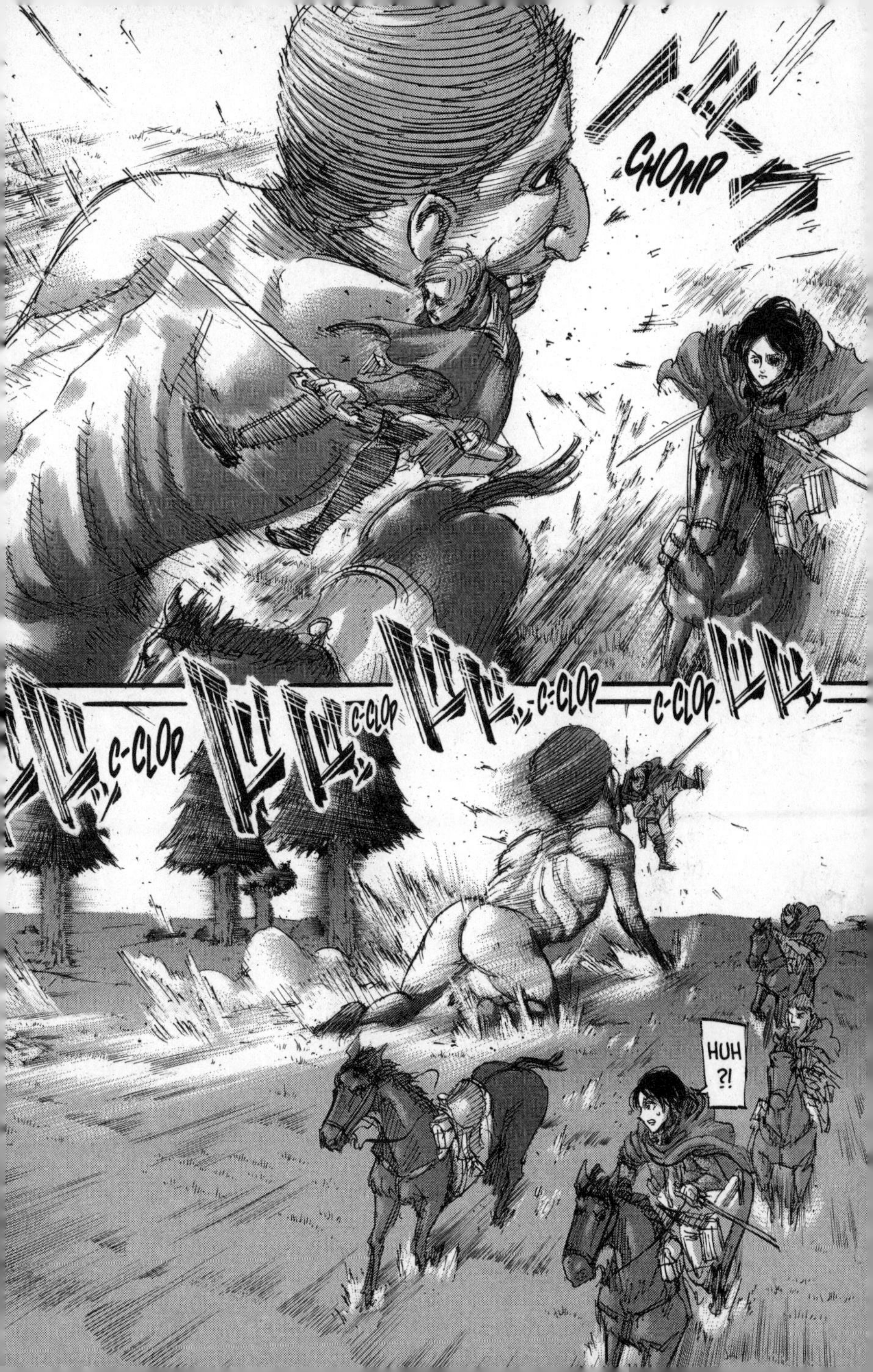
CHOMP
C-CLOP
C-CLOP
C-CLOP
C-CLOP
HUH ?!

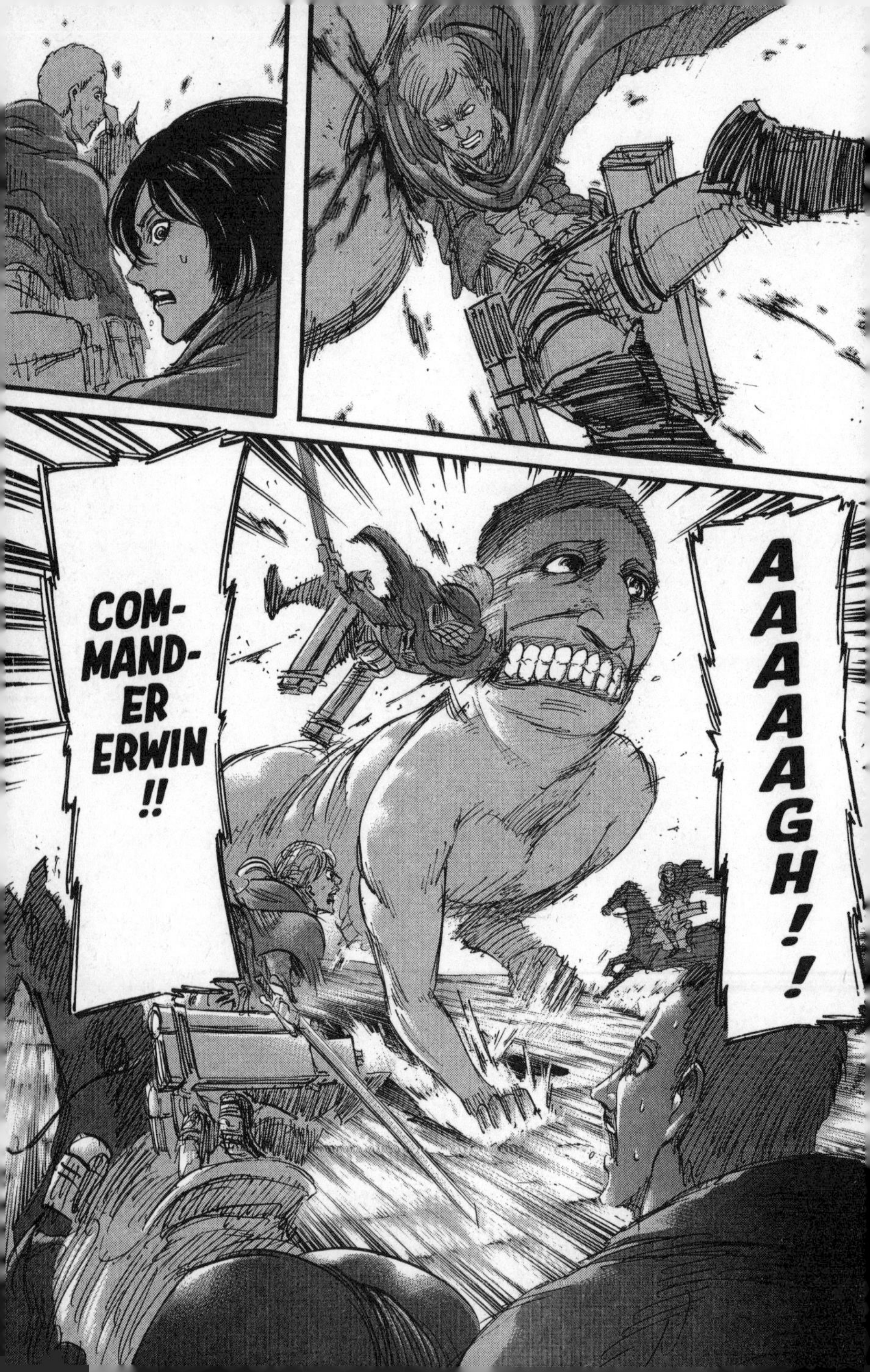
AAAAAGH!!
COM-
MAND-
ER
ERWIN
!!

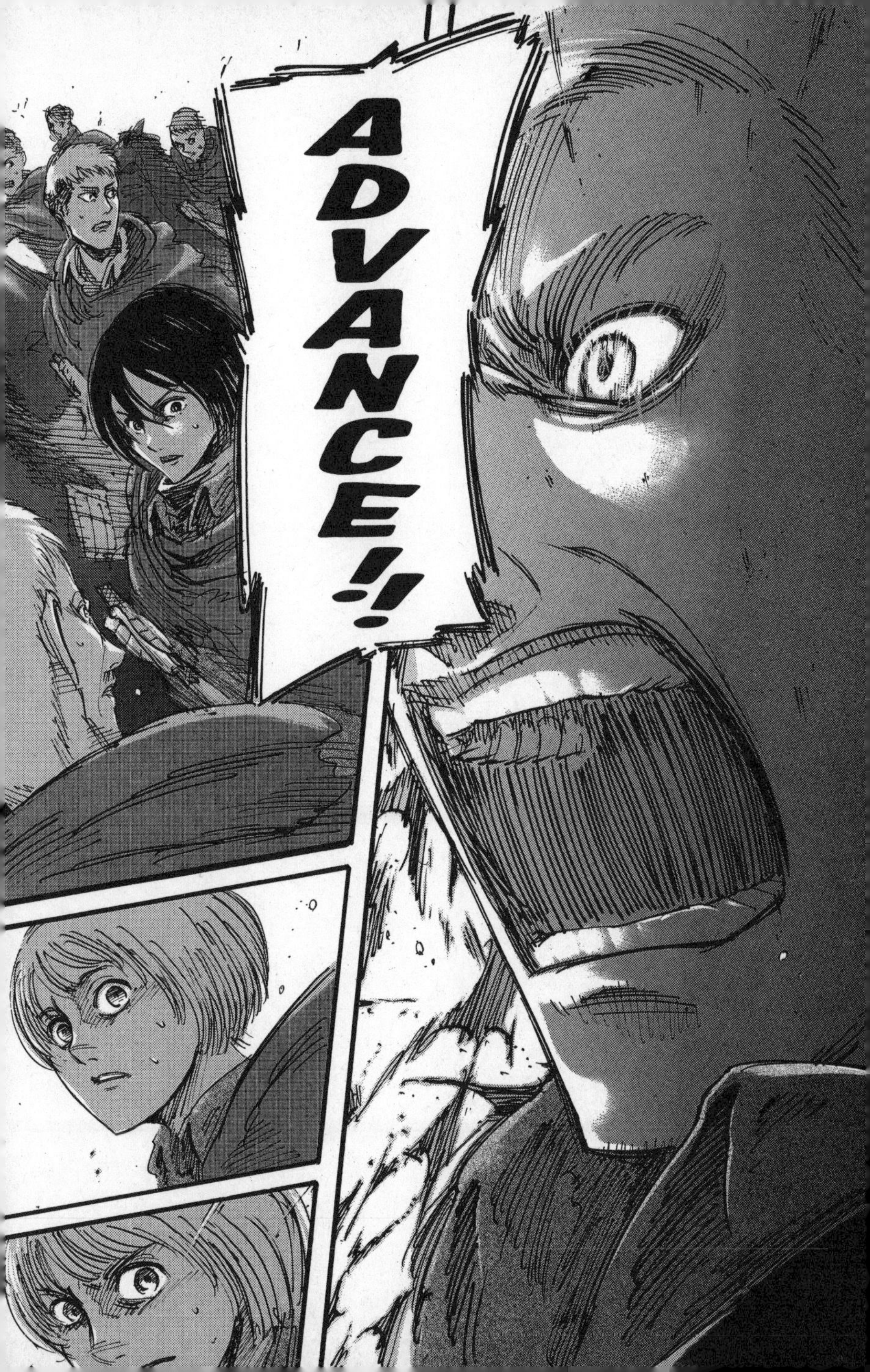
ADVANCE!!

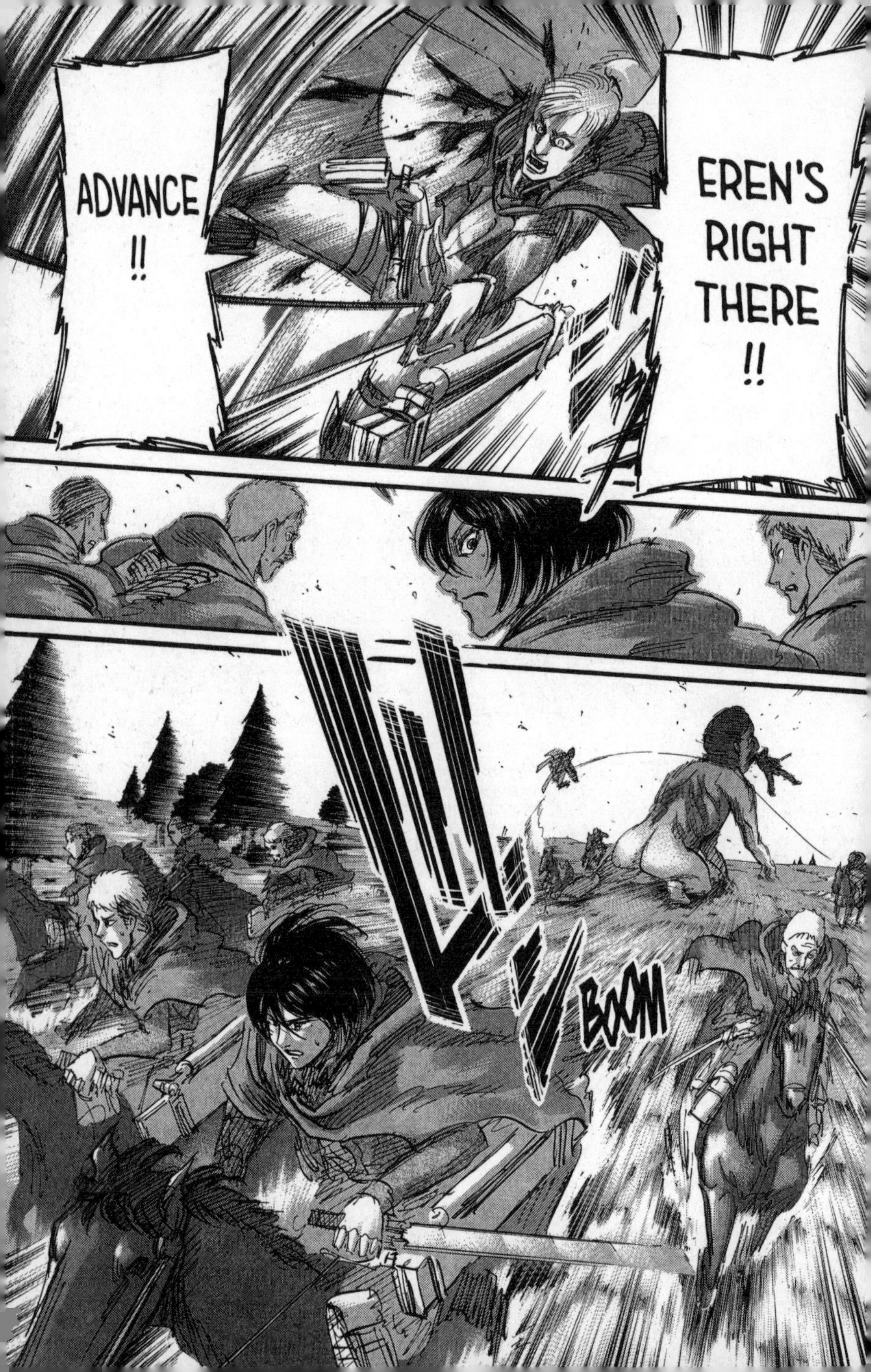
EREN'S RIGHT THERE !!
ADVANCE !!
BOOM

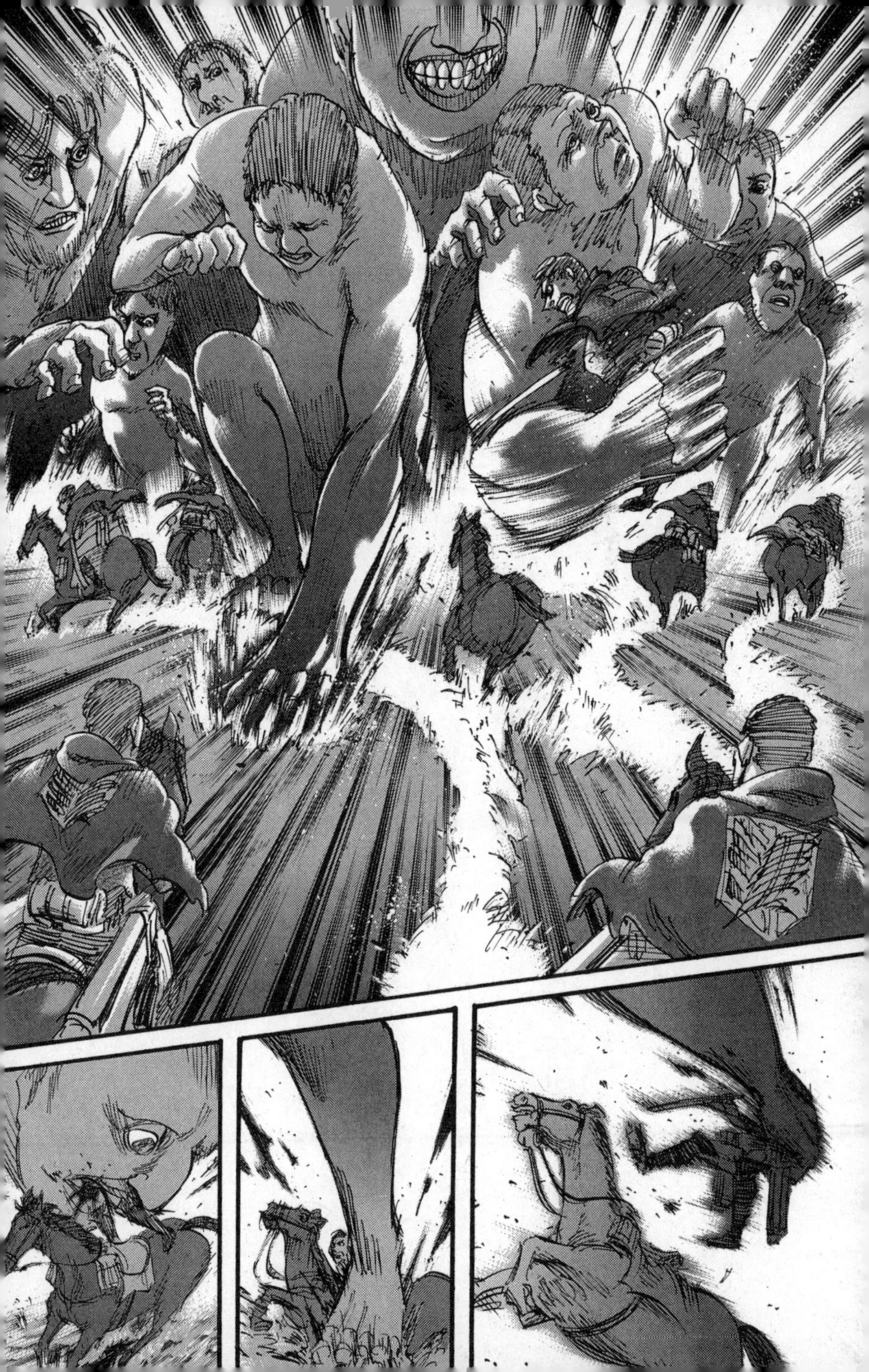

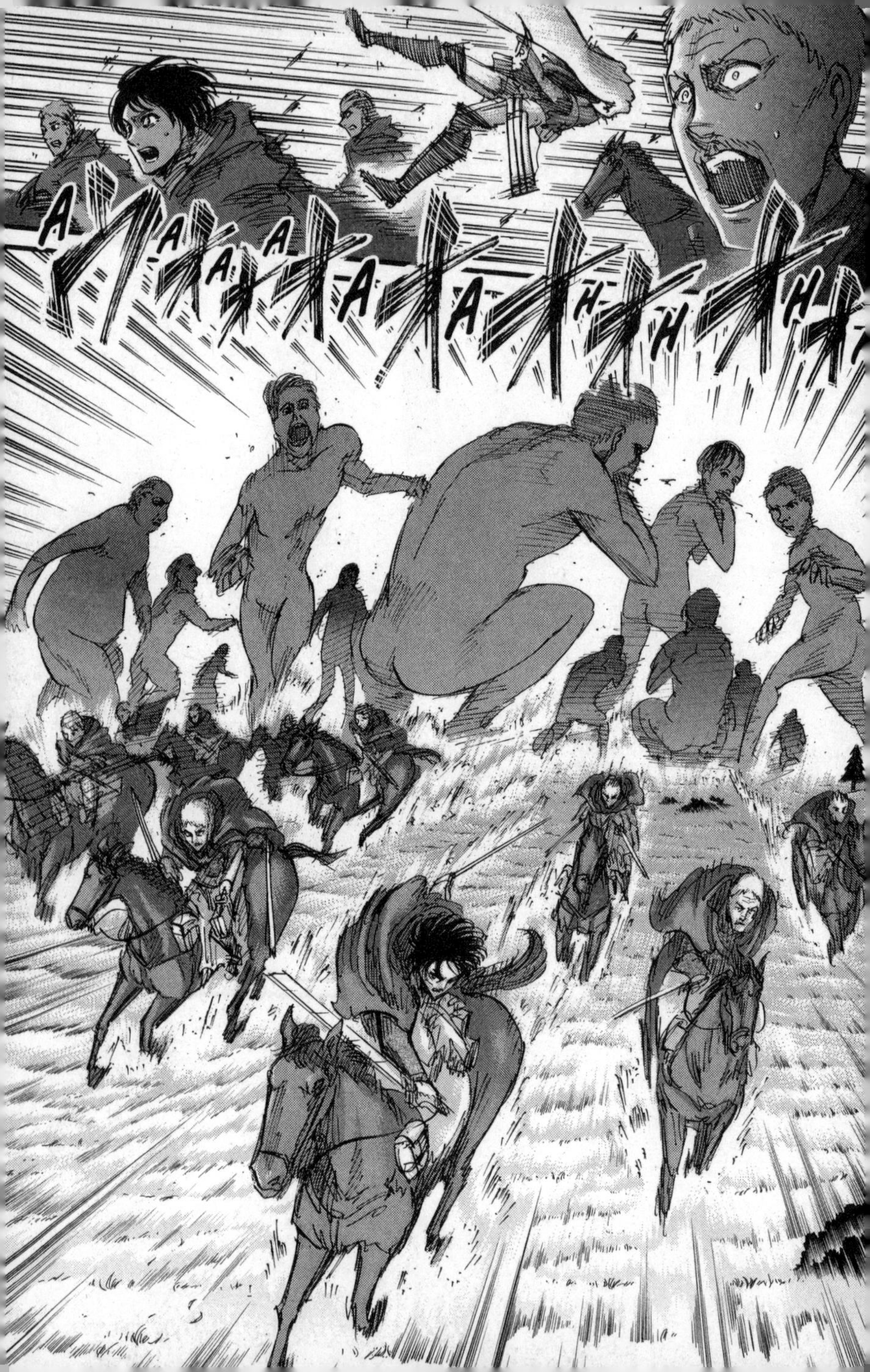
AAAAAAAHHH

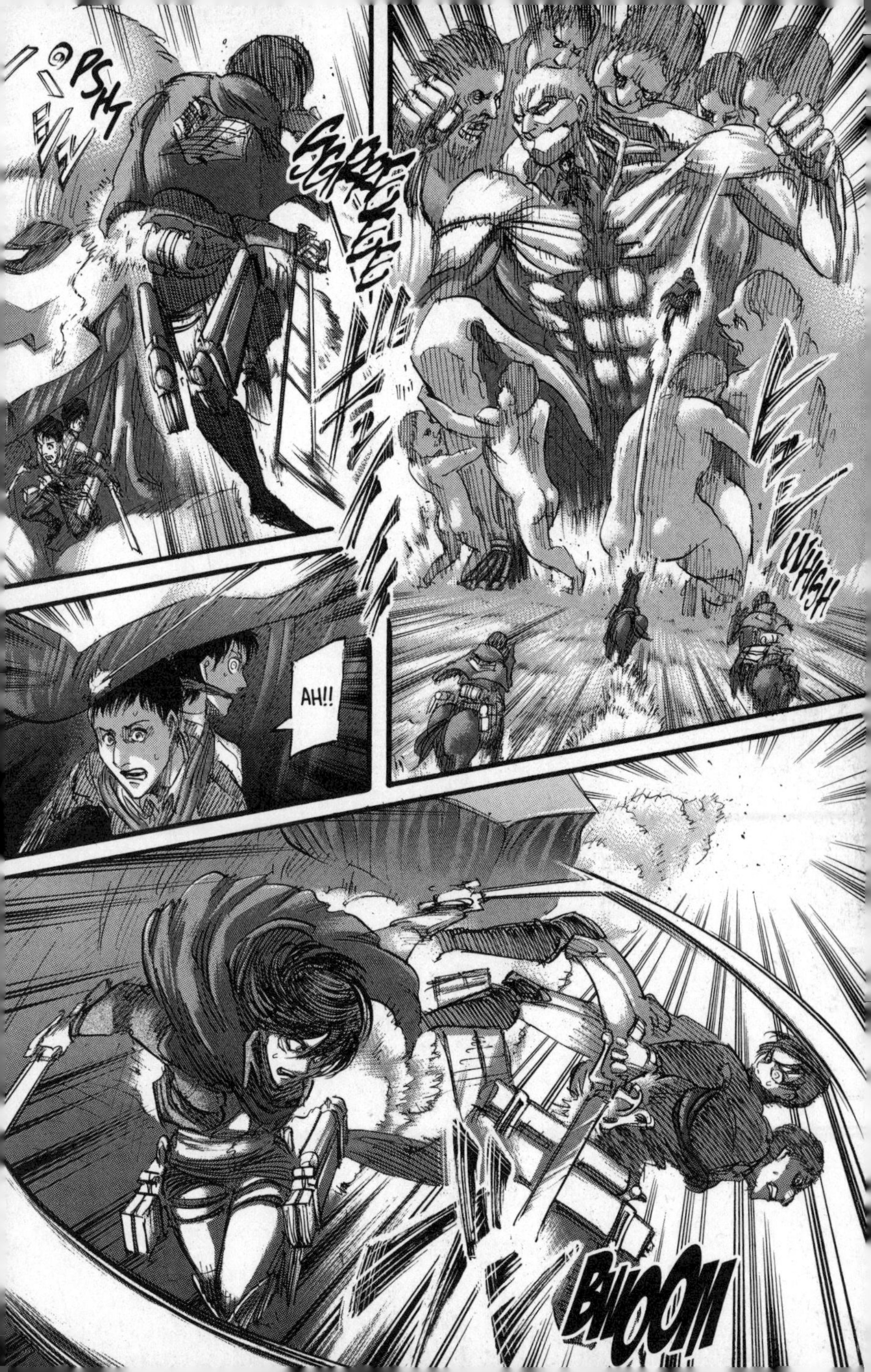
VWHSH
PSHH
AH!!
BWOOM

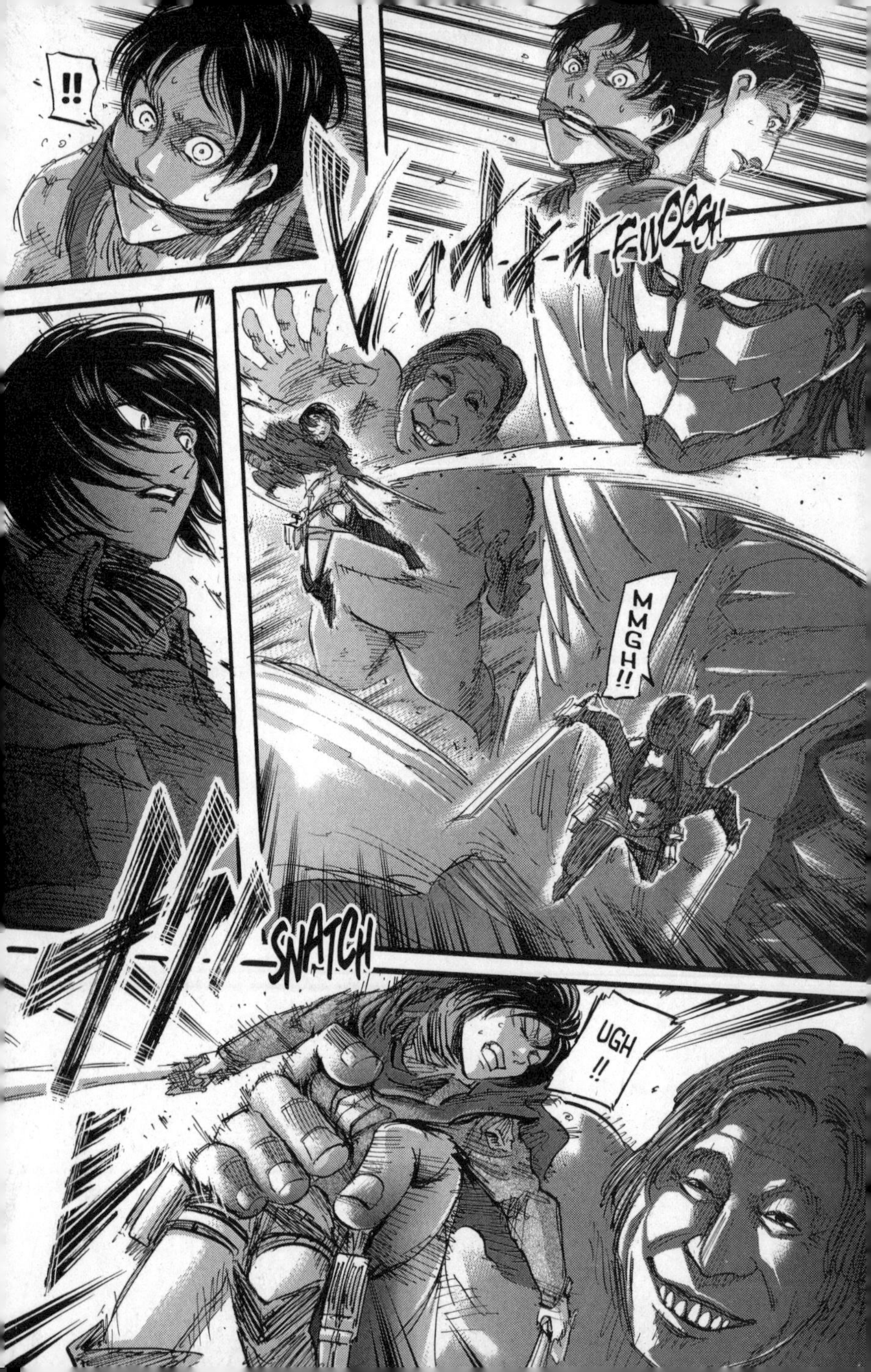
FWOOSH
!!
MMGH!!
SNATCH
UGH!!

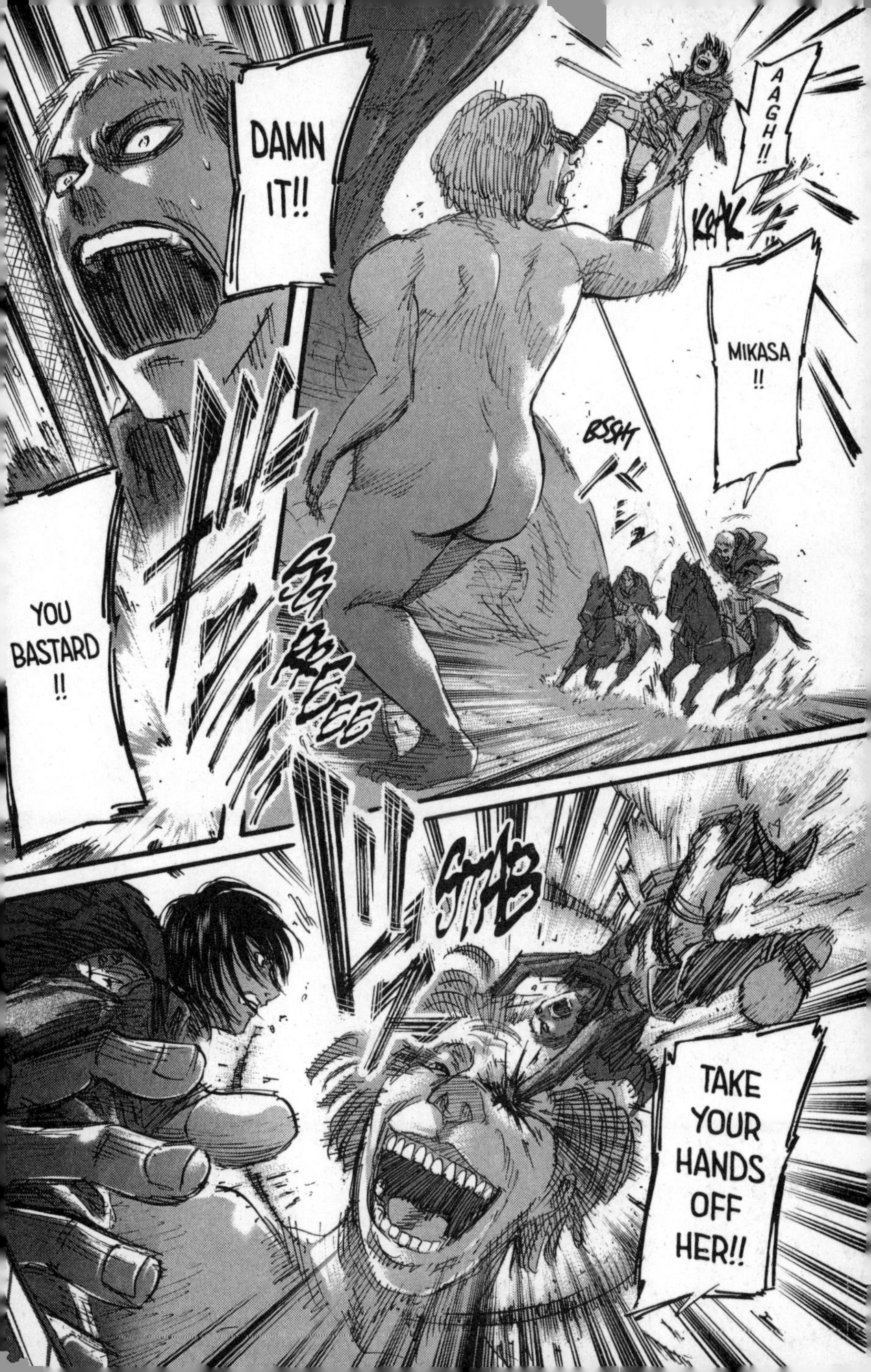
AAGH!!
KRAK
MIKASA!!
BSSH
DAMN IT!!
YOU BASTARD!!
STAB
TAKE YOUR HANDS OFF HER!!

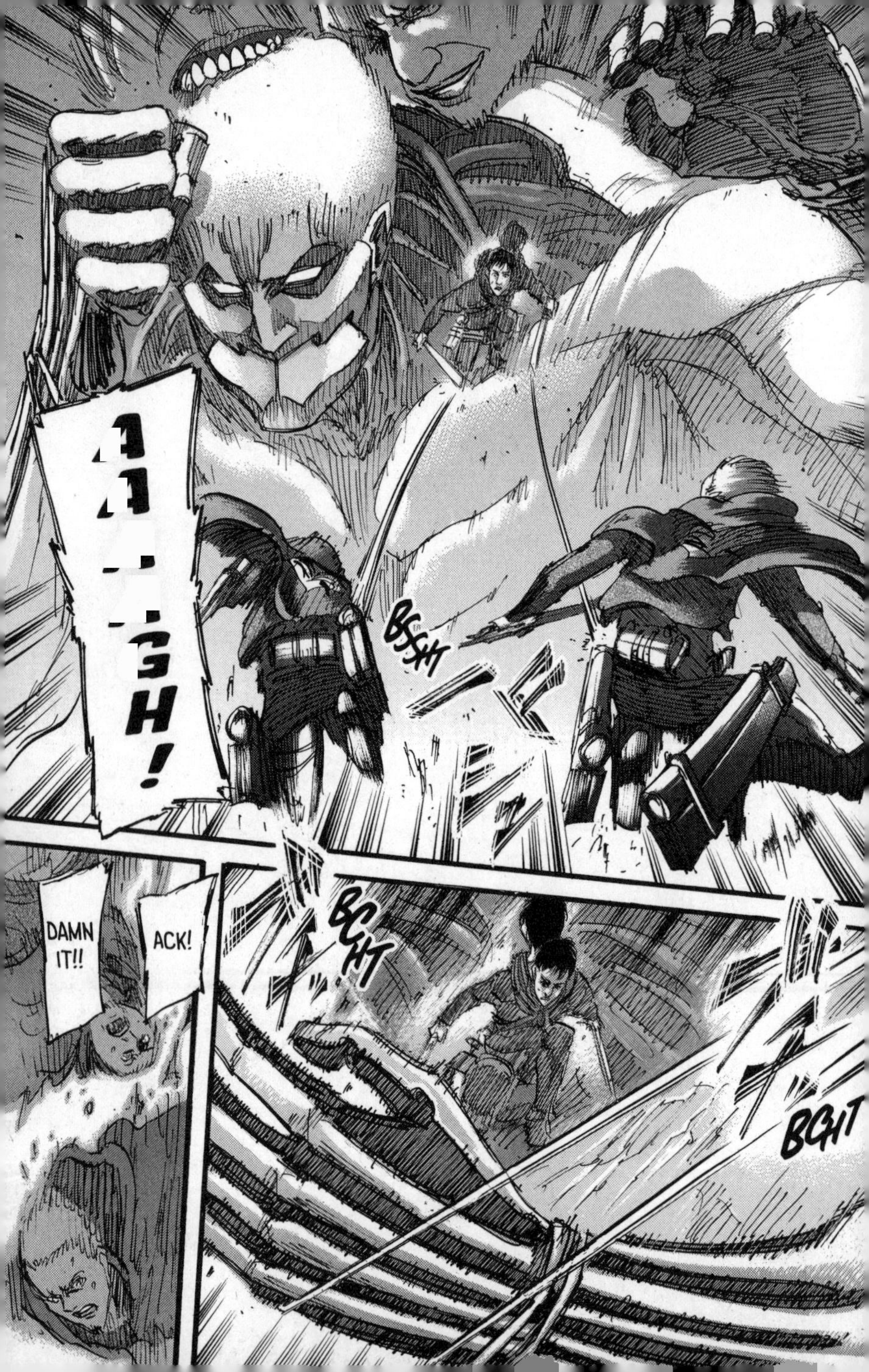
AA
GH!
BSHT
BCHT
BCHT
ACK!
DAMN IT!!

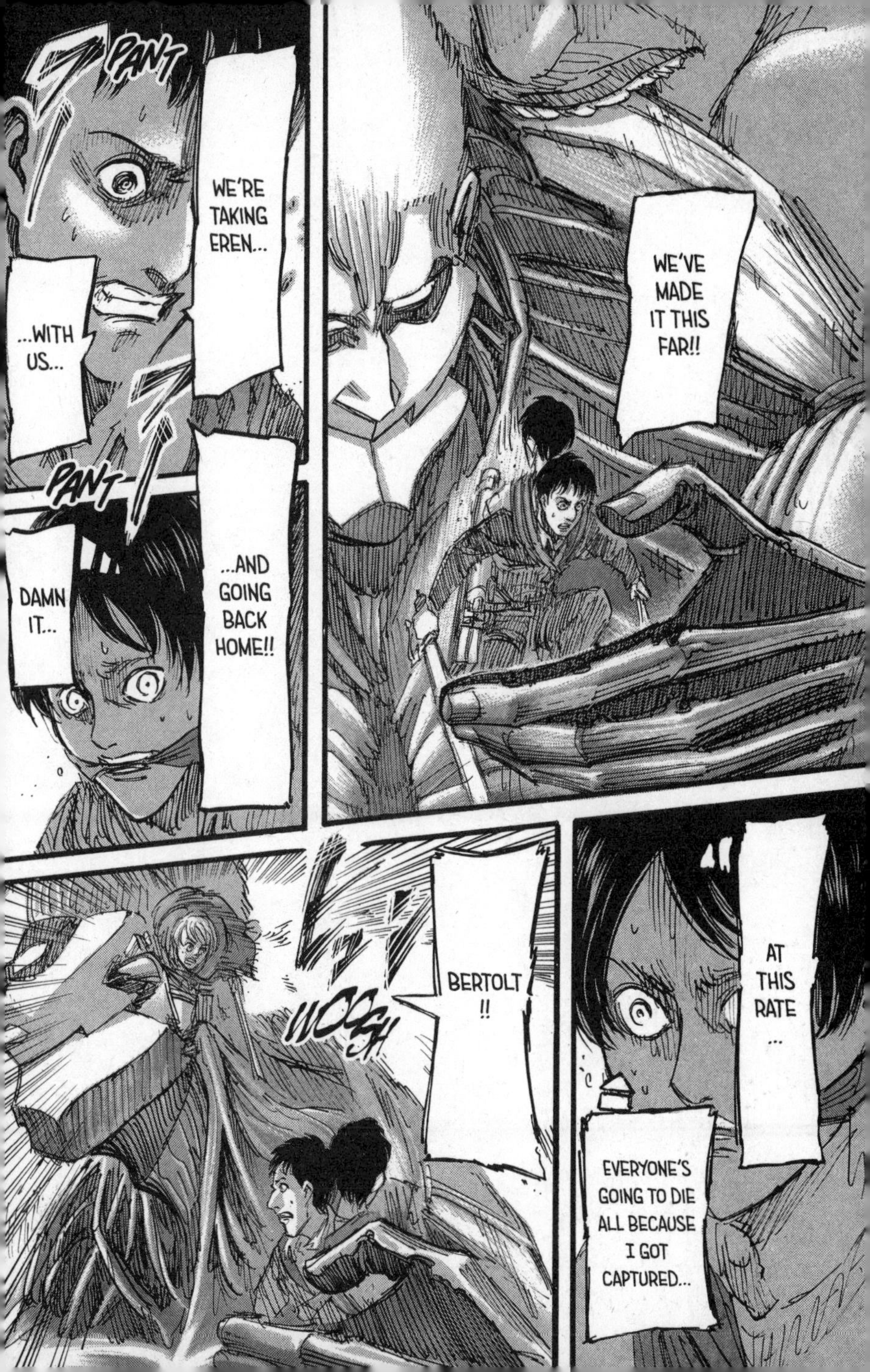

WE'VE MADE IT THIS FAR!!
PANT
WE'RE TAKING EREN...
...WITH US...
PANT
...AND GOING BACK HOME!!
DAMN IT...
AT THIS RATE ...
EVERYONE'S GOING TO DIE ALL BECAUSE I GOT CAPTURED...
BERTOLT !!
WOOSH

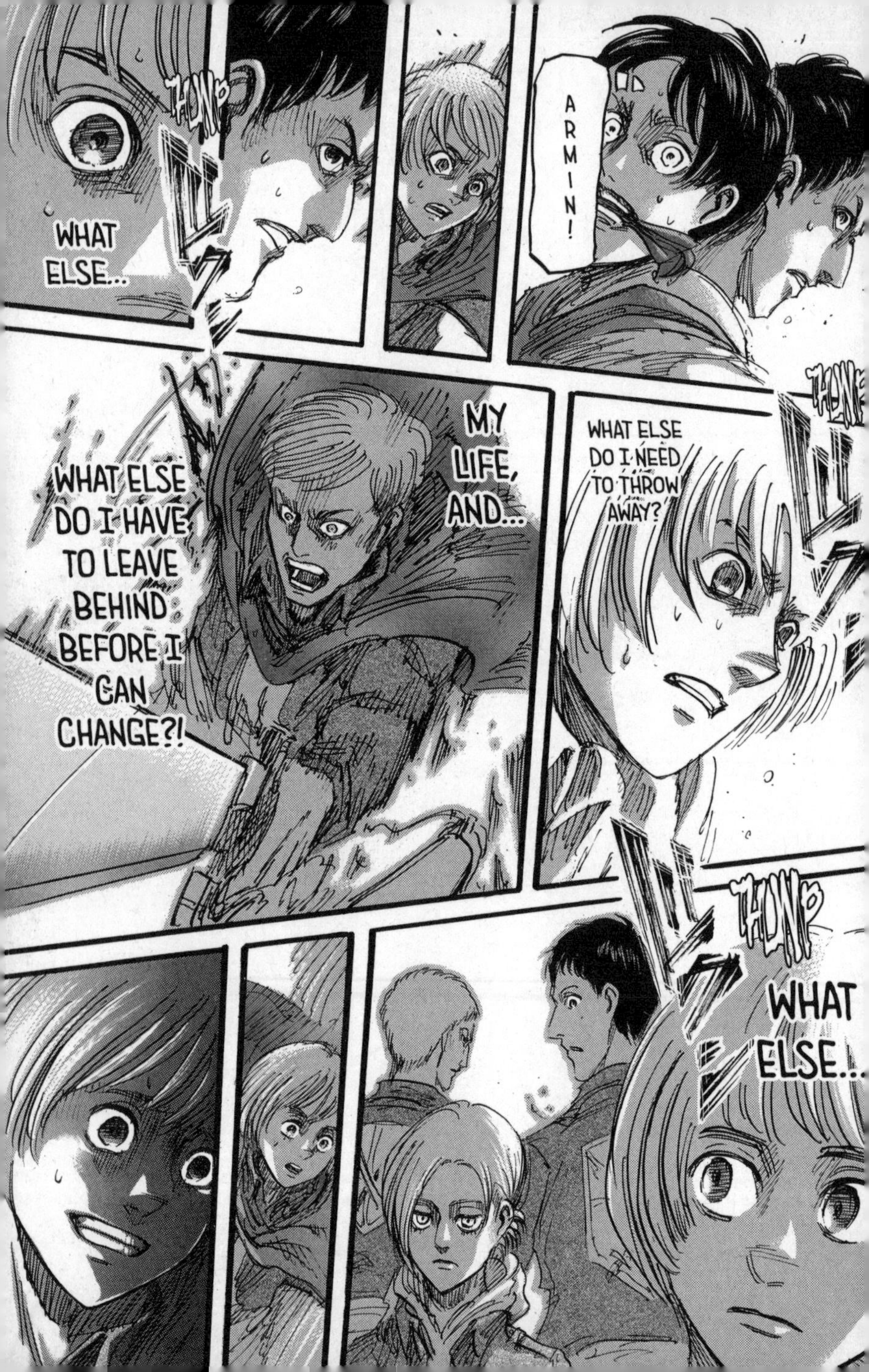
ARMIN!
THOMP
WHAT ELSE...
THOMP
WHAT ELSE DO I NEED TO THROW AWAY?
MY LIFE, AND...
WHAT ELSE DO I HAVE TO LEAVE BEHIND BEFORE I CAN CHANGE?!
THOMP
WHAT ELSE...

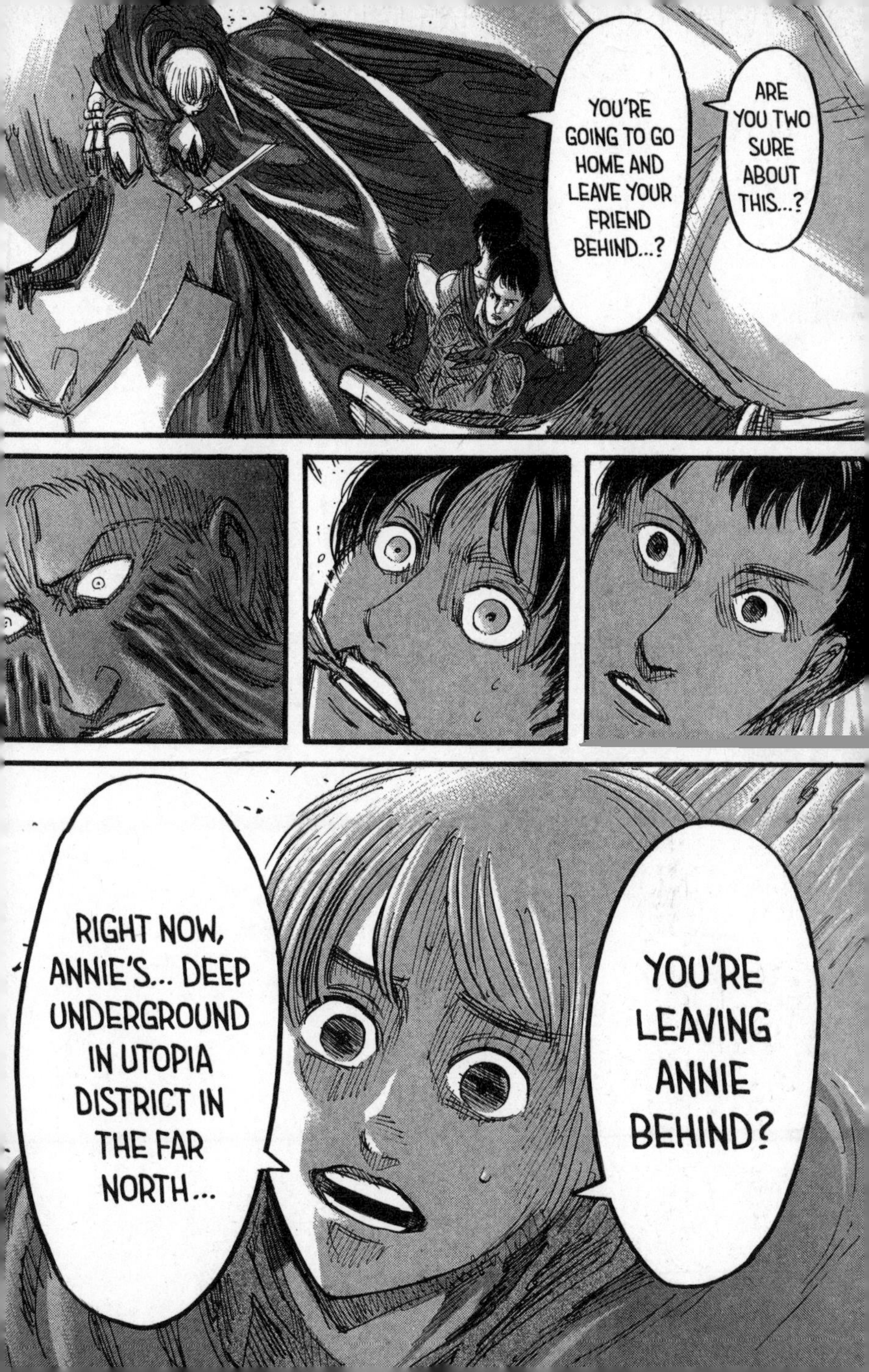
ARE YOU TWO SURE ABOUT THIS...?
YOU'RE GOING TO GO HOME AND LEAVE YOUR FRIEND BEHIND...?
YOU'RE LEAVING ANNIE BEHIND?
RIGHT NOW, ANNIE'S... DEEP UNDERGROUND IN UTOPIA DISTRICT IN THE FAR NORTH...

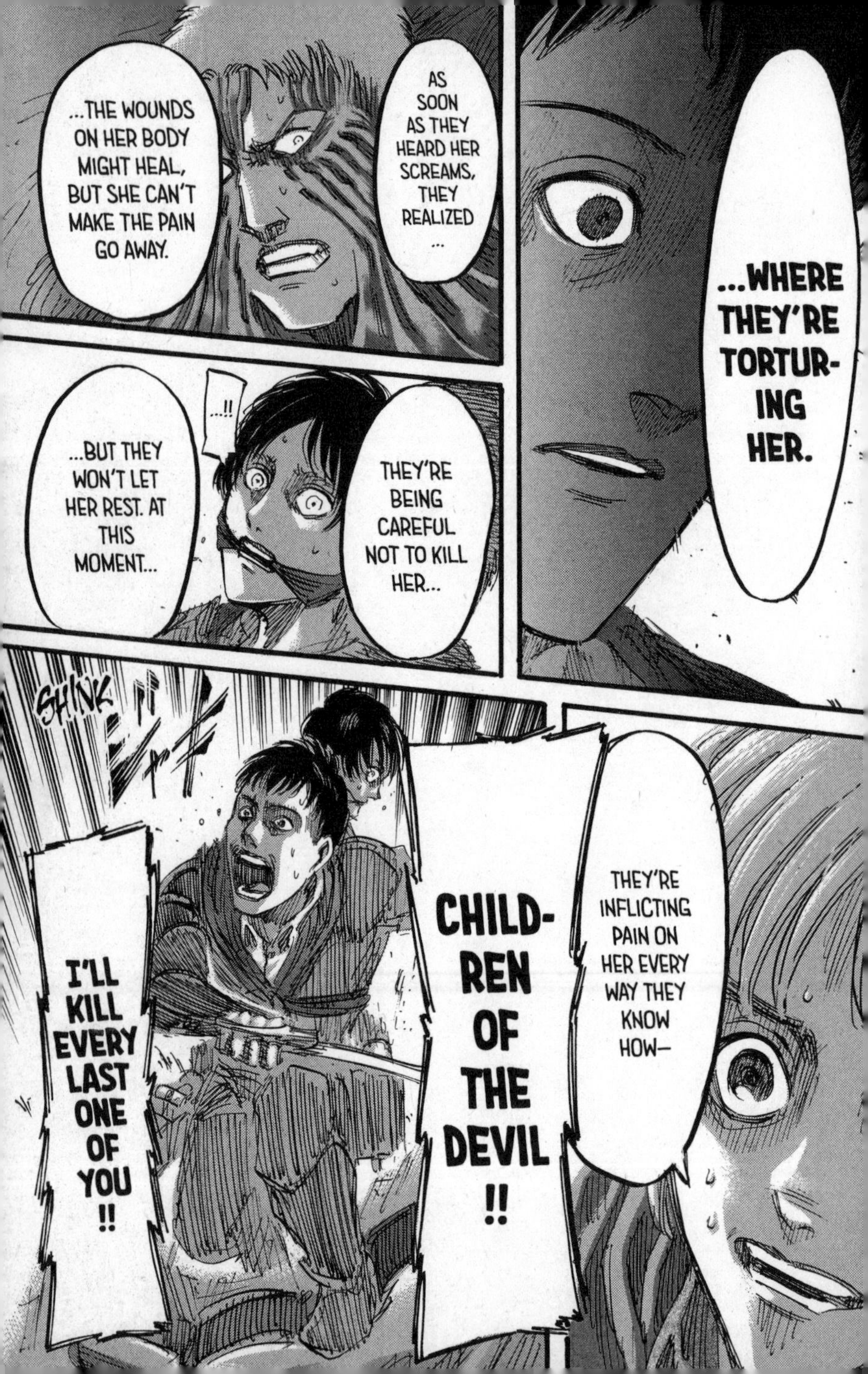
...WHERE THEY'RE TORTURING HER.
AS SOON AS THEY HEARD HER SCREAMS, THEY REALIZED ...
...THE WOUNDS ON HER BODY MIGHT HEAL, BUT SHE CAN'T MAKE THE PAIN GO AWAY.
THEY'RE BEING CAREFUL NOT TO KILL HER...
...!!
...BUT THEY WON'T LET HER REST. AT THIS MOMENT...
THEY'RE INFLICTING PAIN ON HER EVERY WAY THEY KNOW HOW—
CHILDREN OF THE DEVIL !!
SHINK
I'LL KILL EVERY LAST ONE OF YOU !!

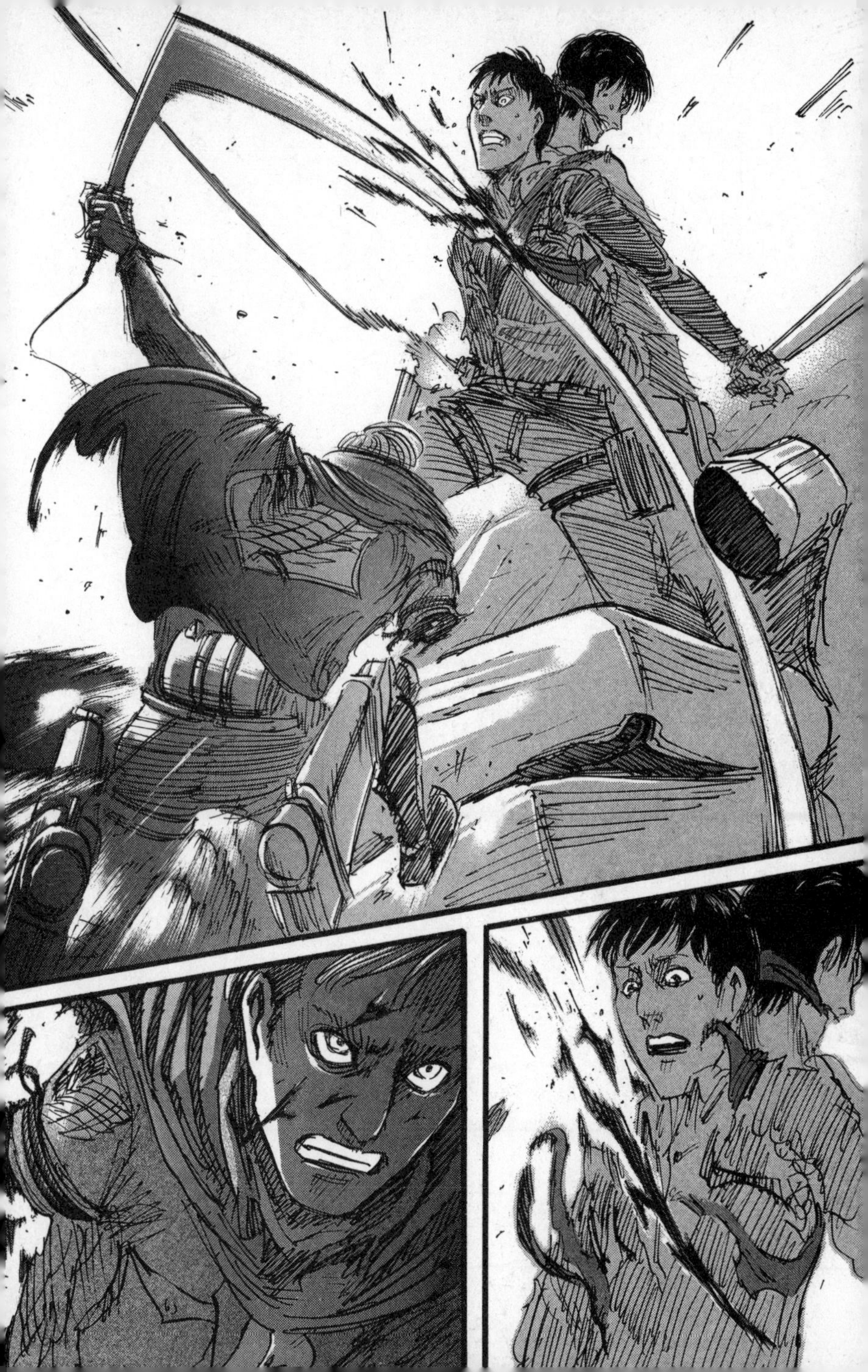

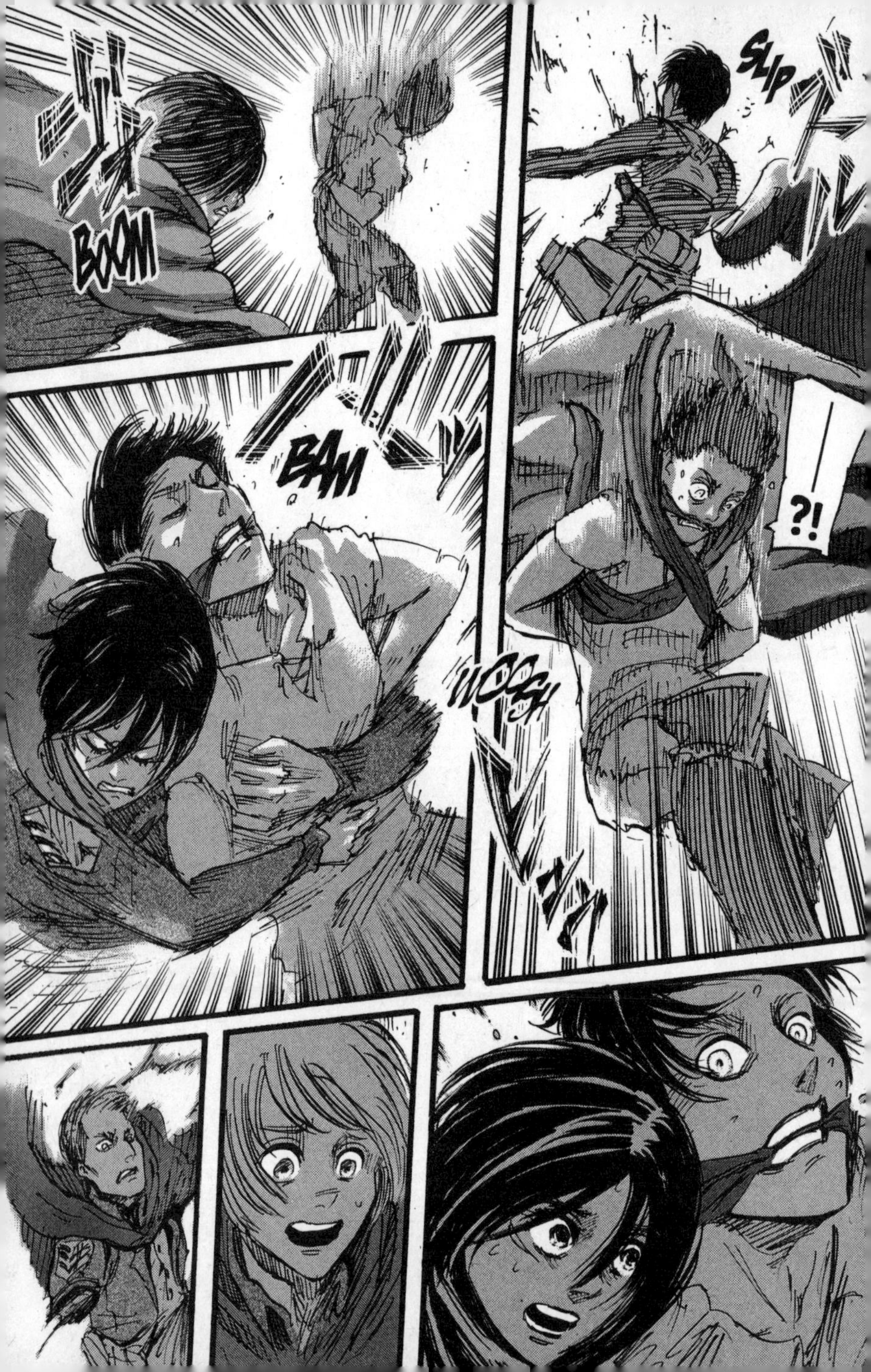
SLIP
BOOM
?!
WOOSH
BAM

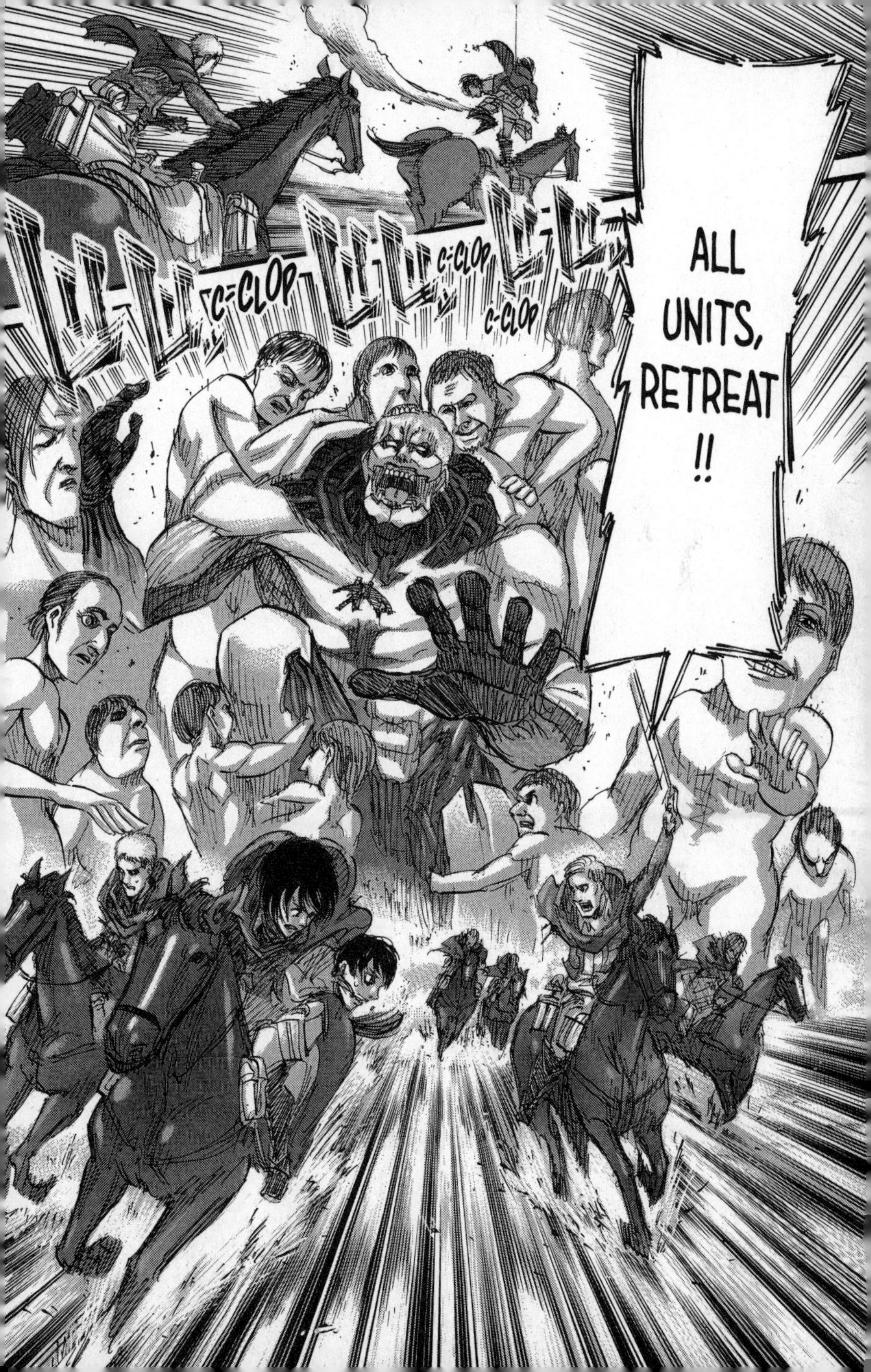
ALL UNITS, RETREAT!!
C-CLOP
C-CLOP
C-CLOP
C-CLOP

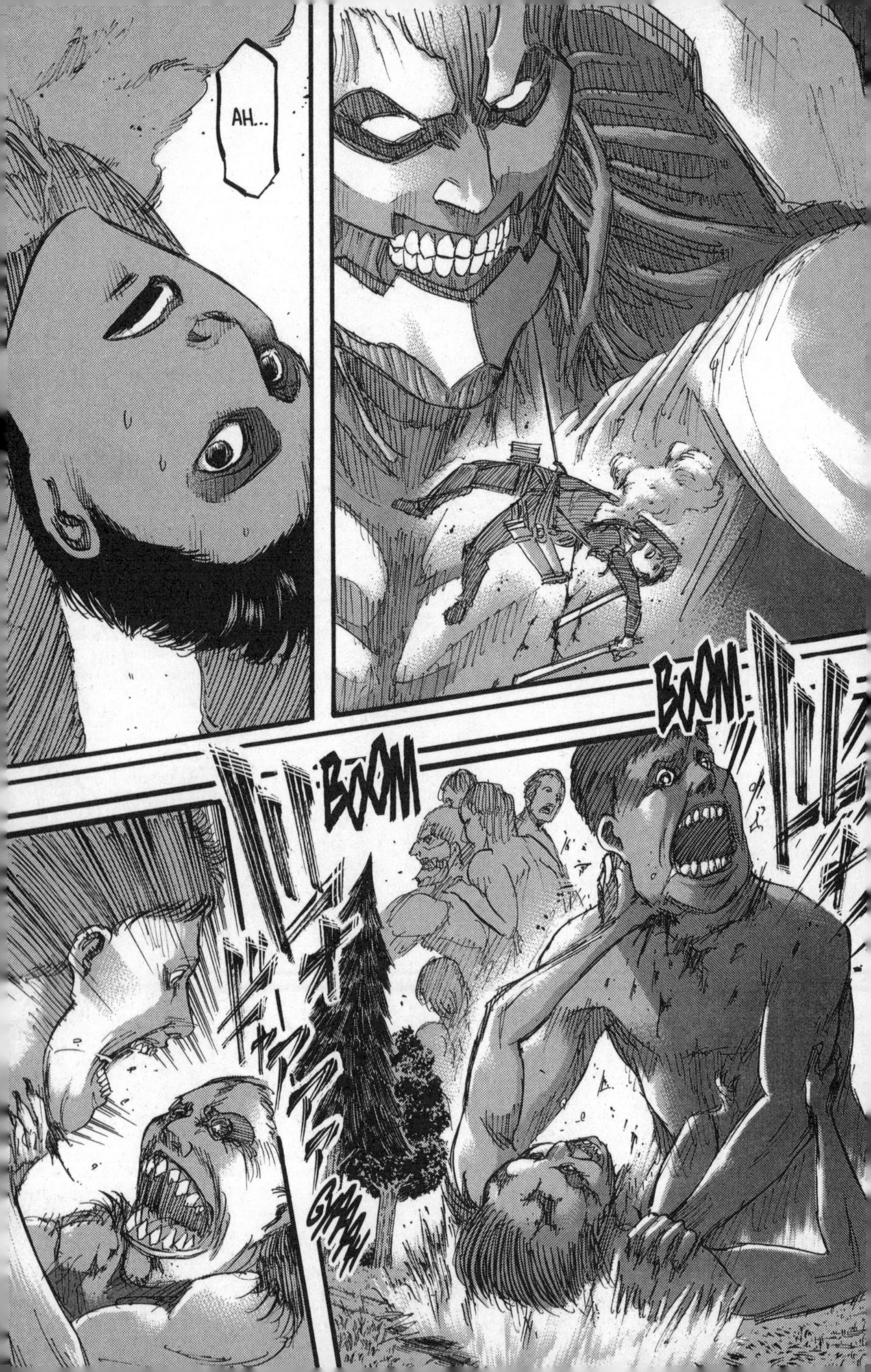
AH...
BOOM
BOOM

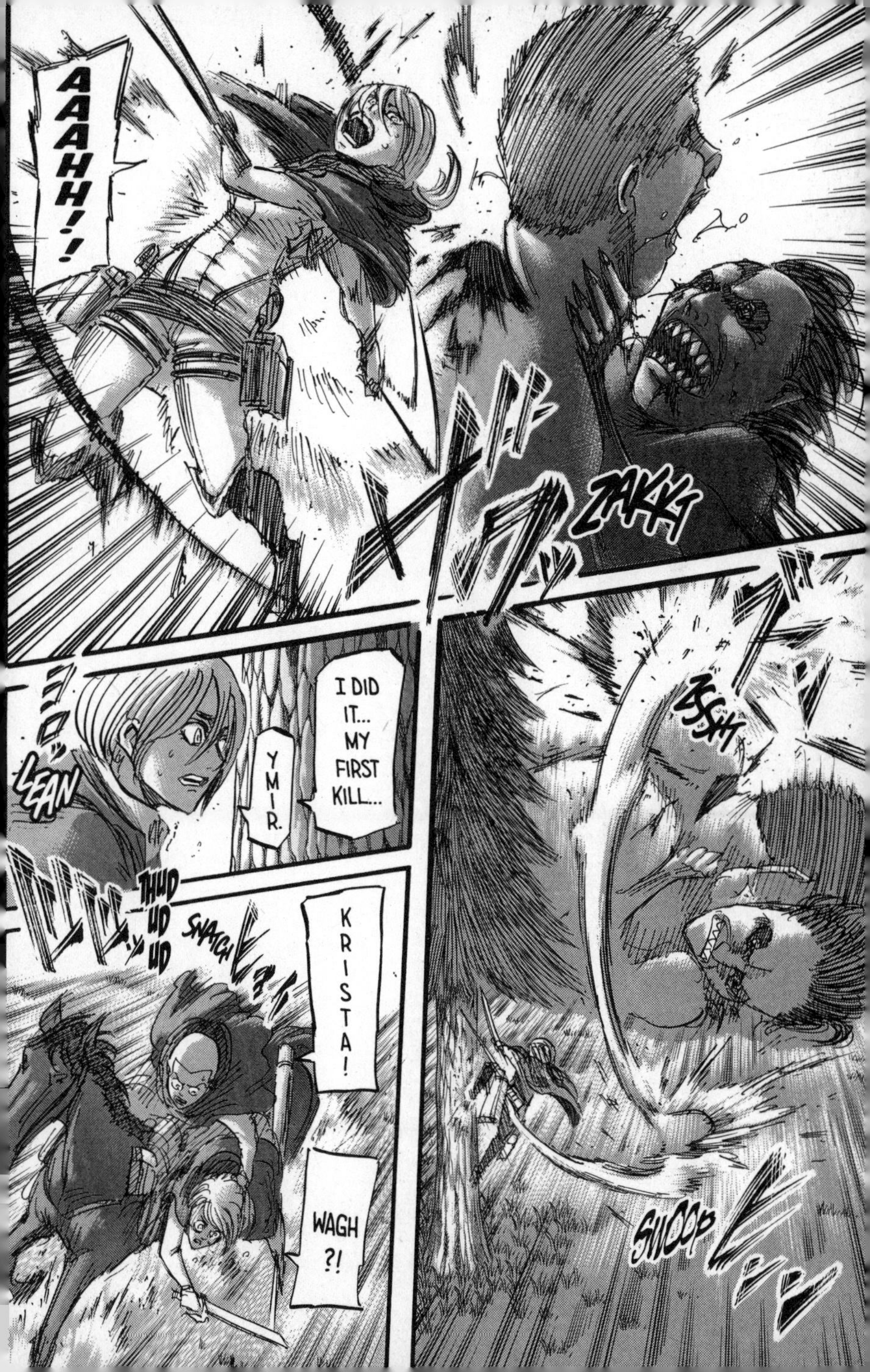
AAAAHH!!
ZAKAG
TSSH
SWOOP
I DID IT... MY FIRST KILL...
YMIR.
LEAN
KRISTA!
SNATCH
THUD UD UD
WAGH?!

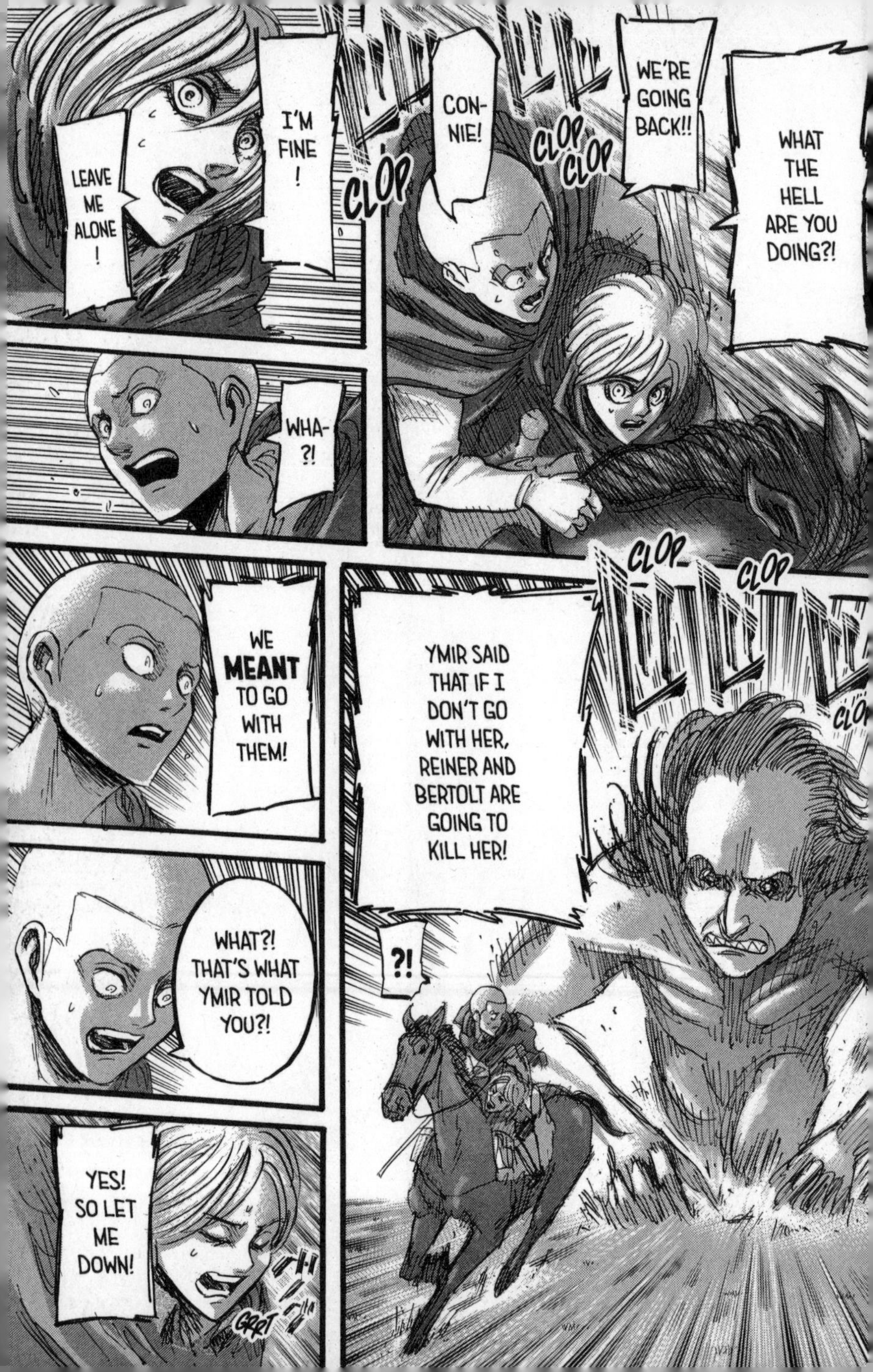
WHAT THE HELL ARE YOU DOING?!
WE'RE GOING BACK!!
CLOP CLOP
CON-NIE!
CLOP
I'M FINE!
LEAVE ME ALONE!
WHA-?!
CLOP CLOP
CLOP
YMIR SAID THAT IF I DON'T GO WITH HER, REINER AND BERTOLT ARE GOING TO KILL HER!
?!
WE **MEANT** TO GO WITH THEM!
WHAT?! THAT'S WHAT YMIR TOLD YOU?!
YES! SO LET ME DOWN!
GRRT

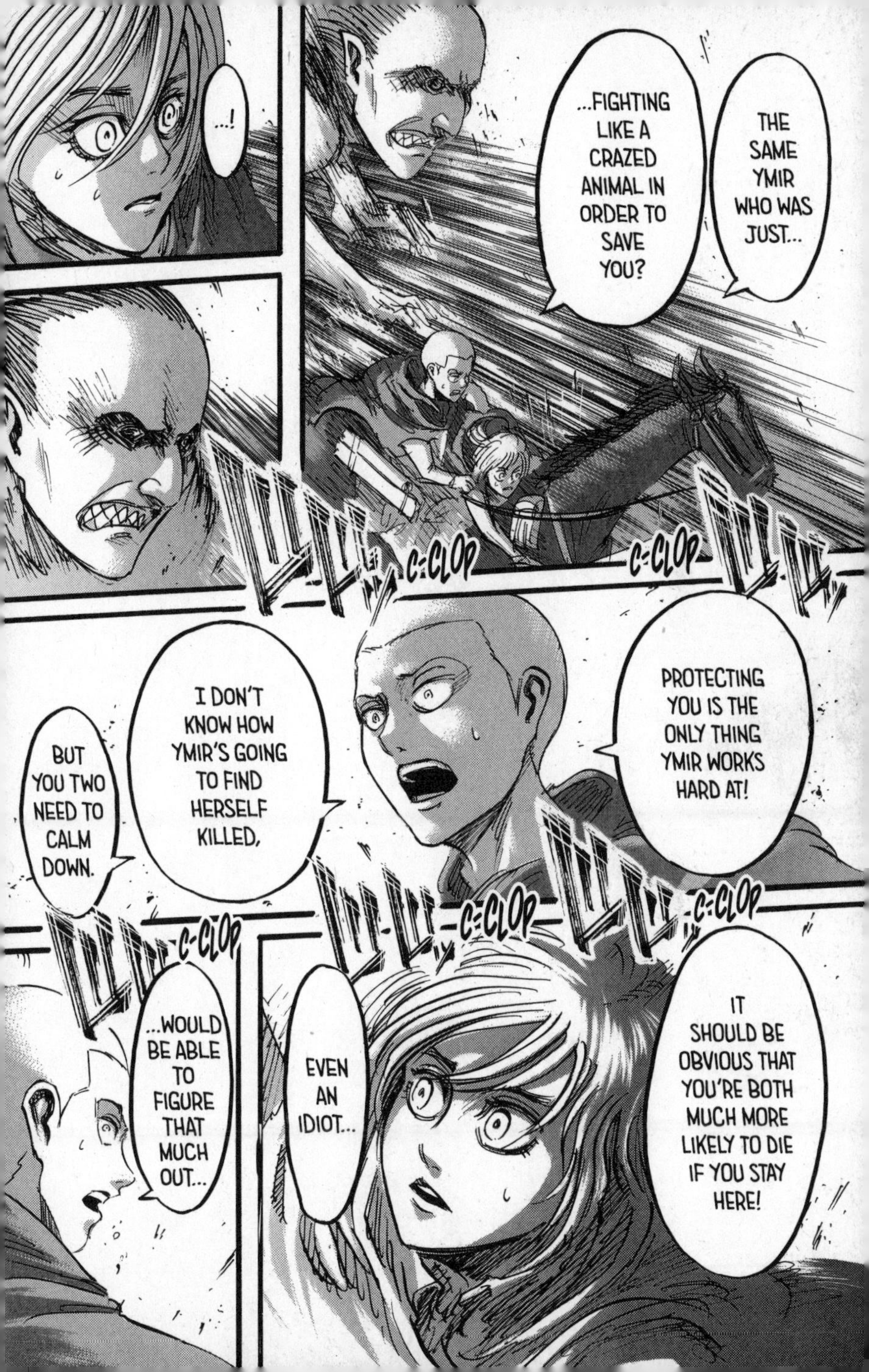
THE SAME YMIR WHO WAS JUST...
...FIGHTING LIKE A CRAZED ANIMAL IN ORDER TO SAVE YOU?
C-CLOP
...!
C-CLOP
PROTECTING YOU IS THE ONLY THING YMIR WORKS HARD AT!
I DON'T KNOW HOW YMIR'S GOING TO FIND HERSELF KILLED,
BUT YOU TWO NEED TO CALM DOWN.
C-CLOP
C-CLOP
IT SHOULD BE OBVIOUS THAT YOU'RE BOTH MUCH MORE LIKELY TO DIE IF YOU STAY HERE!
EVEN AN IDIOT...
C-CLOP
...WOULD BE ABLE TO FIGURE THAT MUCH OUT...

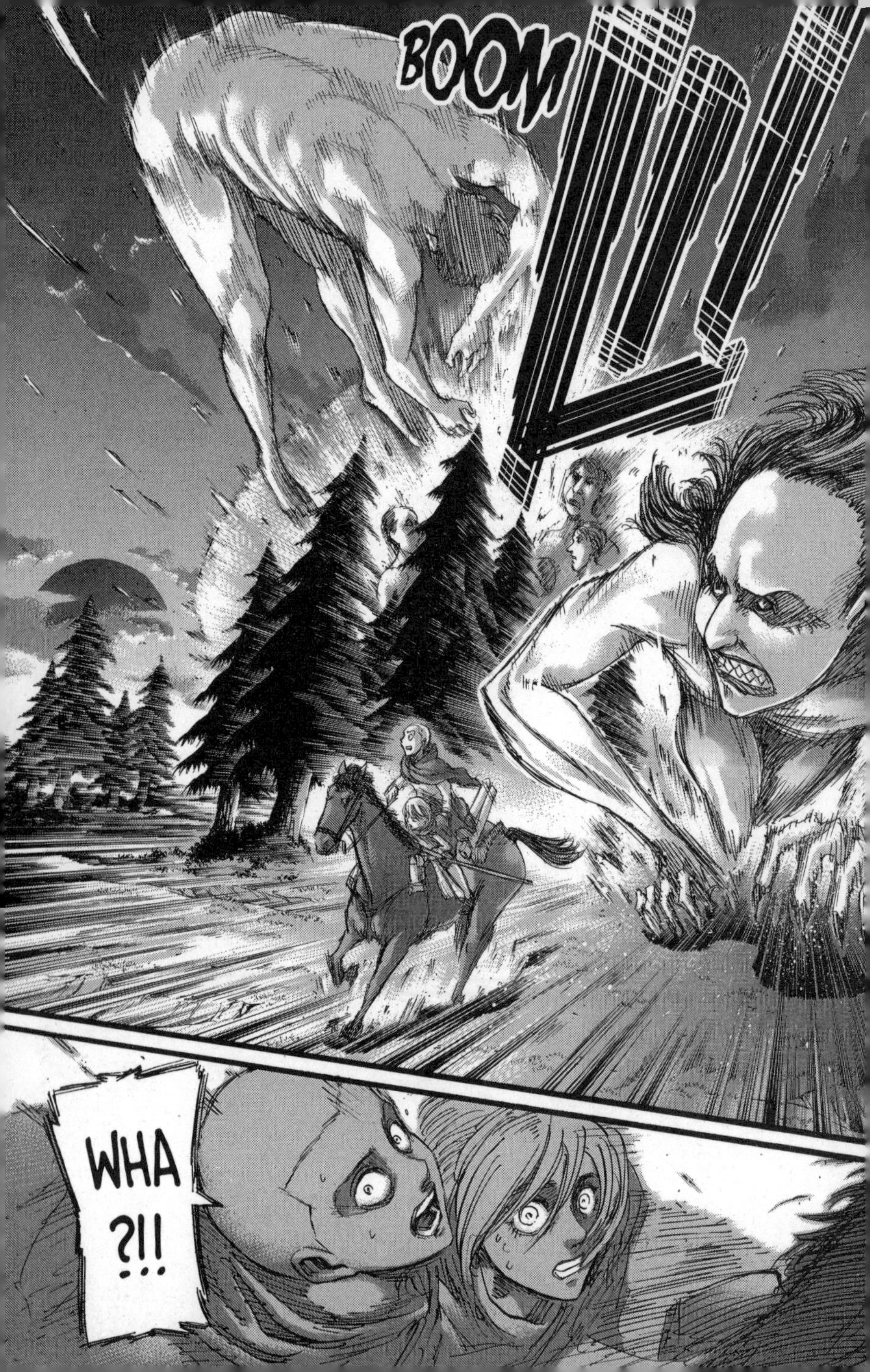
BOOM
WHA ?!!

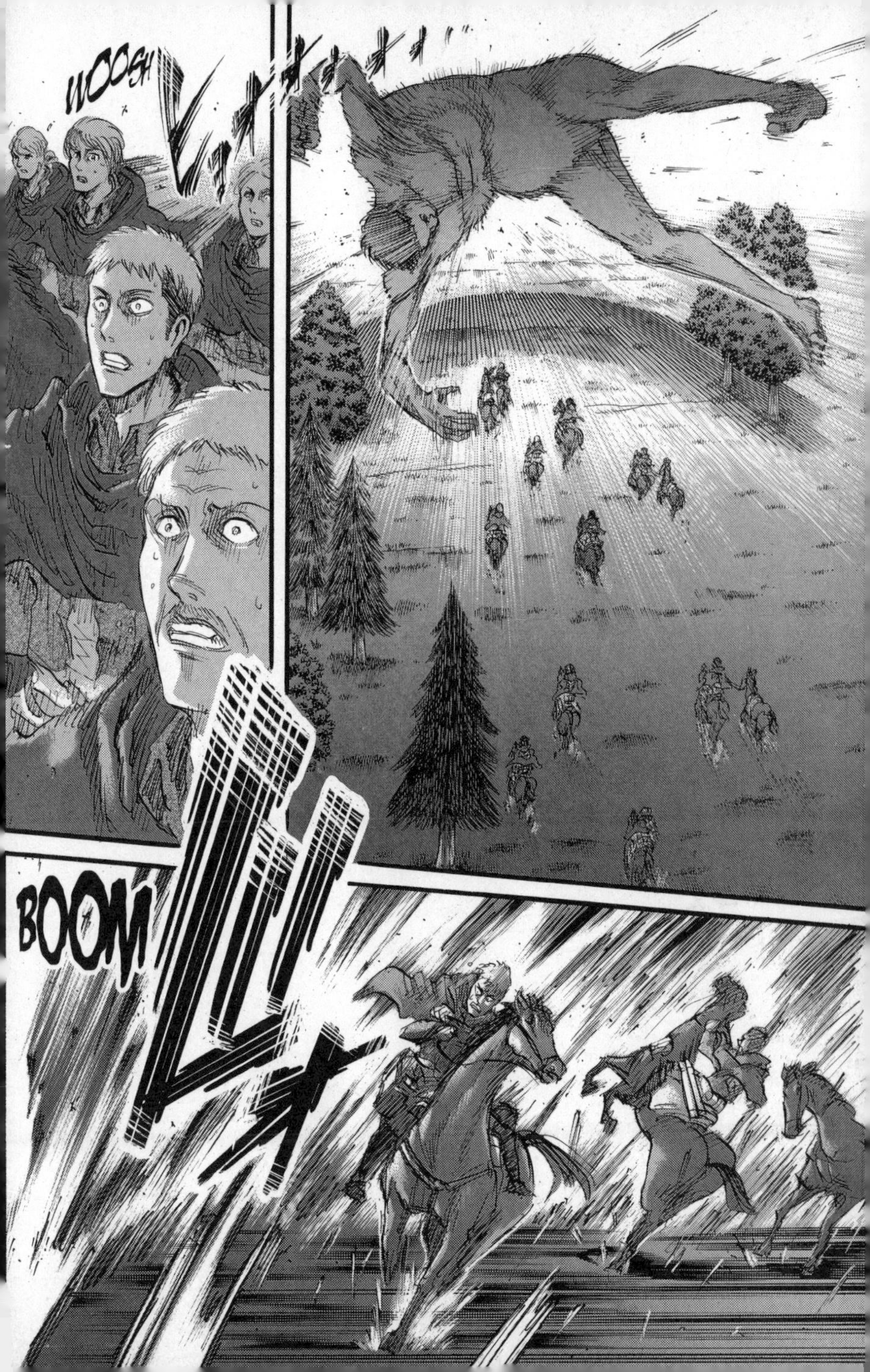
WOOSH
BOOM

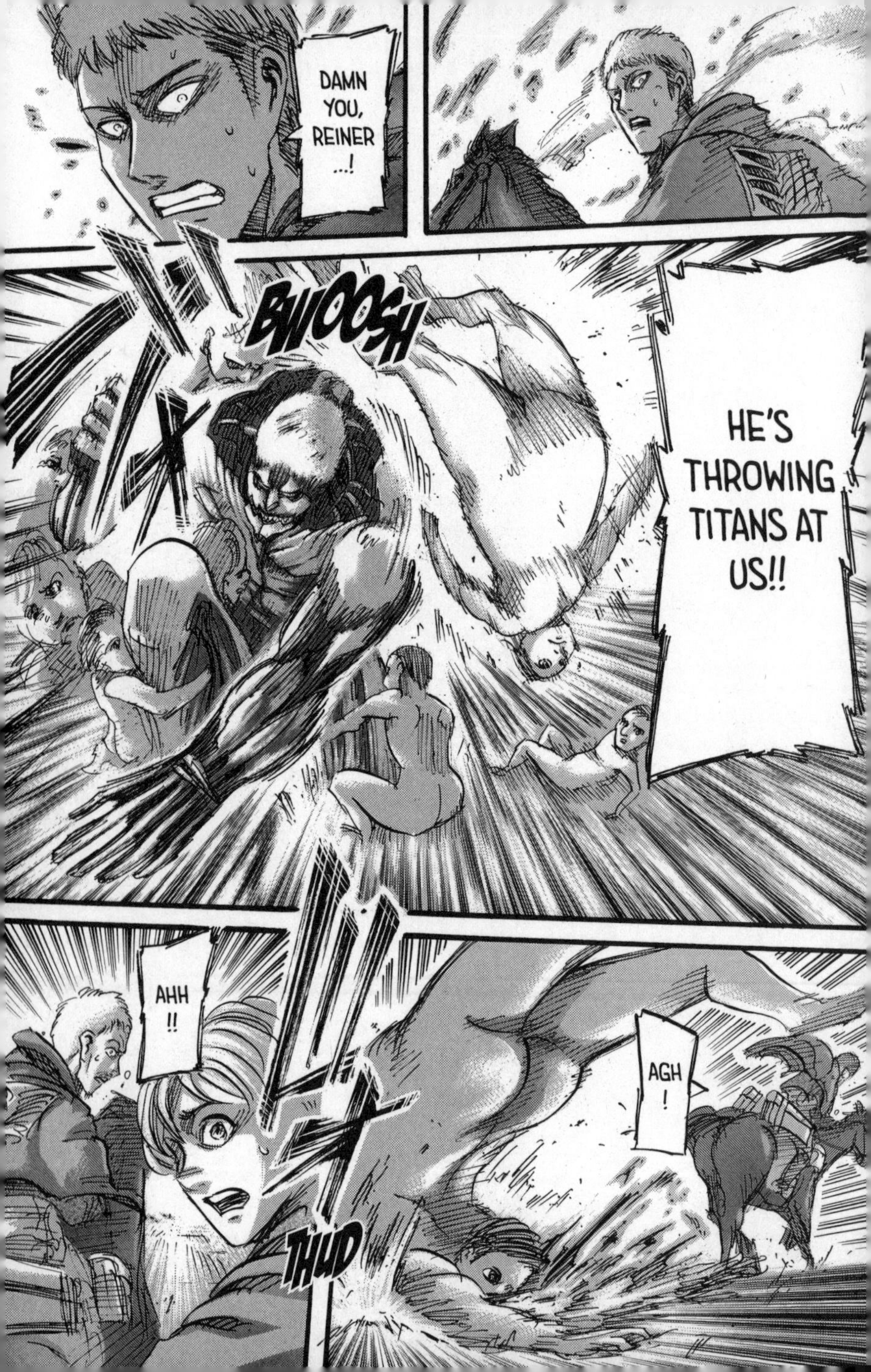
DAMN YOU, REINER ...!
HE'S THROWING TITANS AT US!!
BWOOSH
AGH !
AHH !!
THUD

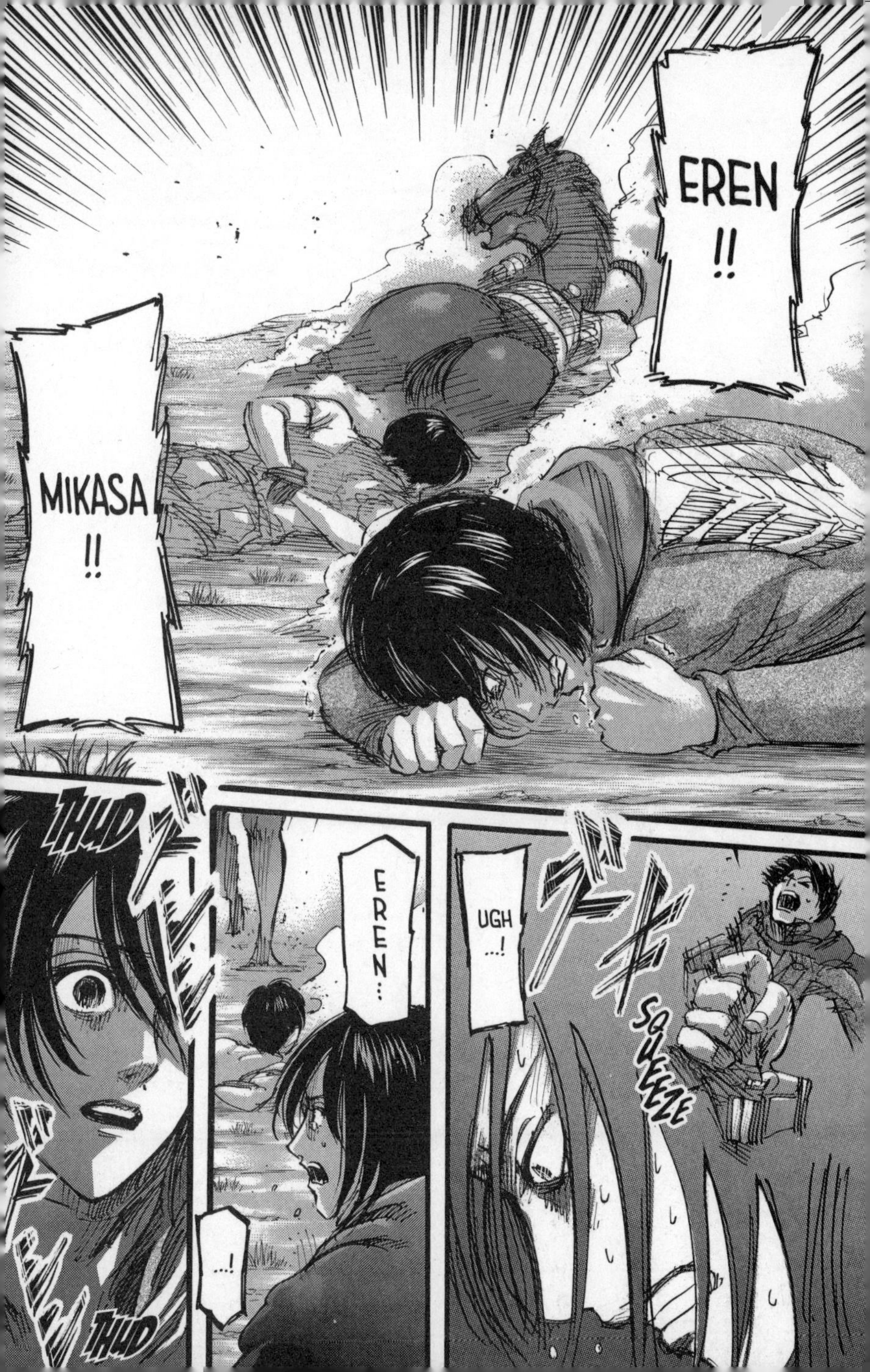
EREN !!
MIKASA !!
UGH ...!
SQUEEZE
EREN...
...!
THUD
THUD

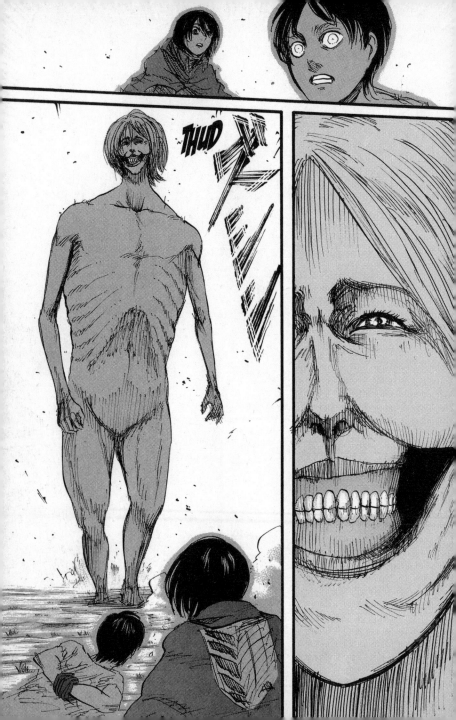

THUD

ATTACK on TITAN

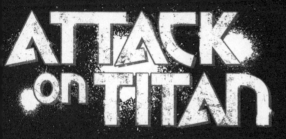

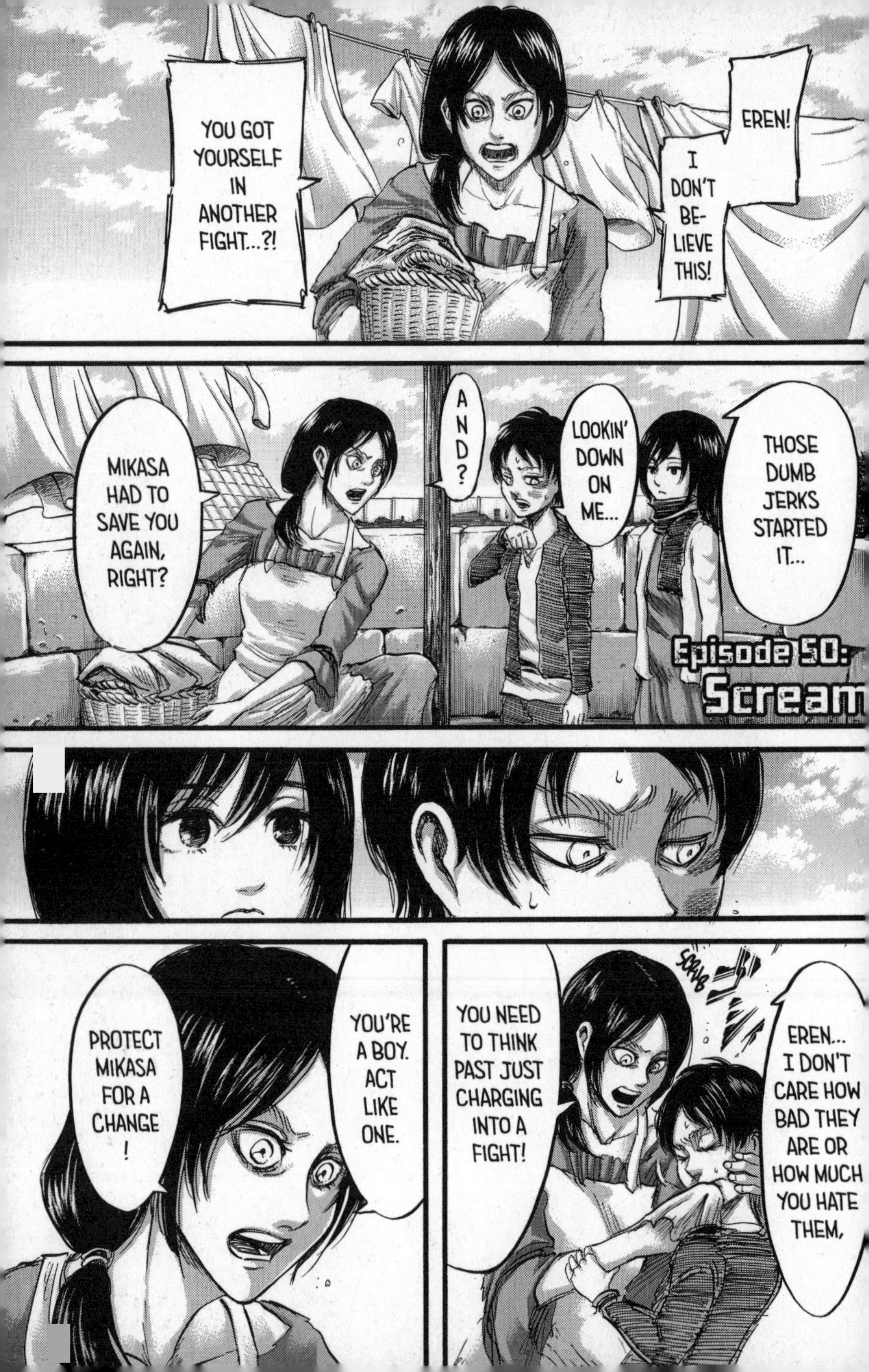
EREN!
I DON'T BE-LIEVE THIS!
YOU GOT YOURSELF IN ANOTHER FIGHT...?!
THOSE DUMB JERKS STARTED IT...
LOOKIN' DOWN ON ME...
AND?
Episode 50: Scream
MIKASA HAD TO SAVE YOU AGAIN, RIGHT?
SCRUB
EREN... I DON'T CARE HOW BAD THEY ARE OR HOW MUCH YOU HATE THEM,
YOU NEED TO THINK PAST JUST CHARGING INTO A FIGHT!
YOU'RE A BOY. ACT LIKE ONE.
PROTECT MIKASA FOR A CHANGE!

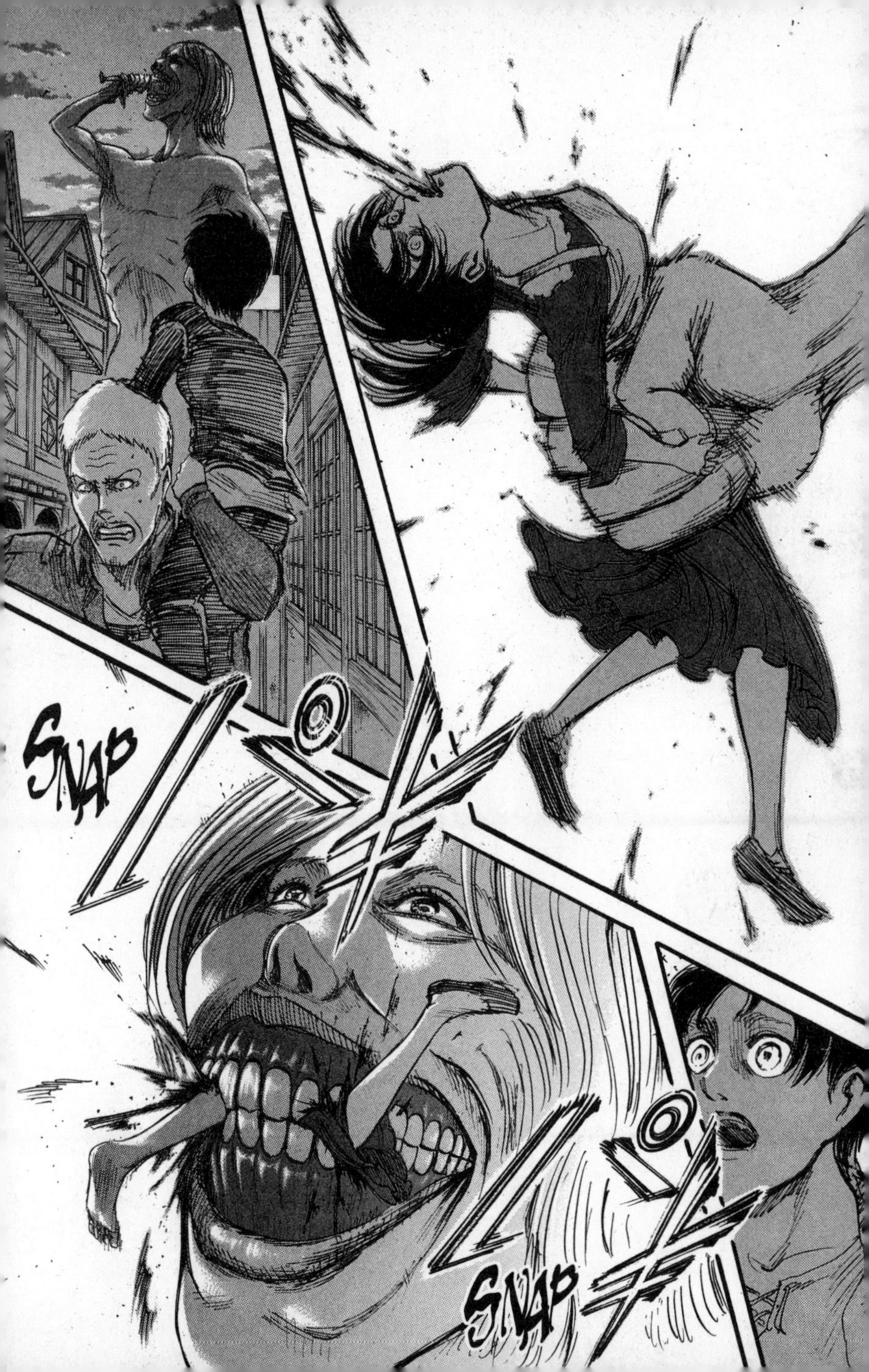
SNAP
SNAP

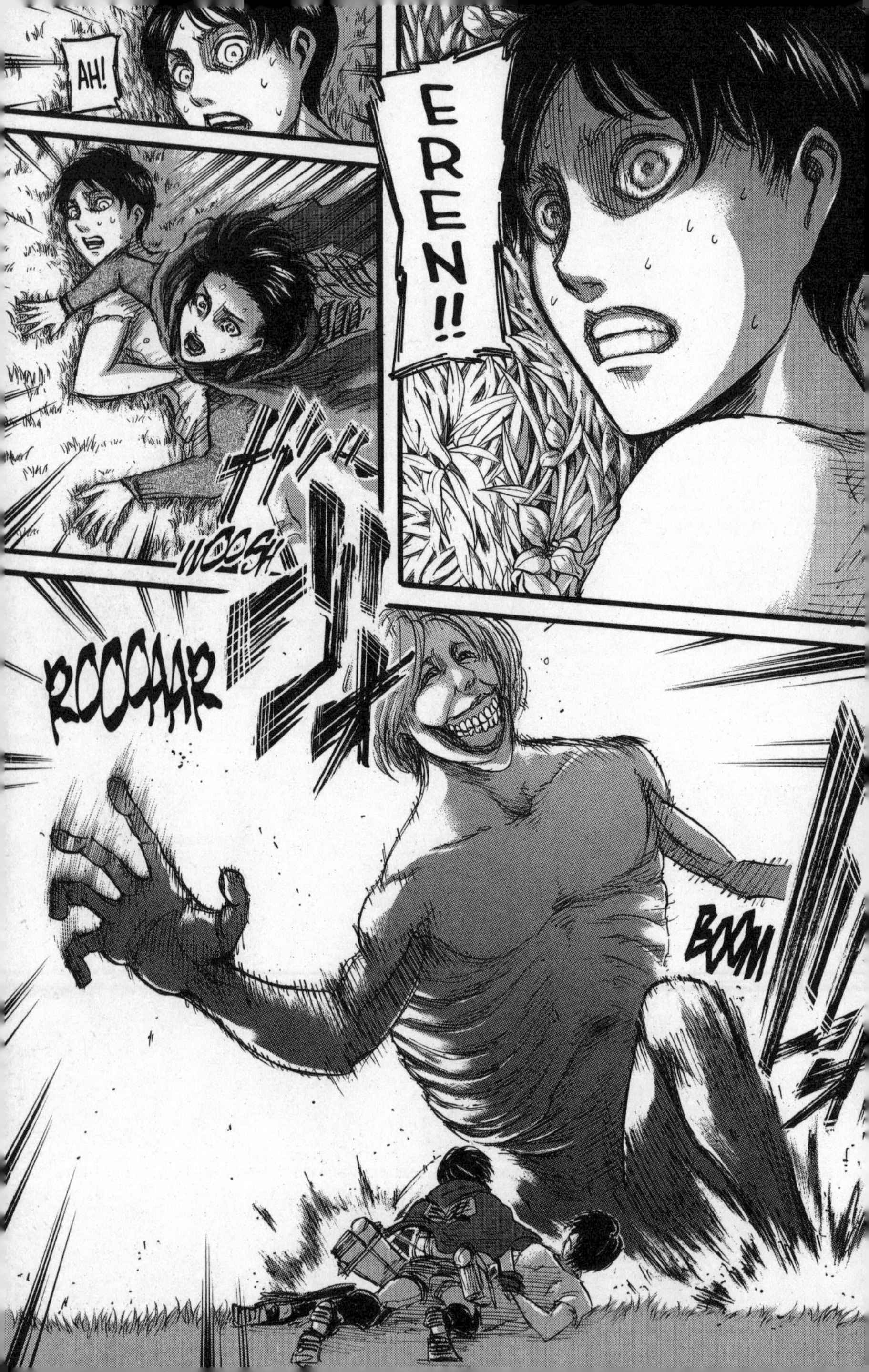
EREN!!
AH!
WOOSH
ROOOAAR
BOOM

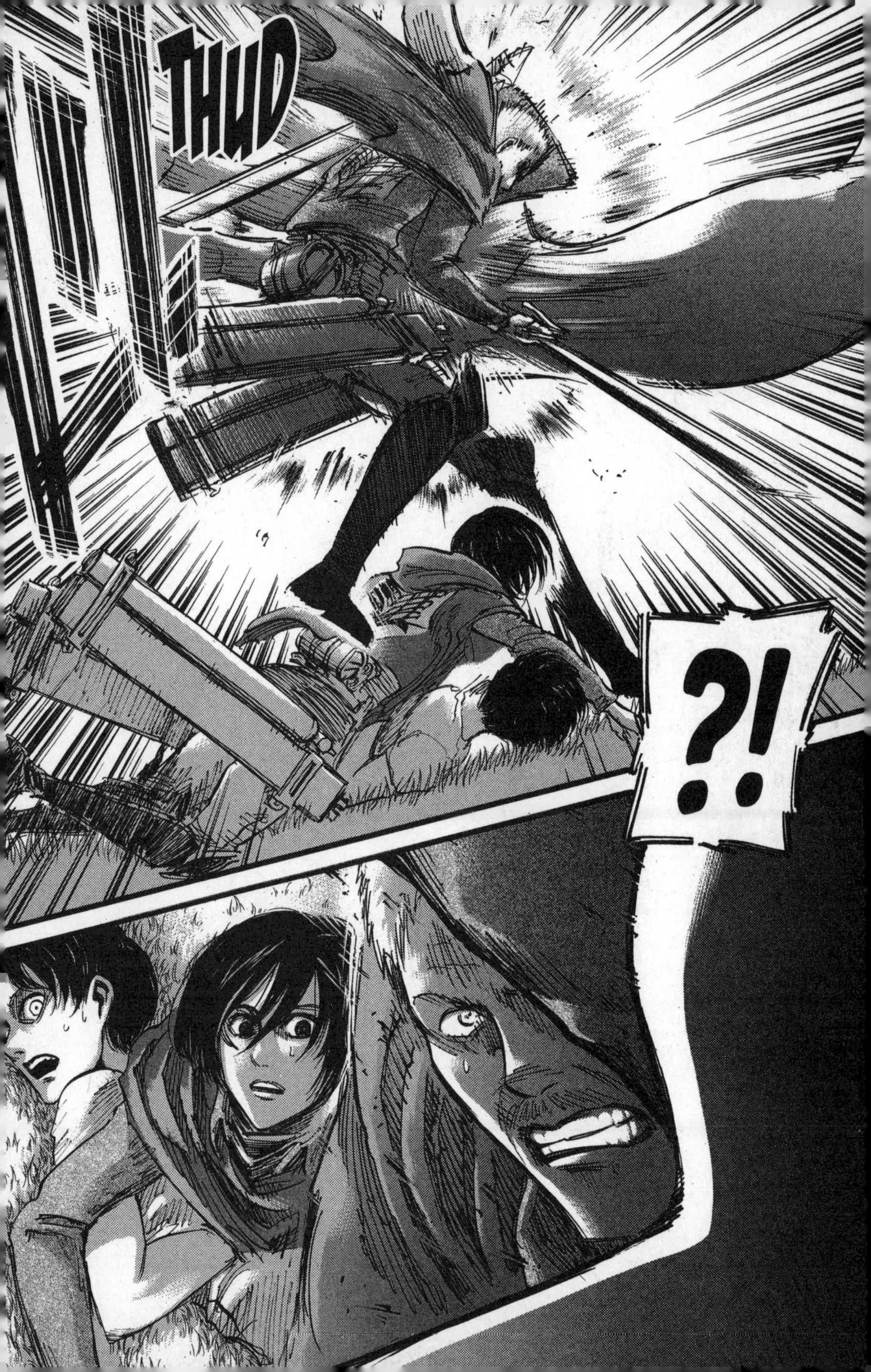
THUD
?!

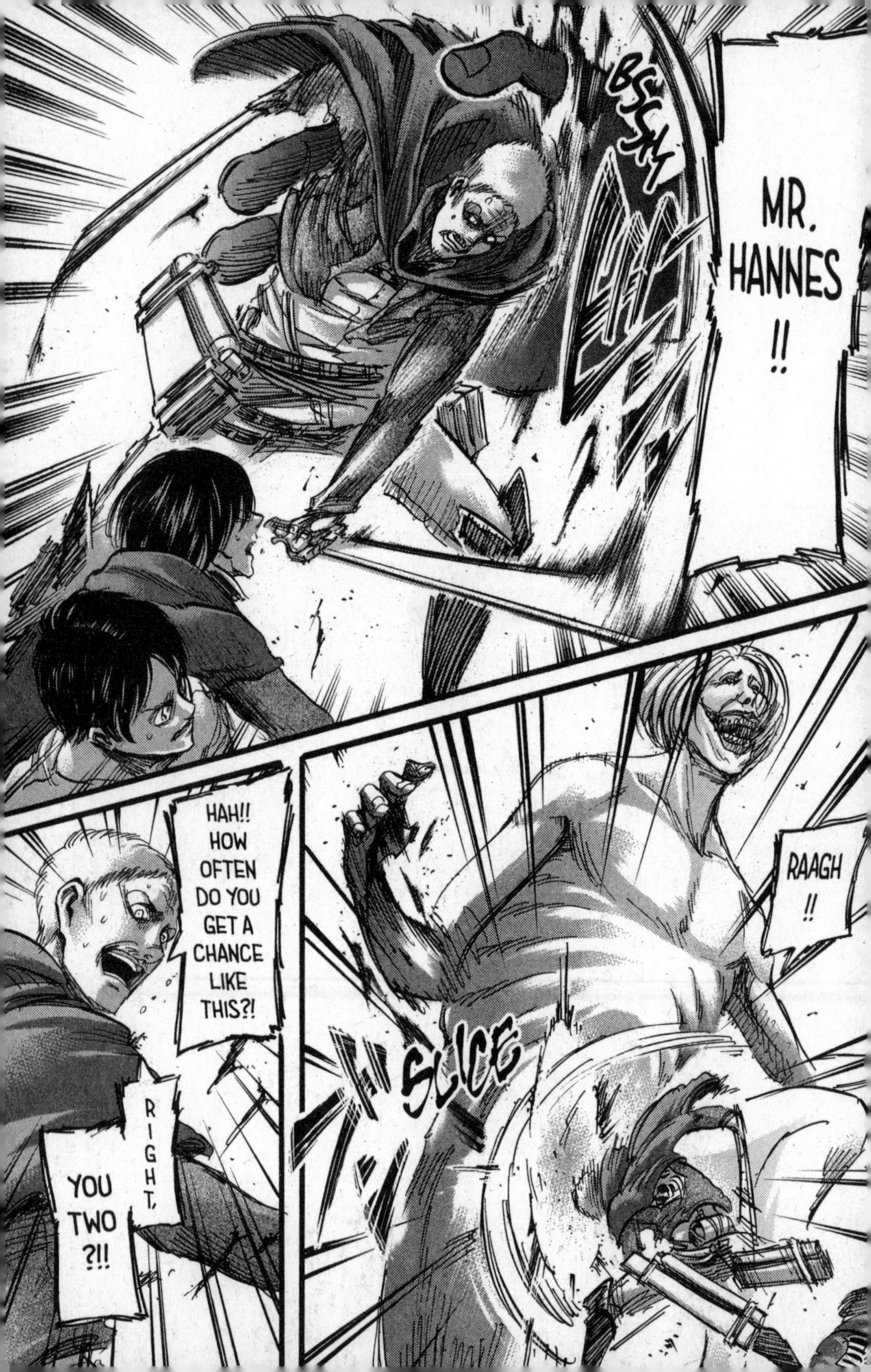
BSCHK
MR. HANNES!!
RAAGH!!
SLICE
HAH!! HOW OFTEN DO YOU GET A CHANCE LIKE THIS?!
RIGHT, YOU TWO?!!

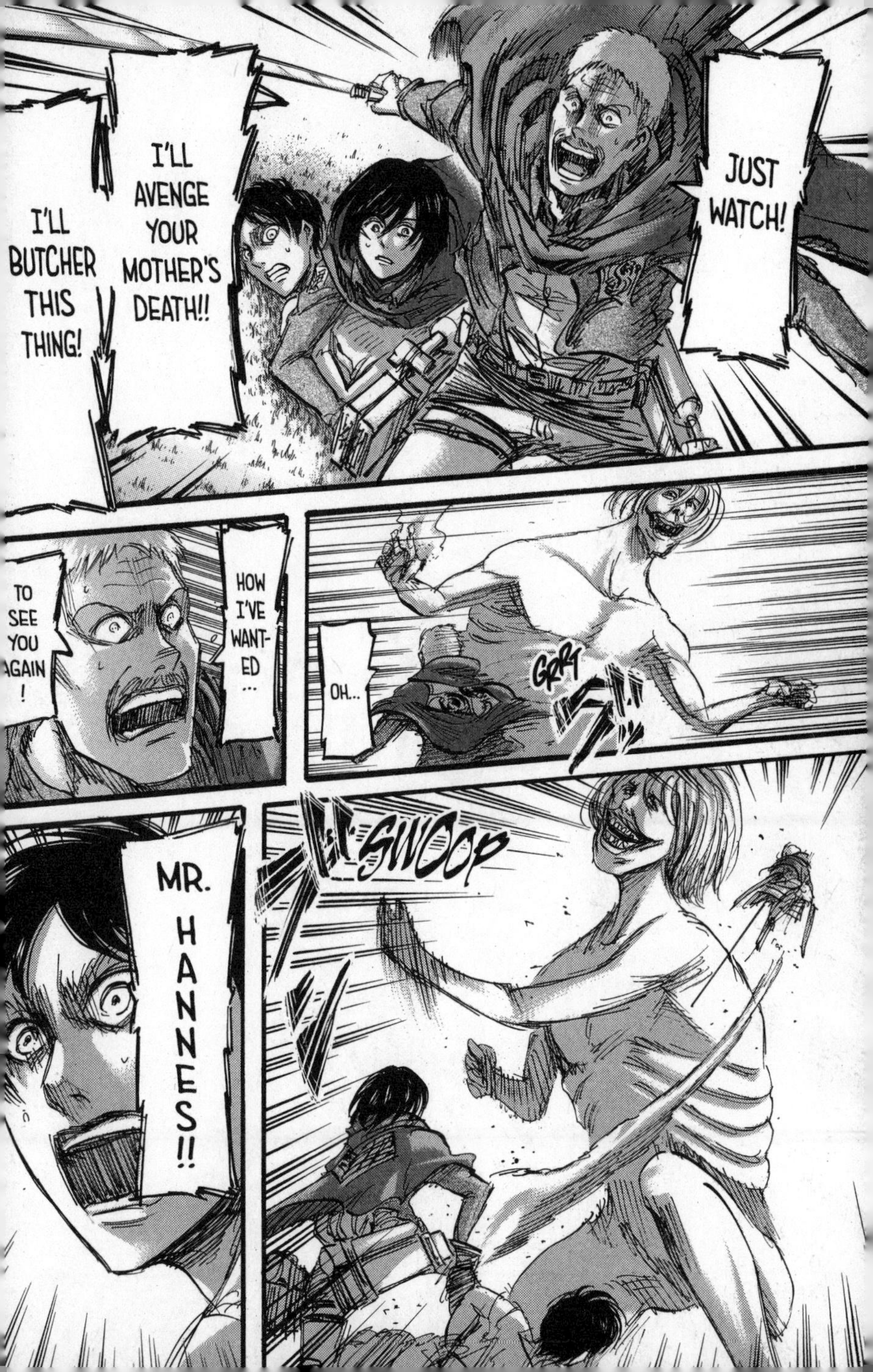
JUST WATCH!
I'LL AVENGE YOUR MOTHER'S DEATH!!
I'LL BUTCHER THIS THING!
OH...
GRPT
HOW I'VE WANT-ED...
TO SEE YOU AGAIN!
SWOOP
MR. HANNES!!

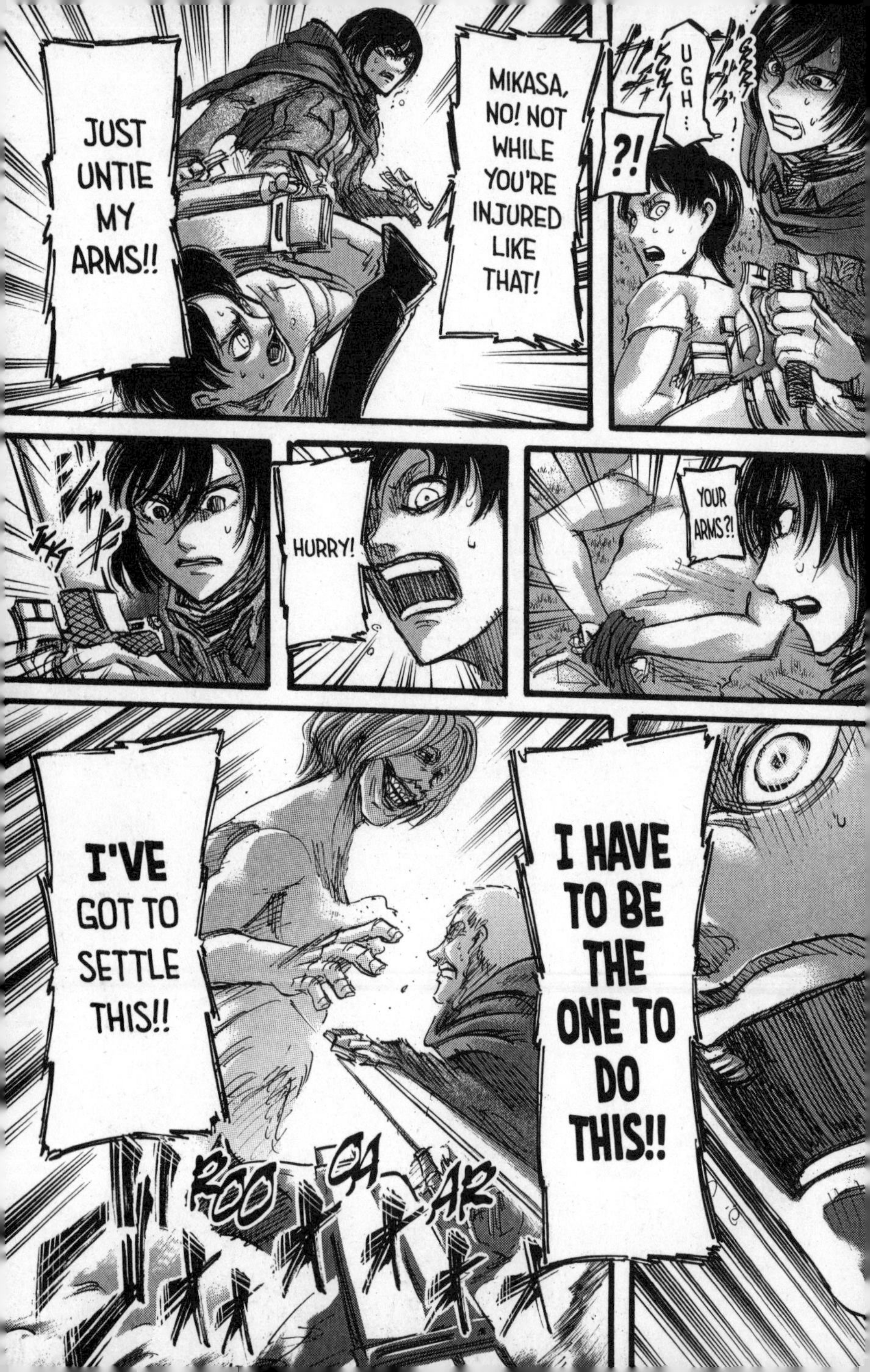
GRRT
UGH...
KCHK
?!
MIKASA, NO! NOT WHILE YOU'RE INJURED LIKE THAT!
JUST UNTIE MY ARMS!!
YOUR ARMS?!
HURRY!
I HAVE TO BE THE ONE TO DO THIS!!
I'VE GOT TO SETTLE THIS!!
ROO OA AR

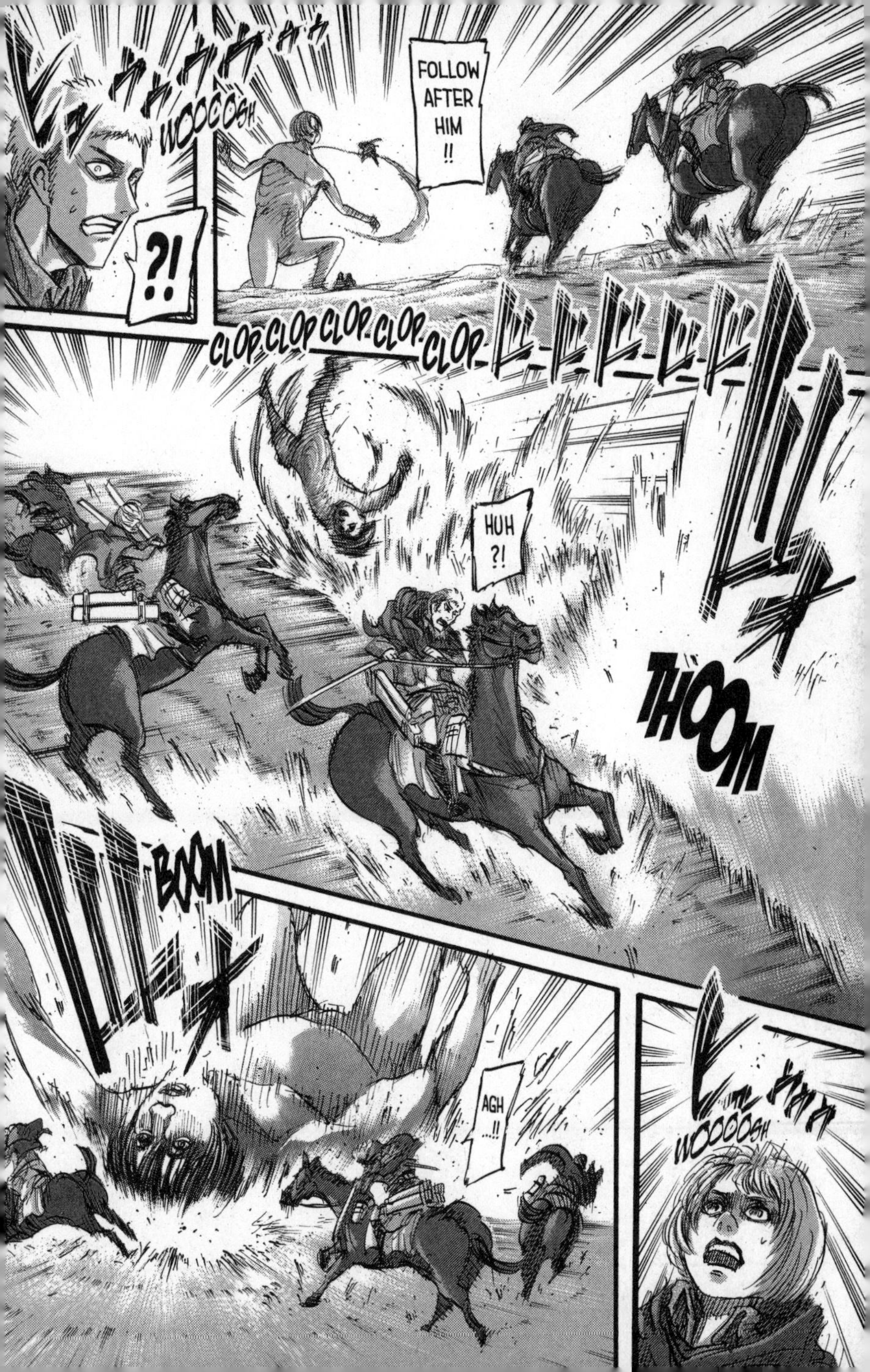
FOLLOW AFTER HIM !!
WOOOOSH
?!
CLOP CLOP CLOP CLOP CLOP
HUH ?!
THOOM
WOOOOSH
BOOM
AGH ...!!

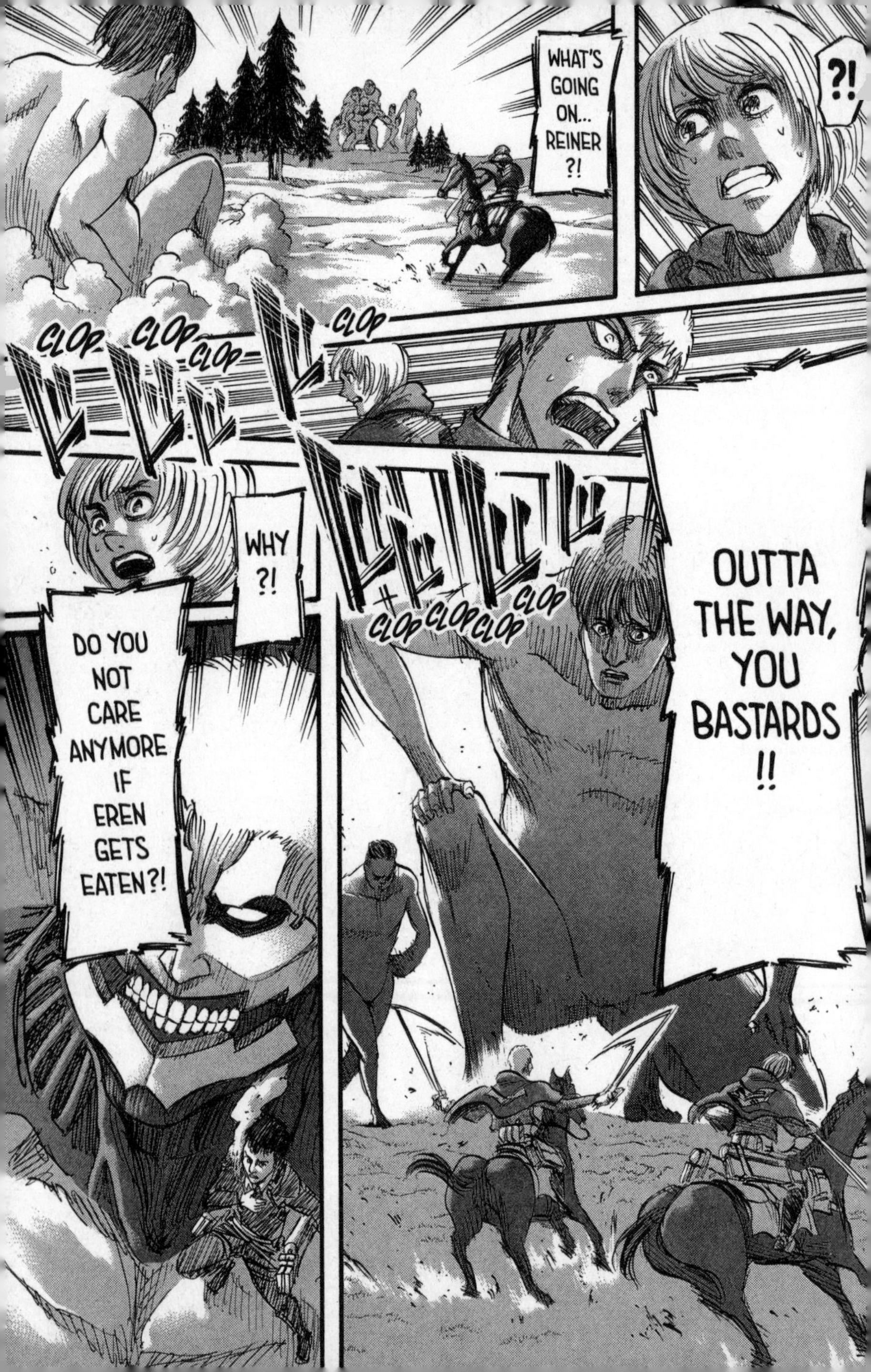
?!
WHAT'S GOING ON... REINER ?!
CLOP
CLOP
CLOP
CLOP
CLOP
OUTTA THE WAY, YOU BASTARDS !!
CLOP
CLOP
CLOP
CLOP
WHY ?!
DO YOU NOT CARE ANYMORE IF EREN GETS EATEN?!

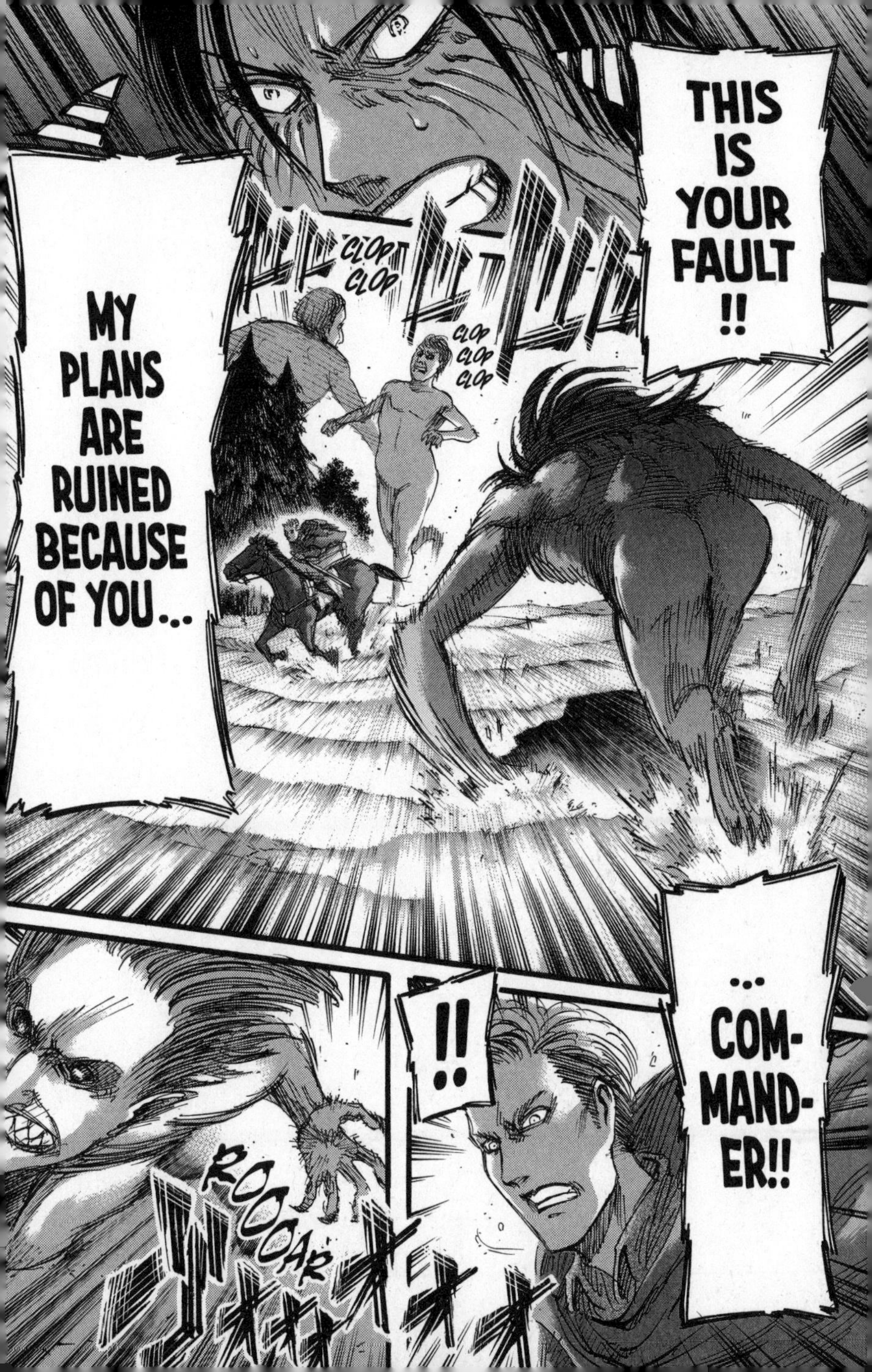
THIS IS YOUR FAULT!!
MY PLANS ARE RUINED BECAUSE OF YOU...
CLOP CLOP
CLOP CLOP CLOP
...COMMANDER!!
!!
ROOOAR

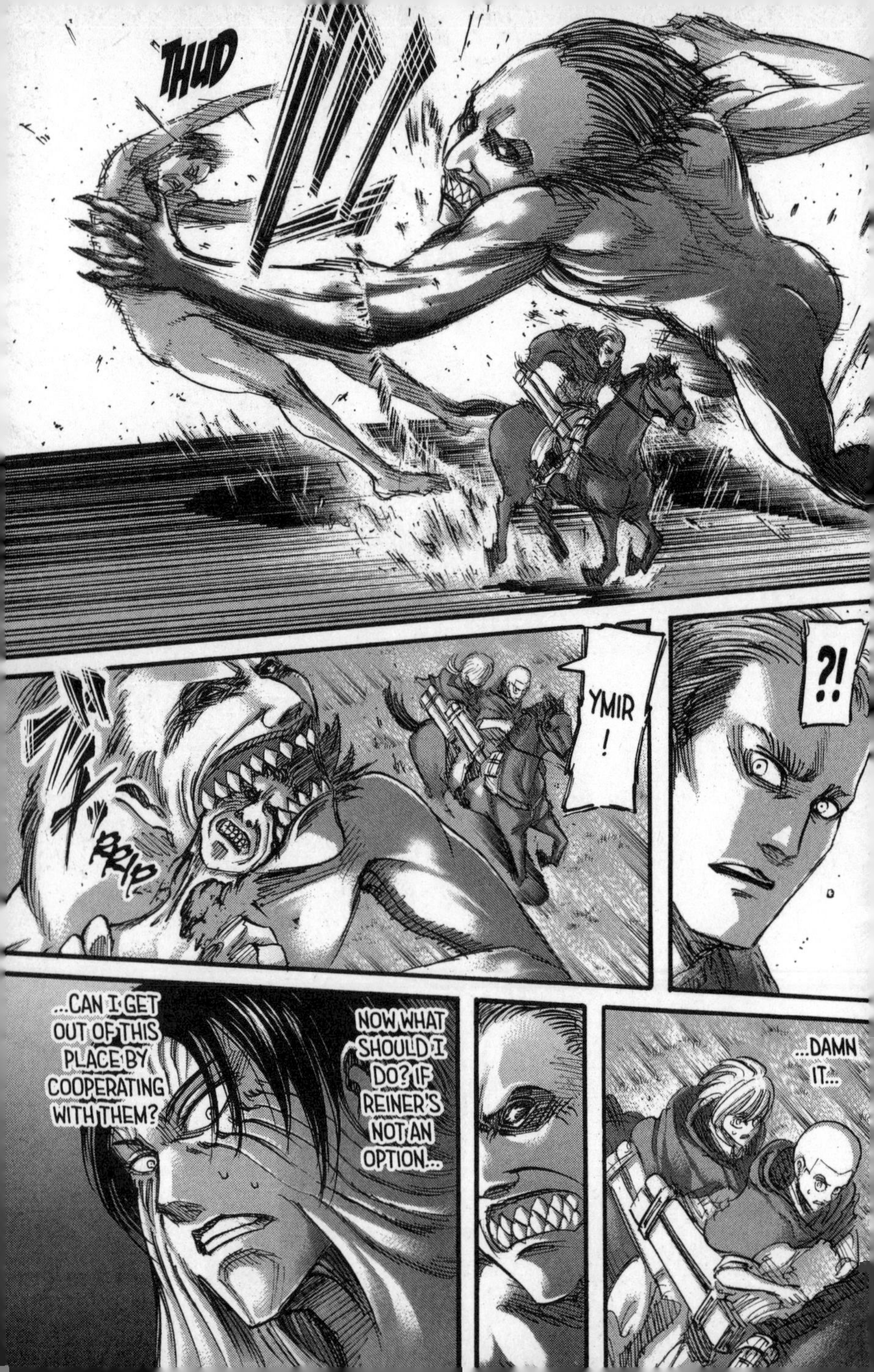
THUD
?!
YMIR !
RRIP
...DAMN IT...
NOW WHAT SHOULD I DO? IF REINER'S NOT AN OPTION...
...CAN I GET OUT OF THIS PLACE BY COOPERATING WITH THEM?

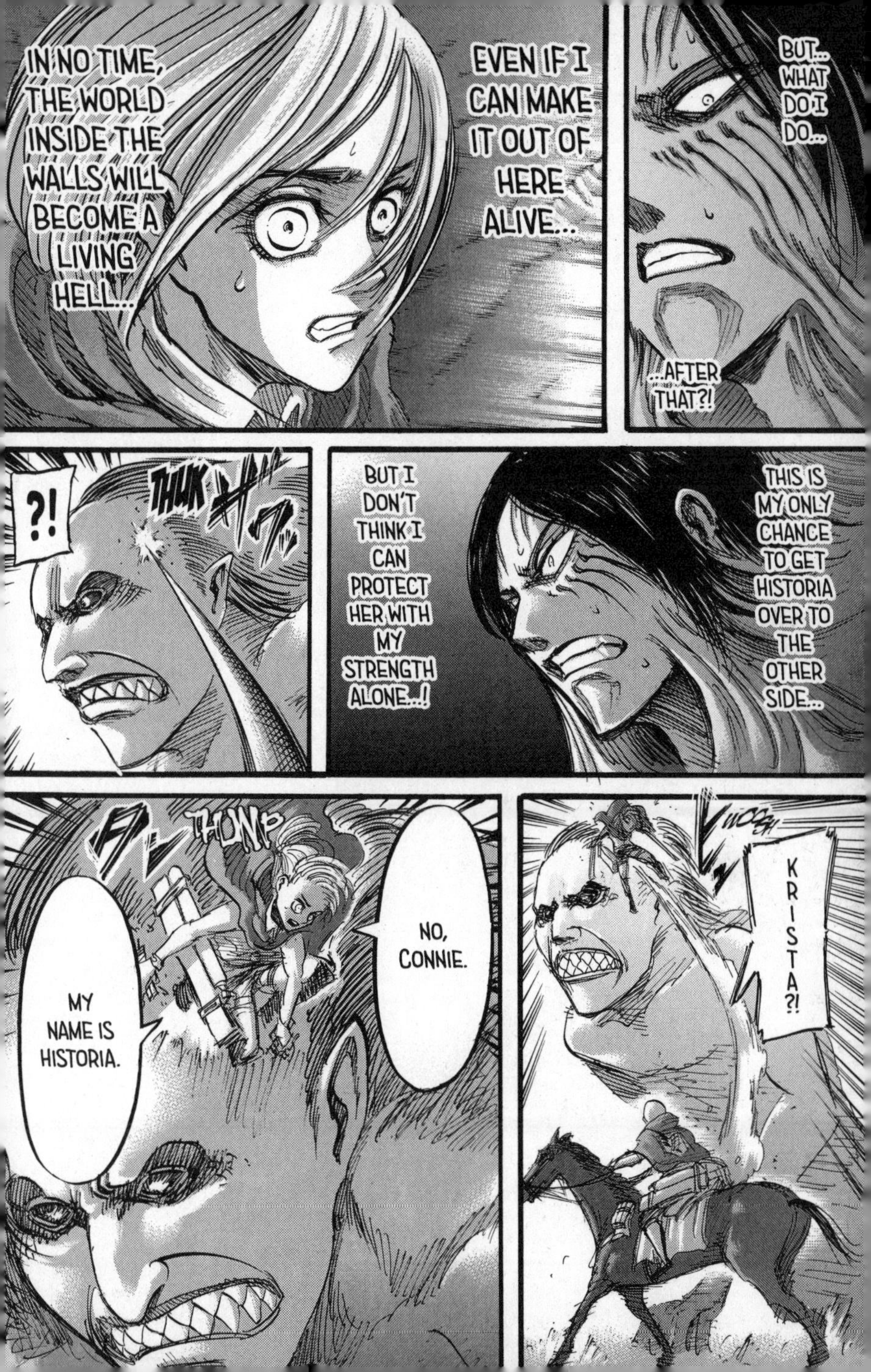
BUT... WHAT DO I DO...
...AFTER THAT?!
EVEN IF I CAN MAKE IT OUT OF HERE ALIVE...
IN NO TIME, THE WORLD INSIDE THE WALLS WILL BECOME A LIVING HELL...
THIS IS MY ONLY CHANCE TO GET HISTORIA OVER TO THE OTHER SIDE...
BUT I DON'T THINK I CAN PROTECT HER WITH MY STRENGTH ALONE...!
THUK
?!
WHOOSH
KRISTA?!
THUMP
NO, CONNIE.
MY NAME IS HISTORIA.

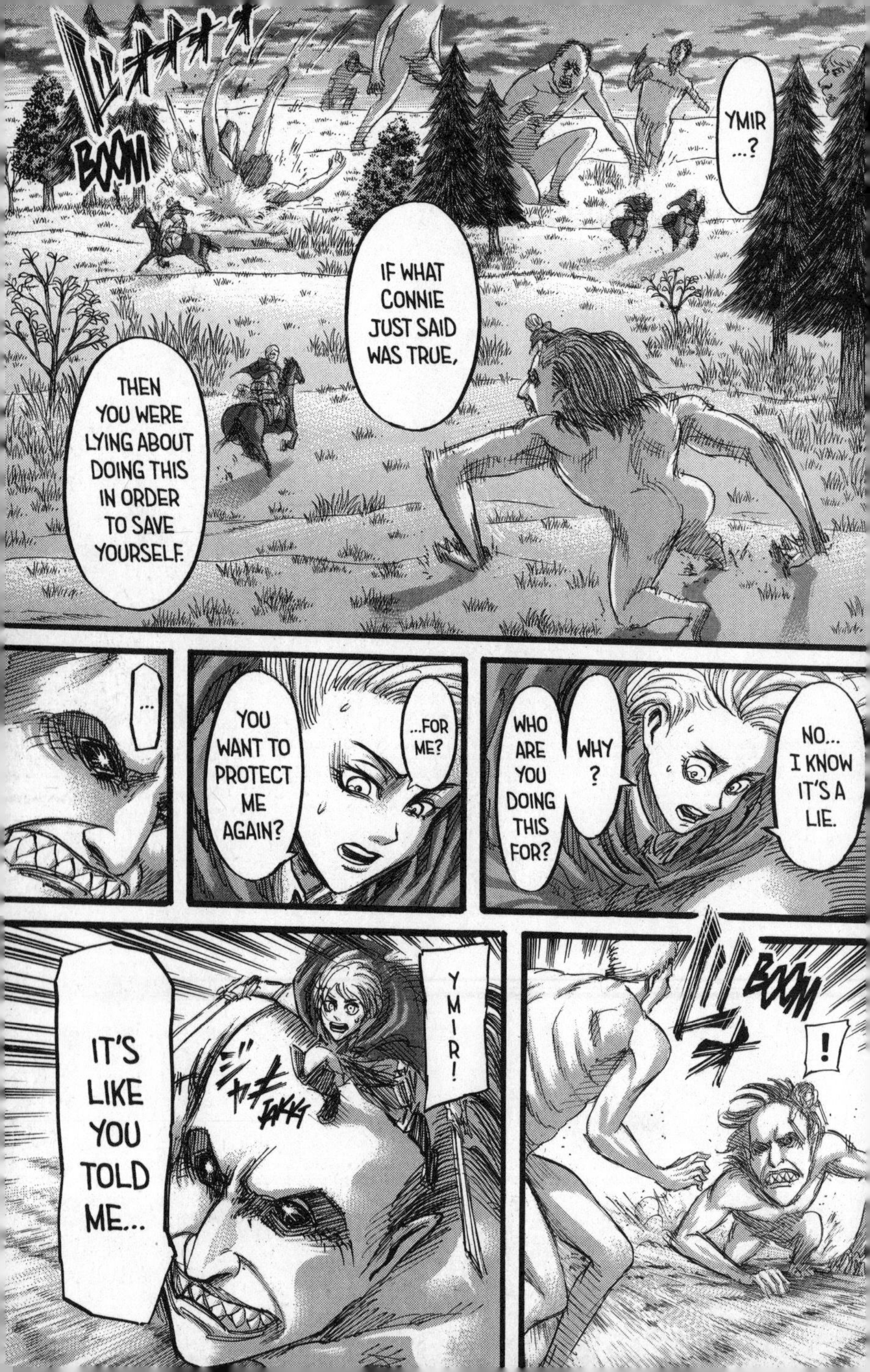
BOOM
YMIR ...?
IF WHAT CONNIE JUST SAID WAS TRUE,
THEN YOU WERE LYING ABOUT DOING THIS IN ORDER TO SAVE YOURSELF.
NO... I KNOW IT'S A LIE.
WHY ?
WHO ARE YOU DOING THIS FOR?
...FOR ME?
YOU WANT TO PROTECT ME AGAIN?
...
BOOM
!
YMIR!
IT'S LIKE YOU TOLD ME...

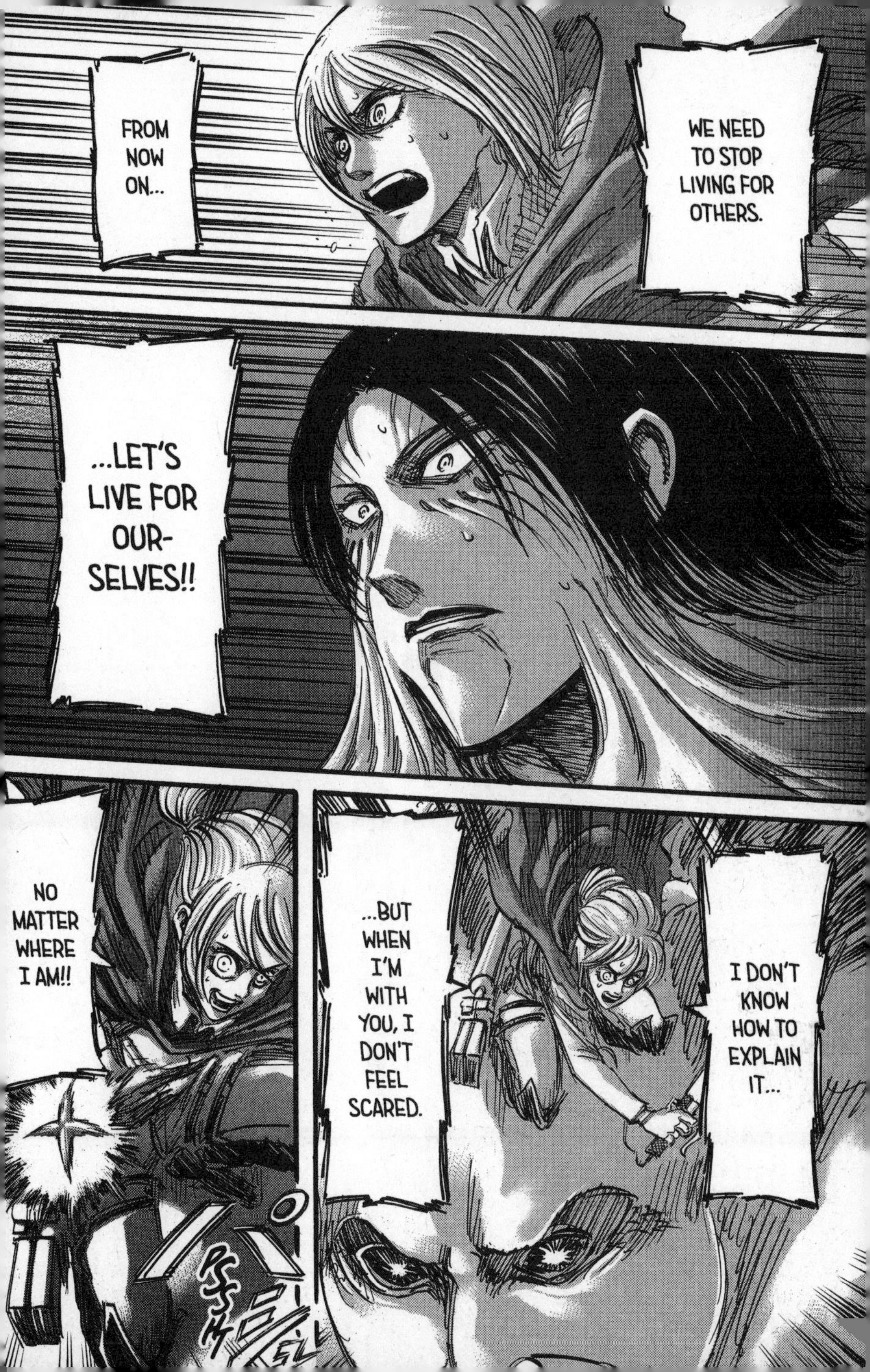
WE NEED TO STOP LIVING FOR OTHERS.
FROM NOW ON...
...LET'S LIVE FOR OUR-SELVES!!
I DON'T KNOW HOW TO EXPLAIN IT...
...BUT WHEN I'M WITH YOU, I DON'T FEEL SCARED.
NO MATTER WHERE I AM!!

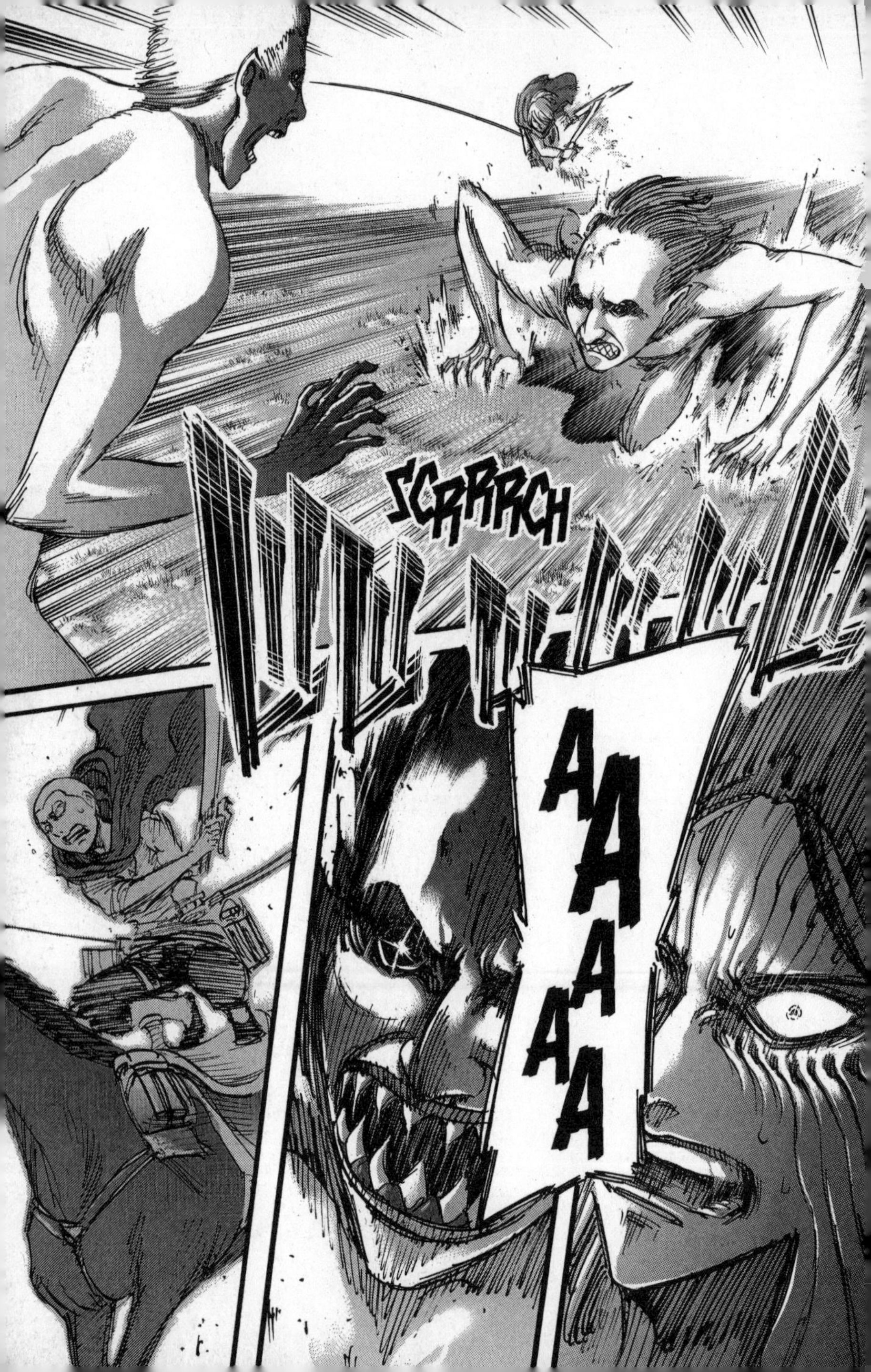
SCRRRCH
AAAAAA

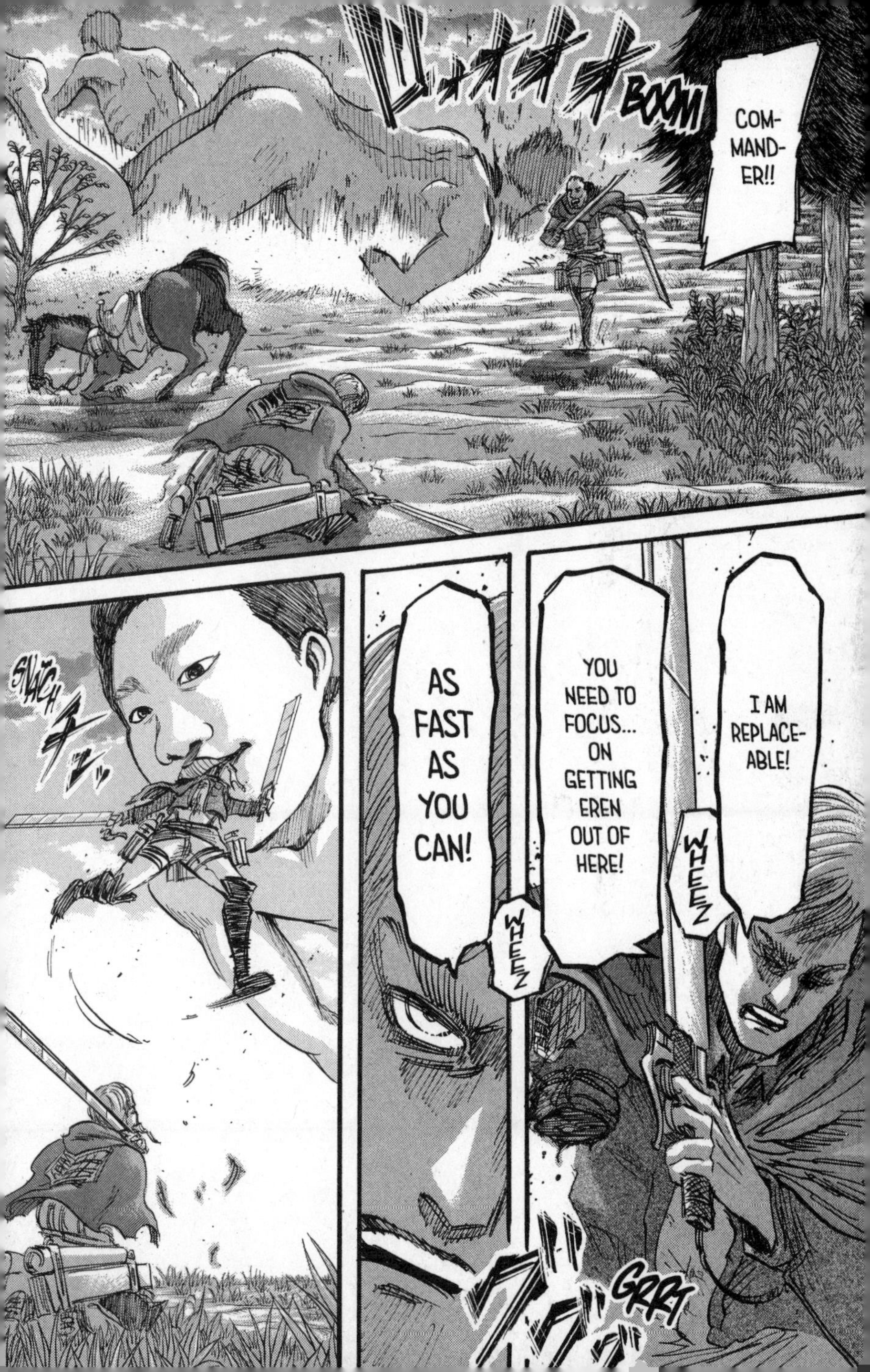
COM-MAND-ER!!
BOOM
I AM REPLACE-ABLE!
WHEEZ
YOU NEED TO FOCUS... ON GETTING EREN OUT OF HERE!
WHEEZ
GRRR
AS FAST AS YOU CAN!
SNATCH

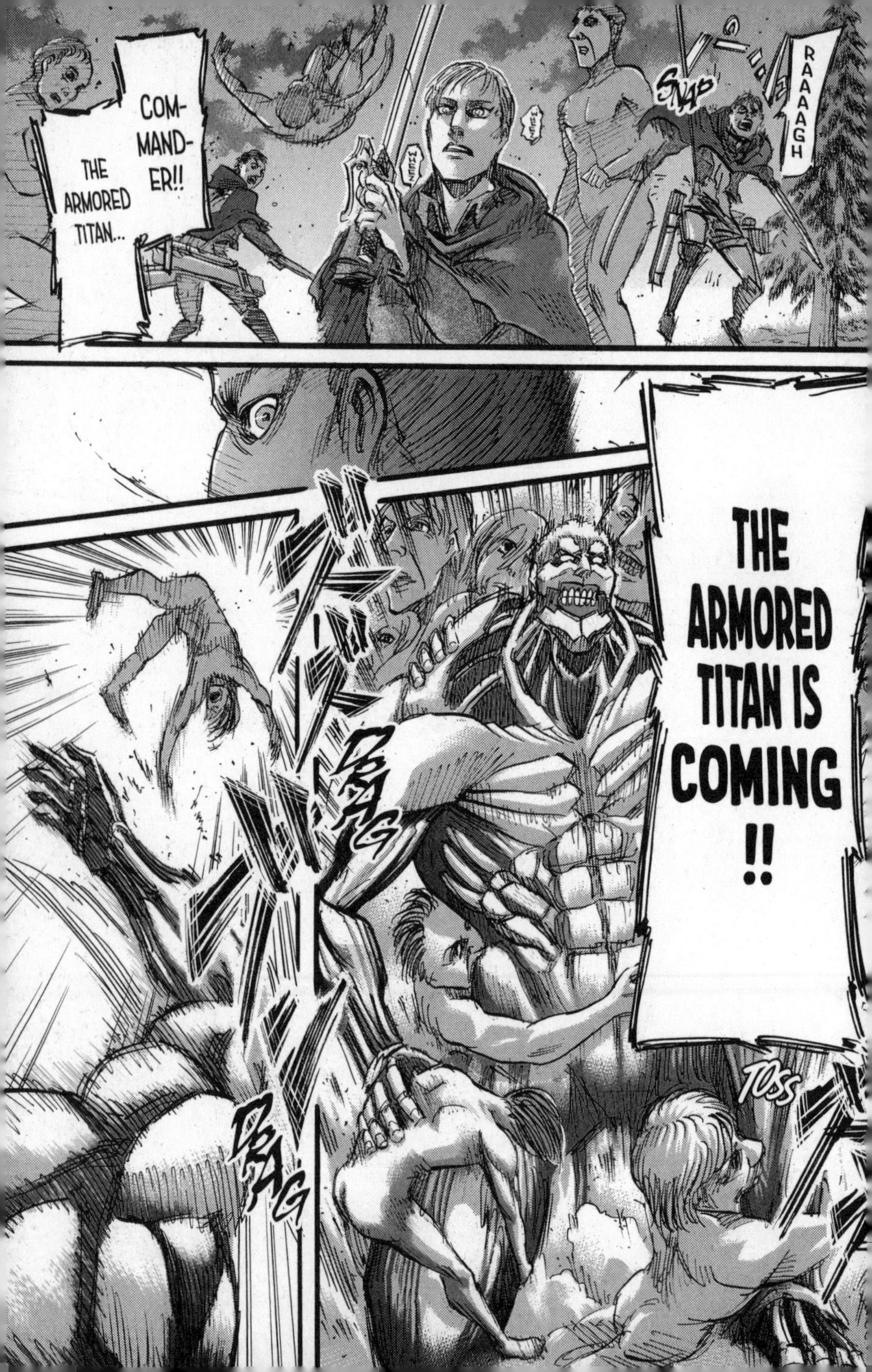
RAAAAGH
SNAP
WHEEZ
WHEEZ
COM-MANDER!!
THE ARMORED TITAN...
THE ARMORED TITAN IS COMING!!
DRAG
TOSS
DRAG

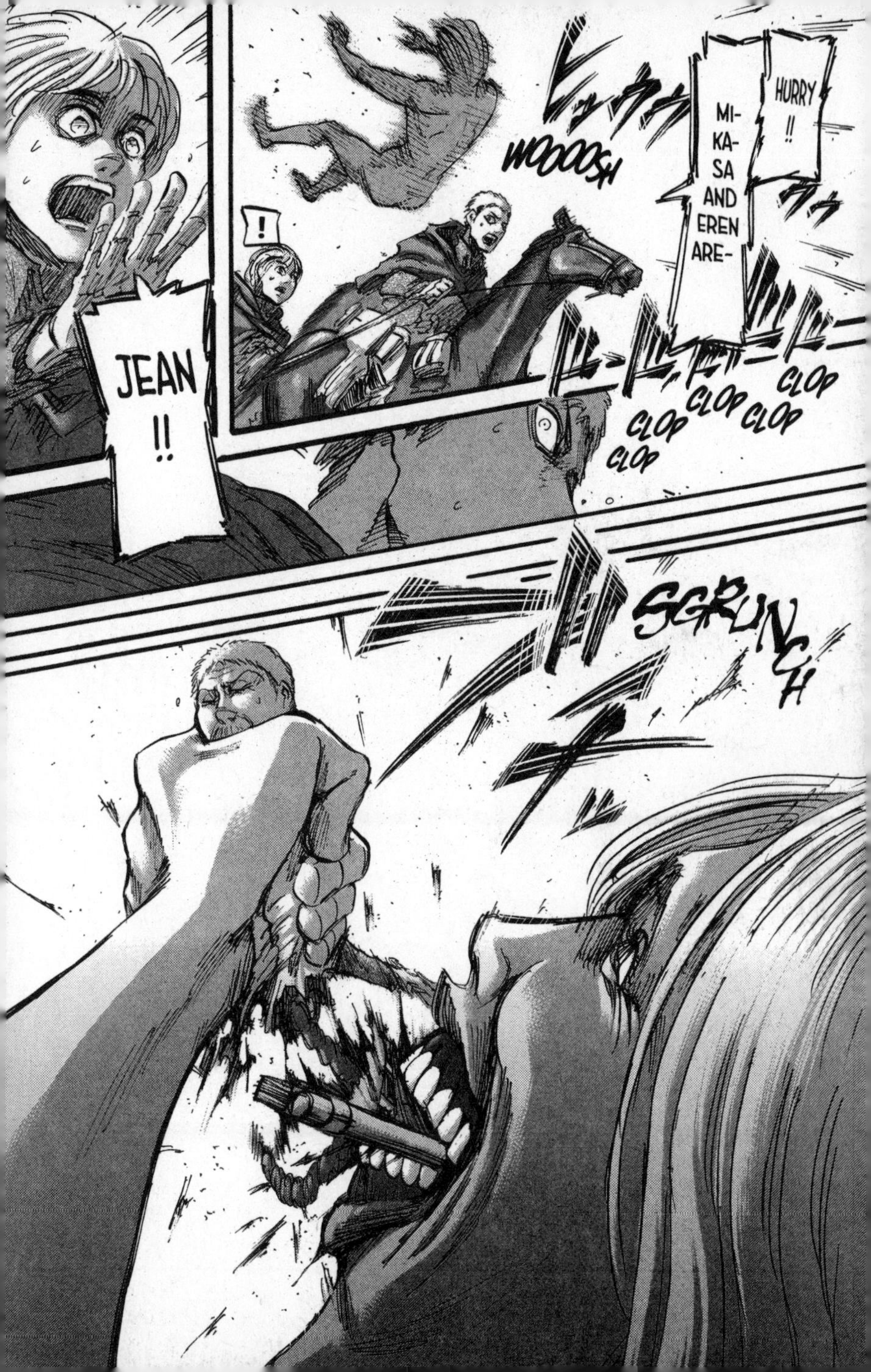
HURRY!!
MI-KA-SA AND EREN ARE-
WOOOOSH
!
CLOP CLOP CLOP CLOP CLOP CLOP
JEAN!!
SCRUNCH

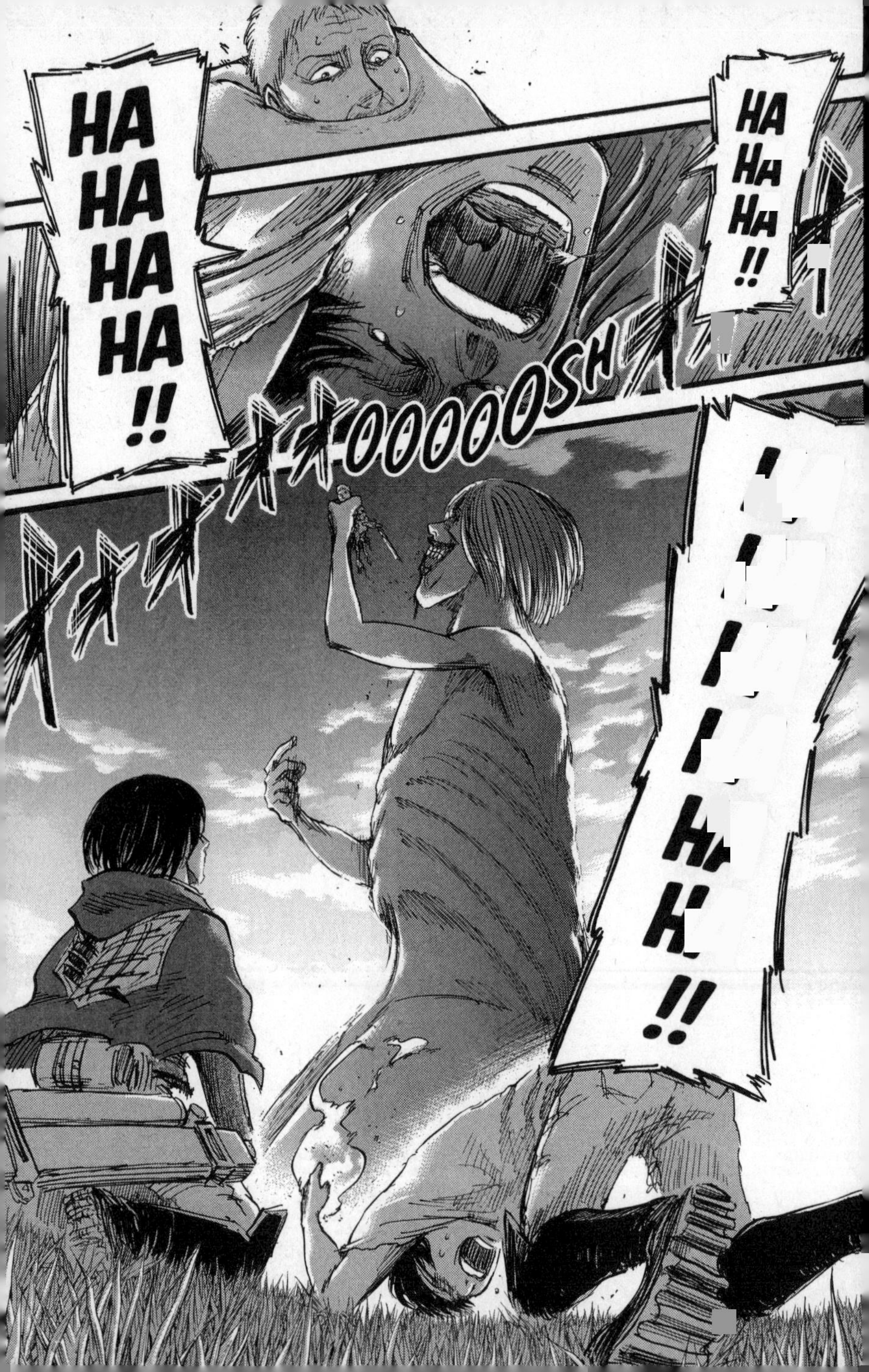
HA HA HA !!
OOOOOOSH
HA HA HA HA !!

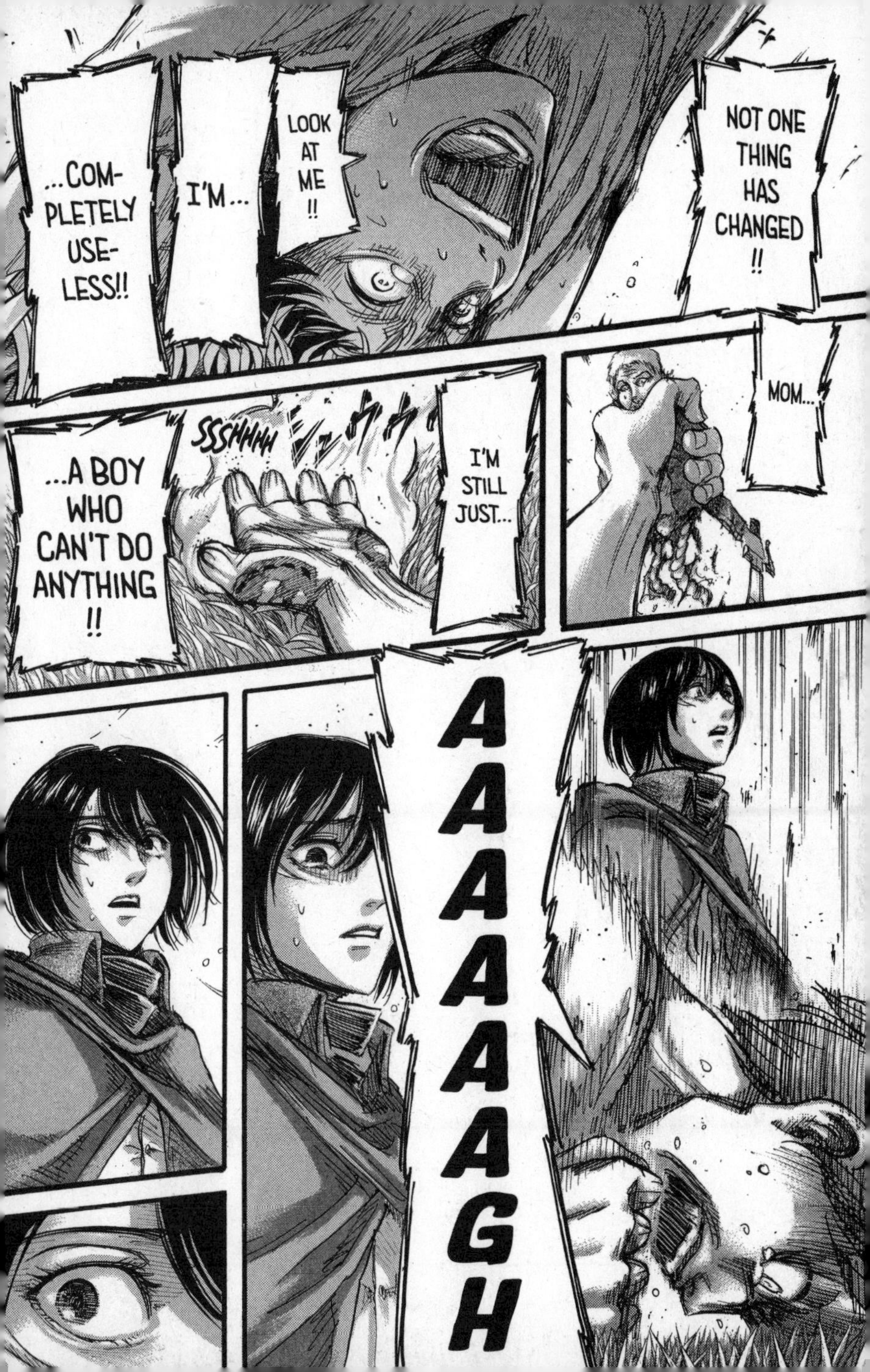
NOT ONE THING HAS CHANGED !!
LOOK AT ME !!
I'M...
...COMPLETELY USELESS!!
MOM...
I'M STILL JUST...
SSSHHHH
...A BOY WHO CAN'T DO ANYTHING !!
AAAAAAGH

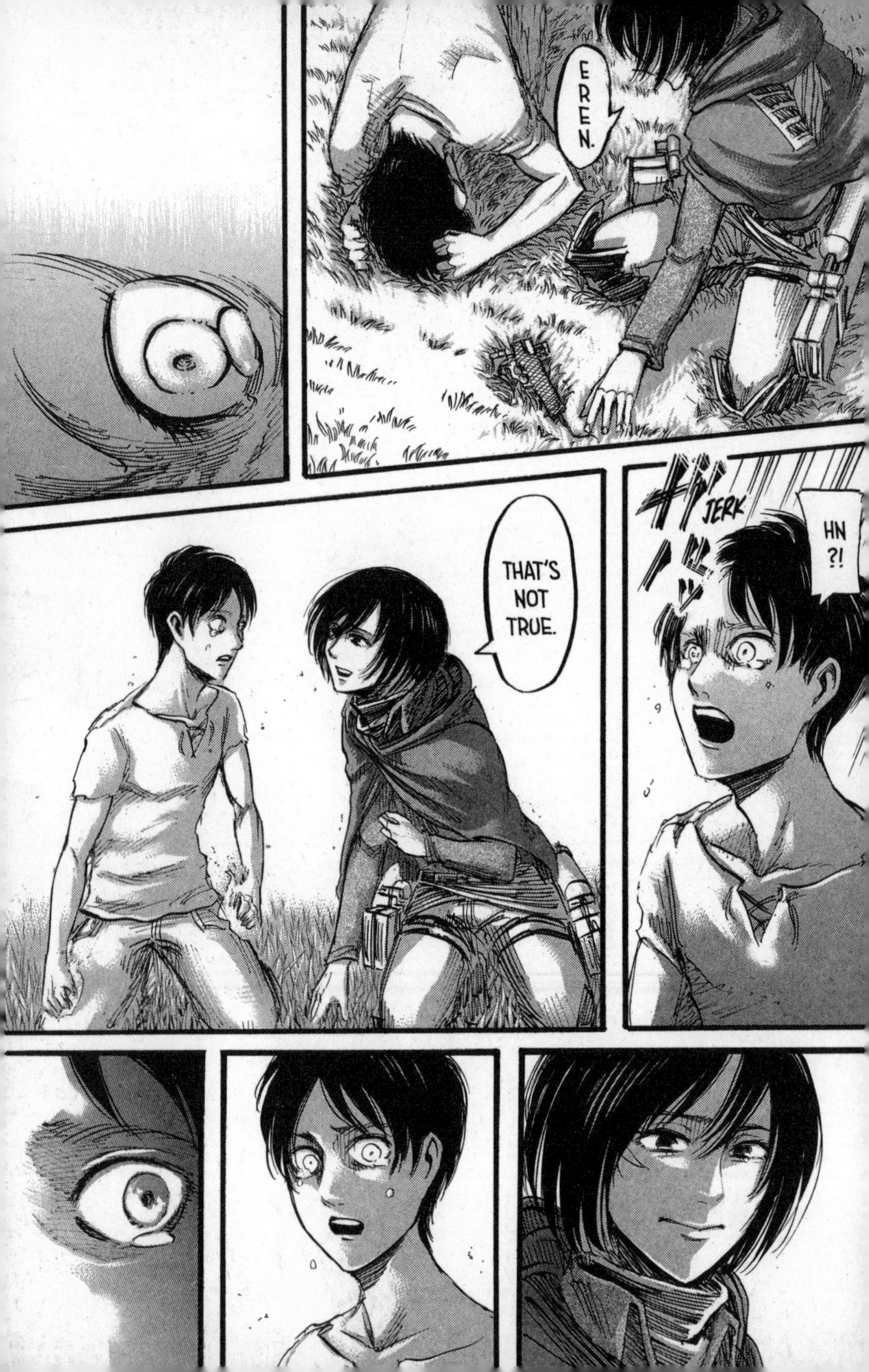
EREN.
HN ?!
JERK
THAT'S NOT TRUE.

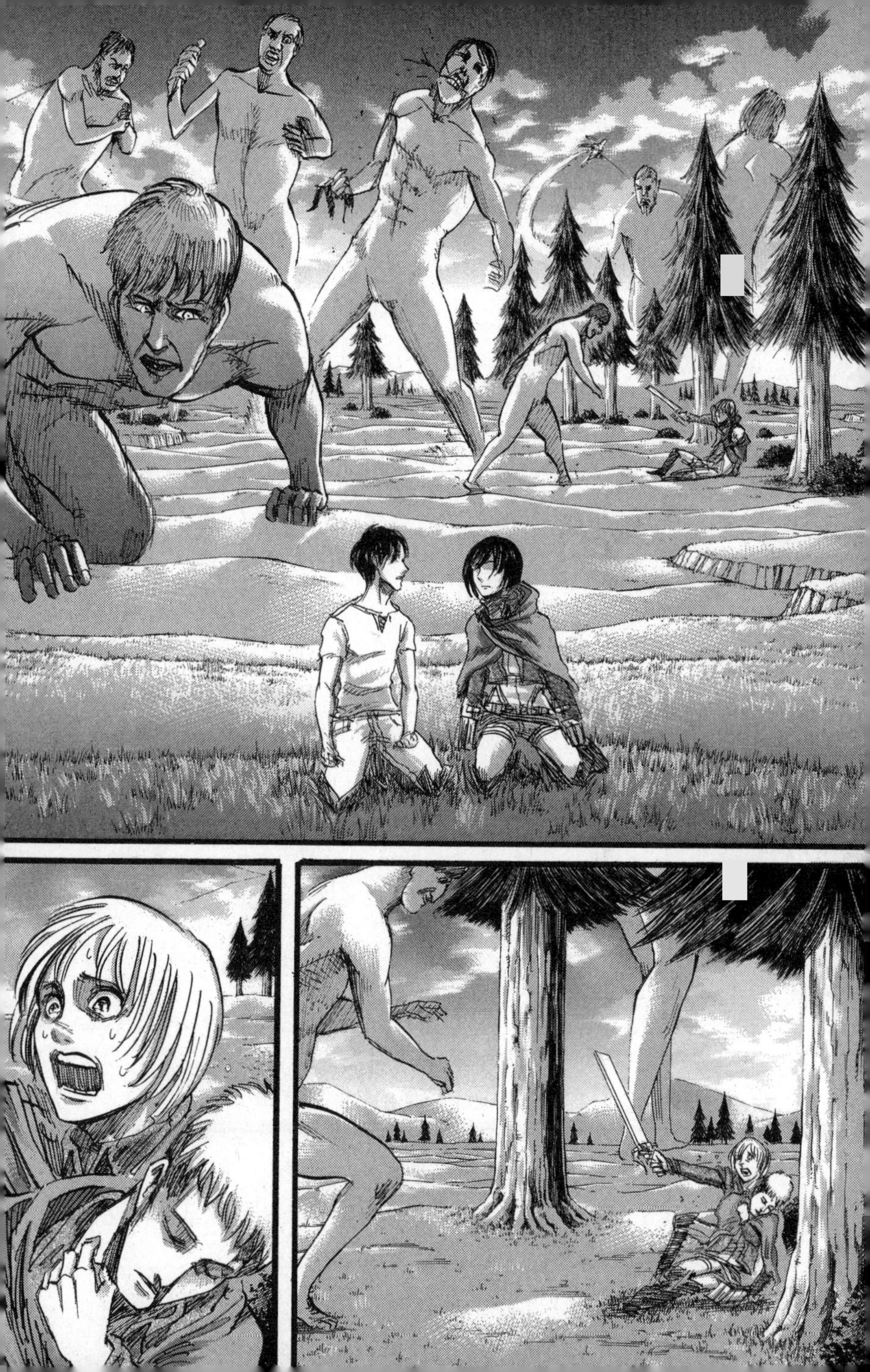

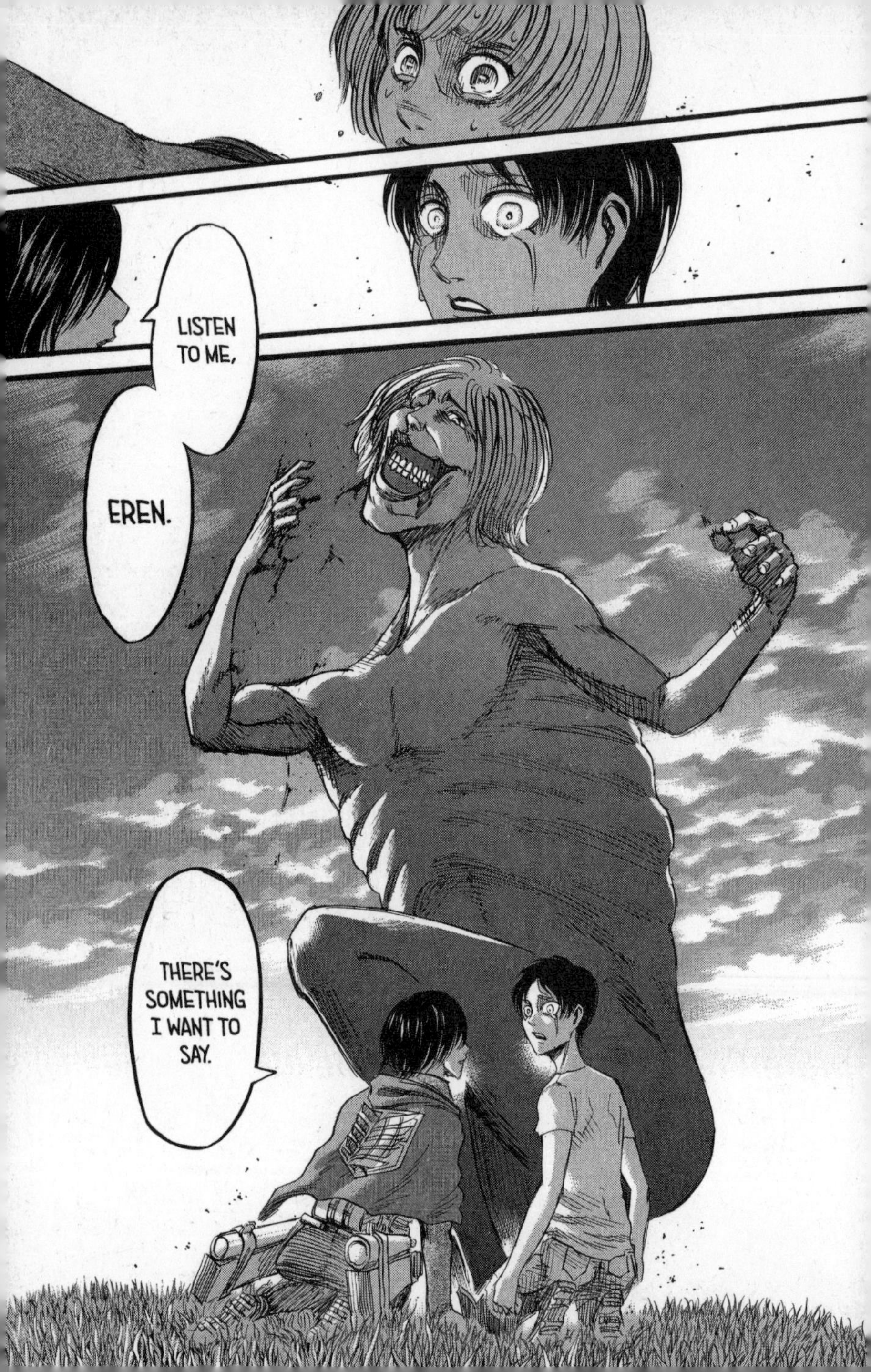
LISTEN TO ME,
EREN.
THERE'S SOMETHING I WANT TO SAY.

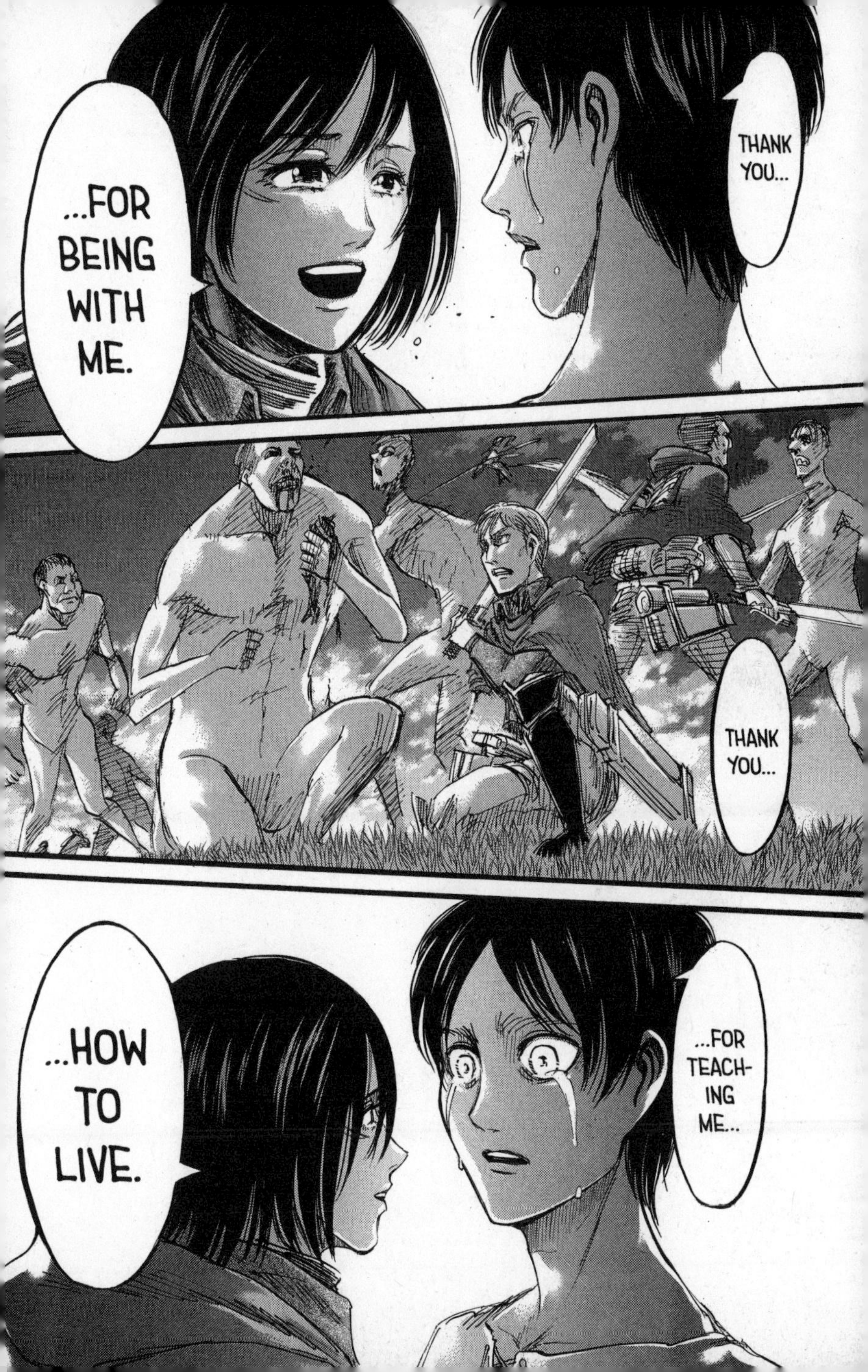
THANK YOU...
...FOR BEING WITH ME.
THANK YOU...
...FOR TEACHING-ING ME...
...HOW TO LIVE.

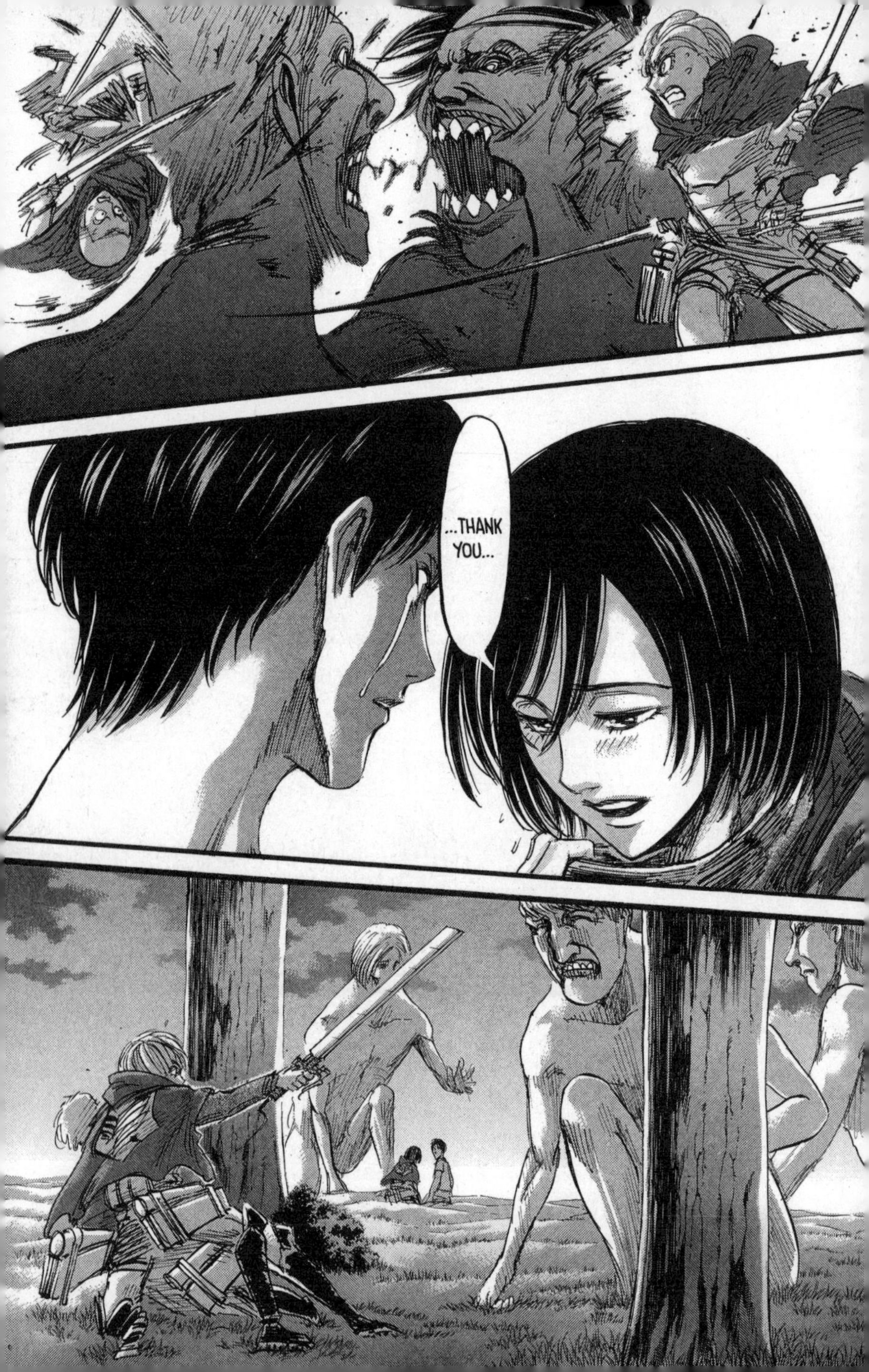
...THANK YOU...

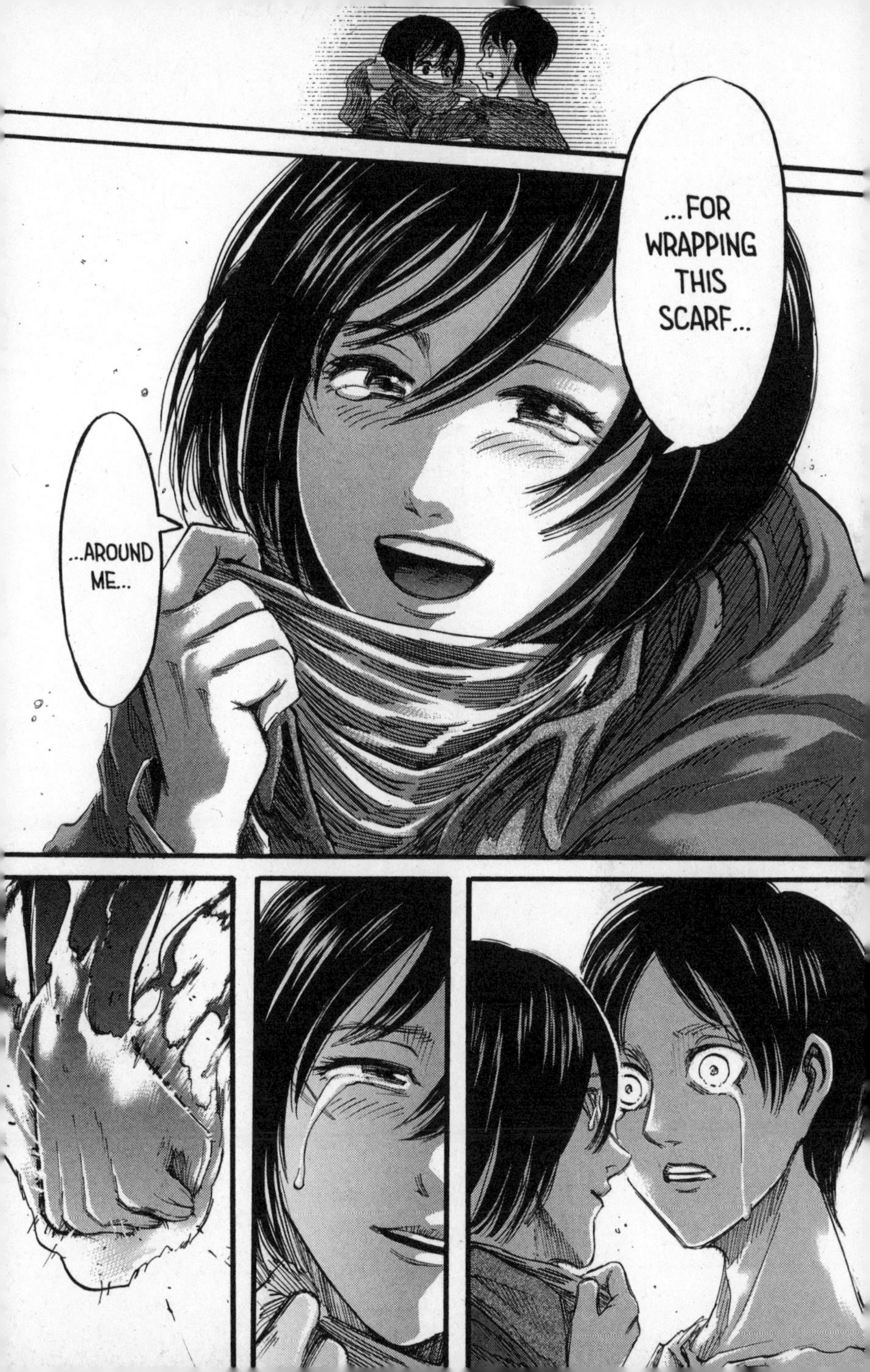
...FOR WRAPPING THIS SCARF...
...AROUND ME...

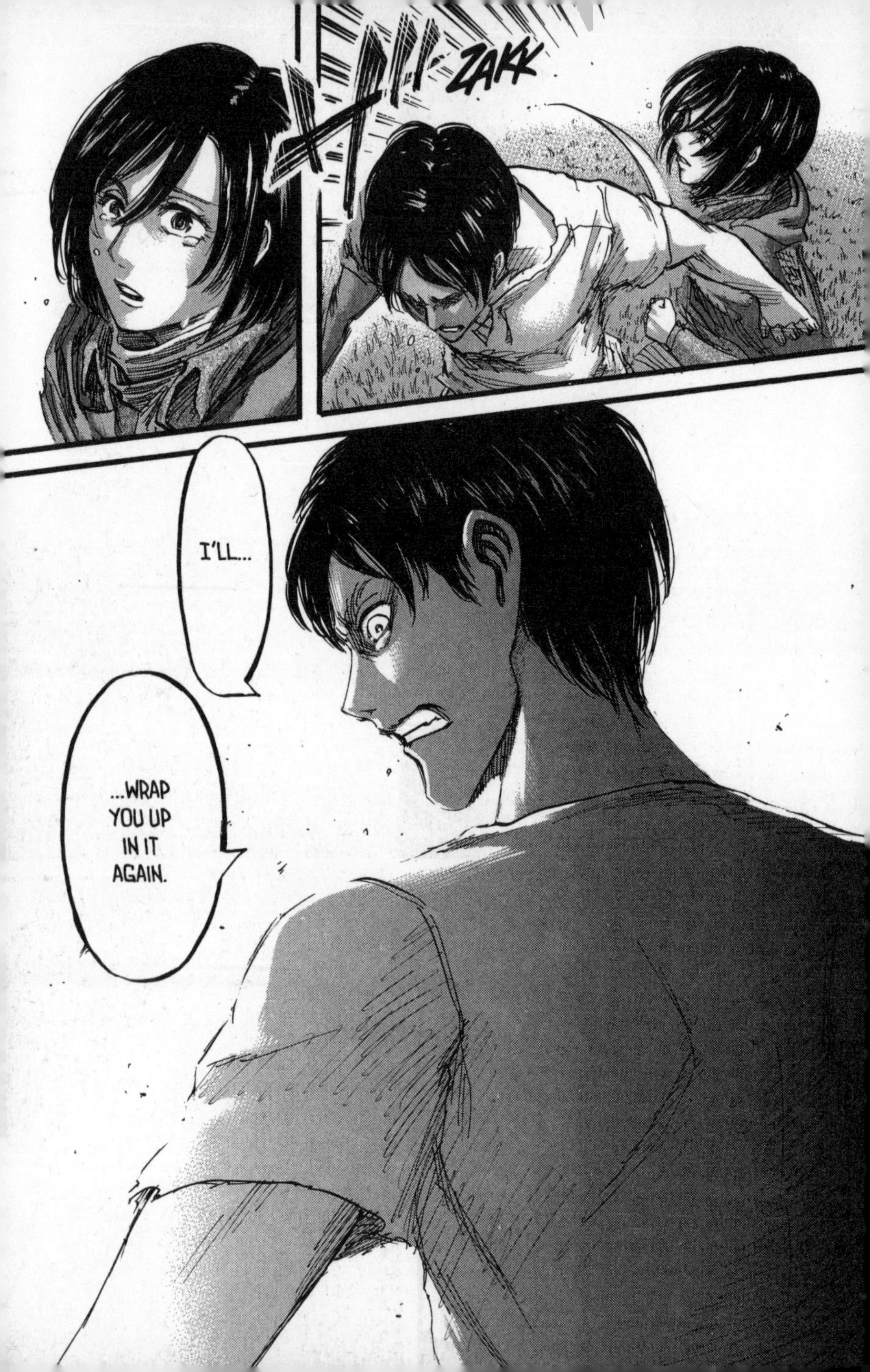
ZAKK
I'LL...
...WRAP YOU UP IN IT AGAIN.

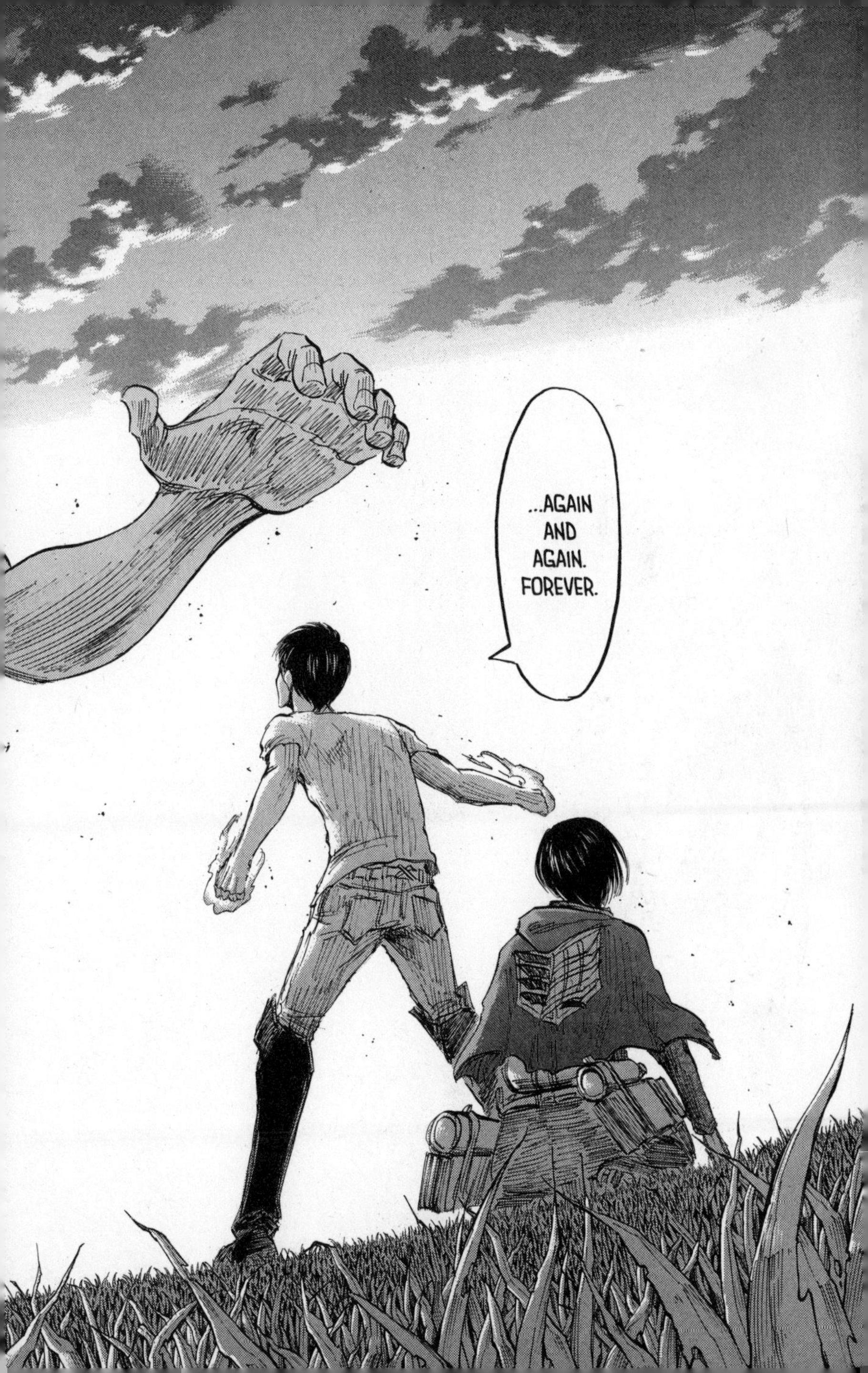
...AGAIN AND AGAIN. FOREVER.

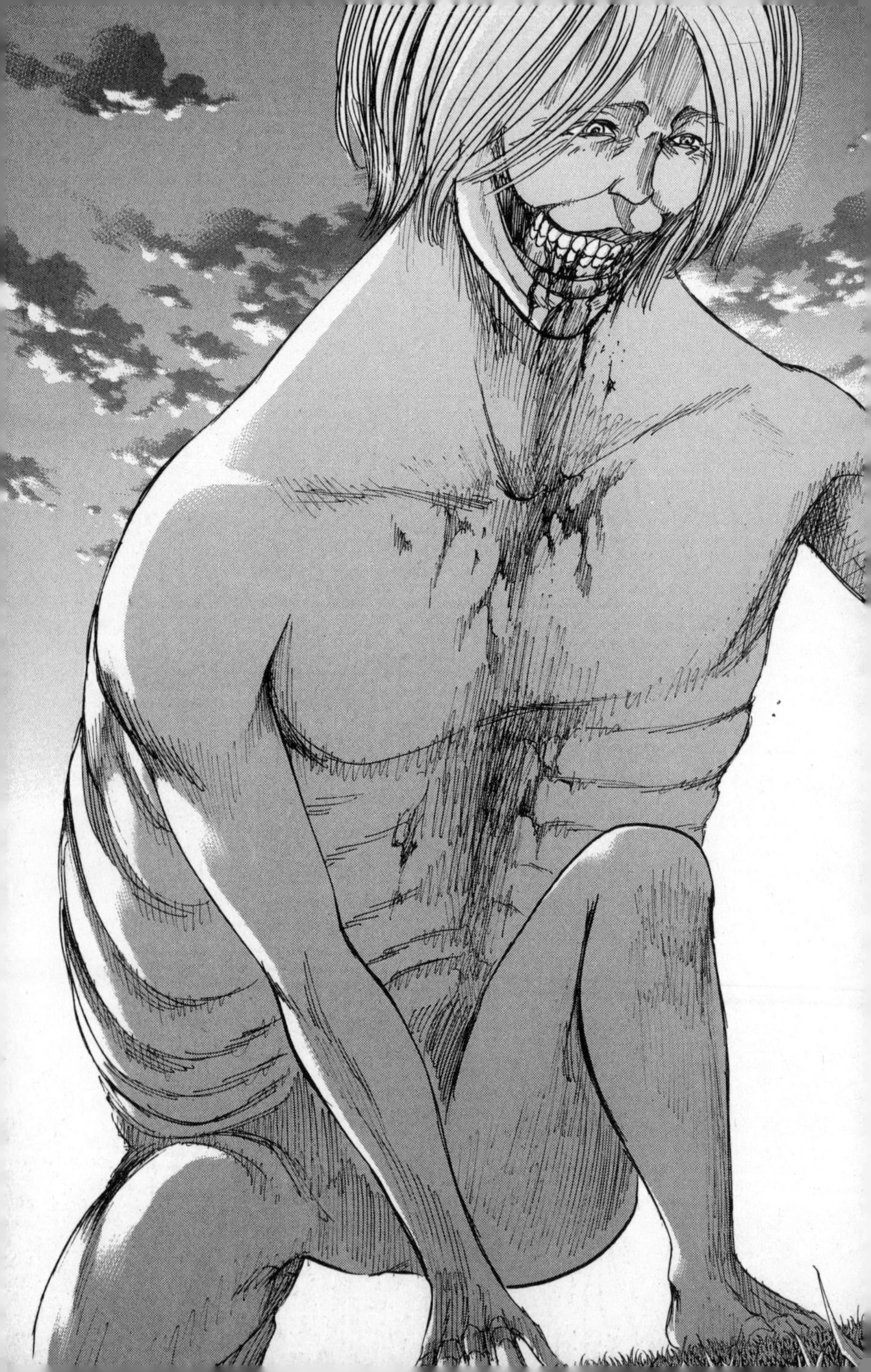

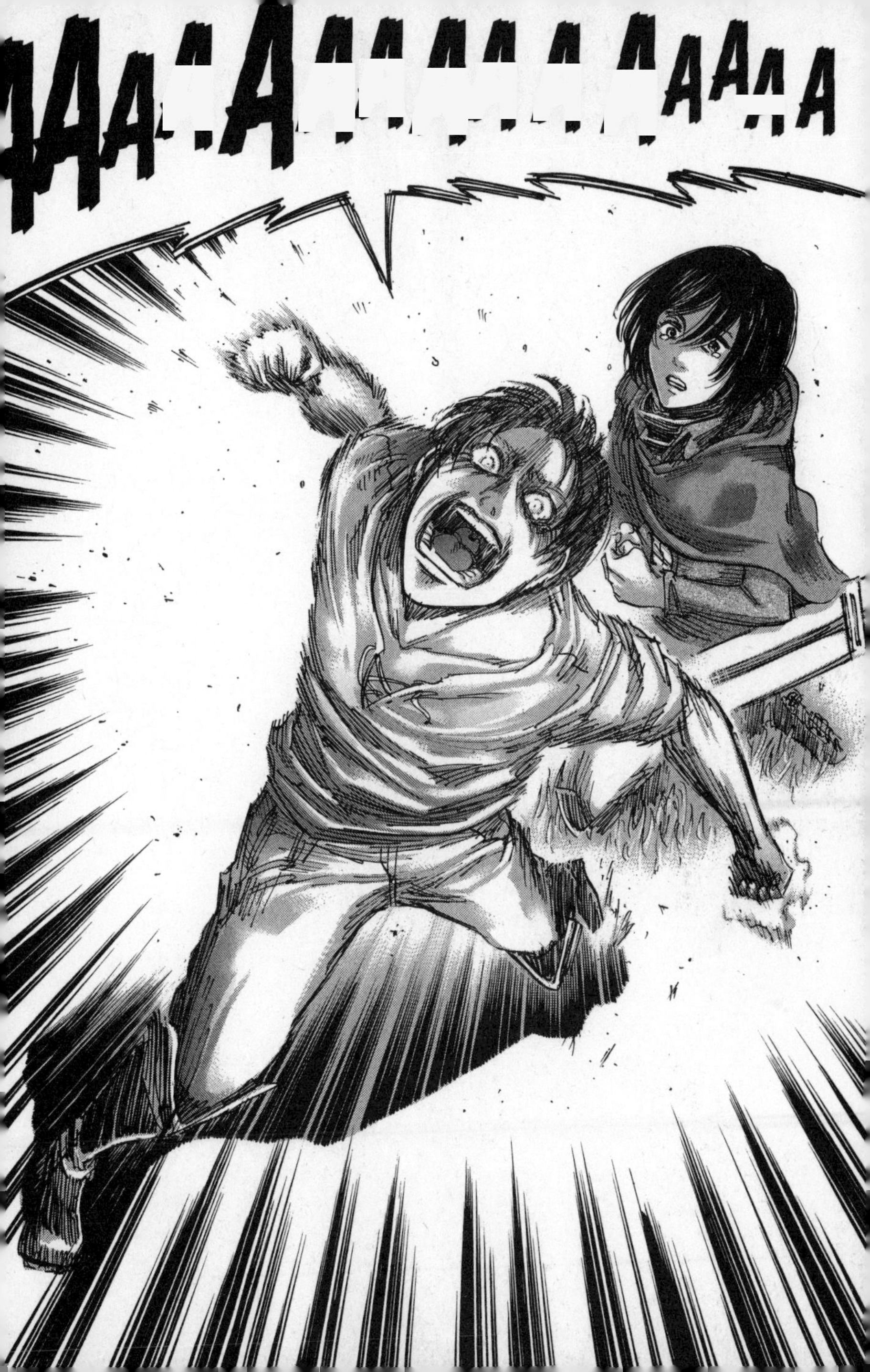
AAAAAAAAAAAA

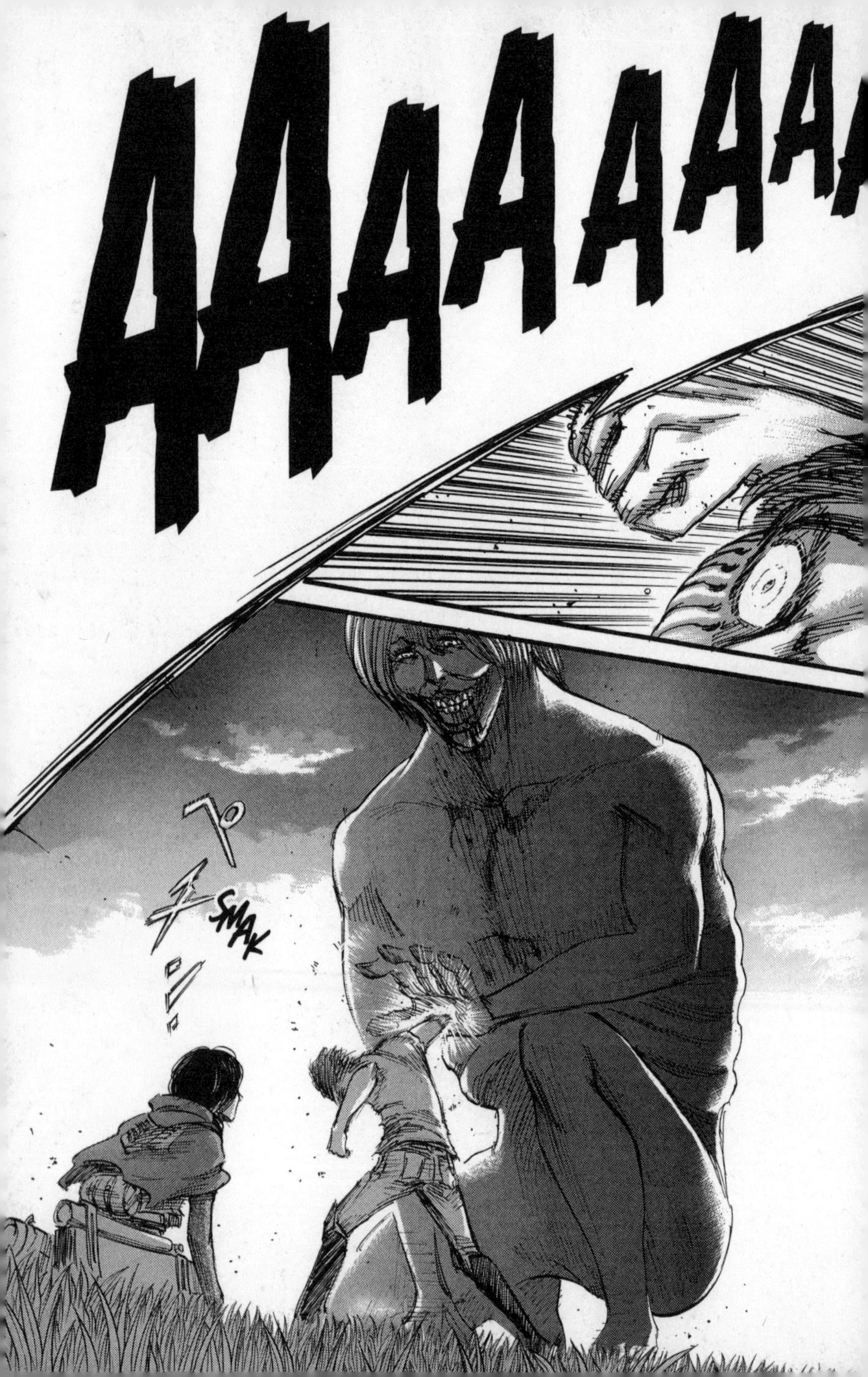
AAAAAAA
SMAK

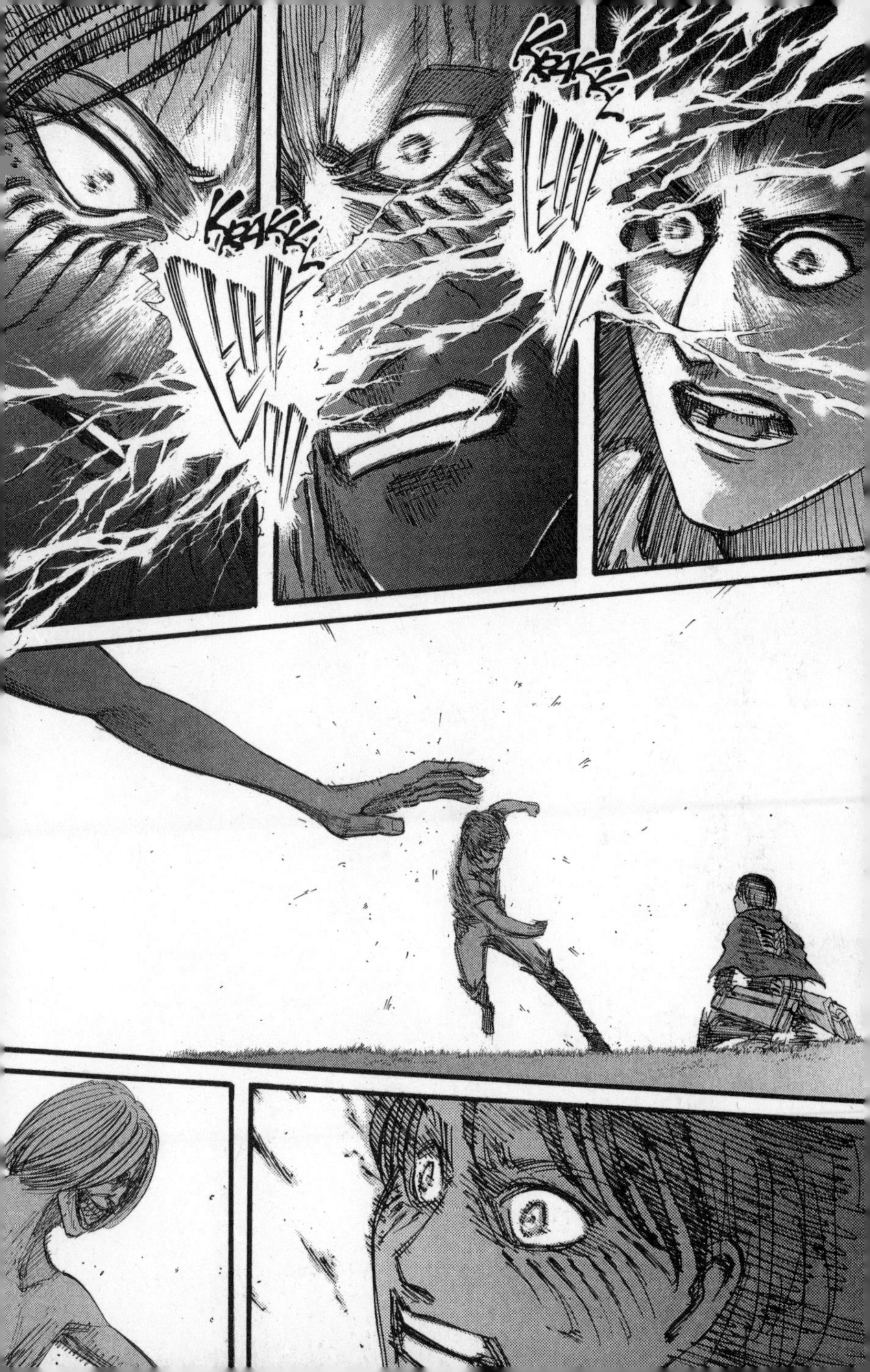
KRAKKL
KRAKKL

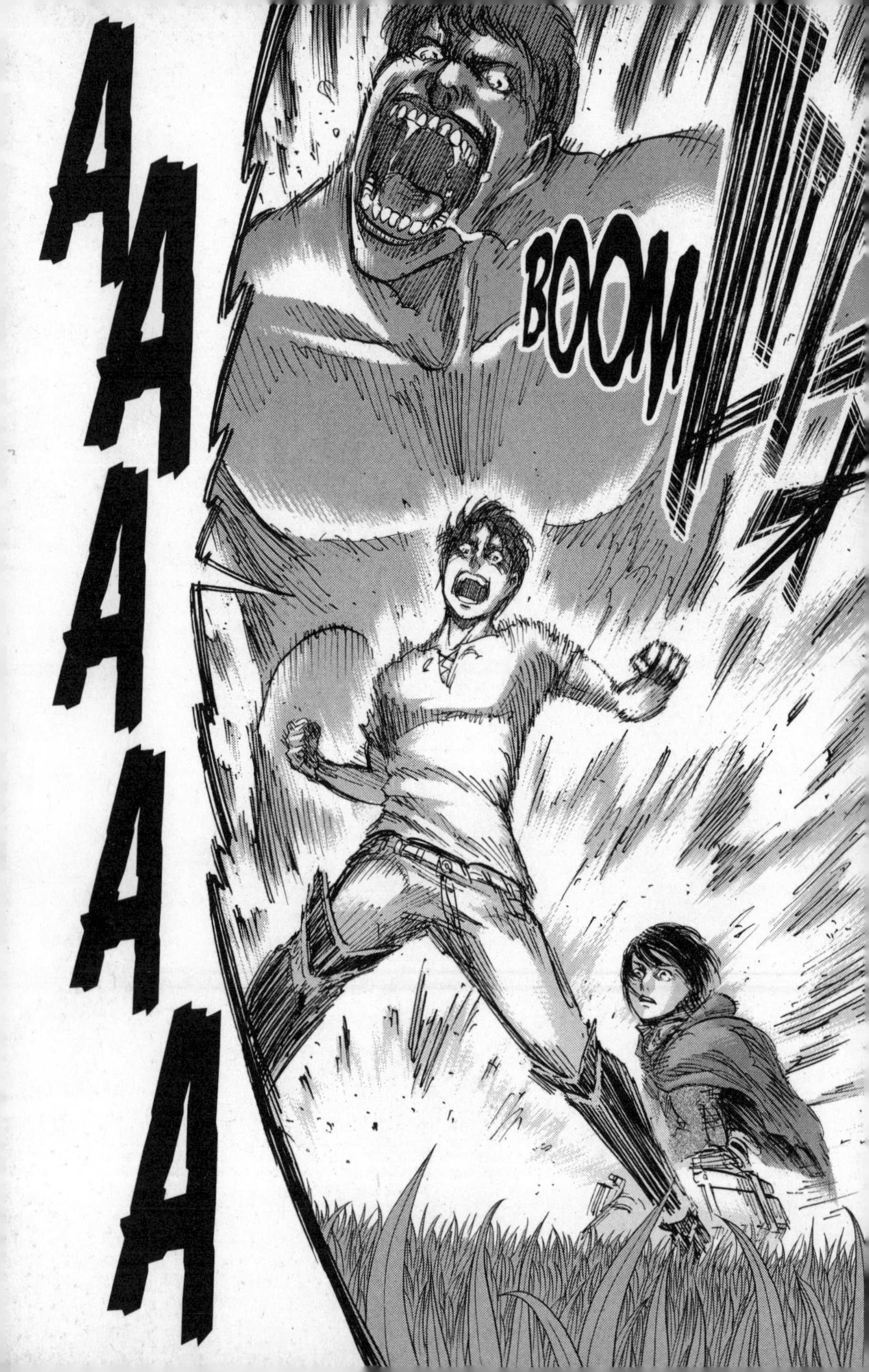
BOOM
AAAAAAA

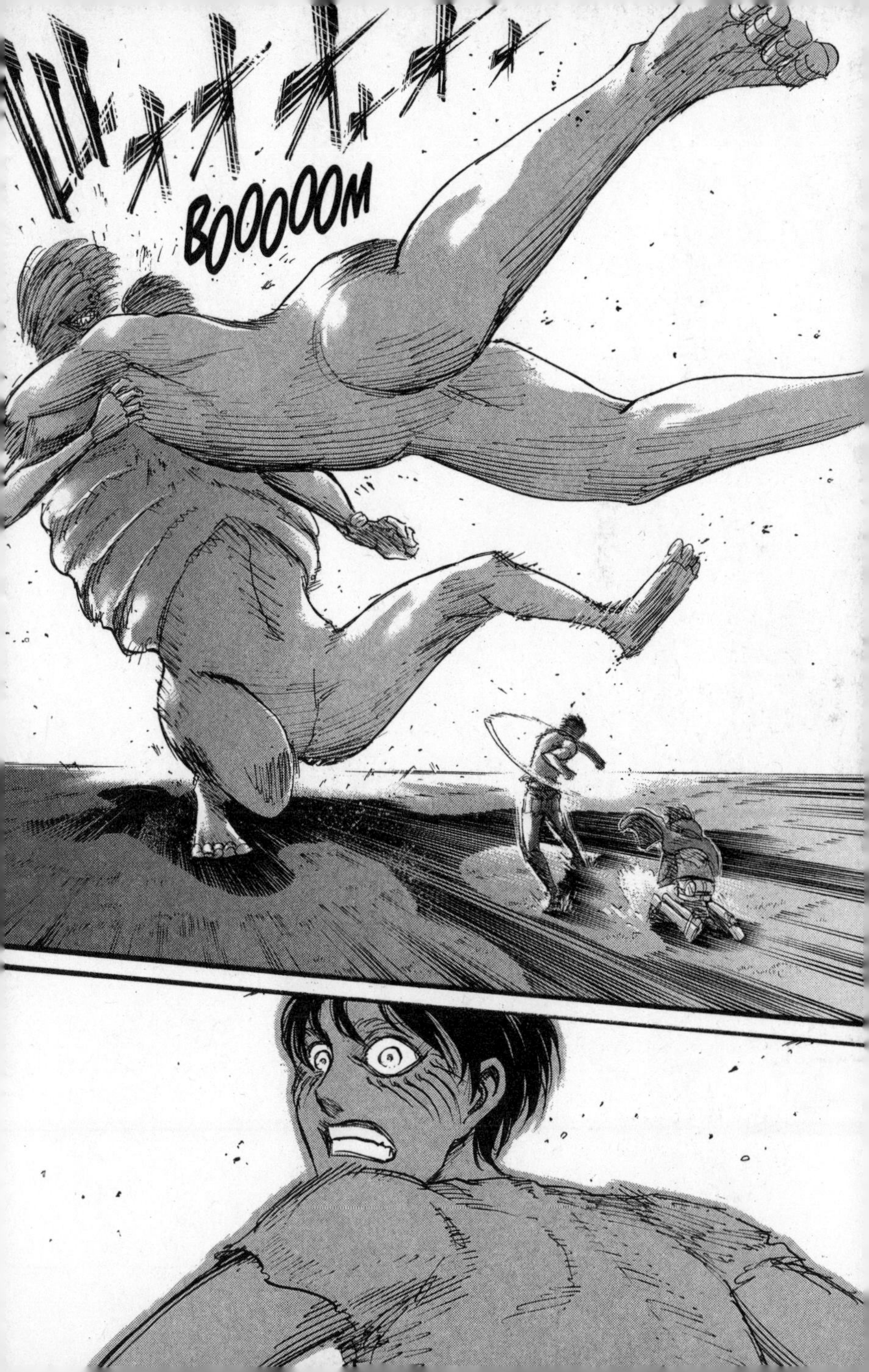
BOOOOOM

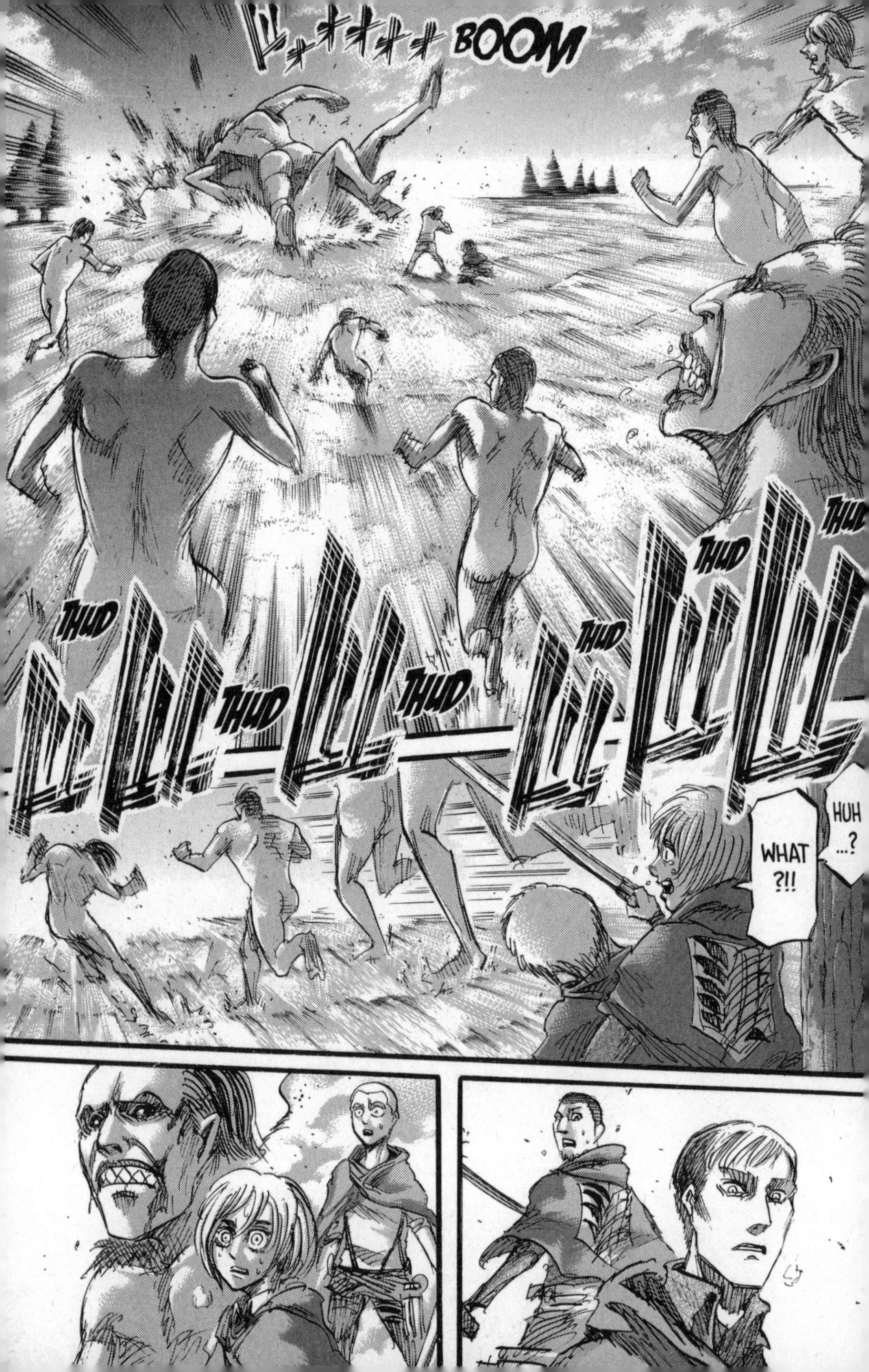
BOOM
THUD
THUD
THUD
THUD
THUD
THUD
HUH ...?
WHAT ?!!

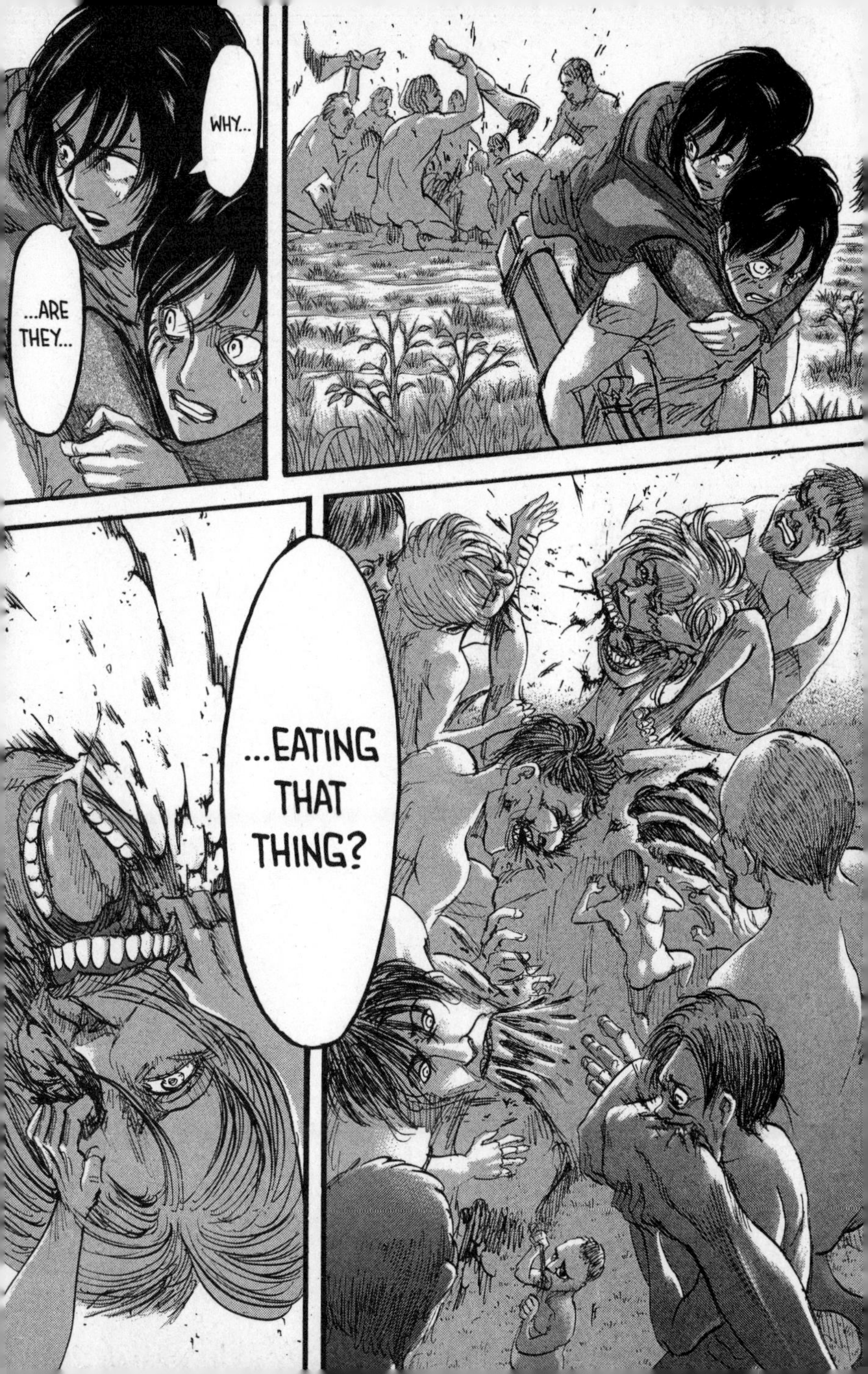
WHY...
...ARE THEY...
...EATING THAT THING?

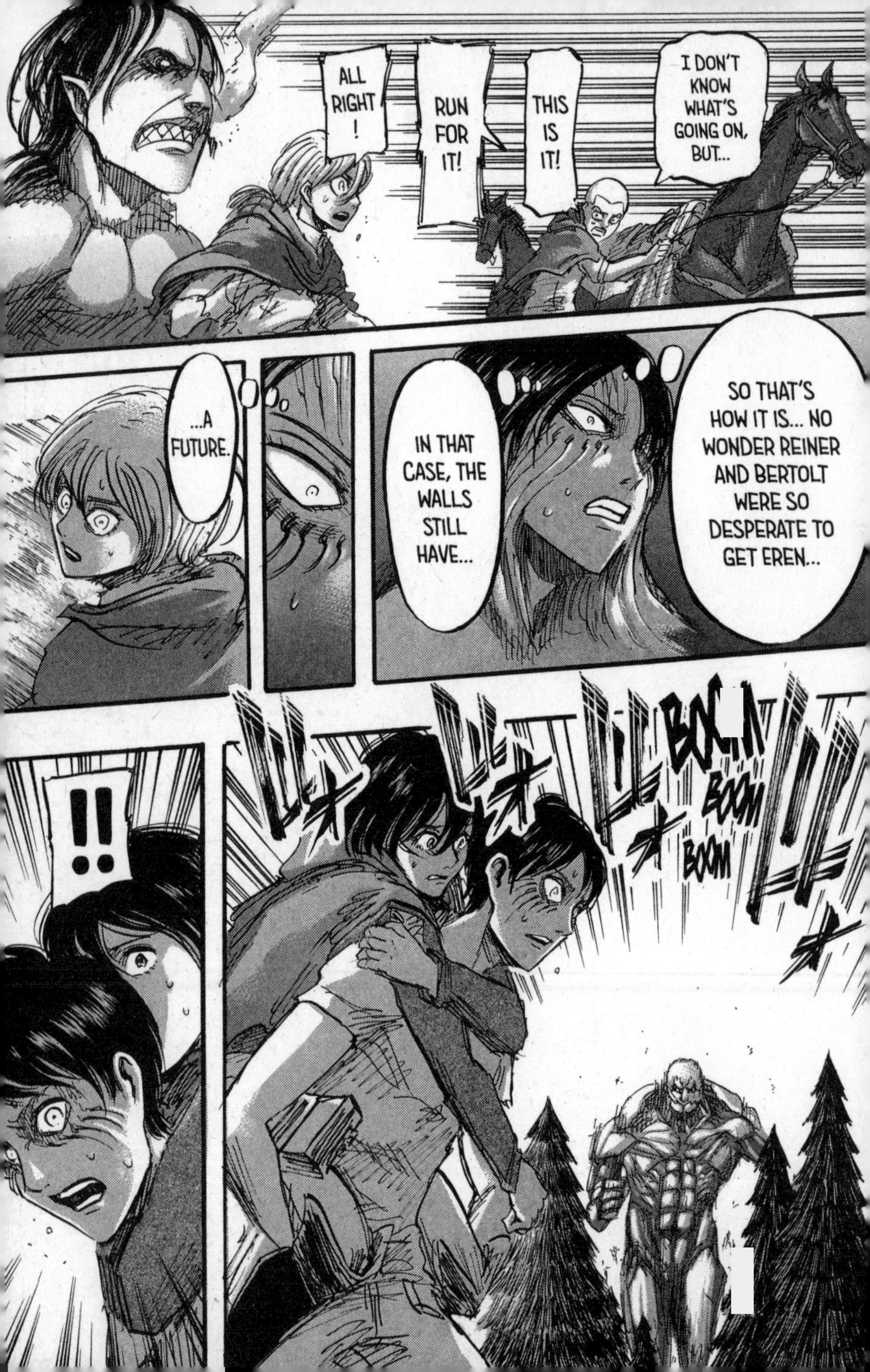
I DON'T KNOW WHAT'S GOING ON, BUT...
THIS IS IT!
RUN FOR IT!
ALL RIGHT!
SO THAT'S HOW IT IS... NO WONDER REINER AND BERTOLT WERE SO DESPERATE TO GET EREN...
IN THAT CASE, THE WALLS STILL HAVE...
...A FUTURE.
BOOM
BOOM
!!

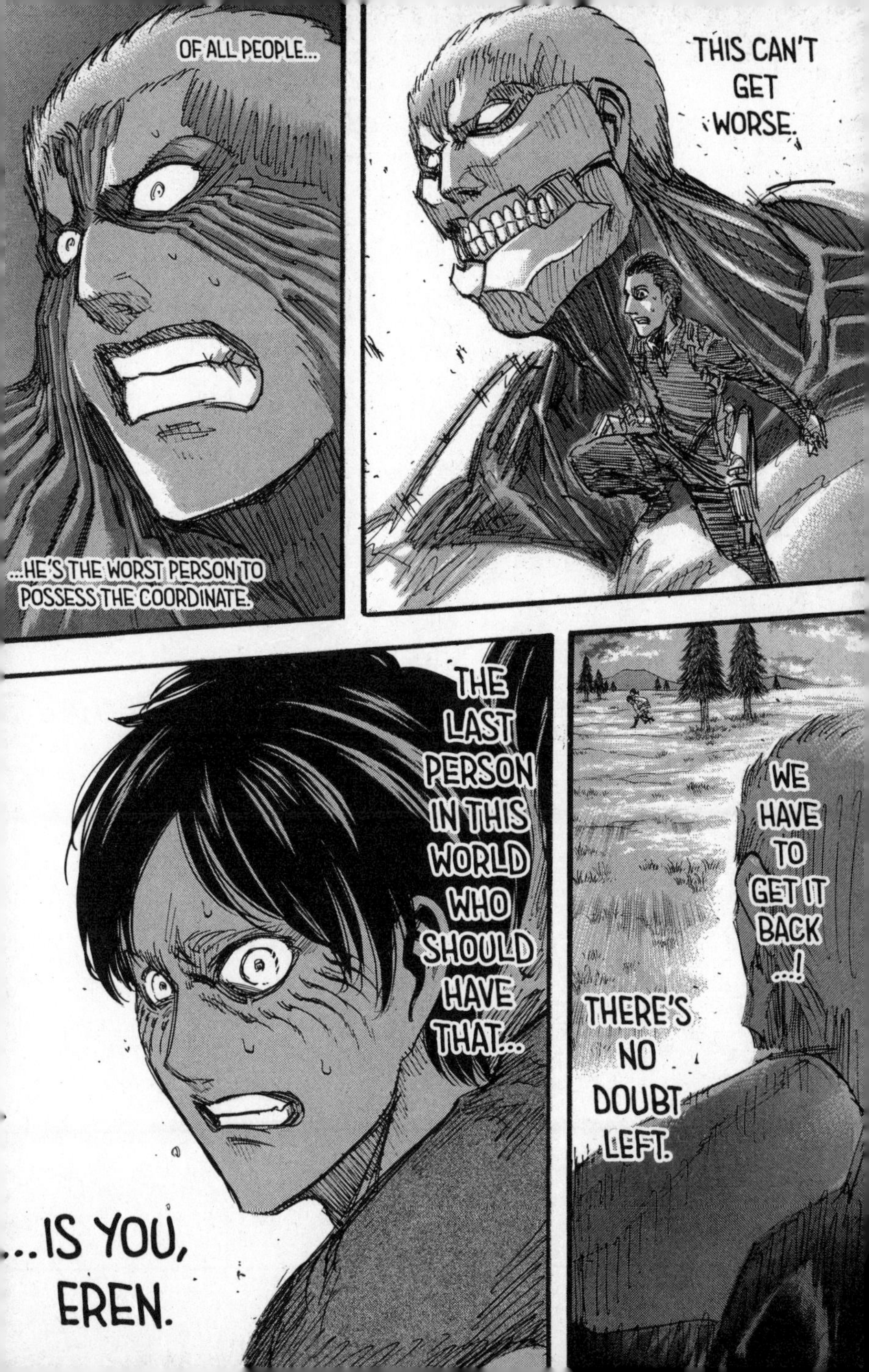
THIS CAN'T GET WORSE.
OF ALL PEOPLE...
...HE'S THE WORST PERSON TO POSSESS THE COORDINATE.
WE HAVE TO GET IT BACK ...!
THERE'S NO DOUBT LEFT.
THE LAST PERSON IN THIS WORLD WHO SHOULD HAVE THAT...
...IS YOU, EREN.

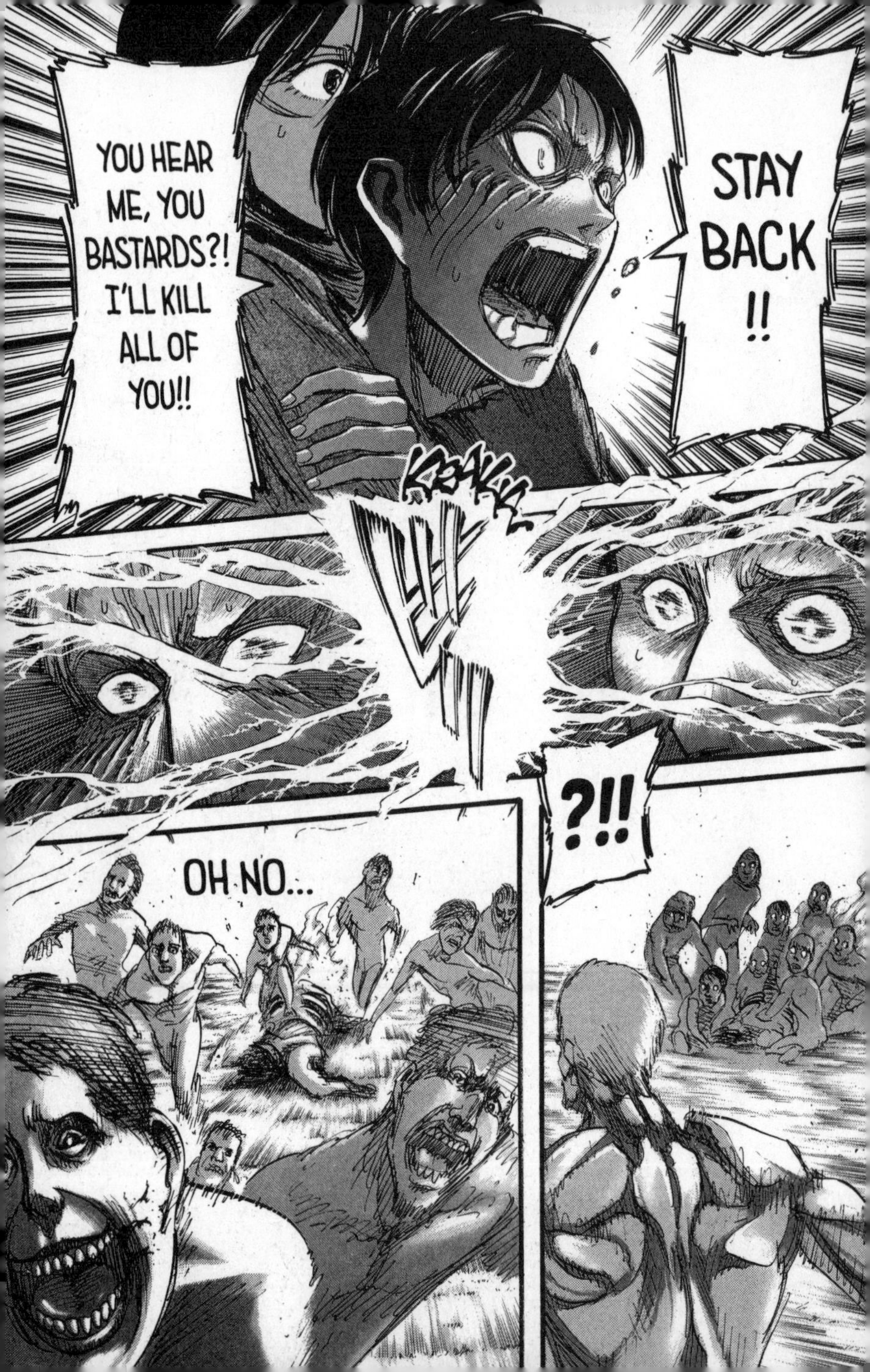
STAY BACK !!
YOU HEAR ME, YOU BASTARDS?! I'LL KILL ALL OF YOU!!
?!!
OH NO...

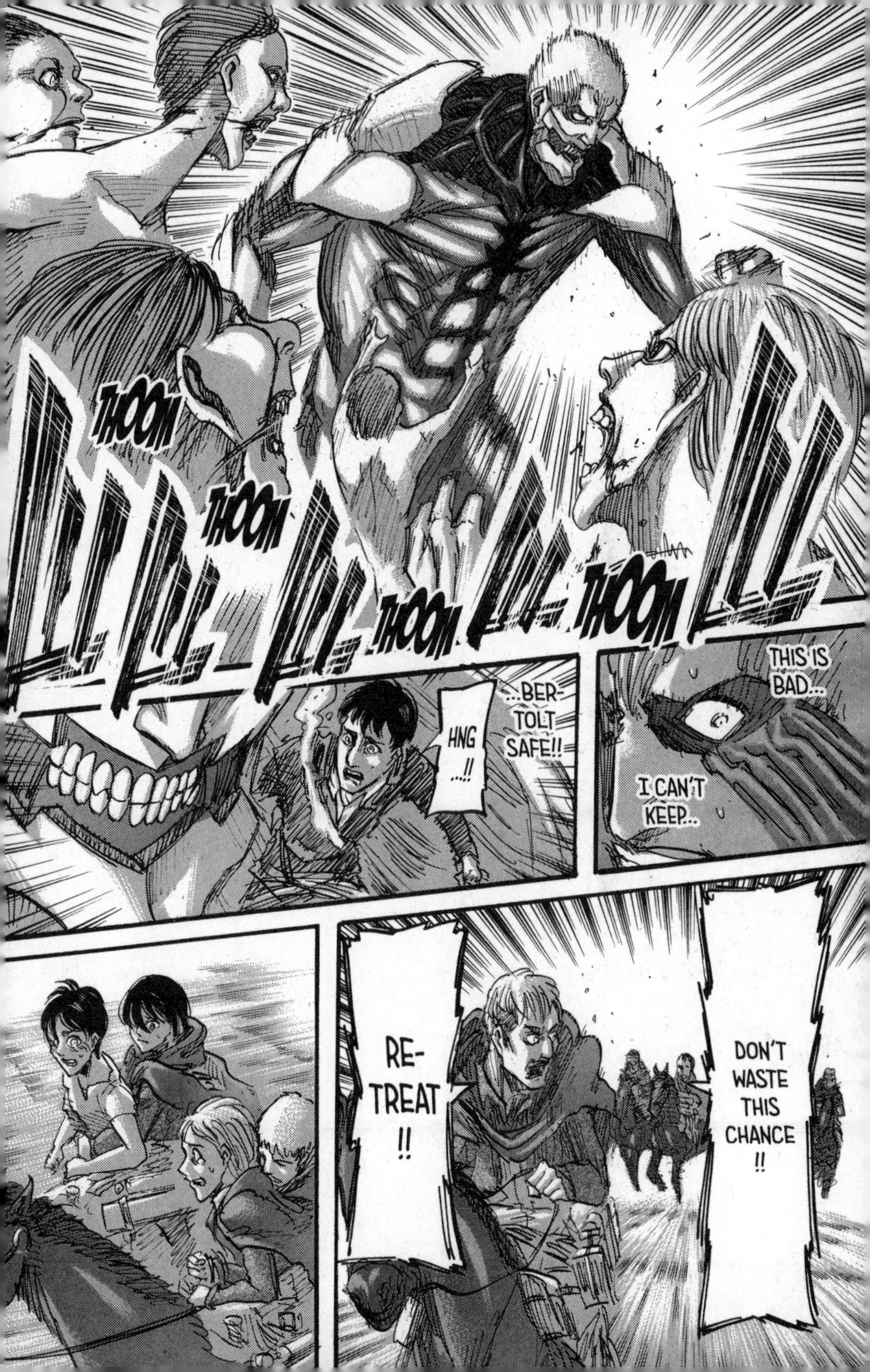
THOOM
THOOM
THOOM
THOOM
THIS IS BAD...
I CAN'T KEEP...
...BER-TOLT SAFE!!
HNG ...!!
DON'T WASTE THIS CHANCE !!
RE-TREAT !!

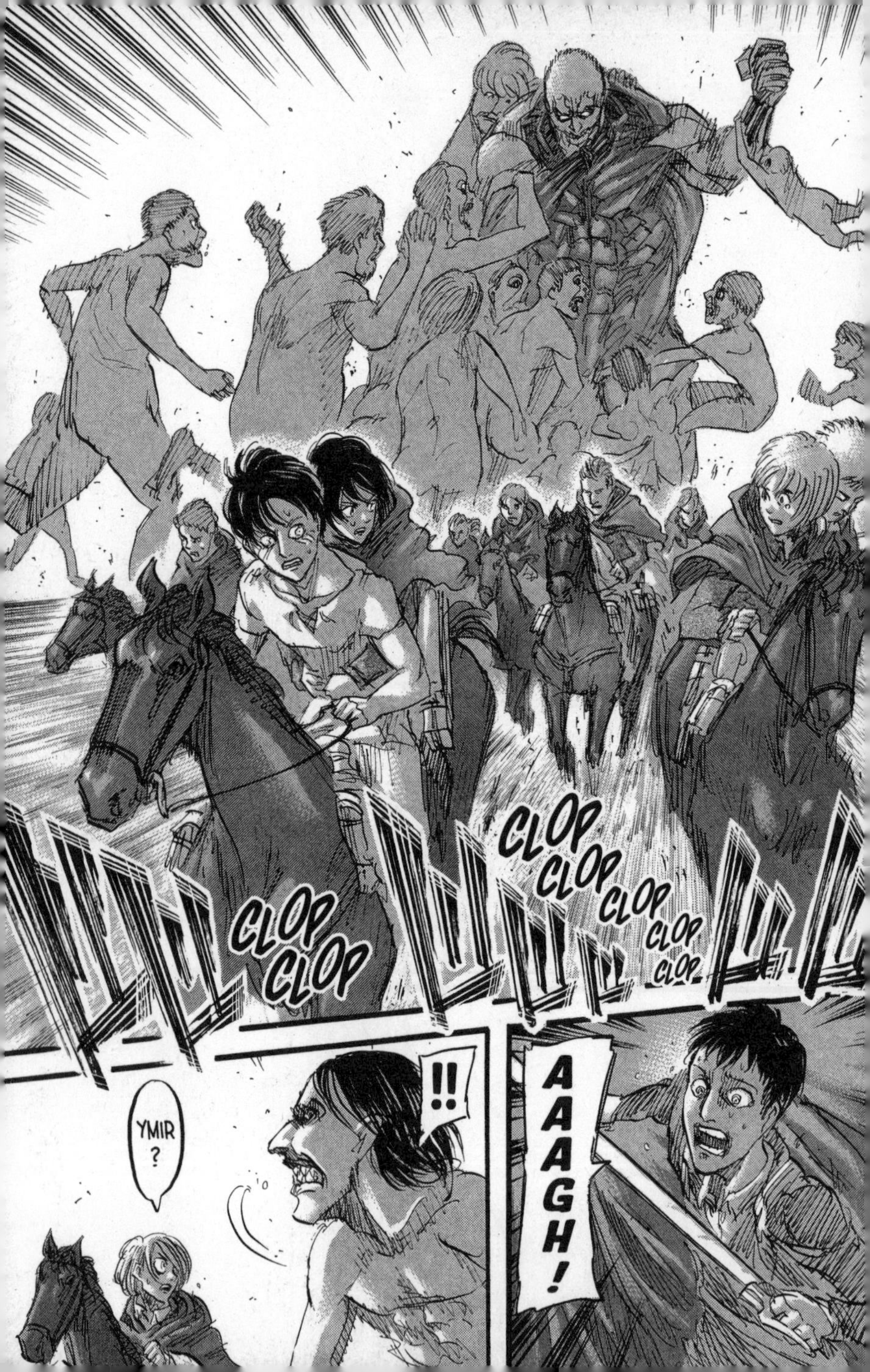
CLOP CLOP CLOP CLOP CLOP
CLOP CLOP
AAAAGH!
!!
YMIR ?

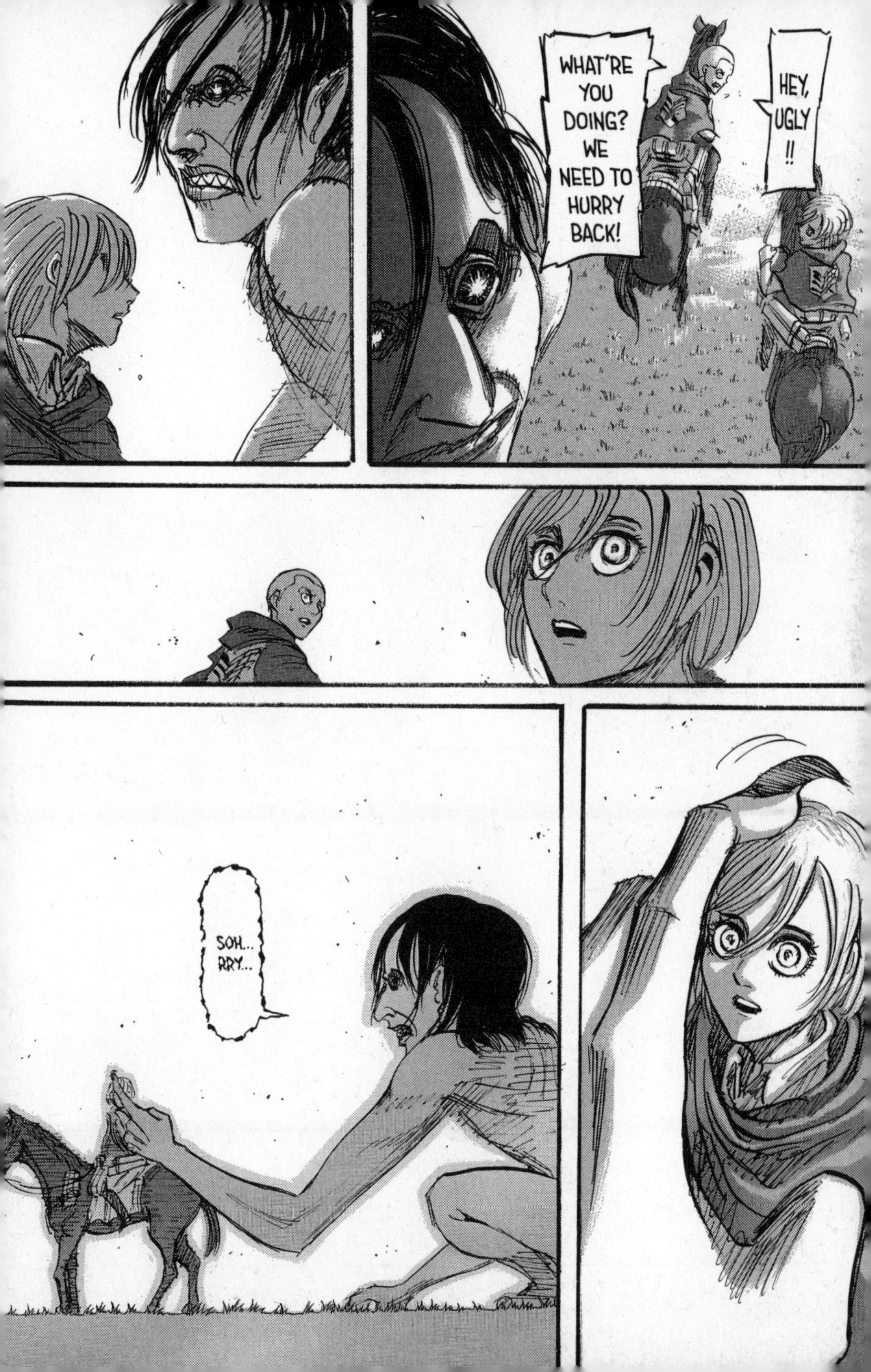
HEY, UGLY !!
WHAT'RE YOU DOING? WE NEED TO HURRY BACK!
SOH... RRY...

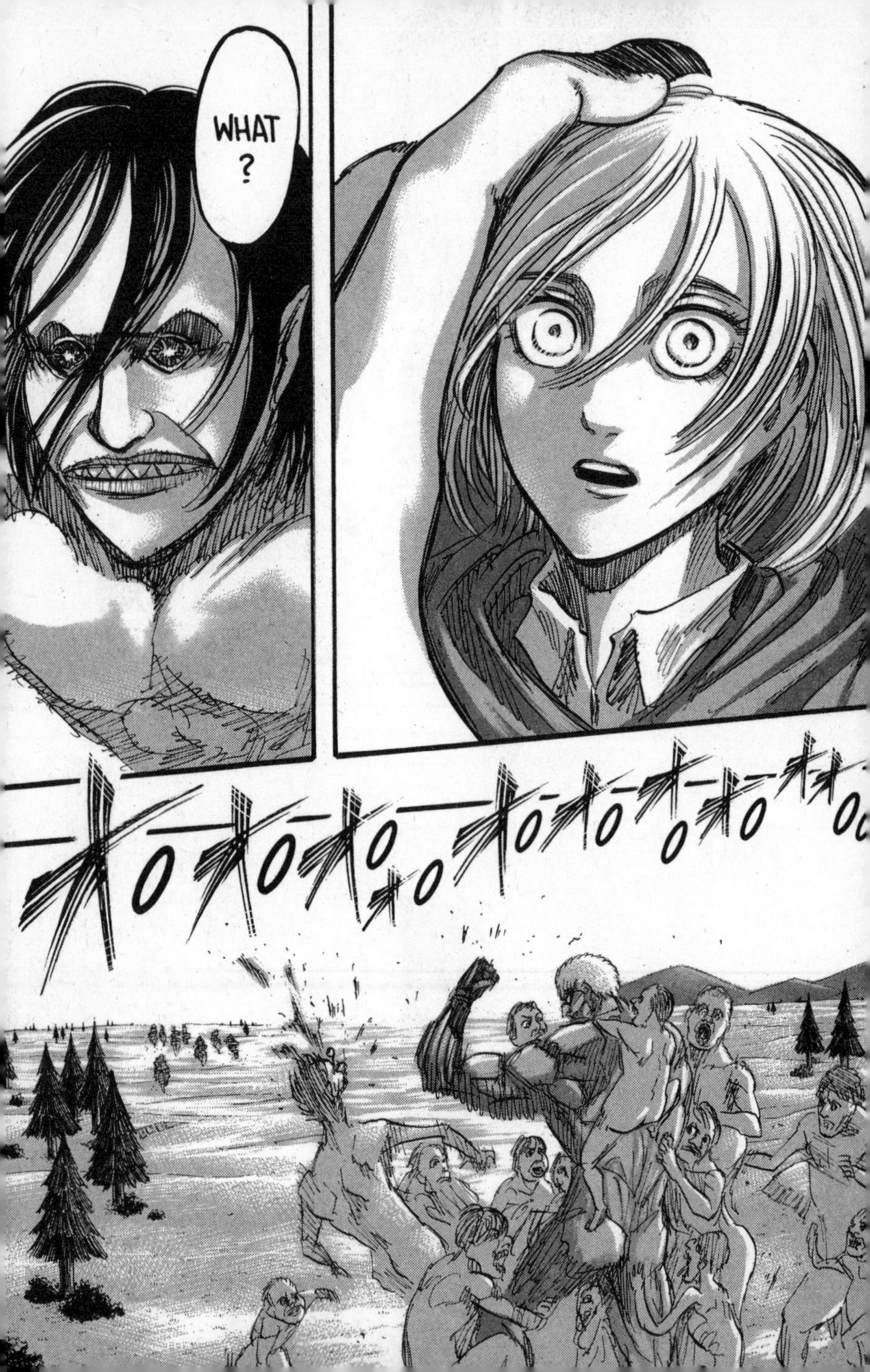
WHAT ?

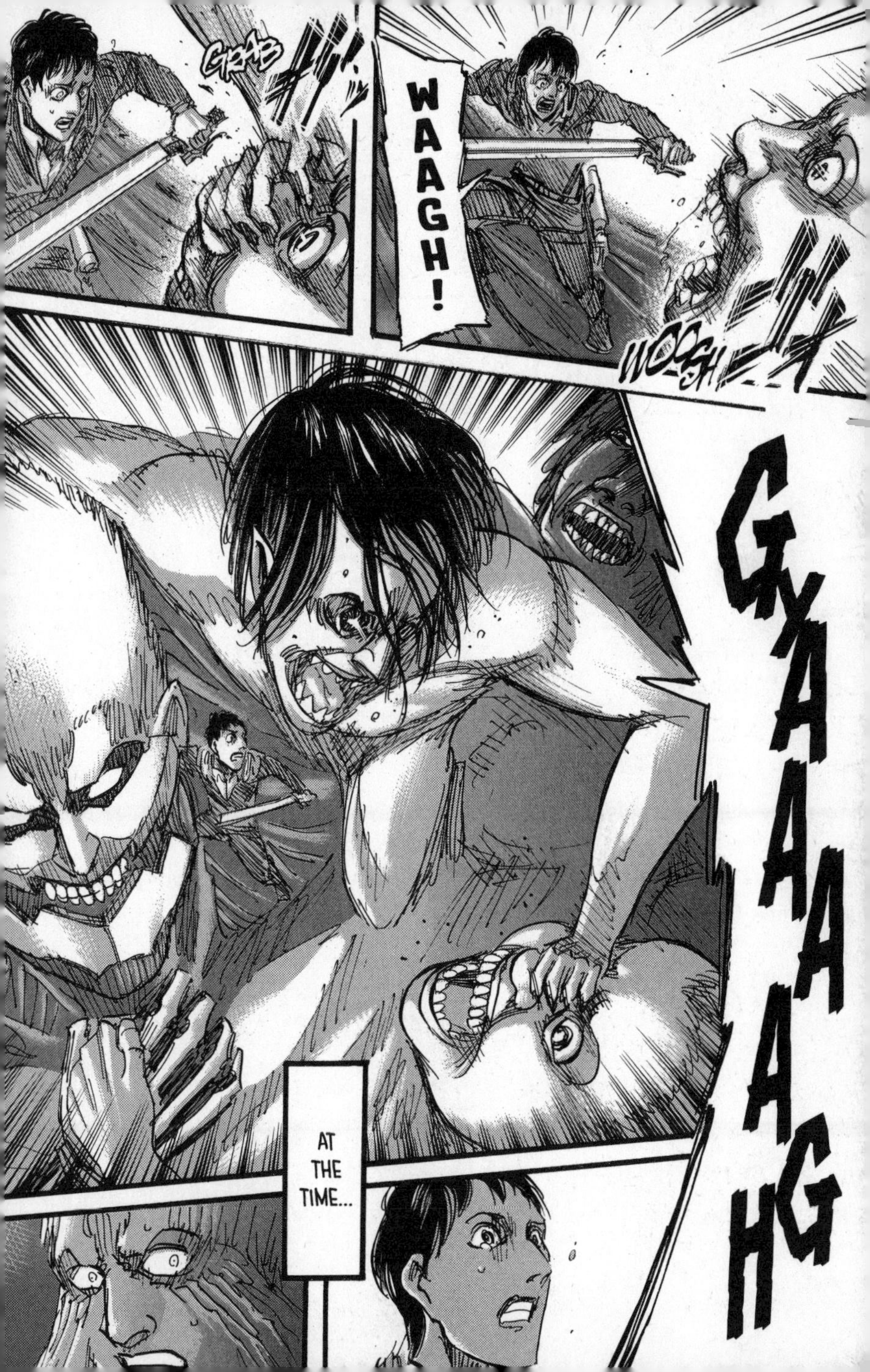
WAAGH!
WOOSH
GRAB
GYAAAAGH
AT THE TIME...

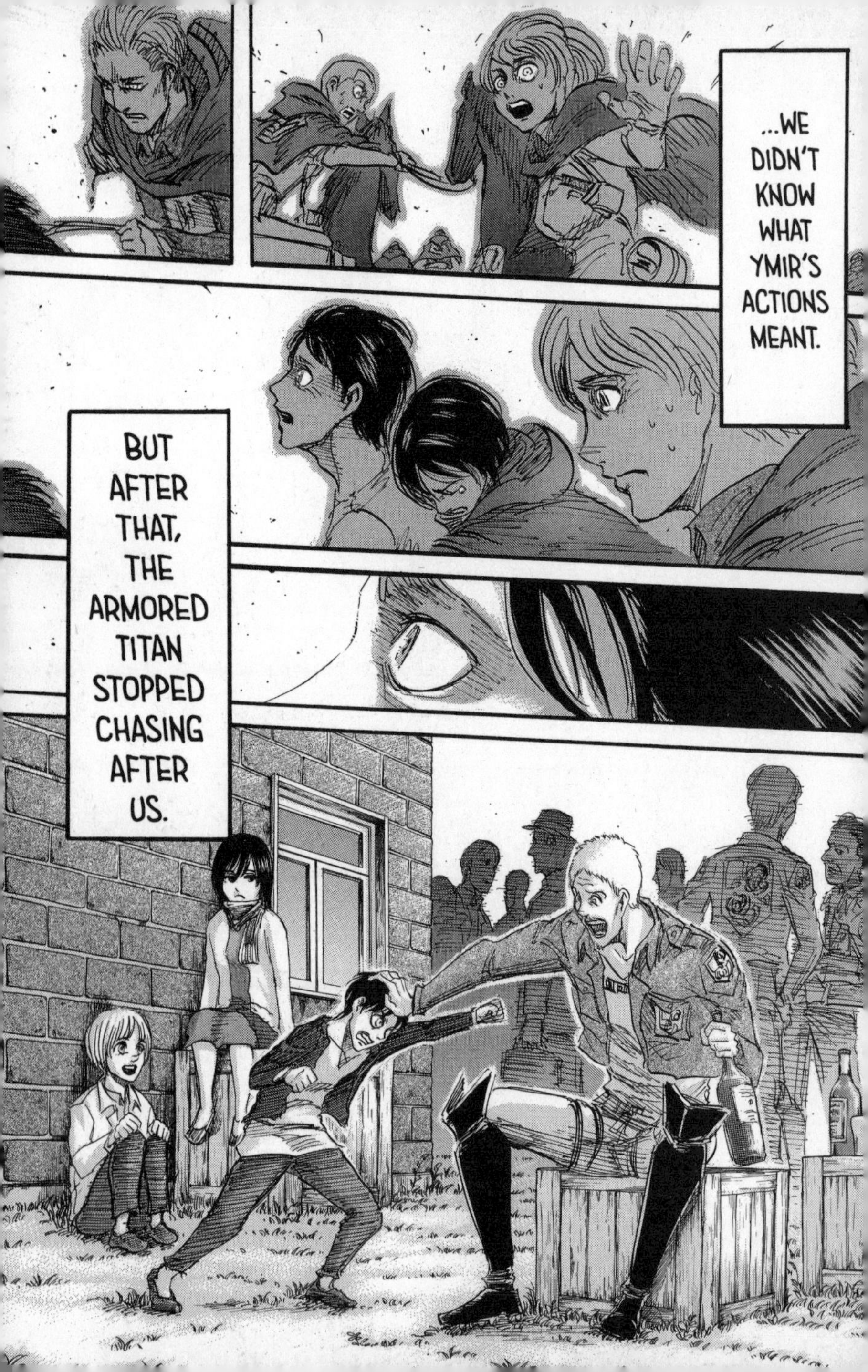
...WE DIDN'T KNOW WHAT YMIR'S ACTIONS MEANT.
BUT AFTER THAT, THE ARMORED TITAN STOPPED CHASING AFTER US.

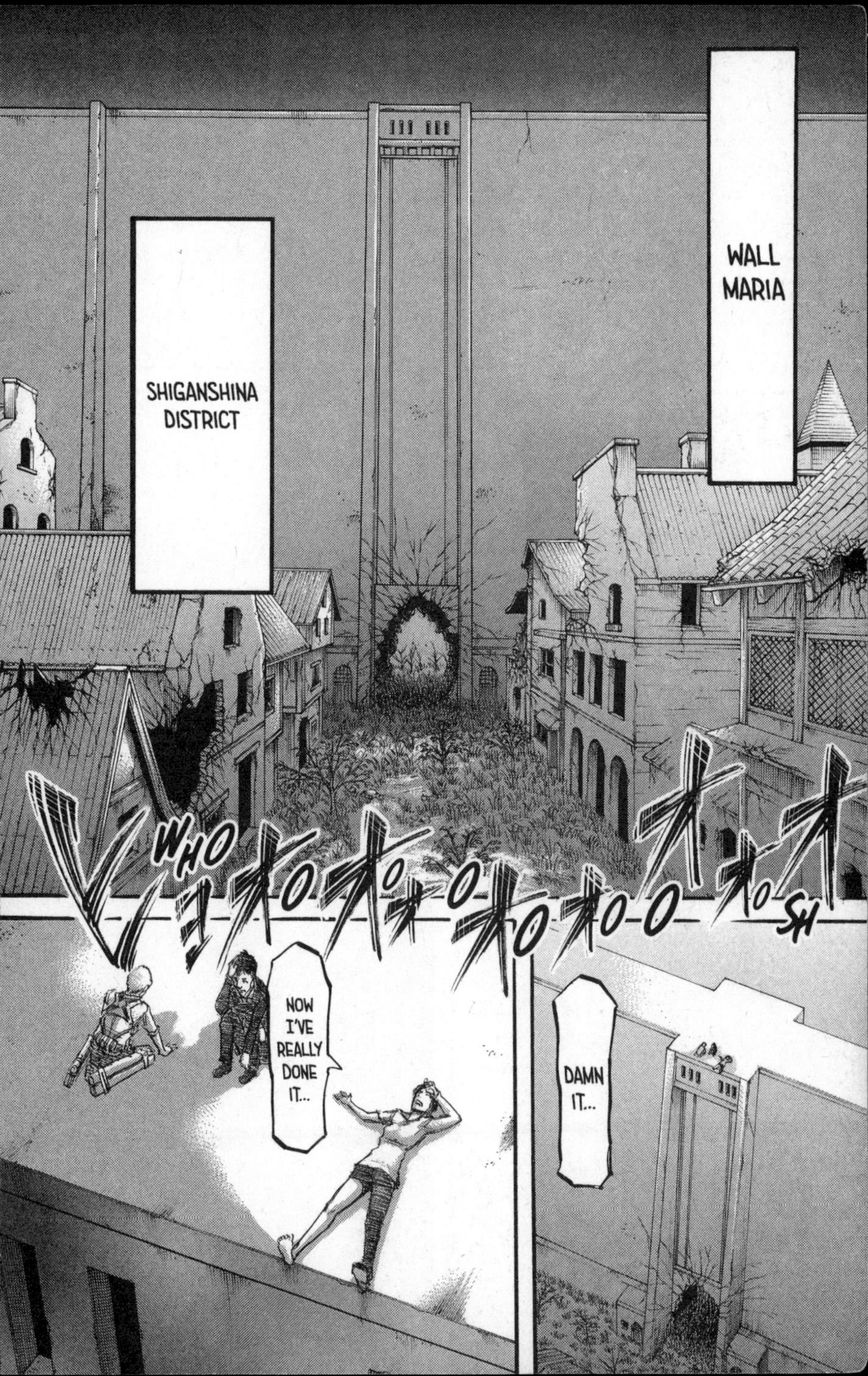
WALL MARIA
SHIGANSHINA DISTRICT
WHOOOOOOOOOSH
DAMN IT...
NOW I'VE REALLY DONE IT...

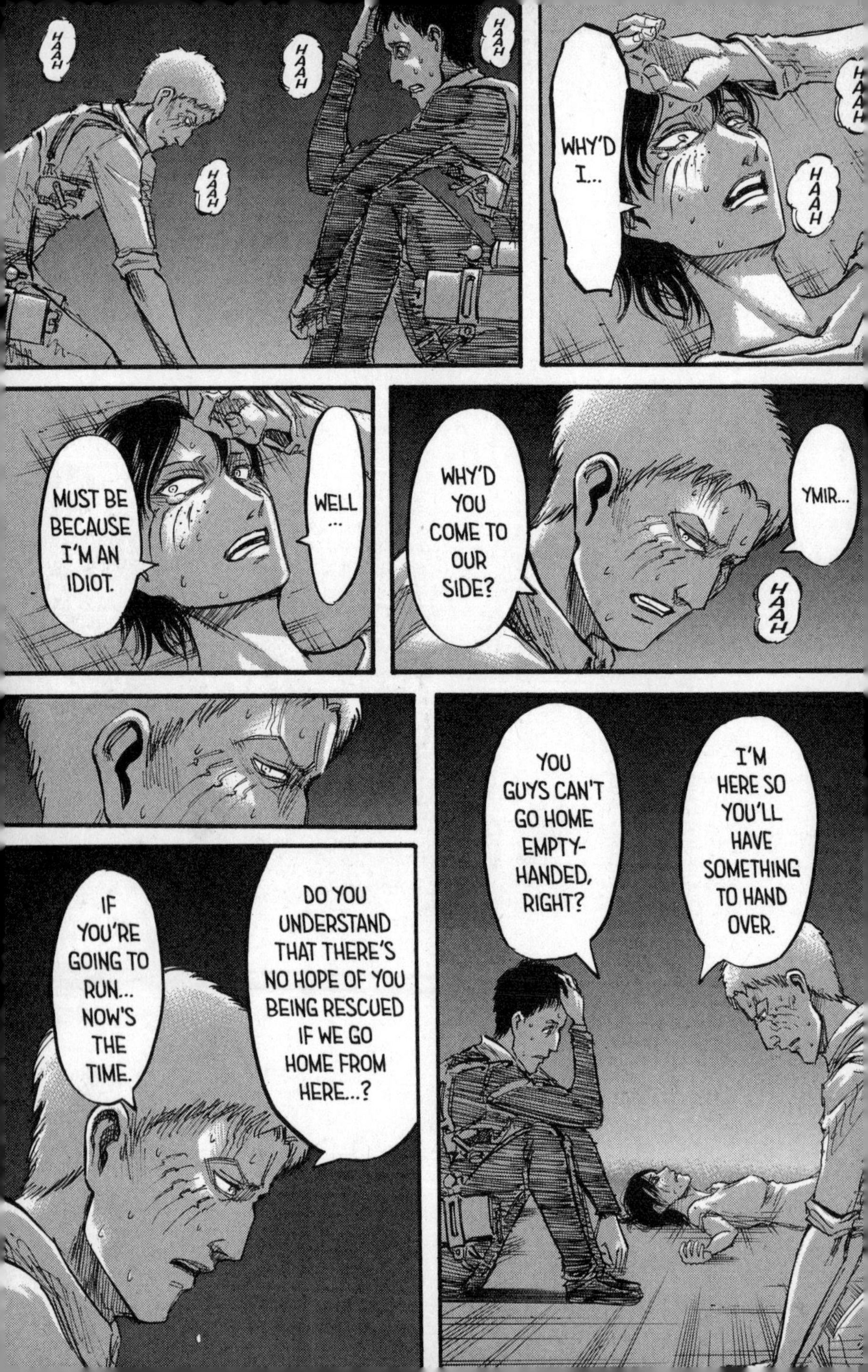
HAAH
HAAH
WHY'D I...
HAAH
HAAH
HAAH
HAAH
YMIR...
WHY'D YOU COME TO OUR SIDE?
HAAH
WELL...
MUST BE BECAUSE I'M AN IDIOT.
I'M HERE SO YOU'LL HAVE SOMETHING TO HAND OVER.
YOU GUYS CAN'T GO HOME EMPTY-HANDED, RIGHT?
DO YOU UNDERSTAND THAT THERE'S NO HOPE OF YOU BEING RESCUED IF WE GO HOME FROM HERE...?
IF YOU'RE GOING TO RUN... NOW'S THE TIME.

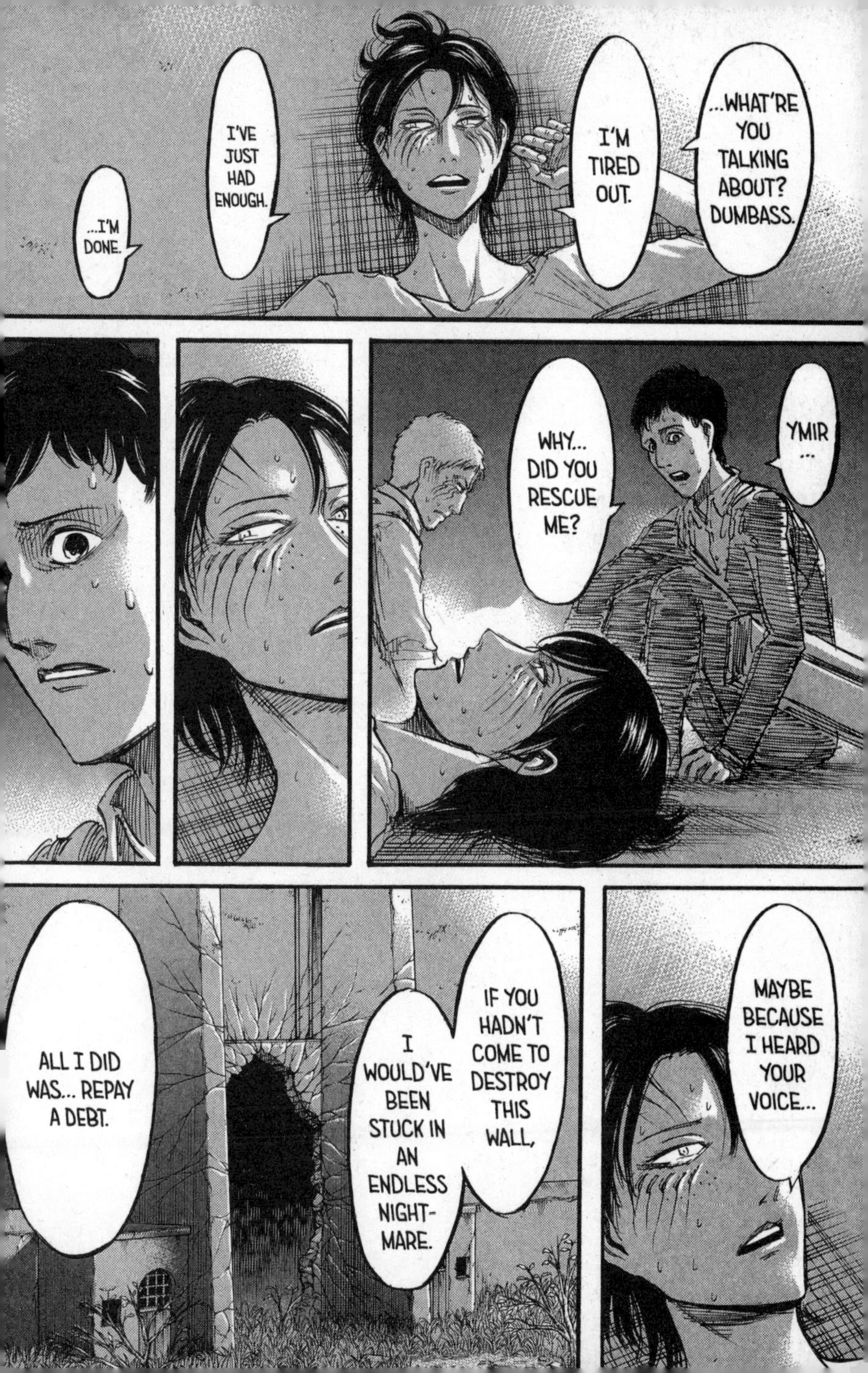
...WHAT'RE YOU TALKING ABOUT? DUMBASS.
I'M TIRED OUT.
I'VE JUST HAD ENOUGH.
...I'M DONE.
YMIR ...
WHY... DID YOU RESCUE ME?
MAYBE BECAUSE I HEARD YOUR VOICE...
IF YOU HADN'T COME TO DESTROY THIS WALL,
I WOULD'VE BEEN STUCK IN AN ENDLESS NIGHT-MARE.
ALL I DID WAS... REPAY A DEBT.

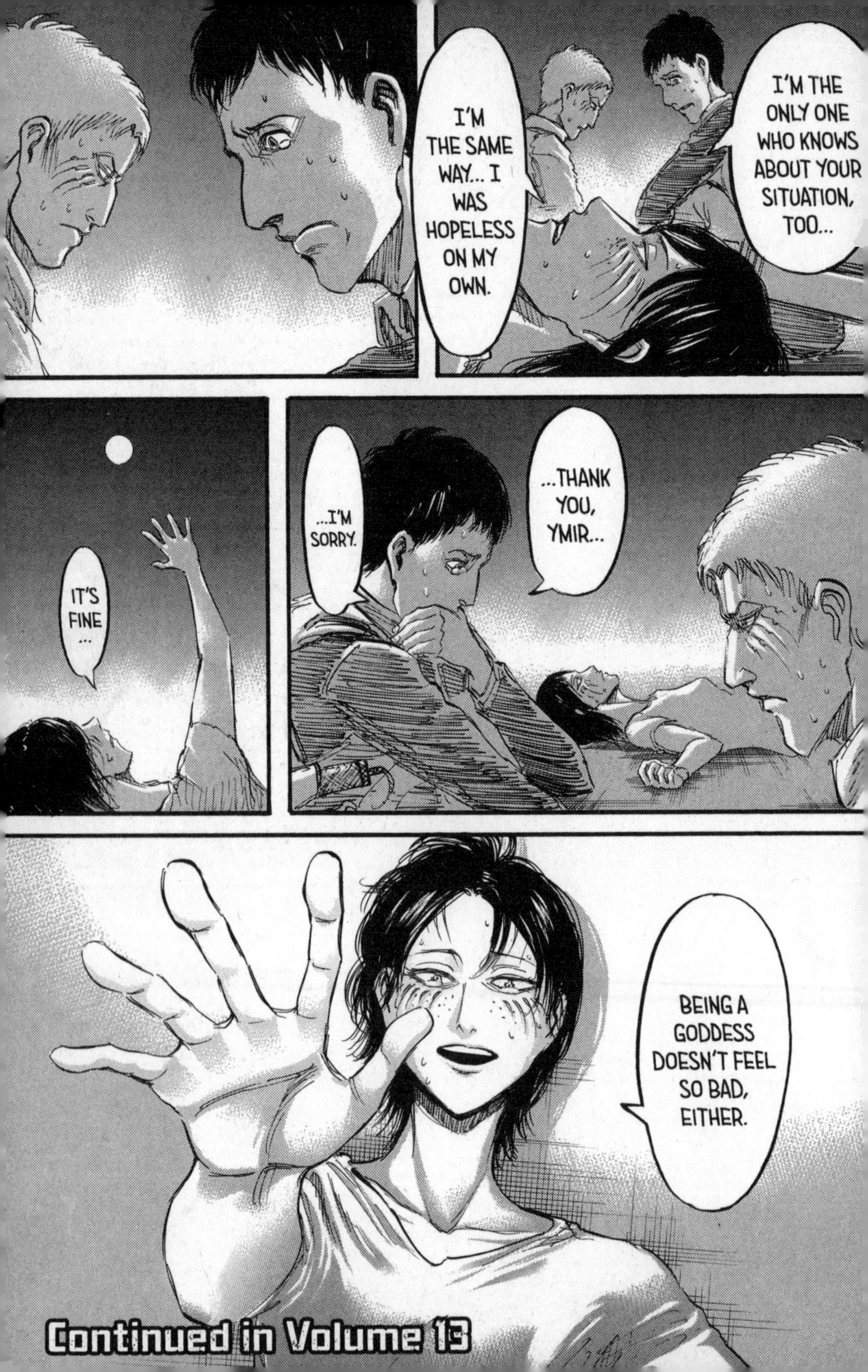
I'M THE ONLY ONE WHO KNOWS ABOUT YOUR SITUATION, TOO...
I'M THE SAME WAY... I WAS HOPELESS ON MY OWN.
...THANK YOU, YMIR...
...I'M SORRY.
IT'S FINE ...
BEING A GODDESS DOESN'T FEEL SO BAD, EITHER.
Continued in Volume 13

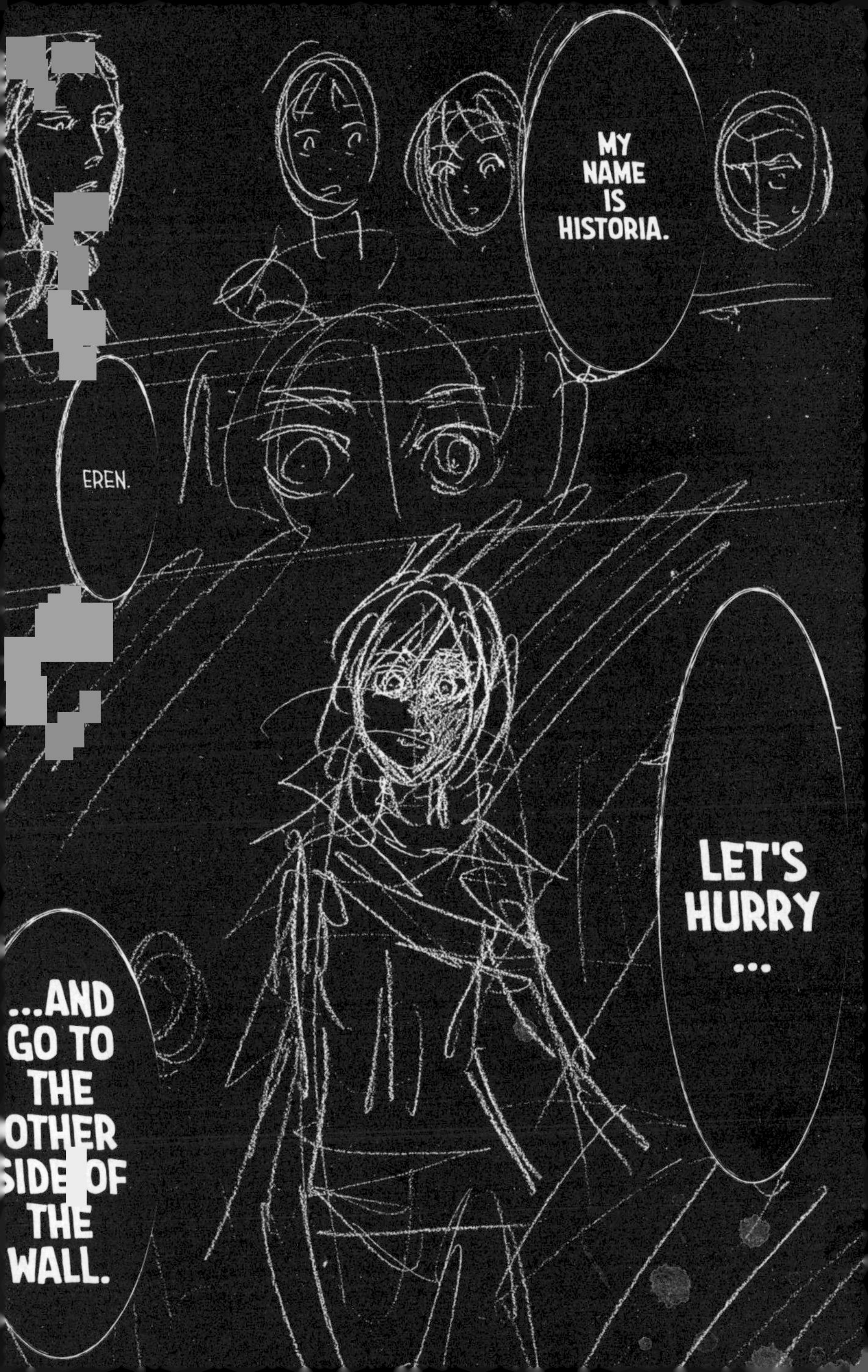
MY NAME IS HISTORIA.
EREN.
LET'S HURRY...
...AND GO TO THE OTHER SIDE OF THE WALL.

VOLUME 13 COMING SOON!

KRISTA LENZ.
REAL NAME: HISTORIA REISS...

THE PERSON WHO HOLDS IN
HER HANDS THE KEY TO THE
WORLD'S GREATEST MYSTERY.

D0032933

A Kodansha Comics Trade Paperback Original
Attack on Titan volume 12 copyright © 2013 Hajime Isayama
English translation copyright © 2014 Hajime Isayama

All rights reserved.

Published in the United States by Kodansha Comics, an imprint of
Kodansha USA Publishing, LLC, New York.

Publication rights for this English edition arranged through
Kodansha Ltd, Tokyo.

First published in Japan in 2013 by Kodansha Ltd., Tokyo
as *Shingeki no Kyojin*, volume 12.

ISBN 978-1-61262-678-9

Original cover design by Takashi Shimoyama (Red Rooster)

Printed in the United States of America.

www.kodanshacomics.com

9 8 7 6 5 4 3 2
Translation: Ko Ransom
Lettering: Steve Wands
Editing: Ben Applegate
Kodansha Comics edition cover design by Phil Balsman